A Matter of Taste

A Matter of Taste

HOW NAMES, FASHIONS, AND CULTURE CHANGE

Stanley Lieberson

YALE UNIVERSITY PRESS

NEW HAVEN & LONDON

Figure 1.1 on page 3 is published by permission from John H. Mueller,
The American Symphony Orchestra (Bloomington: Indiana University
Press, 1951).

Printed in the United States of America

ISBN 0-300-08385-8 (cloth : alk. paper)
Library of Congress Card Number: 00-104460

A catalogue record for this book is available from the British Library.

The paper in this book meets the guidelines for permanence and
durability of the Committee on Production Guidelines for Book
Longevity of the Council on Library Resources.

10   9   8   7   6   5   4   3   2   1

For Patricia
(favorite name, according to a scientific
random sample of one husband)

Contents

Acknowledgments   ix

Prologue   xi

1 Tastes: Why Do They Become What They Become?   1

2 Becoming a Fashion   31

3 How the Social Order Influences Names After They Become
a Matter of Taste—And How It Doesn't   69

4 The Ratchet Effect   92

5 Other Internal Mechanisms   112

6 Models of the Fashion Process   143

7 Ethnic and Racial Groups   172

8 Entertainment and Entertainers   223

9 Broader Issues: The Cultural Surface and Cultural Change   257

Appendix 1: Sources for Graphs in Chapter 2   277

Appendix 2: Use of Ethnic Data in Chapter 7   283

Notes   289

References   303

Index   317

Acknowledgments

This study was supported by a grant from the National Science Foundation to the author (NSF SBR-92-23418) as well as an indirect one (NSF SES-9022192); funds provided by Percy Tannenbaum, then director of the Survey Research Center, University of California; research support from the Demography Center, University of California; a year at the Center for Advanced Studies in the Behavioral and Social Sciences; and Harvard University. I am indebted to many for helpful discussions, references, suggestions, encouragement, or assistance on the project: William Alonso (deceased), Elaine Bachman, Thomas Ballinger, Bernard Barber, William P. Barnett, Daniel Bell, Eleanor O. Bell, Mabel Berezin, Denise Bielby, William Bielby, Judith Blau, Bob Blauner, Debra Boadway, Edyta Bojanowska, Joseph Boskin, Richard F. Boulware, Steven Brint, Margaret Brown (deceased), Rogers Brubaker, James L. Bruning, John Campbell, Daniel Cervone, Leslie Cintron, John Cloninger, Ray P. Cuzzort (deceased), James Davis, Carol Dolcini, Sonja Drobnič, Harry Edwards, Max Epstein, Cleveland K. Evans, Lynne Farnum, Christy Farrell, Jennifer Fehser, Lee Forester, George Murray Friedman, Frank Furstenberg, Lynn Gale, Samuel L. Gilmore, Nathan Glazer, Patrick Goebel, Eugenia Gohrman, Leo A. Goodman, Leah Greenfeld, Avery "Augustus" Guest, T. C. Haldi, Lowell Lavern Hargens, David Heise, Charles "Chuck" Hirschman, Ann Hogan, Stanley Holwitz, Michael Hout, Lani Kask, Deana Knickebocker, Frederick P. Krantz, Manfred Krifka, Kurt Lang, Edwin D. Lawson, Adrienne Lehrer, Leslie Lindzey, Virginia Loo, Virginia MacDonald,

Frank Many, Peter Marsden, James McCann (deceased), Antonio McDaniel, Jean Michel, S. M. Miller, Philip Morgan, Kathleen Much, Francie Ostrower, Nancy Park, Roy D. Pea, Joel Perlmann, Samuel H. Preston, Lincoln Quillian, Michael Relish, Rachel A. Rosenfeld, Paul Rozin, Steven Rytina, Joy Scott, Paul Siegel, Neil Smelser, Roger Smith, Tom Smith, Aage B. Sørensen, David Stark, Percy Tannenbaum, Ralph Turner, Mary C. Waters, Susan Watkins, Dorothy Watson, Ian Watson, Rose-Marie Weber, Lynn White, Sheldon White, Aaron Wildavsky (deceased), James Wiley, Christine L. Williams, Robin Williams, Moiraine Wong, Anne Woodell, Erich Olin Wright, Alison Wylie, Moira Yip, and Morris Zelditch.

I thank especially Lilja Gretarsdottir, Shyon S. Baumann, Susan Dumais, Traci R. Manning, and Kelly Mikelson for extensive research assistance on the project; Howard Becker and the late Zvi Grilliches for innumerable discussions; Catherine Kenny and Mami Suzuki for help not only in preparing the manuscript, figures, and tables but also for many suggestions and corrections; and Cheri Minton and Nancy Williamson for extraordinary help in all facets of data crunching (not the least being the creation of special programs that took into account the unusual problems encountered when working with data of the sort not usually encountered in sociology). Last, there are those Harvard undergraduates whom I have encountered through the years in my junior tutorial on names and my lecture course on the social underpinnings of taste. Many (albeit far from all) have been a pleasure to have had in the courses, and I have benefited from their enthusiasm and stimulation—even if they are terribly resistant to naming their first son "Stanley." In my seminar I have also appreciated Harvard graduate students' discussions about broader issues in cultural analysis.

Next door is Mary Quigley, who has been working far beyond the call of duty in helping me prepare this manuscript for Yale University Press. I am grateful, and indebted. Glen Hartley is an extraordinary agent, and I have enjoyed working with him—not the least because of his excellent criticisms and suggestions about purely intellectual features of the book. His partner, Lynn Chu, also helpfully advised me on contractual matters. Howard Becker, Bonnie Erickson, and John R. Sutton provided detailed and extremely helpful comments about the manuscript; all three will find their influence on these pages. My dealings with Yale University Press have been amazingly pleasant. Starting with Susan Arellano, my acquisitions editor, continuing on with Judith Adkins and Jenya Weinreb (editorial assistant and manuscript editor, respectively), and capped by associate managing editor Laura Jones Dooley's magnificent review of the manuscript, I have benefited from their enthusiasm, professionalism, and advice.

Prologue

My wife and I are a conventional couple; when our first child was born, we gave her a name. Although we didn't know it, other parents were choosing the same name for their daughters. We found out soon enough, though; from nursery school on, our *Rebecca* almost invariably encountered peers with the same name. What intrigued me was that neither my wife nor I had had any idea that we were picking such a popular name. We and these other parents, without talking about it, were "independently" reaching the same decision at the same time. Obviously, the choice was not independent—it had to reflect social influences. But it seemed as if something "in the air" was leading different parents to make the same choices. Being a sociologist, of course this fascinated me. Unlike many other societal tastes, the popularity of the name *Rebecca* did not reflect commercial or organizational interests: there was no advertising campaign sponsored by the NRA—the National Rebecca Association—let alone an effort to demean those who preferred a competitor. The ascent of *Rebecca* and the decline of another name was not the same as the intense competition between Pepsi and Coca-Cola. Neither Walmart nor Neiman Marcus were promoting the name as part of a newborn daughter's fashion ensemble. And there was no factory rebate for naming your daughter *Rebecca*.

I suppose you could say that my wife and I *liked* the name, and probably so did the other parents. True enough, but that explanation is not sufficient. Not too many years before this, few parents had *liked* the name—at least enough to give it to their daughters. And, not so many years later, the number who liked the name was again in decline. How could this naming pattern be explained? It seemed, in a certain sense, to be the ultimate example of a social process. A name does not change, but its appeal does. Parents at a given time and place were resonating to certain names. In different periods, they would resonate to other names. At that time, I had no idea that parents using other names also had a *Rebecca*-like experience; they gave their baby a name, unaware that many other parents had the same idea in mind.

This fascinated me, but for many years it remained an idle curiosity. Only after I received an unexpected telephone call offering me funds to hire a research assistant did I start on the long path that led to this volume. At the time of the call, I was occupied with another project, yet I was not about to refuse a free research assistant—academic greed, you know. The ensuing work with my new research assistant, Eleanor Bell, led to a paper on first names, "Children's First Names: An Empirical Study of Social Taste" (Lieberson and Bell 1992). But it did not address my initial curiosity about *Rebecca*.

Delving deeper into the topic, I began to appreciate that my curiosity about *Rebecca* in particular, and names in general, was really part of a broader set of issues involving *fashion* (throughout the book I use the term interchangeably with *taste*). Until then, I had never reflected on people's resistance to taking fashion seriously, stemming from what the sociologist Herbert Blumer describes as a widespread belief that fashion is "an aberrant and irrational social happening, akin to a craze or mania" (1969, 276). Because fashions are viewed as frivolous, fickle, and bizarre, they "rarely seem to make sense in terms of utility or rational purpose; they seem much more to express the play of fancy and caprice." There is also, according to Blumer, a general belief that fashion applies primarily to clothing and adornment (275). In fact, an element of fashion is present in many areas:

> It is easily observable in the realm of the pure and applied arts, such as painting, sculpture, music, drama, architecture, dancing, and household decoration. Its presence is very obvious in the area of entertainment and amusement. There is plenty of evidence to show its play in the field of medicine. Many of us are familiar with its operation in fields of industry, especially that of business management. It even touches such a relative sacred area as that of mortuary practice.... it is unquestionably at work in the field of science.... fashion appears in such redoubtable areas as physical and biological science and mathematics.... To limit it to, or to center it in, the field of costume and adornment is to have a very inadequate idea of the scope of its occurrence. [275–276]

Not only do fashions and tastes occur in an enormous variety of contexts, but fashion is often an important influence in these many domains. For example, Blumer writes, "the styles in art, the themes and styles in literature, the forms and themes in entertainment, the perspectives in philosophy, the practices in business, and the preoccupations in science may be affected profoundly by fashion" (276). The topic of fashion is neither trivial, nor do the processes operate in a haphazard manner.

Beyond this, fashions provide an extraordinary opportunity to study issues of social change more generally. As Rolf Meyersohn and Elihu Katz put it, "The study of fads and fashions may serve the student of social change much as the study of fruit flies has served geneticists: neither the sociologist nor the geneticist has to wait long for a new generation to arrive" (1957, 594). The broad spectrum of extraordinarily rich data sets on names helped me appreciate the exceptional opportunity to go beyond broad assertions about fashion sometimes based on rather flimsy evidence.

First names are of interest in themselves; they are not just one fashion among many. Unlike many other cultural fashions, no commercial efforts are made to influence our naming choices. Compare this with the organizational impact on tastes in such diverse areas as soft drinks, clothing, popular entertainment, automobiles, watches, rugs, lamps, vacations, food, perfumes, soaps, books, and medications—to name just a few. This is crucial: the naming process provides an excellent opportunity to understand fashion mechanisms (what I shall call "internal mechanisms") that drive tastes even in the absence of commercial influences. (In fact, these mechanisms do also mold and direct the movement of tastes in the presence of commercial and organizational efforts, but it is a little harder to sort them out at first.) Advertisements, for example, operate best when they harmonize with the same principles that influence tastes in noncommercial and nonorganizational activities, such as giving names to one's children. The key point, though, is that names provide an exceptional opportunity to study internal mechanisms of taste without the need to disentangle the powerful commercial forces that strive to mold fashion.

This is important because there are, broadly speaking, two major influences on taste: external social forces and internal mechanisms of change. The first category includes what are probably the most commonly used explanations for cultural events generally and fashions in particular. Namely, there is a disposition to explain changing tastes by looking at social and cultural developments in the surrounding society. An example of this is the influence of the changing social order in the Netherlands on Rembrandt's paintings. Less obvious is that tastes have their own internal mechanisms that cause fashions to change in specific directions. Even in the presence of external influences, these internal mechanisms affect the outcome (in Chapter 7, for example, I describe how Mexican-American parents in the United States adapt to "American" names in ways that are linked to a widespread internal mechanism based on how fashion changes). Although this book focuses on internal mechanisms relevant for first names, many of these mechanisms influence other fashions, too. The ratchet effect, the mutation analogue, the enhancement-contamination effects, and the expansion model are only a few of the mechanisms I propose here that have wider significance. The model of how individual dispositions generate fashions among subsets of a population, as well as create their eventual decline (see Chapter 6), also has broader applications.

Internal mechanisms—once set in motion—will generate new preferences indefinitely without the addition of any external influences. This entails a somewhat counterintuitive perspective—namely, fashion will change (in orderly ways, no less) without the operation of *any* external social or cultural shifts. This proposition has massive implications for the way popular culture is often explained. Instead of routinely searching for a social change that will provide an ad hoc account, it is best to consider that changes can occur without any external developments. In that respect, when internal mechanisms are operating to generate such a change, the event has no meaning—at least in the conventional way that *meaning* is usually employed as a reference to some external event. Because the change occurs in the absence of any changes in these external influences, the *meaning* is found in identifying and understanding the internal mechanism. Again, this applies to more than just shifting fashions in first names. (Of course, social conditions are often necessary for internal mechanisms to operate. And both types of influence can be important for some fashion shifts. But these are modifications of the simple truth that fashions will change in the absence of social or even cultural changes.)

Naming data are also helpful for dealing with a tendency to confuse a *plausible* explanation with a *correct* explanation. The various explanations offered to account for the decline of men's fedoras (Chapter 3) illustrates this problem. All are plausible speculations about what could have been the cause, but the evidence shows that virtually none can account for the long-term changes in the popularity of fedoras. Indeed, the ad hoc explanations for hats overlook the existence of a broad change in tastes away from the formal to the informal. This exercise, I hope, will serve as a warning to commentators on popular culture who deceive themselves into thinking that *plausibility* is a synonym for *truth*. The advantage provided by the data on names is that they allow for systematic tests.

When there are many different names to consider, along with information about changes for each succeeding year, an ad hoc interpretation of a single cultural event based on minimal documentation of what precedes or follows it cannot be a sufficient explanation. For example, *Marilyn* was once a common name for daughters in the United States. Hardly surprising, you might say. After all, Marilyn Monroe was an exceptionally popular actress, so it is really only a matter of finding out why parents found her name so appealing. Perhaps something about the role of women at the time and how Monroe fit or challenged that role? Very nice, except the data prevent such a facile interpretation; *Marilyn* was already very popular when Norma Jeane Baker adopted it as her stage name. And in fact, the name steadily declined in popularity in the years following Monroe's debut. All right, you might say, that's not really a problem—a mere technical correction is needed to explain this. We can think about why Marilyn Monroe was an unattractive persona when it came to naming daughters. Perhaps parents in that era didn't want to give their daughters names associated with a woman who displayed such open sensuality. Didn't a strong prudish streak run through American culture in that era? Or perhaps this was a period when parents were beginning to think of new roles for women-roles that were the antithesis of the persona Monroe projected. Yes, *perhaps*, but again, if we look at the data we will see that *Marilyn* was already in decline at the time of the actress's debut; it was still a popular name, but becoming less so. In effect, because there is more precise information about the developments, a plausible explanation alone cannot suffice. In fact, the clue to the popularity of *Marilyn* lies in the expansion of a suffix, *lyn-line*, which was added to a variety of existing names. We shall see that this is a common mechanism for taste development that can operate independently of external events.

Rather than dismissing fashion altogether, one of the joys in this research is to see that tastes do follow fairly orderly processes and principles. When viewed correctly, they are not the erratic, arbitrary, or ephemeral phenomena that some would have you believe. Granted, this is by no means comparable to the precision that allows us to be confident about the Earth's yearly course around the

Sun. Yet there is enough order reported in the examples given in this book for the author (and it is hoped the reader) to appreciate the existence of regularities in how tastes change and are replaced by newer ones.

Finally, returning to my initial curiosity about my daughter's name, in retrospect I understand why my earlier work on names did not address this question, for it is one that cannot be answered glibly; one must first develop a deeper understanding of the complicated ways that tastes operate. A variety of preconditions and mechanisms help us address this simple curiosity. I had never even thought about the most basic of these conditions--although, again in retrospect, it is terribly obvious. *All of these preferential shifts are predicated on names first becoming a matter of taste.* What leads this to occur? Although a fashion element has been present in names for a long time, the extraordinary role of fashion in naming is a relatively recent development, reflecting social changes associated with modernization. (In Chapter 2 we shall examine the rise in naming fashions and: the growth in cities and industrialization, a concomitant decline in smaller communities and agriculture, increasing levels of education and migration, technological changes, radical shifts in family structure, and many other indications of normative change.) In the end, in Chapter 8, I was able to tackle the *Rebecca* question with the intellectual tools necessary to provide what I hope is a sound answer. It is my hope, too, that this book will be a guide to many other questions about names in particular, fashion and tastes more generally, and broad elements of cultural change.

1 Tastes: Why Do They Become What They Become?

I see a sweater that I *like*, others leave me indifferent, and some are definitely unattractive. Similarly, certain cars appeal to me and others don't. And I can say the same for: movie stars, television shows, magazine covers, book jackets, typefaces, breakfast cereals, landscaping, furniture, wristwatches, people's faces, the voice and diction of unseen radio announcers, foods, music, photographs, cutlery, and even smells. In the course of each day, we all encounter objects that we like, dislike, or are indifferent to. Similarly, among the people we pass on the street, some are attractive to us, others are definitely not, and many generate no strong response one way or the other. What shapes our tastes? Why do we like what we like? Sometimes we can immediately explain the basis of our response or, at the very least, make a guess if asked. Something about the color of the sweater, the knit, the pattern, the material, or the shape is appealing. Or perhaps it's a combination of features. Likewise, when considering people, their manners, clothing, walk, accent, "looks," or attitudes may be noticeably annoying or just the opposite. It is still hard—even in these cases—for us to say *why* these criteria are what they are. Why one color, but not another? Often we find it hard even to say what qualities we're responding to, only that the object in question is attractive or unattractive—hardly much help in finding out *why* that should be. And yet, as we shall see, it is possible to infer in a reasonably rigorous manner the societal underpinnings of tastes, even at the extreme, when most people are unable to say what it is that makes something attractive or unattractive to them. But it is a challenge.

The aesthetic rules that operate in society may help us understand the prominence of particular tastes or certain standards. To take the example of our sweater, some color combinations *clash;* there are *classical* sweater shapes; natural fibers may appeal more than synthetic ones (particularly when the sweater is an *obvious* imitation); the skill and care of the production process may affect the impression the sweater gives, even if one can only respond subliminally to the garment, knowing, for example, that it hangs well, but not exactly understanding the tailoring involved; and there are rules of harmony. Because these aesthetic criteria change over time, however, there is no use arguing that some inherent set of aesthetic rules creates our tastes. If I find a certain color attractive, after all, this just pushes us back to the next question: Why is the color presently attractive when at an earlier time other colors were popular for the same item of clothing? Likewise, if certain cuisines are growing in popularity in the United States (say, Thai or Mexican) and if others are declining (say, Greek), I cannot explain this as purely a change in the biology of human senses. In fact, our responses to smells as unattractive or attractive may well be learned, not inherent in our biological disposition (Corbin 1986). To put it another way, if natural wood finishes inside homes are appealing in certain eras, this is not always the case. People who buy older houses, for example, often encounter wooden doors and trim covered by layers of paint.

The crux lies in two interrelated questions: Why do we like what we like, and why do our tastes change over time in the manner that they do? The music and composers favored in classical concerts change over time—not simply because new composers appear on the scene but also because the popularity of composers long dead waxes and wanes. A remarkable—and sadly neglected—study by John Mueller of changing tastes in the music played by American orchestras traces the decline between 1875 and 1950 in the importance for symphony repertoires of six composers (see fig. 1.1). During this span, even Beethoven's popularity declined substantially (Mueller 1951, 183–187), and the relative popularity of specific works by Beethoven also shifted. One symphony, for example, that was among Beethoven's most popular works during his lifetime, the program piece *Wellington's Victory,* op. 91, was largely neglected by 1950. There was a corresponding decline during the same span—albeit less spectacular—in the popularity of his Ninth Symphony (186–187).[1]

It is easy to find convincing evidence that tastes have a deep societal dimen-

Fig. 1.1. Life spans of composers in the repertoire (Source: Mueller 1951, 235)

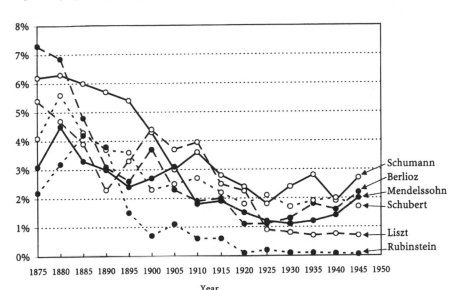

sion: their sheer time-bound nature makes this clear. Go to an old movie and you'll see all sorts of "dated" fashions that don't have the same impact on our senses as they undoubtedly did to earlier audiences. Women's dresses, eyebrow shapes, hats and gloves, lipstick colors and lip shapes, shoes, and hairdos will all differ from contemporary tastes. The characters' manners will be different, also reflecting changing tastes in the behavior appropriate for different segments of the population. Because of the story we will figure out that a particular character is being portrayed as very fashionable, assertive, attractive, gaudy, flamboyant, and so forth. Likewise, we will guess the meaning of someone's automobile or living room furniture—both from the story and in comparison with others shown. So we will guess what is going on in terms of how a past audience might have viewed these portrayals and, in turn, respond roughly in the intended manner. (Indeed, we learn to view the story in its time context so that the meaning we attach to the fashions is different from the meaning we would attach to a contemporary who followed the same tastes.) This temporal impact on tastes is so significant that period movies with costumes meant to represent that era need to be altered ever so slightly to adjust to current tastes (see Maeder 1987). In effect, any completely accurate film rendition of earlier fashions in clothing, hair, and so forth will work counter to the intended illusion because it will fail to take into account the perspective of contemporary tastes. Earlier

fashions must always be modified subtly if the illusion is to work when audiences with radically different tastes view the movie.[2]

The impact of fashion on society is everywhere. Take, for example, the French
and Turkish upholstery styles that were so popular in parlors during the Gilded
Age: rococo design, elaborate, curved shapes, ornately carved frames, over-
stuffed seating, tassels and other ornamentation, extensive tufting, and complex
tapestry-like fabrics in a variety of surfaces, colors, materials, and images.[3]
Those aesthetic rules are no longer present. Indeed, the *parlor* itself which we
now call the *living room,* no longer functions in the same manner. From a
perspective that only time can give us, all the individual tastes of that period are
secondary to the tastes of the period itself—personal choices are significant
variations, to be sure, but they are variations around a common thread—one
that is alien to our time. So when we say that so-and-so has good taste or
someone else does not, what we really mean is that we like or dislike their choices
(say, in clothing) within the context of the tastes available now.

Why do tastes change over time as they do? This question encompasses two
different meanings. One we usually take for granted, although it is the more fundamental starting point. By definition, the term *fashion* is not applied to tastes
that *never* change. What, then, causes an unchanging practice in one period to
become a matter of fashion in a later period? This is not usually what we have in
mind when we think about the causes of changing tastes, but all sorts of shifts in
taste that fascinate us can occur only after the practice in fact is open to fashion.
On this score, observe that fashion incorporates a quantitative dimension because the rates of change may themselves shift over time. To use the example of
sweaters again: we have to ask first what leads sweaters to move from a more or
less constant form (consisting of an unchanging shape, pattern, and color) into
a garment that changes over time? Then we can ask about the rate of change *and*
what causes the specific shapes, colors, and patterns that are favored at a particular time? It is not difficult to understand why this first issue—the movement
from constancy to fashion—involves social developments (I include economic
and political facets as well). And we will see this in operation in Chapter 2 when
we turn back to an era when the giving of first names was not a matter of taste.
But it seems as if specific tastes that come and go in sweaters are the product of
individual tastes coupled with the efforts of organizations with a commercial
interest in the newest fashions. For example, there are sweater manufacturers
and retailers, and there are consumers. At first blush, we may ask if the explanation lies merely in the appeal a cultural artifact has for each individual. Can we

simply say that people like or do not like an object, and that is the beginning and end of it? An individual's distinctive preferences are obviously important, but they are really the last factor to consider in analyzing tastes, for individual responses are molded by the standards of a specific time and place, as well as by the individual's activities and membership in a variety of subgroups and organizations. Individual choices, then, are made within two frameworks, one of the existing broad set of fashions and a more specific one of their own subgroups.

At the end of a very successful career, the American-born movie actor Issur Danielovitch Demsky described how he decided after college to change his name. "I went back to the Tamarack Playhouse the summer after graduation. Every day, we all played the game of deciding what name would lead me to fame and fortune. 'Norman Dems' was considered. I wanted a last name that started with 'D,' that wasn't Danielovitch or Demsky. Somebody suggested 'Douglas.' I liked it. The first name took longer. Finally, someone suggested 'Kirk.' It sounded right. I liked the crisp 'k' sound. I didn't realize what a Scottish name I was taking" (Douglas 1988, 77). His friends and he thought of different stage names. Demsky liked the sound of *Douglas* and resonated to what he saw as the crispness of *Kirk*. Another appeal apparently came from the fact that both names sounded very Scottish. Purely a matter of individual taste? In a sense the answer is yes, but we have to ask whether any social underpinnings provoked this choice. Was it equally likely that a young aspiring actor named Kirk Douglas would change his name in the opposite direction and use Issur Danielovitch Demsky for his stage name? A rhetorical question, and unanswerable, but the point is clear: some underlying tastes were certainly operating here. Did *Kirk Douglas* have some special appeal for a young Issur Demsky? Yes. Is that appeal idiosyncratic? No. It is not by chance that it is part of a broad disposition in a specific direction. The stage and original names of a selection of popular entertainers makes this clearer (table 1.1). Many of the name changes for white entertainers appear to either hide ethnic or religious origins, particularly for those from southern, central, and eastern Europe. Others are efforts to add a certain glamour through changes in last or first names—or both. As in the case of Kirk Douglas, the movement toward using surnames associated with British origins is striking (see also Baltzell 1964, 46–48).

To be sure, these examples contain idiosyncrasies; we differ from one another in what we find attractive in the same way as we vary in skills, interests, and habits. If a group of men are each given the same amount of money to buy a

Table 1.1. Original and stage names of selected entertainers

Stage Name	Original Name	Stage Name	Original Name
Edie Adams	Elizabeth Edith Enke	Cher	Cherilyn Sarkisian
Eddie Albert	Edward Albert Heimberger	Patsy Cline	Virginia Patterson Hensley
Alan Alda	Alphonso D'Abruzzo	Lee J. Cobb	Leo Jacoby
Jane Alexander	Jane Quigley	Claudette Colbert	Lily Chauchoin
Fred Allen	John Sullivan	Mike Connors	Kreker Ohanian
Woody Allen	Allen Konigsberg	Robert Conrad	Conrad Robert Falk
Julie Andrews	Julia Wells	Alice Cooper	Vincent Furnier
Eve Arden	Eunice Quedens	David Copperfield	David Kotkin
Bea Arthur	Bernice Frankel	Howard Cosell	Howard Cohen
Jean Arthur	Gladys Greene	Elvis Costello	Declan Patrick McManus
Fred Astaire	Frederick Austerlitz	Lou Costello	Louis Cristillo
Alan Autry	Carlos Brown	Joan Crawford	Lucille Fay LeSueur
Lauren Bacall	Betty Joan Perske	Michael Crawford	Michael Dumble-Smith
Anne Bancroft	Anna Maria Italiano	Tom Cruise	Thomas Mapother
Brigitte Bardot	Camille Javal	Tony Curtis	Bernard Schwartz
Gene Barry	Eugene Klass	Vic Damone	Vito Farinola
Orson Bean	Dallas Burrows	Rodney Dangerfield	Jacob Cohen
Bonnie Bedelia	Bonnie Culkin	Bobby Darin	Walden Robert Cassotto
Pat Benetar	Patricia Andrejewski	Doris Day	Doris von Kappelhoff
Robbie Benson	Robert Segal	Yvonne De Carlo	Peggy Middleton
Tony Bennett	Anthony Benedetto	Sandra Dee	Alexandra Zuck
Busby Berkeley	William Berkeley Enos	John Denver	Henry John Deutschendorf, Jr.
Jack Benny	Benjamin Kubelsky	Bo Derek	Mary Cathleen Collins
Joey Bishop	Joseph Gottlieb	John Derek	Derek Harris
Robert Blake	Michael Gubitosi	Susan Dey	Susan Smith
Victor Borge	Borge Rosenbaum	Angie Dickinson	Angeline Brown
David Bowie	David Robert Jones	Bo Diddley	Elias Bates
Boy George	George Alan O'Dowd	Phyllis Diller	Phyllis Driver
Fanny Brice	Fannie Borach	Diana Dors	Diana Fluck
Charles Bronson	Charles Buchinsky	Melvyn Douglas	Melvyn Hesselberg
Albert Brooks	Albert Einstein	Bob Dylan	Robert Zimmerman
Mel Brooks	Melvin Kaminsky	Sheena Easton	Sheena Shirley Orr
George Burns	Nathan Birnbaum	Barbara Eden	Barbara Huffman
Ellen Burstyn	Edna Gillooly	Ron Ely	Ronald Pierce
Richard Burton	Richard Jenkins	Chad Everett	Raymond Cramton
Red Buttons	Aaron Chwatt	Tom Ewell	S. Yewell Tompkins
Nicolas Cage	Nicholas Coppola	Douglas Fairbanks	Douglas Ullman

Table 1.1. Continued

Stage Name	Original Name	Stage Name	Original Name
Michael Caine	Maurice Micklewhite	Morgan Fairchild	Patsy McClenny
Maria Callas	Maria Kalogeropoulos	Alice Faye	Ann Leppert
Vikke Carr	Florencia Casíllas	Stepin Fetchit	Lincoln Perry
Diahann Carroll	Carol Diann Johnson	Sally Field	Sally Mahoney
Cyd Charisse	Tula Finklea	W. C. Fields	William Claude Dukenfield
Ray Charles	Ray Charles Robinson	Peter Finch	William Mitchell

Source: Hoffman 1992, 364

wardrobe, we can be confident that they will differ in what they choose and in the way they combine colors and styles. They will even differ in what stores they choose to shop at. Moreover, a set of judges will differ from one another on how much they like each man's choices. No surprise here. Still, within the context of the broader society, subgroups have varying tastes and interests in fashion and different abilities to express their tastes—that is, money and access.[4] For either men or women, for example, people of a comparable age, social class, and other background characteristics will still differ from one another in the clothing they purchase, but less than they will on average from those of different backgrounds. Individual differences in preference are the final step, but they operate within the context of broad societal and subgroup influences. It is not a question of individual choice *versus* social determinism; it is a matter of individual choices operating within the context of social influences. As Fred Davis (1992) observes, even if we go out of our way to intentionally violate contemporary fashions, what he calls *antifashion*, we need to be aware of the tastes that we are to reject and avoid. Indeed, those seeking to announce their opposition often have their own fashions. Those engaged in antifashion are very different from those who are *oblivious* or otherwise *unconcerned* with fashion.

As an individual, it is perfectly appropriate to say simply that one "likes" or does not like a particular cultural product. If we ask ourselves the scientific question of what leads these tastes to be of the form that they are at a given time, place, and for specific subsets of the population, then more is going on than merely the sum of random individual decisions. And this is not just because the aggregate of individual decisions shifts over time, although it does. Rather, it is because there are orderly movements which suggest that some set of principles must be operating to drive these changes. Our goal, then, is to understand the principles (insofar as they exist) that both drive changes in taste and lead the tastes to take the forms that they do.

AN APPROACH TO SOCIAL AESTHETICS

In seeking to learn what causes fashions to change and why the fashions take the specific form that they do, we shall not describe a set of rules for determining beauty or harmony or what is *intrinsically* appealing. Instead, we will use prosaic everyday behavior (mainly the naming of children) to infer the social processes that lead us to like what we do at one time and then to change that taste at a later time. This is by no means a deterministic viewpoint, but rather one that attempts to consider how various social factors influence tastes. Note that I say *influence*, not *cause*—individual choices are of consequence, even if they operate within the framework of these socially driven influences.

Are there principles to help us understand why tastes change? Are there rules that lead tastes to take the form that they do? The answer is a resounding "yes." The first step toward analyzing these questions, however, is to avoid the temptation to think that there is a fixed answer such that tastes are the product of a single causal factor, or even the product of an invariant relationship among several causes. Keep in mind changes in fashion are not inevitably an essential feature of any particular part of either material or symbolic culture. In many countries today it is hard to imagine the absence of fashion changes when considering clothing or the way homes are furnished and decorated or the types of foods that are eaten. Yet *changes in fashion* are different from the *existence of customs*. A specific type of clothing, say, may be associated with a given group and is not purely utilitarian in the sense that features of this garment are inherently separate from its ostensible function. If, however, the garment is rather static and unchanging, then it is not a matter of fashion.

Because it is not inevitable that fashion exists as an essential feature of any given attribute—whether it be the clothing we wear or how we furnish our homes or choose our food—we can ask why is an attribute fashionable? Why is there a steady change of tastes associated with a given attribute that are not linked to its inherent utilitarian function? In effect, we ask for the factors that lead tastes to change. As Fernand Braudel observes about the development of modern Western society:

One cannot really talk of fashion becoming all-powerful before about 1700. At that time the word gained a new lease of life and spread everywhere with its new meaning: keeping up with the times. From then on fashion in the modern sense began to influence everything: the pace of change had never been as swift in earlier times.

In fact, the further back in time one goes, even in Europe, one is more likely to find the still waters of ancient situations like those we have described in India, China and Islam. The general rule was changelessness. Until towards the beginning of the twelfth century costumes in Europe remained entirely as they had been in Roman times: long tunics falling straight to the feet for women and to the knees for men. For century upon century, costume had remained unchanged. Any innovation, such as the lengthening of men's clothes in the twelfth century was strongly criticized. . . .

The really big change came in about 1350 with the sudden shortening of men's costume, which was viewed as scandalous by the old, the prudent and the defenders of tradition. . . .

In a way, one could say that fashion began here. For after this, ways of dressing became subject to change in Europe. [1981, 316–317]

In other words, a given society (or subset) may have distinctive jewelry, music, clothing, homes, furnishings, food, manners, and the like. Unless, however, there is a regular pattern of change, by definition these are *customs* rather than *fashions*. Even so, they are not intrinsically customs, and hence they may develop into fashions at some later point. When clothing, for example, becomes a matter of fashion, then people will change their clothing even if there is no utilitarian reason to do so. The old garment still serves its function to keep us warm or to cover certain parts of our body or repel the rain, but it is discarded because it no longer looks *right* (even though it once did) in ways that are irrelevant to utilitarian function. The color, width, pattern, weave, length, number of buttons, and decorative additions of garments may change through the years without necessarily improving on their function. Every time we put aside a garment because we no longer like the way it looks, then we are treating clothing as a representation of aesthetic issues rather than judging it exclusively from its nondecorative role. It is not inevitable, of course, that clothing and fashion be linked. Indeed, this linking requires enough affluence so that one can replace clothing—even if still serviceable—without giving up another necessity such as food or shelter. Fashion in clothing becomes an affordable consideration when either we earn more or the cost of producing the clothing declines or the price of other "needs" drops.[5]

The second issue pertains to the form fashion takes. This is linked in part to the first question in the sense that whatever causes fashion to change might well influence the direction that fashion takes. Yet it provides only a partial answer at best. The new forms of fashion are not entirely explained by what causes fashion to change; other rules of fashion direct its newest outcomes. As we discuss the relevant literature in this chapter, it will become clear that some of the most important theories of fashion are not wrong—but they are often lopsided and incomplete, helping us understand only *some* of the conditions that lead fashions to change or take a particular form. Three types of influence—external events, internal mechanisms, and idiosyncratic historical developments—affect fashion changes, and we shall consider them in turn.

External Events

By "external events" I mean the impact of various organizational, institutional, political, technological, and cultural changes on fashions. This includes broad, sweeping shifts as well as narrower ones. Among broad shifts, we can think of the sweep of democratization, industrialization, the decline of formality, technological revolutions, changes in gender and race relations, literacy, increased social mobility, the rise of computers, and urbanization. Among narrower shifts, it is easy to think of how a specific development—say, an invention—influences tastes. Examples are color television or the ability to record sounds and thereby to replay music in the absence of musicians and at will. The influence is *external* because the social change is not caused by its fashion consequences. Such external events as war or the development of space travel or economic depression, for example, can alter various features of fashion, but they occur regardless of any possible consequence for fashion.

And yet, it may not seem so clear that technological developments such as those permitting the reproduction of music would have occurred independently and, hence, whether this is an *external* event. Clearly, the technological ability to reproduce music in virtually any locale, culminating in portable battery-powered radios and compact disk or cassette players, has had a profound impact on music. But it is an external event in the sense that it has consequences for fashion in music, not that it was produced in order to change these fashions. Consequences for fashion or not, we can assume that the invention would have occurred if only to reproduce existing music.

It is easiest to grasp the role of broad external changes by examining earlier popular tastes that—by today's standards—might be rather unappealing. Ignoring fashion for the moment, consider the influence of external forces on three examples of what the public once found to be entertaining. The first deals with technology alone, the second combines a technological change with normative standards in an earlier period, and the last reflects the joint influence of political standards, an economic depression, and behavior that people once found acceptable.

The Cyclorama, built in Boston in 1884, was a 127-foot-diameter dome, second only in size in the United States to the Capitol building. Exhibited here was a single painting, four hundred feet long and fifty feet high, depicting the Battle of Gettysburg in realistic detail. To enhance the illusion of being at the battle, viewers climbed a stairway to stand in the middle of the painting, cannons and soldiers were placed in the foreground, and the painted sky was illuminated (Campbell and Vanderwarker 1994). Imagine how bland and ineffective the Cyclorama would seem today in comparison with the that contemporary technology would create the illusion of being in the battle (the building now serves as exhibition space for the Boston Center for the Arts).

Our tastes are changed and molded by far more than technology. The exhibition of babies in their incubators illustrates how earlier standards of behavior made it possible for a medical innovation gradually also to become a successful form of commercial recreation. The development of infant incubators toward the end of the nineteenth century was a clear step in reducing the mortality of premature infants. To publicize this medical innovation and gain hospital space for incubators, six of them were exhibited at the Berlin Exposition of 1896. So far, nothing counter to today's tastes. Yet the machines were not merely being demonstrated: there were babies in them. A distinguished obstetrician supplied the newborns for the incubators from a charity hospital in Berlin. Spectators to the *Kinderbrutanstalt* (child hatchery) were charged a fee to pay for the expenses, and it proved to be quite profitable. A year later, a similar display opened at an exhibition in London. The British medical community objected to the public display of premature infants and offered none for exhibition. Yet three wicker baskets of infants were shipped from Paris to the exhibit, and it was a great success, attracting as many as 3,600 visitors a day. Similar exhibits began to appear at a variety of expositions and world's fairs. Eventually a showman picked up the idea and started a permanent incubator exhibit first at Coney Island and then other amusement parks. Keep in mind that the medical standards of care at these exhibits were high and that incubators per se were a major step forward in the care of premature babies. Still, this display had become a show, one involving infants. At one point at the Coney Island show, the admission was two and a half times greater than the going rate at other attractions.

Although the exhibit was challenged, it never was declared illegal, and it finally closed only in 1943 (see Brown 1994).

Last, many readers know little about the Dionne quintuplets. Born to French-Canadian parents in rural Ontario in 1934, they became:

> Canada's biggest tourist draw, bringing 6,000 visitors a day to Quintland, the theme park operated by the Ontario government where the five little girls were put on display like carnival geeks or pandas in a zoo.
>
> Ontario raked in hundreds of millions of dollars from the Depression-era throngs that made the pilgrimage to North Bay, Ontario—home of the Dionne quintuplets—to gawk at Cecile, Annette, Yvonne, Emilie and Marie, the first five-of-a-kind babies to live more than a few days. [Nickerson 1995, 2]

The Dionne quintuplets were on display for the first nine years of their lives, and nearly three million people visited them at the remote location of Quintland, some 250 miles north of Toronto (Berton 1977, 11–12). The parents lost all rights to their children and underwent an eight-year legal battle to regain them, the little girls were exhibited in what amounted to a glorified fishbowl, and they were treated more or less as simple commercial property as they were transformed into a tourist attraction. It is hard to see, by today's standards, how such behavior could have been tolerated. Yet as Ontario's premier said in 1995, "Things were done back then which would not be tolerated today" (Nickerson 1995, 2; see also Berton 1977 and Came 1994). Again, we readily see how changes in social standards for the treatment of infants and small children have changed through the years, making such a response—at least in its crudest form, and given the publicity accorded to these children—unlikely at present. Today, of course, additional issues that would surface would be parental rights, the protection of the children's rights, and the appropriate role of the government.

The possibilities of considering fashions as a response to external social changes—of either a broad or a narrow nature—is not only tempting but surely often an appropriate step. One may well wonder: How can it possibly *not* be the case that these fundamental events affect fashions? What else but some distinctive and powerful social conditions could account for the dominance of a particular fashion at a specific time? Shifts in artistic and intellectual movements, for example, are often linked to a society's zeitgeist, its spirit of the times. As John Mueller (1951) has observed for music and Florian Znaniecki (1952) for the arts in general, such artistic developments often accompany nationalistic movements. The thrust to create a nation-state or to glorify one's group often generates musical fashions that emphasize the "distinctive roots" of a culture and revive these earlier musical themes directly or by incorporating them in modern forms. Writing of the nineteenth-century nationalist movement in music, Mueller states that "after the old feudal aristocracy had been destroyed, most European nations, large and small, turned to the musical forms of the simple folk, their songs and dances, as well as their myths and legends, which were viewed as grass-root emanations of their national spirit. These were then appropriated as the basic elements of their new art forms. . . . These were either presented "straight" or more commonly incorporated and absorbed into standard forms of song, symphony, and opera, on which they bestowed a national flavor" (1951, 253).

This assertion seems straightforward enough, but there are several difficulties. First, it is all too easy to find *some* plausible connection between a fashion change and developments within a society. Contentions like this need to be evaluated more rigorously. Second, one would want to understand the specific mechanisms whereby broad events are connected (or not connected) to a given fashion outcome. Otherwise, the explanation is all rather simplistic. As Levin Schücking observes, an artistic fashion is more likely to be linked to a specific subgroup of society than to the general outlook within that society. He argues, in fact, that advanced industrialized nations have relatively little commonly shared perspective: "a new taste appearing anywhere is the expression not by any means of the 'spirit of the age' but only of the spirit of a particular group, which may fail to represent the spirit of the age" (1944, 75). This perspective accords with Howard Becker's observations (1982) of the central role of relevant groups (what he terms "collective action") in generating artistic innovations. In any case, because there are many possible external influences on either a given fashion or a change in fashion, one cannot—without rigorous study—blithely attribute causality. Last, as we shall see, fashions change or take the form that they do through more than external events. Fashion developments cannot be attributed either to the spirit of the times or to some specific societal development without serious effort—even if there is a general reason to believe that such external conditions may play a role.

External events certainly account for some developments in taste. In some instances, the evidence is extensive; in other cases, though not extensive, it is compelling. As we shall see in Chapter 3, for example, a modest increase in the popularity of *Herbert* coincides precisely with the election of Herbert Hoover, and the name's decline a few years later occurs during the Great Depression. Likewise, *Franklin* goes up with Roosevelt's election in the midst of the

Depression. Occasionally there is neither an abundance of evidence nor a precision in the timing. In some cases, we can see how internal mechanisms influence the outcome even with the assumption that strong external influences are operating. There is evidence of tastes being generated by internal mechanisms *even if* you assume a powerful external influence. The discussion of the naming tastes among African Americans, Asian Americans, Mexican Americans, and various ethnic groups of European origin (largely in Chapter 7, but also in Chapter 3) makes assumptions about the role external events played at such different times as slavery, assimilation, protest, and ethnic assertion. These are subject to the same criticism as other plausible external causes of taste (they may or may not be true, but such a determination must rest on more than fitting the realm of possibility). I do not delve into the assumption of external causes here because there is an opportunity to describe the importance and pervasiveness of internal mechanisms even under the assumption that powerful external forces are operating. An internal mechanism, for example, provides a compelling explanation for which Anglo girls' names Mexican-American parents in Texas favor —while avoiding other equally popular names. This accounting can be employed even if one assumes that assimilation is a driving force. In similar fashion, a related internal mechanism helps us understand the linguistic nature of newly invented African-American names—even accounting for the roles that black nationalism and black protest play in driving this development.

Internal Mechanisms

Fashions are affected by more than just external influences; they will alter and take new forms even when external influences do not change.[6] Internal mechanisms are at work in such situations to generate new fashions even in the absence of social or cultural change. Incidentally, the existence of such internal mechanisms means that one can all too easily overinterpret the social meaning of a change in tastes—some changes have no meaning other than that they are changes in fashion. Unlike the influence of external events, a standard way of explaining changes in taste, the notion of internal mechanisms is less commonly understood. The model of class imitation that follows here is a clear and plausible example of how such an internal mechanism might operate. The magnitude of its impact is a separate empirical question we shall consider later.

Class Imitation The hypothesis that the fashions adopted by higher classes are then imitated by the classes below them is an internal mechanism that, when applicable, would continuously spew out new fashions. The following quotation from Fernand Braudel is a good illustration of this widely cited fashion imitation model, originally suggested by Georg Simmel in 1904 and considered by Bernard Barber and Lyle Lobel (1953).

> I have always thought that fashion resulted to a large extent from the desire of the privileged to distinguish themselves, whatever the cost, from the masses who followed them; to set up a barrier. "Nothing makes noble persons despise the gilded costume so much [according to a Sicilian who passed through Paris in 1714] as to see it on the bodies of the lowest men in the world." So the upper classes had to invent new "gilded costumes," or new distinctive signs, whatever they might be, every time complaining that "things have changed indeed, and the new clothes being worn by the bourgeois, both men and women, cannot be distinguished from those of persons of quality" (1779). Pressure from followers and imitators obviously made the pace quicken. [1981, 324]

Here is a three-step internal mechanism that generates continuous changes in taste: (1) the "upper" strata seek to set themselves off by adopting the latest fashions in clothing; (2) the classes below promptly imitate their fashions; (3) this thereby forces the upper strata to adopt new fashions. Clearly, this mechanism can apply to a wide variety of taste shifts. How widespread this mechanism is, as well as how it operates today, is an empirical question that we will consider in a relatively rigorous manner for at least one taste.

Not only does the class imitation model operate indefinitely to change fashions—even if society otherwise remains constant in all of its external elements—it has two other important features. First, it requires the presence of certain external conditions, though they need not change. In this case, there needs to be a combination of sufficient affluence and low-cost technology that allows changes in clothing fashions to be accessible to a vast part of the population—that is, possibly for more than one subset of society. Second, this mechanism provides no basis for the particular fashion itself. It implies only that upper-strata members of society wear clothing not worn by others. When the fashion is widely copied, and hence no longer distinguishes this group, then some new fashion must be introduced. What that new fashion will be is not generated by the model; indeed, it is ignored. This fact is worth keeping in mind.

Idiosyncratic Historical Developments

By "idiosyncratic historical developments" I refer to two influences on taste. First, the tastes (or fashions) existing at the initial point of an analysis themselves have the power to exert a strong influence on later tastes; as a result, these initial tastes are a fundamental starting point for understanding the tastes that follow. Even if an external social development leads us to expect a radical shift in tastes, we need to consider the influence of the existing fashions on what follows. And, in order to avoid infinite regression in time, it is convenient to take the existing tastes as given, looking at the influence they exert on later developments and considering how they are modified by external changes and internal mechanisms. Existing tastes affect later tastes. Indeed, new fashions are usually variants of preceding fashions. For this reason, one often cannot even understand the appeal of a new taste without first considering the existing practices. We can model an internal mechanism that converts existing tastes into new tastes (see the discussion of ratchets in Chapter 4), but it has to start with these initial events as a given. The tastes that are present, when important external social events occur, are best viewed as an "unexplained" combination of events that affect the tastes that follow.

Idiosyncratic historical developments also include events that influence a *specific* taste—as contrasted with a general movement in tastes—but that are also best viewed as unpredictable. Because we can develop a very plausible explanation after the fact but could not even remotely propose to view this as a "predictable" event, it is best that these be taken as *givens* in understanding some feature of fashion, rather than as either a *condition to be explained* or as simply some *external event*. In some instances, this type of idiosyncratic occurrence may profoundly affect fashion movements more generally, but again it is best to view its specific cause as idiosyncratic, even though the types of mechanisms are generalizable.

The popularity of a name, for example, is often influenced by specific events, which themselves cannot be explained. By contrast, the shift in popularity of a name can be understood as a product of these idiosyncratic events. Changes in the popularity of the first names *Marcus, Jacqueline, Donald,* and *Adolf* in the United States reflect events that cannot be explained in any generalizable way— linked as they are to events surrounding Marcus Garvey, Jacqueline Bouvier Kennedy, Donald Duck, or Adolf Hitler. Paradoxically, the processes responding to these unique events are themselves generalizable. One cannot predict what taste will next experience a jolt upward or downward in popularity owing to some historically specific event. It is possible, however, to understand the ensuing shifts as the product of a specific mechanism whereby symbols are contaminated or enhanced (see Chapter 5).

Because existing tastes tend to affect later tastes, we can use initial tastes to help account for later fashions without necessarily trying to understand how the tastes at the starting point came into being. Rather, starting with the existing tastes, we can ask what bearing they have on later fashions. We have to think about how historical events can be incorporated into an understanding of the development of fashions without falling prey to the undoable task of explaining the idiosyncratic events themselves. These events are best viewed as owing to chance and therefore in themselves of no inherent long-lasting significance (although indirectly they may have an important impact). In the case of Adolf Hitler, for example, we would have no difficulty understanding why his rise to power might reduce the popularity of *Adolf*—and this itself represents a model of taste change that we can generalize rather nicely. The attempt to understand why Hitler's name is *Adolf*, however, would be unproductive.

Interactions and Complexities

In practice, of course, these influences operate in complex ways. People do not live in a laboratory setting, where each influence can operate with the others held under control. When considering real events we often need to think about how tastes change when all three types of influences are operating at once. Consider the variety of influences affecting the design of Cadillac automobiles in the years after World War II, when they were exceptionally prestigious. It was during this period "when to call anything 'the Cadillac of its class' meant that it was the best" (Stern and Stern 1990, 62). The famous fin-tail design sported by Cadillacs of the late forties and much of the fifties was part of a general thematic emphasis on the rapid development of aircraft and the technological events of the fifties. But several different factors were in operation, as the tail fin was copied and then exaggerated in other cars, and this eventually undermined the initial marking function that was first served when tail fins appeared on the 1948 Cadillac. The following quotations from David Gartman's social history of car design, *Auto Opium*, tell the story.

> In 1948 Harley Earl [then head of styling at General Motors] fired the first volley in the postwar style war with the introduction of the fabulous new Cadillac, inspired by the P-38 Lightning aircraft [a well-known American fighter plane in World War II]. The nose of the car was rather pointed, like the plane, and accented by two protruding bullets on the bumper. And the dummy chromed scoops on the rear fenders simulated the functional air entries on the P-38. But the most distinctly aeronautical feature of the new luxury car was the little fin on each rear fender. The initially controversial

tail fin was placed there not merely as a symbol of airborn[e] escape but also of distinction. As Earl stated: "Cadillac owners realized that it gave them an extra receipt for their money in the form of a visible prestige marking for an expensive car." Earl's airplane allusions also resonated with the nationalist ideology of the postwar era, for they symbolized America's military superiority over past and present enemies. . . . Between 1950 and 1956, Harley Earl and his GM Styling Staff extended and intensified these entertaining themes of aeronautics and escapism, setting the styling pace for the other automakers to follow. [162, 163]

And follow they did: "Stylists in the two other major American automakers slavishly followed Earl's fantastic path of design. Ford styling caught on quickly, replacing its smooth, clean, envelope body of 1949 with chromed-up collections of airplane clichés, replete with hardtops, curved windshields, bullet grilles, tail fins, and jet-exhaust taillights. After a slow start in the 1950s styling race, Chrysler stylists picked up their pace in 1955 and raced to the forefront in 1957" (163). We also see the influence of several external changes. Not only did the global conflict influence Americans' postwar attitudes, but airplanes made rapid technological advances during the war. These changes soon spread from the P-38 model's new styling to other related themes. Other General Motors cars "did not yet have fins, but their squared-off rear fenders suggested rudderlike formations. And a new aeronautic motif appeared on the Buick, the infamous portholes. Named Venti-Ports, the holes in the sides of the front fenders were reminiscent of the exhaust ports on fighter planes" (162). This trend then expanded and shifted when the Chrysler cars got into the airplane motif. General Motors had employed the World War II warplane theme, which reflected Americans' positive feelings about winning the war.. Chrysler, by contrast, used the jet age as inspiration for its automobile designs. (It is, by the way, not a matter of chance that advertisers described the car drivers as getting into their "cockpits.")

Americans' affluence in this period is also a crucial external condition—after all, these designs added cost to the cars without offering mechanical improvements, superior comfort, or better gas mileage. In terms of gas mileage, in fact, note that these developments occur during a period of relatively cheap gasoline, before the formation of the Organization of Petroleum Exporting Countries (OPEC).

The evolution of tail fins illustrates how the impact of social changes on tastes may occur at a time when internal mechanisms are also generating changes and the influence of the past, too, is affecting the outcome. Fashions change owing to some form of the imitation mechanism we have described. Initially distinctive features found, for example, in expensive and prestigious cars are then copied in less expensive cars: even the same advertising themes are copied to show that consumers can obtain equivalent quality for much less. This imitation in cheaper cars in turn causes the initial producer to seek novel features to again set the automobile apart from others.

The analysis of fashions is complicated for several reasons: more than one internal mechanism can affect fashion; societies are increasingly subject to the simultaneous occurrence of external changes that can potentially affect tastes; and current fashions have historical underpinnings that influence the impact of both internal mechanisms *and* external changes on new fashions. For example, it would be reasonable today to speculate that the women's movement has influenced the names given to children, but the actual impact of this exogenous social force is influenced both by ongoing shifts in taste caused by the "pure" principles of fashion and by existing tastes. It is worth our while to examine the role of each of these three types of influences and, in turn, to consider the complicated interactions among them.

The Net Result: A Multilayered, Probabilistic, and Asymmetrical Approach

To examine changes in taste, we will need to take into account the three types of influence described above: external events of social, political, and economic significance; internal mechanisms of taste that generate changes even when the external environment remains constant; and the unique historical conditions of a fixed point in time. This suggests that we take a multilayered, asymmetrical, and probabilistic approach. It is multilayered because we visualize a set of influences of differing consequence: broad influences set bounds on what is acceptable and unacceptable, while narrower ones shape specific tastes within the confines of these bounds. It is probabilistic because no simple deterministic cause-and-effect model operates; rather, the likelihood of different outcomes is altered by the continuity of a currently popular name and/or the chances of a new set of names (Lieberson 1992). The broad influences in turn permit the operation of other influences that affect the specific tastes that are chosen. It is asymmetrical because the processes are not simply reversible (Lieberson 1985, chap. 4). If we could reverse the historical conditions leading to a given set of tastes, those tastes would not return to their previous nature. Internal mechanisms would move them in a different direction.

There should, of course, be some correlation with major political and social events, but it would be a mistake to think that political and social events could "cause" the resulting tastes. Social events may generate a decline in existing patterns of taste, but not they do not specifically drive the tastes that replace them. (Those new tastes would be the product of other mechanisms.) Can we say that a broad political or social change has a greater effect on existing tastes than on new tastes? More often than not, yes. I am suggesting here that external events may create openings for new tastes as well as limits on what they may be, but that is not the same as causing them in a simple fashion. Yet what about the existing tastes? It is unlikely that any social change, no matter how monumental, will completely destroy existing patterns. It is far more likely, it seems to me, that even a massive social change will itself be deeply affected by critical features of existing tastes, rather than radically altering them. And yet, features irrelevant to the central focus of the external changes will not be altered but instead will fit into the matrix of existing practices. I will elaborate on this approach and evaluate its utility as we examine empirical data in ensuing chapters.

AND WHAT DO WE ALREADY KNOW?

As one might expect, through the years researchers have made a number of valuable efforts to account for the nature of fashion. They have addressed a variety of important questions about fashion, among them, the causes of fashion; the role of organizations on fashion; the impact of social, political, and economic changes; the influence of mass media and popular culture; the symbolic nature of fashion; the linkages of fashion to features of the stratification system; the different domains of fashion; imitation; long-term patterns change; and the role of such specific sources of fashion as France, California, Milan, New York, and London.

As we shall see, much of the earlier work is useful *if* we ask the right questions. Rather than evaluating contributions in terms of whether they adequately account for tastes, even if the theory presented makes such a claim, it is useful to regard each contribution from the perspective of suggesting an internal mechanism, an exogenous force, or a complex interaction between the two (along with historical circumstances) to account for either changes in taste or the nature of the tastes. We can think of these theories as inherently incomplete. They are incomplete certainly because each emphasizes not all of the possible influences on fashion changes usually just one. Each theory likewise tends to emphasize either external or internal sources of change, rarely both. And they are incomplete insofar as they cannot account for the role of unique, idiosyncratic events and historical influences on the outcome. All of these theories are true in the limited sense that they sometimes operate, but they can be put together as part of a fundamentally different way to approach taste (with applications to many other kinds of change as well, as developed in the final chapter). These are ideas about what may play a role in driving tastes.[7] They may be helpful in any given context. If they are, that's fine, and we are happy to use them. If they aren't, it doesn't mean that the ideas are worthless or wrong. Rather, they don't seem to work in the context of the particular conglomeration of historical and external and internal conditions. That is all one can say. All we can try to do is to address fashion changes in context to see if we can discover what is driving these tastes and, then, hopefully develop an analysis that will help us understand the structure of linkages. The structure may hold for a long time or a short time; it may hold for many societies or just one. It is no more right if broad than if narrow; it is simply a question of understanding how the existing structure operates, and then setting some bounds on its applicability (see Lieberson 1992, 7–11).

From this point of view, consider Thorstein Veblen's landmark discussion of conspicuous consumption. This notion, which he formulated a century ago, in 1899, remains a useful tool for understanding domains of taste ranging from automobiles to works of art. In a nutshell, Veblen realized, expensive products are consumed as a way of demonstrating wealth. Many material goods, therefore, are expensive *not* because they are attractive and fashionable; rather, they are attractive and fashionable *because* they are expensive. Material wealth is thus a powerful nonorganizational influence on taste. As James Davis observes, "esthetic norms and pecuniary norms are highly correlated in this society, for it is remarkable how, despite constant change in taste, a material object considered to be in 'good taste' at a given moment is also hideously expensive" (1958, 11). Interesting spin-offs from this line of thought are such questions as what happens to the aesthetic enjoyment of previously expensive objects that—through technological or other changes—are no longer costly. And yet, except for explaining changes in taste because of either their decline in cost or their imitation by other social classes, conspicuous consumption will not help us understand why one expensive taste is preferred over another expensive taste, whether this be one automobile versus another or one clothing fashion versus another. At best, it sets a limit on what may occur. If the Cadillac is replaced by the Mercedes and the BMW (or they in turn by such upscale Japanese as the Lexus and Infiniti), the changes probably cannot be explained simply as expressions of wealth.

Should we conclude that Veblen was *wrong* because the idea of conspicuous consumption fails to account for the decline of the Cadillac? We should view his theory as contributing an important mechanism for accounting for tastes—to wit, expensive goods tend to be more attractive because they allow the buyer to display wealth. Does this concept hold for all expensive things? For all subsets of the population? Only for expensive things? These are perfectly fine questions, yet all the idea of conspicuous consumption says is that this is *one* basis whereby people find goods attractive. Conspicuous consumption is a powerful tool for understanding the basis of tastes and, by implication, why tastes can change when something previously expensive is no longer high-priced and so is no longer as a marker of wealth and attainment. All ideas should do as well.

Another example of a valuable contribution to this field is Pierre Bourdieu's discussion of cultural capital.[8] Cultural capital is the high value that some classes place on certain tastes, knowledge, and the arts—especially when other classes are less likely to have the background to understand these tastes and interests. Those who have this knowledge, asserts Bourdieu, believe that it allows them to enjoy a higher status than those who lack it. The more complex and difficult to acquire the knowledge is, the greater value it has. Cultural capital is thus interpreted as allowing "higher classes" to mark others as both different and inferior. This idea has appeal for our purposes, since esoteric knowledge in the arts can become a commodity for marking and displaying one's background and position.

Nevertheless, the idea of cultural capital has limitations. For example, there would be no reason for the knowledge emphasized to change at all over time—except when initially esoteric knowledge becomes knowledge held by all. Take the elements that make up a college education. The basic curriculum of American colleges has changed enormously through the centuries, with massively less emphasis on Greek and Roman (whether it be knowledge of the languages and of the Classics written in these languages or even the histories of the Roman Empire and the Greek city-states). Could this knowledge be a class marker? I think so. Clearly, then, cultural capital does not readily account for the changing tastes in a college education. Likewise, in comparing the culture of the French and American upper middle class, Michèle Lamont finds (1992) that cultural capital goes a lot further in explaining the recreational activities of the upper strata in France than in the United States. Further, class differences in the use of art in homes in New York are far greater than can be explained by class differences in cultural capital (Halle 1993). For her part, Bonnie Erickson (1996) has shown that the use of cultural capital at the workplace need not always use forms linked to either class origin or education. And, of course, John Hall (1992) provides reason to believe that there is more than one type of cultural capital, such that different subsets of the population will have different capital and thus differ in their evaluations and currency. In sum, is cultural capital a useful idea? Yes. Should we evaluate it as providing a total account? No.

If we keep in mind the inevitable incompleteness of any mechanism, any external force, or any single basis for understanding taste or its level of change, then we shall better appreciate each element's help for understanding the questions posed here. More than that, we will be closer to thinking of a more appropriate and realistic model of how and why tastes change if we distinguish between causes of change per se from what causes the new tastes to take the form that they do. And it will not hurt us to understand that different types of causes are always operating.

FIRST NAMES

Why study first names? First names provide a unique opportunity to address questions about taste.[9] Compared with fashions in clothing, cars, and sodas, the naming process can be studied without worrying about the effect of organizations dedicated to influencing these tastes. Likewise, the effect of external forces, internal mechanisms, and historic factors are more easily seen. Certainly, the mass media play a role in the outcome (for example, a movie star name, or a name in the title of a hit song may influence the disposition to use a specific name), but these are not intentional organizational efforts to affect fashions. Contemporary changes in first names is a form of collective behavior that operates, as much as any taste can, without being the product—in part or whole—of formal organizations that attempt to affect current and future tastes.

Organizational influences do, however, exist. For example, nations vary in the ease with which parents are permitted to give newly invented, "foreign," or "nontraditional" names to their children. Some religions likewise have rules affecting parental choices, as for example Roman Catholics and Jews. But even these formal restrictions still allow followers a variety of options (Catholics may choose a name from an enormous number of saints, and Jews often tend to select a name that has the same first letter as a deceased ancestor). As I have earlier observed (Lieberson and Bell 1992, 514), organizations linked to children are not affected by the names given to them—only by whether a child is born. Also, although the mass media and popular culture can and do affect naming

practices, these influences are an unintended by-product rather than an organized effort to direct and mold tastes.[10]

The observed *expression* of many other tastes, moreover, will vary not simply
by dispositions but by the financial ability to buy what one most likes. It is a
common mistake to infer that observed class differences in consumption are
necessarily due solely to differences in taste that can be linked to education or
family background, although such taste differences between these subsets are
likely in many contexts. So far as subsets of the population differ in income
and, in turn, income affects purchases, however, subsets will *appear* to differ in
their tastes even when they are identical. Take the example of designer homes.
Only the affluent can act on their "champagne tastes" for distinctive architect-
designed homes built in desirable locations. Others may have identical preferences but are obliged to live in tract houses or in trailer homes for the simple
reason that they cannot afford more (to say nothing of those who cannot afford
to buy a home at all). Under these circumstances, before attributing an observed
difference solely to taste, one must account for wealth as a prerequisite for acting
on that taste. In this regard, names pose no problems. If groups differ in their
giving of names, we can be confident that these differences reflect variations in
tastes. It costs no more in dollars and cents to name a daughter *Lauren* or
Elizabeth than it does to name her *Crystal* or *Tammy*.

The pattern of name usage reflects a combination of influences: the imagery
associated with each name, the notions parents have about the children's future,
estimates of others' responses to a name, the awareness and knowledge of names
through the mass media and other sources, parents' beliefs about what names
are appropriate for people of their status, and institutionalized norms and pressures. As the role of the extended family, religious rules, and other institutional
pressures declines, choices are increasingly free to be matters of taste, and they
reflect corresponding differences among subsets of the population. In this regard, shifts in naming practices can be analyzed in terms of the combined
impact of exogenous forces, internal mechanisms of fashion change, and idiosyncratic historical conditions.

Studying fashion through the naming process has important technical advan-
tages. Names provide an exceptional opportunity to consider, in a relatively
rigorous way, how culture changes over time. The name data in this book are
based mainly on birth certificate data registered with government bodies or
listed in parish records. This permits us to analyze the names given to *all* children born in a given area—or even nation—over a span of years. Moreover, we

have every reason to assume that the data are at least as accurate (if not more accurate) than most sources of information on fashion. These sources provide relatively high-quality information for a wide variety of settings, with substantial numbers of cases, and often for relatively long spans.[11] Birth certificates, for example, list names along with such other attributes as race, birthplace, ethnicity, the mother's marital status, and the parents' education, economic status (inferred usually through other characteristics), and age. Unlike some of the remarkable long-term quantitative studies of high fashion in women's clothing (Kroeber 1919; Richardson and Kroeber 1940; Young 1937), we need not worry about how many people are actually responding to the fashions shown. Each child is given a name, and we know what that name is.[12] Of course, cultures and societies differ in their naming practices, although some customs are fairly common. Most societies, for example, give names that delineate the child's sex (Alford 1988, 65–66). Although the predominant source of our information on names is the United States, historical comparisons are made for *some* patterns in a number of other countries (particularly in Chapter 2).

Another especially attractive characteristic of first names in the United States and many other Western nations is their relative permanence; they are largely a once-in-a-lifetime proposition. To be sure, in some societies names change over a life span (see Alford 1988, table 4.2.1)—and this can occur in the United States—but generally people keep their given names. (The use of nicknames and diminutives is another matter, of course.) This means that when we look at changing fashions in names, the nature of these shifts is less complicated than for many other fashions. Unlike furniture, denim jeans, or breakfast cereals, changes in naming fashions focus on the names parents give their newly born infants, a lifetime association.

First names can also help us think about change more generally. The eminent geographer Wilbur Zelinsky, writing about the difficulty of measuring the subtle features of what he calls "the core of culture" (and, later, "the identity of the invisible heart of a culture"; 1970, 744), argues that first names form an ideal cultural metric. They yield "significant amounts of information about the essential nature of the culture," are found throughout time and space, have data that can be obtained for the past with no serious measurement and counting problems, are not contaminated by noncultural factors, and are relatively easily to gather. Zelinsky is fully aware of the difficulty in stating that there is such a thing as *the essential nature of the culture,* let alone deciding whether first names provide a desirable vehicle for uncovering that essential nature. And, as we shall see, he may be overly optimistic about how easy it is to use name data for different periods and places. Nevertheless, his analysis of changes between 1790 and 1968 in regional naming patterns in the eastern United States reveals characteristics of naming data and their utility for rigorously describing core features.

Other studies show how naming patterns can reveal subtle features of a culture. Alice Rossi's investigation (1965, 499–500) of differences between white middle-class boys and girls uses naming data to show differences in the treatment of sons and daughters when it comes to naming them after relatives or other significant people. Rossi discovered that sons are more closely linked to familial continuity and hence are far more likely to be named after a relative. Daughters' names, in contrast, tend to respond more to fashion in the sense that they are less linked to the family (in either an extended or a narrower sense). Rossi also stratified the data in her survey by birth decade, demonstrating that this gender difference has declined over time.

Obstacles

First names provide a magnificent opportunity to get at the nature of fashion and tastes, but they do face numerous stumbling blocks.

I Like the Name People cannot always tell us why a name appeals to them. It's easy to see why. First, they are almost certain to have unclear notions about the broad social conditions that are necessary prerequisites for their behavior; second, often they have no clear idea of what there is about a specific name that makes it appealing to them—they just *like* it. Likewise, the answer "named after a relative" is deceptive, simple as it may appear. Is the child named after someone regardless of whether the name in itself appeals to the parents? Or is it because the parents find a name attractive that they choose this particular relative's name? To put the question another way, how often do parents select a name that they flatly dislike, even though they wish to honor the person by giving their child that first name? Using an unattractive name as a middle name is a separate issue, because this does become a matter of taste, though in a negative way in the sense that the parents are able to avoid giving it to the child as a first name.[13]

Consider how entertainer Dana Carvey and his wife decided on their son's name: "They have a 21-month-old son named Dex—a shortened version of the word 'dextrose.' It seems Carvey was visiting his wife after she'd given birth and saw a bottle with that word on it. 'We hadn't picked a name yet, and it sounded good,' he explained" (Rader 1993, 5). We can't overanalyze any specific individual's behavior, but this anecdote clearly suggests how naming tastes incorporate a variety of forces: What are the existing cultural features that make *Dex* attractive? Is a name like *Dex* as likely to be given to a daughter? Do underlying conditions "free" the parents to follow their own impulses and, beyond that, to select a name that does not exist in the repertoire of names? Have names given to children always been a matter of parents *liking* or *not liking* the name?[14] Carvey's reason is undoubtedly an honest one, but a bevy of preconditions influence parents' decisions as to whether they like a name or not. (Another consideration, as we shall discover, is whether this sound cluster fits into broader movements in sound preferences for boys' names.)

Implicit Imagery and Connotations Names, as we will see, have imagery. Names differ in their connotations of intelligence, strength, assertiveness, honesty, humor, stuffiness, social class, masculinity or femininity, and a variety of other attributes. Accordingly, they can be selected—or rejected—simply because of the appeal these images have for their parents. These influences may often be implicit rather than explicit in the naming process.

Consider the collective processes that arise in the use of words associated with American Indians as nicknames for sports teams. Drawing on a study by Ray Franks (1982), Frank Nuesell reports that two of the ten most common nicknames for college sports teams are of this nature, *Warriors* and *Indians*. In addition, many teams often pick names belonging to specific Indian tribes, such as the *Illini*, *Hurons*, *Apaches*, and *Mohawks*, use names based on stereotyped images, such as *Redskins* or *Tomahawks*, and evoke other Indian associations in names such as *Chieftains*, *Chiefs*, or *Tribe*. Why is this so? If one looks at the eight other most frequently chosen names for sports teams, the usage of Indian names becomes clearer: they refer to animals. In declining order, the other most popular names are: *Eagles*, *Tigers*, *Cougars*, *Bulldogs*, *Lions*, *Panthers*, *Wildcats*, and *Bears*. In popularity, *Warriors* falls between *Bulldogs* and *Lions*, *Indians* between *Panthers* and *Wildcats*. According to Nuessel, these animals are all associated with "vicious or predatory tendencies. Most sports fans consider these to be characteristics that competitive athletic teams ought to possess. Two of these terms, *Indians* and *Warriors*, however, refer to American Indians who, presumably, also possess these traits" (1994, 101). In other words, the Indian references are based on stereotypes. Nuesell continues: "Because of their competitive nature, sport teams prefer nicknames that connote speed, strength, heroism, and courage. Most often these designations refer to animals (*Bears*, *Bulls*), natural disasters (*Cyclones, Hurricanes*), objects (*Jets, Bullets, Rockets, Spurs*), occupations (*Buccaneers, Kings*), and other phenomena, products, or people that signify those attributes that opposing athletic teams need to win games and championships" (Nuessel 1994, 102–103). Interestingly, although there is no formal rule about the imagery to be sought through the nicknames given to teams, a certain theme nevertheless develops. References to a specific Indian tribe or an aggressive animal are often linked to a school's location. Of course, many names are based on other associations, such as school colors (*Maroons, Crimson*) or geographic or historic ties (*Ducks, Quakers, Owls, Engineers, Cornhuskers, Boilermakers*). Yet it is clear that many high schools and colleges have "independently" arrived at the same thematic image in naming their sports teams. Likewise, the names given to car models are often of animals, places, astronomical objects, royalty, racetracks, and other images with connotations meant to appeal to buyers (Lehrer 1992, 129–132).

Historical Difficulties It is hard enough to understand the viewpoint and perspective of our contemporaries. The further we go back in time, the harder it becomes to gain a reasonable grasp of people's visceral responses toward names. In the case of *Ethel*, for example, a name not favored today in the United States, it is hard for us to see how people may have approached *Ethel* when it first arose as a pet form for names like *Etheldred, Ethelinda*, and *Ethelburg* (Withycombe 1977, 107–108). Because these longer names are not in common usage today, we cannot understand the imagery of *Ethel* as a diminutive when these names were themselves known, and we have no sense of the connotation this shortened form had. And even though *The Oxford Dictionary of English Common Names* tells us that *Ethel* became very fashionable after it appeared in midnineteenth-century novels by William Thackeray (*The Newcomes*) and Charlotte Yonge (*The Daisy Chain*), it is still hard to see what distinctive features of *Ethel* in these novels made the name resonate with readers. Yet this problem, though difficult, is not insurmountable. When, in Chapter 8, I discuss the influence of past movie stars on the popularity of first names, I attempt to show why some stars' names appeal and others do not. The results are promising.

Ad Hoc Conclusions May Be True, But How Do You Know? Ruth provides another example of the difficulties in developing a rigorous interpretation of a taste, even in the case of names. The name *Ruth* was fairly popular among Puritans in the United States and ranked in the top 10 for female births in Boston in the seventeenth century (Stewart 1979, 226, 15). Knowledge of the idiosyncratic conditions the Puritans faced in the New World suggests a plausible interpretation for the popularity of *Ruth*. The Puritans were unquestionably well acquainted with the Book of Ruth in the Old Testament, the story of a woman who leaves her own people (she had been a Moabite) never to return. What is the appeal? Patrick Hanks and Flavia Hodges speculate in *A Dictionary of First Names* that the meaning of the term *ruth,* compassion, was especially appealing to the Puritans (1990, 290–291). George Stewart reaches a similar conclusion in *American Given Names* about the possible appeal of this meaning and suggests a parallel between the biblical Ruth's life and that of early women in the colony:

> One detail of Ruth's story came especially close to that of the early American women. Like her, they had migrated, and they faced the problems of being "strangers in a strange land," and along with all this they faced the heartbreaking dilemma of "to go or to stay" when families had to be forever divided. An occasional man, as merchant or seaman, might visit England, but a woman had no such hope. Not as empty rhetoric would the emigrating woman read the words: "whither thou goest, I will go; and where thou lodgest, I will lodge: thy people shall be my people, and thy God my God." [1979, 226]

By the same token, however, Stewart also observes, that it is much harder to interpret the continuity in popularity for most of the other names. So we are attracted to the interpretation because it is *plausible,* but it is little more than an ad hoc explanation. Again, there is the difficulty in understanding earlier thought processes in order to understand the mechanisms and the external social changes affecting tastes. We shall see that in some cases inferences can be drawn with a certain degree of confidence.

BY WAY OF SUMMARY

As we go forward, we are prepared to address two questions: What causes tastes to change? Why do the new ones take the form that they do? A distinction is drawn among three types of influences: *external, internal,* and *idiosyncratic historical developments.* This leads to the following propositions:

- Changes in external conditions can cause fashions to change.
- However, it does not follow that a fashion change is necessarily due to a change in external conditions.

- This is because fashion has its own internal mechanisms that generate changes even in the absence of societal change. Indeed, it can be shown that internal mechanisms lead fashions to change indefinitely without the operation of any new societal changes.
- It is therefore treacherous to casually use an external social development to explain an observed change in fashion.
- Under any circumstance, external changes do not operate in a vacuum but are formed and channeled by both the ongoing changes driven by internal mechanisms and the legacy of existing tastes.
- There is an important distinction between the factors that cause fashions to change and those that lead to new fashions.

Becoming a Fashion

The word *fashion* means many things and encompasses many criteria. As we shall use it here, *fashion* entails aesthetic, nonessential changes to a physical object or concept. Fashion changes do not improve the ostensible functions of products or make them less expensive or allow for new features. Conversely, it is *not* simply fashion if new ideas replace older ideas solely because the new ideas are superior in their power and intellectual utility. An aesthetic change occurs because something is now more attractive than what was previously deemed attractive. If these aesthetic changes grow more frequent, then it means that fashion is becoming an increasingly central feature of the product. In practice, the distinction is sometimes blurred between changes caused by nonessential aesthetic matters and changes in the improvement in the function of the material or nonmaterial object. For example, an object's function may be to display the aesthetic skill of the purchaser or creator (as in many forms of jewelry that are not simply markers of wealth). Or the improvement of the ostensible function may have an aesthetic dimension (as, say, purchase of new appliance with "bells and whistles" that have an appeal beyond what is due sheerly to any functional improvement).

Putting this arbitrary quality aside, we see that this view breaks down changes in a product into two components. One is fashion, an attribute based on the rate of change for aesthetic reasons. This contrasts with changes related to the product's ostensible function. By definition, *fashion* is not applicable to aesthetic preferences that *never* change. And yet, what is not a matter of fashion in one period may become so at a later time. Moreover, fashion changes entail an additional quantitative issue, because rates of change themselves may shift over time. Although it is often convenient to talk about the presence or absence of fashions, this is really a matter of degree—and this matter of degree may shift over time. At one end of the spectrum are cultural aesthetics that barely change in one's lifetime. At the other extreme, we can conceive of aesthetic changes that occur several times in one year. In investigating the development of a fashion, we are really considering a movement over time on a continuum from virtually no change for aesthetic reasons to constant aesthetic change.

Fashion has both an individual and an aggregate dimension. Individual responses can vary; for some, simply to learn that something *is in fashion* is to give that item an aesthetic attraction. What is declared to be in fashion is, by that simple matter, automatically attractive to the element of the population whose pleasure is in knowing that they are in fashion. For others, fashion is more complex; somehow, somewhere, many of us find something attractive, whereas only a few years before this, either we (or our predecessors) did not find it attractive. And not too long from now, we or our successors will again cease to find it attractive.

Following Herbert Blumer, I approach fashion as a property of both material and nonmaterial features of culture:

> Although conspicuous in the area of dress, fashion operates in a wide assortment of fields. Among them are painting, music, drama, architecture, household decoration, entertainment, literature, medical practice, business management, political doctrines, philosophy, psychological and social science, and even such redoubtable areas as the physical sciences and mathematics. Any area of social life that is caught in continuing change is open to the intrusion of fashion. In contrast, fashion is scarcely to be found in settled societies, such as primitive tribes, peasant societies, or caste societies, which cling to what is established and has been sanctioned through long usage. [1968, 342]

Although it is customary to think of many material objects as having this element of fashion, it would be a mistake to neglect its relevance for nonmaterial culture. Such nonfrivolous matters as intellectual investigation in the sciences and elsewhere can also have a fashion element. Many intellectual changes, of course, are not fashion changes but reflect discoveries that open up new problems and provide a new intellectual view or investigative procedure, such as improved telescopes or microscopes. There is an element of fashion, however, in many intellectual endeavors where some problems and topics are rejected without intrinsic reason and others are preferred without offering greater intellectual promise (what Fujimura [1988] calls a "bandwagon" in her analysis of cancer research). This distinction is not always clear and can be more complex. Matters of fashion sometimes dictate the functional features of material and conceptual developments. Consider a winter garment, for example. A material improvement in the warmth of this clothing is likely to be adopted fairly rapidly—certainly if there is no impact on existing fashion. Yet it is much less likely that the improved material will be adopted if it can be produced in only one color or adds exceptional bulk to the garment. This is because the ostensible function of a cultural item often includes a strong decorative dimension.

Fashion can also be viewed as a form of collective behavior (see Smelser 1963; Turner and Killian 1987; Park and Burgess 1921; Coleman 1990; and Blumer 1968). Following James Coleman, we can think of three general properties of collective behavior that apply to fashion: (1) they involve a number of people carrying out the same or similar actions at the same time; (2) the behavior exhibited is transient or continually changing, not in a a state of equilibrium; and (3) there is some kind of dependency among the actions—individuals are not acting independently (1990, 198). When we observe a set of individuals whose tastes are changing in a certain direction at the same time (as opposed to merely fluctuating in some unordered, random way), these changes are not independent events. From the perspective of the collectivity, there is fashion; at the same time, from the perspective of individuals, a new taste is replacing an older one. So we have fashion referring to a collective outcome, and we have tastes referring to individual changes.

Names: From Custom to Fashion

As I noted in Chapter 1, it is neither inevitable nor essential that any object or concept becomes a matter of fashion. It is essential that we have clothing, dwellings, and food. And it is certainly advantageous that we have the mobility provided by motor vehicles. Likewise, music has its pleasures for many of us, and forms of self-decoration are found just about everywhere. But it is not *necessary* that there be an arbitrary element of fashion to our clothing, houses, food, cars, music, or jewelry—they can exist without the dimension of fashion. Some readers may find this concept hard to accept, not only because fashion is such an important element in contemporary Western societies but because even less developed societies appear to have distinctive styles of clothing and self-adornment.

The distinction between custom and fashion is helpful here. Many styles of clothing, jewelry, and housing are found throughout the world as well as among subgroups within societies. If these forms are stable and unchanging, then by definition they are not fashions. Rather, these are styles or customs that may even distinguish subsets of a population from one another, say, classes, regions, ethnic groups, or occupations. If, however, these features barely change, then these distinguishing features are not necessarily a matter of fashion. For fashion is inherently a *quantitative* attribute that may vary in its *rate* of change. By this standard, for example, there is a fashion element in military uniforms and in baseball, basketball, tennis, and golf clothing. A look at old baseball pictures immediately points up differences from contemporary uniforms. Yet the changes take place much more slowly as compared with daily wear. We can say, then, that there is a fashion element in the uniforms worn by professional athletes, but less so than in other types of clothing. And in fact, clothing intended to represent continuity with the past and tradition is almost certain to have a far smaller element of fashion.

The fashion we are concerned with, of course, is naming practices. In what follows, we will trace the causes and development of naming fashions in Denmark, England and Wales, France, Germany, Hungary, Iceland, Scotland, and the United States. This comparative approach permits us to determine if the experiences in several contexts are repeated in a more or less comparable way.

Naming Customs

Most societies have some traditional naming rules that tend to be *conservative,* meaning that the net effect of the rule is to reduce the likelihood of change. Edwin Lawson (1984, 48), for example, describes the Eskimo custom of naming a child after a deceased person so that the spirit of that person will live on. Such a rule reproduces the existing set of names into the future or, at most, generates a very slow change that itself could conceivably involve a small element of fashion. Customs in which children are named after either living ancestors (for example, among Sephardic Jews), religious figures (as, say, saints in Catholicism), the day of the week in which the child is born, or the conditions of the child's birth—to name only a few—are in varying degrees likely to generate a distribution of names for the newly born that will be fairly similar to the names among adults and will have a relatively slight fashion dimension. In effect, such conventions exclude the issue of whether parents—or anyone else—*likes* the name. It is simply a custom or obligation that has nothing to do with aesthetics.

A description of naming patterns in a Cretan town does more than provide another example of a custom that would minimize temporal changes in prominent names. Although the rules are not inviolate, whether the name is one that parents like in aesthetic terms is of minimal importance:

> The child whose name a father almost always insists on choosing is the first male, who should bear his paternal grandfather's name. . . . Again, the first daughter is likely to be named for her father's mother.
>
> The second child of each sex may take the appropriate maternal grandparent's name. . . . After that, the godparent's right to choose the name is rarely contested, unless one of the parents has recently lost a sibling; the sponsor, too, may confer the name of a recently deceased kinsperson. When the sponsors are willing, these secondary offspring may also receive names from the father's *soi* (group of agnates) or the mother's natal family. [Herzfeld 1991, 131–132]

This seemingly rigid pattern, however, allows for a number of exceptions, particularly if the sponsor has much higher status. "The actual disposition of names thus encapsulates personal histories and relationships. It reflects both the obligations that are expected to subsist among children, parents, and sponsors, and the particular variations that circumstances and idiosyncrasies have wrought on these normative patterns" (133).

In many cultures, relatives and ancestors on the father's side are favored as name sources for both daughters and sons. This is not the only pattern, however. A study of Dutch families in Schenectady, New York, from 1680 to 1800 found a bilineal orientation, in which both parents' families are the naming sources (Tebbenhoff 1985). By contrast, the nuclear family dominated early naming practices in Hingham, Massachusetts, and so children were named for their parents rather than grandparents in the period from 1640 to 1880 (Smith 1985). A similar practice is reported for a working-class area of East London following World War II: "In the past it was not uncommon for children, and especially sons, to be given the same Christian names as their parents, the eldest son often taking the father's and the eldest daughter the mother's name" (Young and Willmott 1957, 10).

Other conditions can also create minimal change in names. For example, naming patterns can serve to connect extended families. As William Williams observes in his study of an English village, the naming process "symbolizes the close tie between the youngest generation and those that have gone before" (1956, 80). In this regard, Georg Søndergaard (1979) summarizes Danish naming es: "Naming children after family members used to be the universal naming principle, which among other things resulted in a very limited number of names to choose from. Since the middle ages it has dominated the choice of names so that the name repertory until one hundred years ago had decreased to scarcely more than thirty names." Names also serve social functions in some settings that constrain the development of naming fashions. The maintenance of existing names, for example, can mark groups off from one another. George Stewart (1948, 123) suggests that the presence of the French in Canada, for example, had the effect of leading the English settlers in New England to retain traditional English names as a reminder of their non-French origins.

Through the Years (and Centuries)

Western nations show remarkably similar movements from virtually no fashion in names to today's situation of an increasingly rapid turnover in popular names. This development from no fashion to a high level of fashion is so robust that it shows up even when the available information is less than ideal (not totally comparable between nations, and sometimes not totally comparable through the years *within* the nation).

A simple measure used to gauge the level of fashion in a nation and changes over time is: the rapidity with which the leading names are replaced. In the absence of any replacement, then obviously there is no fashion operating (at least to the point where fashion affects prominent names). At the other extreme, rapid replacement of leading names is strong evidence that fashion is a major influence. This approach, and the necessary computations, can be illustrated with changes in Scotland, between 1600 and 1650. Of the 25 most commonly given boys' names in 1600, all but 3 are also in the comparable list for 1650, for annual rate of change of just .06.[1] By contrast, 3 of the top 25 boys' names in Scotland in 1990 drop out two years later in 1992, for a tremendously higher annual rate of change, 1.5.[2]

If we look at fashion trends for names in eight nations, a fairly common pattern emerges (fig. 2.1). The leading names given to children are little changed until the late nineteenth century or early twentieth century. Until the twentieth century, moreover, fashion for girls' names is no more pronounced than it is for boys. Yet in the twentieth century we see both a growing fashion dimension in the naming of children manifested in the acceleration in the replacement of names, and a markedly greater level of fashion turnover for girls' names. In France, for example, turnover rates were both extremely low and barely increas-

Fig. 2.1a. Turnover in the top 10 boys' and girls' names, France, 1619–1989

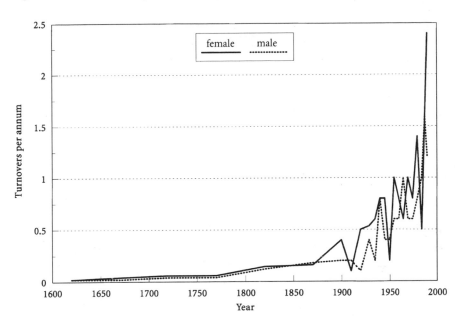

ing until the last quarter of the nineteenth century, but since then they have moved up at a progressively more rapid pace. In the most recent period analyzed, 2.5 of the 10 most frequently given girls' names on average drop from the top 10 category in the following year. Gender differences that were virtually indistinguishable for centuries now display a substantial gap. The turnover level among boys is now 1.5 names per year—much higher than in the past, but well below the girls' 2.5 names per year.

The pattern of change is not identical for each nation, of course, but the similarities are greater than the differences. Other places besides France with noteworthy gender differences in naming fashions are Scotland, Germany, England and Wales, Hungary, and California.[3] Likewise, we should not make too much of modest differences in the yearly turnover rate.[4]

California and, to a lesser extent, England and Wales are somewhat problematic because they appear to deviate from these general patterns. This fact is not so worrisome, however, because there is no reason to expect a valid proposition to include all possible cases—even if the data were of better quality. (To do so is to fall victim to an overly deterministic form of reasoning that is actually counterproductive.)[5] Yet we can learn something from these cases. The results for England and Wales are remarkable. Between 1700 and 1800, there is no indication of

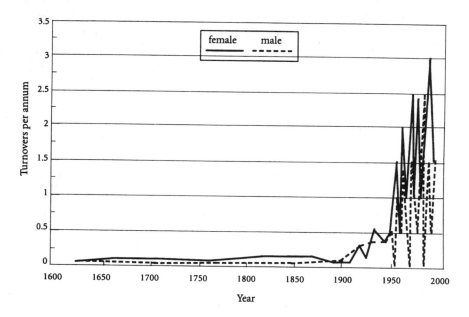

Fig. 2.1b. Turnover in the top 25 boys' and girls' names, Scotland, 1625–1987

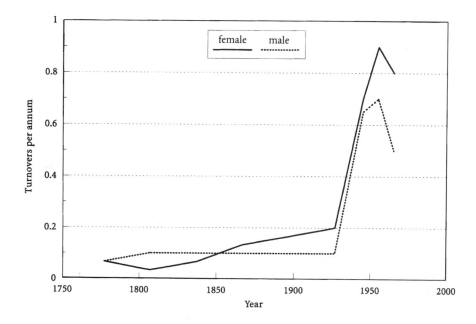

Fig. 2.1c. Turnover in the top 10 boys' and girls' names, Germany, 1760–1970

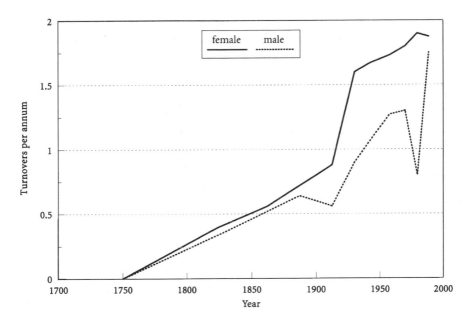

Fig. 2.1d. Turnover in the top 50 boys' and girls' names, England and Wales, 1750–1989

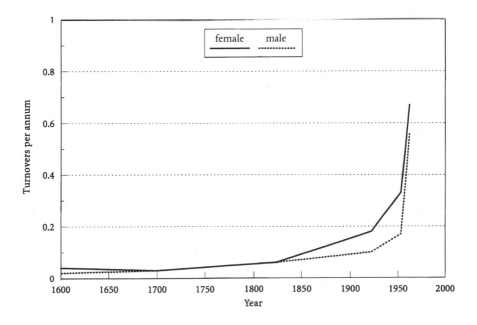

Fig. 2.1e. Turnover in the top 15 boys' and girls' names, Hungary, 1600–1972

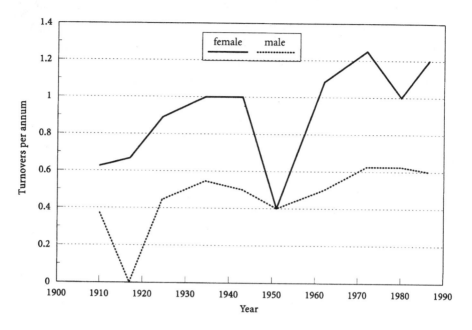

Fig. 2.1f. Turnover in the top 20 boys' and girls' names, California, 1910–1986

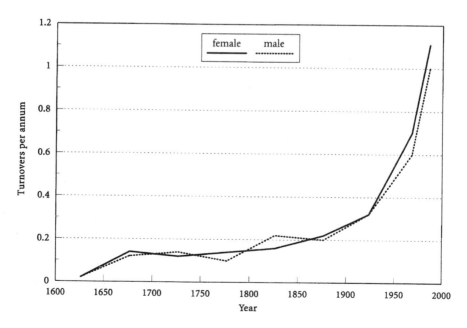

Fig. 2.1g. Turnover in the top 20 boys' and girls' names, Denmark, 1625–1991

Fig. 2.1h. Turnover in the top 25 boys' and girls' names, Iceland, 1075–1980

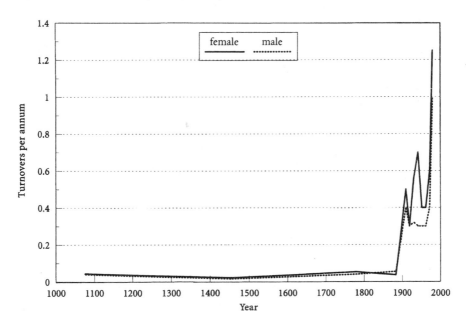

a significant influence on choices stemming from matters of fashion: not one of the 50 most common boys' or girls' names occurring in 1700 is absent from the top 50 in 1800.[6] Then, however, the role of fashion for names in England and Wales starts earlier than elsewhere. Because England led the Industrial Revolution, this may be a possible external cause of the shift toward fashion. England and Wales's strange-looking graph is, in fact, not all that odd. Turnover in daughters' names is clearly upward, though at a slower rate in recent decades. The odd spike for sons' names is essentially caused by one major reversal, the drop in turnover for sons' names in the decade 1975–1985. Incidentally, the level of turnover for girls in twentieth-century England and Wales is higher than for boys—also a feature in most of the other locations. England and Wales's pattern is not as "simple" as elsewhere, but it is harmonious with the overall conclusions.

Last, there is California. Although information is available here and there for earlier periods in the United States, nothing matches the long-term opportunity California's solid data set going back to almost the beginning of the twentieth century. For both girls' and boys' names, fashion is increasingly important in California during the twentieth century. Although California is the least regular of our eight cases, there is definitely an upward movement (a way of determining if fashion turnover increases through the years, the Spearman rank order correlation, is .71 between turnover and year for daughters' names and .82 for sons').[7] California's gender gap is especially large, with turnover twice as frequent for girls in recent years. California's turnover rate (particularly among female names) is high, but not extraordinarily so when compared with Scotland, England and Wales, or France.

The role of taste in the choice of names, then, is a relatively recent development. Before the late nineteenth century or early twentieth century, the most common names of boys or girls changed little, and fashion played a minimal role. The occasional reports of massive changes in names generally originate in the rise and fall of religions in nations and as such don't fall under the rubric of fashion. We need here to remember the greater power of religions in earlier times—particularly the power inherent in state religions.

EXTERNAL INFLUENCES

The next question is obvious: What forces are responsible for the declining influence of custom and the growth of fashion in influencing naming practices? Note that customs are a *declining* influence, but not an entirely *irrelevant* one. Not all choices are based exclusively on changing aesthetics; other traditional influences still occur, though their importance is declining. What societal developments have generated this expansion of fashion in naming choices? We turn to shifts in basic attributes that are often seen as critical for social changes, among them education, urbanization, and family structure. In addition, because we are dealing with a matter of fashion, the influence of mass media (radio, movies, television) must also be considered as far as possible. Because of the difficulties in obtaining information on the long-term changes of external forces in Hungary and Germany, my analysis is confined to France, Scotland, England and Wales, California, Denmark, and Iceland (even then, external data for specific attributes are often unavailable for all six). At the outset, I will confess a bias. I am not one to assume that it is really possible to sort out different influences when considering a handful of nations, even though other comparative historical studies deem this possible. We should not think that a possible external cause can be eliminated if it fails to operate in, say, all six of the nations under study. (Briefly, the reasoning is not that complicated if one recognizes: (1) we live in a world best viewed as probabilistic, if only because the quality of data is less than ideal; (2) events best viewed as chance also play a role; (3) more than one attribute can cause a given outcome; and (4) there is no reason to assume that any cause is so powerful that it can lead to a given outcome regardless of other conditions that are driving the outcome in a different direction. This is not the place to elaborate on this topic; for a fuller development, see Lieberson 1991, 1992, and 1997.)

Urbanization and Education

Urbanization and education are general measures of a nation's development. They may also directly influence the development of fashions. At a minimum, education means literacy and hence exposure to a much wider variety of names than would occur through local face-to-face contacts. Newspapers, for example, give readers a constant flow of reports about events and the names of figures far removed from their immediate contacts. Literacy likewise permits a far more extensive contact with names occurring in fictional stories from far and wide than what is likely when one is illiterate and dependent on storytellers. Of course, as people's level of education expands, names become known from an even wider variety of sources. Early settlers in the American South, for example, often gave their slaves Classical names (see Chapter 7). Perhaps as important as an educated populace's access to names beyond the repertoire of the community, education may increase the disposition to break with tradition. Education leads to greater independence in judgment—reducing the inclination to follow existing practices simply because they are traditional.

In a similar manner, urbanization increases exposure to a greater variety of tastes.[8] Because urban growth typically reflects the populace's migration from smaller settlements and farms to larger communities, the strength of extended family ties and smaller community pressures will weaken and reduce the disposition toward traditional naming usages—particularly practices in which children are named for relatives.

The closest fit between accelerating fashions and either urbanization or education is found in Denmark (fig. 2.2). The expansion of fashion is strikingly parallel for both increasing education (throughout the twentieth century) and urbanization (beginning in the second half of the nineteenth century).[9] Urbanization and education tend to influence the intensity of fashion trends in other countries as well—although not as closely as in Denmark.[10] Educational changes in particular are generally more closely linked to fashion changes. In France, the growth of fashion for names is paralleled by growing urbanization, whereas the association between education and turnover is weak.[11]

In the four other locations, the results do not contradict the propositions, but

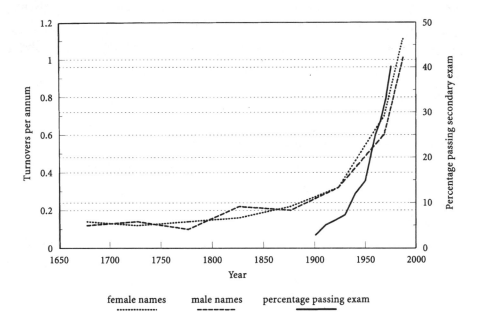

Fig. 2.2a. *Percentage passing secondary school exams and changes in the top 20 girls' and boys' names, Denmark, 1677–1986*

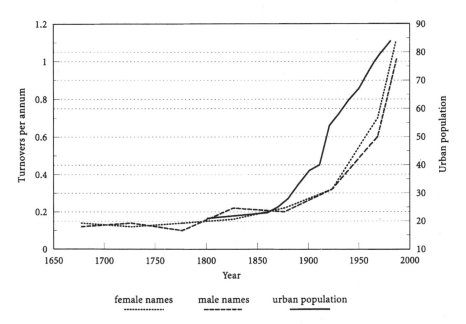

Fig. 2.2b. *Urban population as percentage of total population and changes in the top 20 girls' and boys' names, Denmark, 1677–1986*

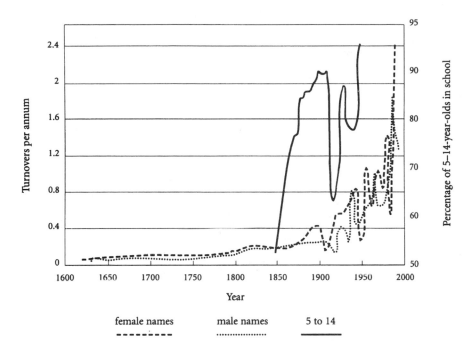

Fig. 2.2c. Percentage attending school (ages 5–14) and changes in the top 10 girls' and boys' names, France, 1619–1989

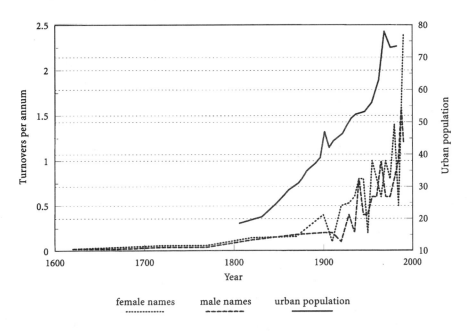

Fig. 2.2d. Urban population as percentage of total population and changes in the top 10 girls' and boys' names, France, 1619–1989

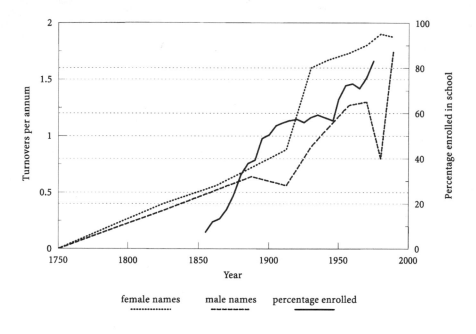

Fig. 2.2e. Percentage attending primary and secondary school (ages 5–19) and changes in the top 50 girls' and boys' names, England and Wales, 1750–1989

female names   male names   percentage enrolled

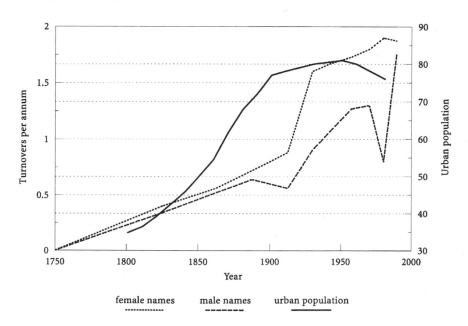

Fig. 2.2f. Urban population as percentage of total population and changes in the top 50 girls' and boys' names, England and Wales, 1750–1989

female names   male names   urban population

Fig 2.2g. Percentage enrolled in public schools (ages 5–17) and changes in the top 20 girls' and boys' names, California, 1905–1989

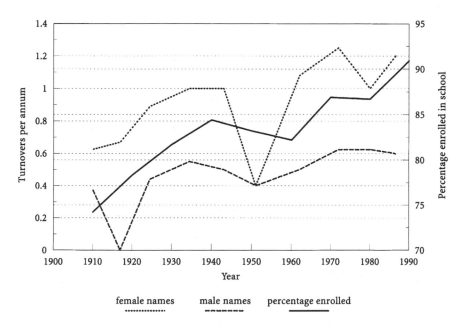

Fig. 2.2h. Urban population as percentage of total population and changes in the top 20 girls' and boys' names, California, 1910–1986

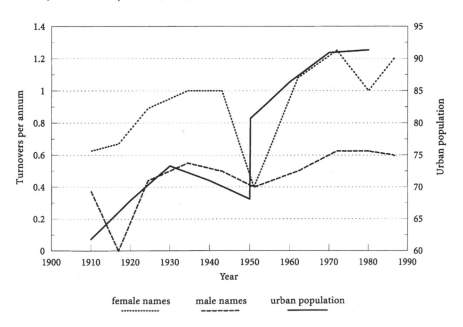

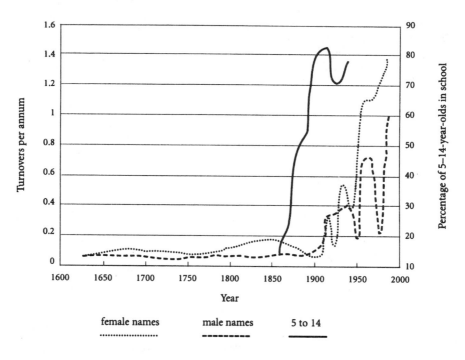

Fig. 2.2i. Percentage attending school (ages 5–14) and changes in the top 25 girls' and boys' names, Scotland, 1625–1987

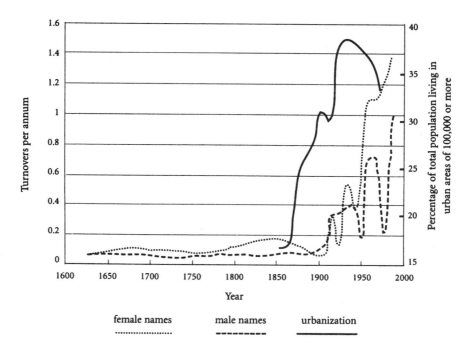

Fig. 2.2j. Urban population as percentage of total population and changes in the top 25 girls' and boys' names, Scotland, 1625–1987

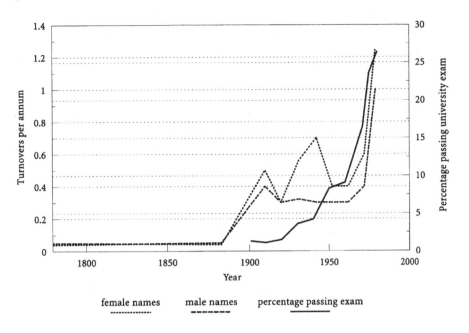

Fig. 2.2k. Percentage passing university entrance exam (age 20) and changes in the top 25 girls' and boys' names, Iceland, 1779–1980

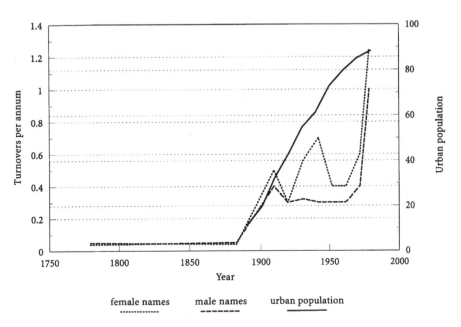

Fig. 2.2l. Urban population as percentage of total population and changes in the top 25 girls' and boys' names, Iceland, 1779–1980

their influence is often murky. In England and Wales, if you stare at the graph long enough, increasing education *and* urbanization can be described as accompanying a rise in turnover for girls' names. At best, however, they seem to have little bearing on the shifts for boys' names. In any case, there is hardly a parallel movement between turnover and either education or urbanization of the sort exhibited in Denmark. Changes in California during the twentieth century suggest that growing urbanization roughly accompanies increasing turnover in names for both boys and girls, as does changing percentages of children enrolled in public schools. In Scotland, the upward movement in fashions also occurs when urbanization rises rapidly, and the growth in turnover for girls' names is impressively linked with education.[12]

The results for boys' names in Iceland fail to support either hypothesis. To be sure, the lowest and highest rates of turnover occur, respectively, at the lowest and highest points of either urbanization or education. But the long-term upward shift in urbanization throughout the twentieth century appears to have no obvious influence on the turnover of boys' names. The upward movement in education, beginning about 1920, likewise is not accompanied by obvious parallel development in the turnover of male names. For girls' names, increasing turnover accompanies, in a somewhat parallel fashion, the upward shift in education and urbanization.[13]

Family

There is reason to expect the extended family to play a central role in maintaining tradition and continuity in the names given to children (thereby countering the development of fashions in names). As in religion, whereby a rules restrict choices, traditions requiring that children be named after ancestors tend to minimize new names because parents' choices roughly repeat the names used in the past. The decline of the extended family's influence in society—particularly the increasing distance between ancestors and descendants, declining contact with living ancestors, and reduced knowledge about ancestors—should free parents to ignore the pressures to assign certain names from their parents, grandparents, and other relatives. Of course, the influence of such a factor varies from country to country. Internal migration within the small nation of Denmark will have very different consequences than in the vast spaces of United States, for example. In Denmark, internal migration is less of a barrier to continuity and interaction than in the United States, where enormous distances can minimize face-to-face interaction.

Fig. 2.3a. Divorce rate and changes in the top 20 girls' and boys' names, Denmark, 1676–1986

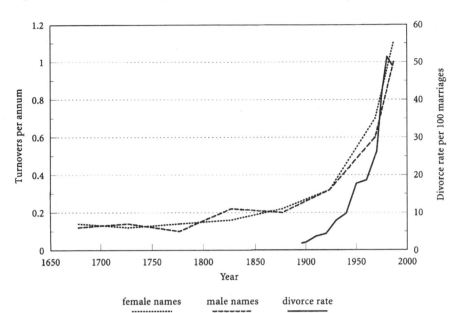

female names   male names   divorce rate
·················   – – – – –   ───────

Long-term data on shifts in the level and nature of individuals' contact with the extended family are unavailable. But two less desirable variables are at least vaguely related to the decline of the traditional family, and hence its role in influencing naming patterns. One is divorce rates in each society, and the other is household size. In the case of divorce, turnover for names in both boys and girls appears to parallel shifting divorce rates in France (a country for which most of the other variables we are examining appear to show little influence of a precise nature) and in Denmark. Girls' names in California, Iceland, and Scotland also correlate with divorce rates, but trends in England and Wales show no correlation (fig. 2.3). A decline in traditional family relationships also occurs when fashion in naming takes off. Bear in mind, however, that this connection between increases in fashion and in divorce is by no means certain. It could simply be the influence of whatever factors are causing increasing divorce rates (of which, see Phillips 1991), rather than family instability per se. In turn, none of this may be directly linked to declines in the extended family.

Another family measure, average household size, also appears to be linked to most shifts in the turnover rate for names: for both sexes in Denmark, England and Wales, Scotland, and—to a certain extent—in California and Iceland

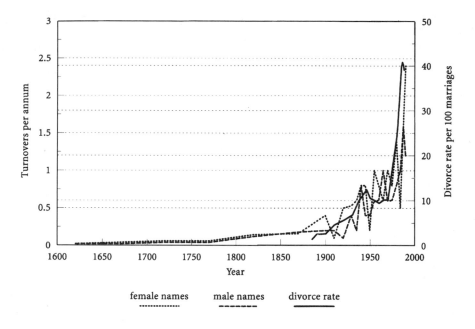

2.3b. *Divorce rate and changes in the top 10 girls' and boys' names, France, 1619–1989*

Fig. 2.3c. *Divorce rate and changes in the top 50 girls' and boys' names, England and Wales, 1750–1984*

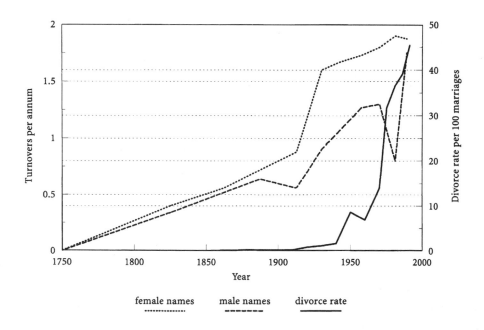

Fig. 2.3d. Divorce rate and changes in the top 20 girls' and girls' names, California, 1905–1989

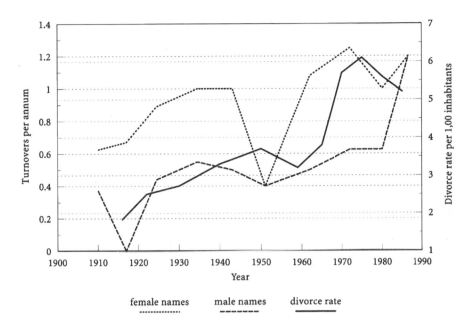

Fig. 2.3e. Divorce rate and changes in the top 25 girls' and boys' names, Scotland, 1625–1987

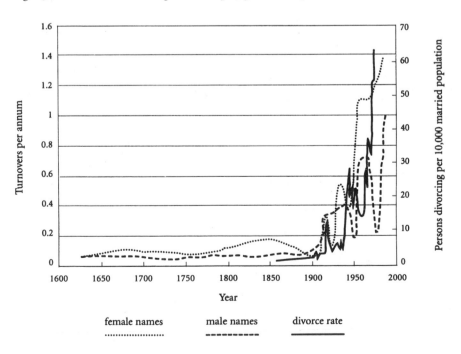

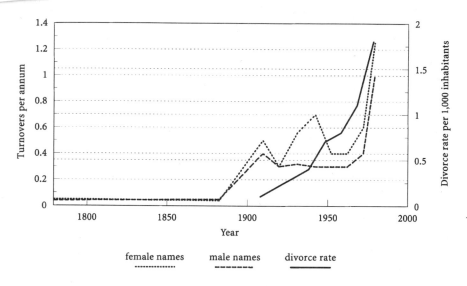

f. Divorce rate and changes in the top 25 girls' and boys' names, Iceland, 1779–1979

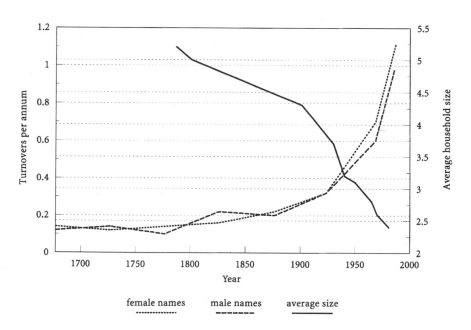

Fig. 2.4a. Average household size and changes in the top 20 girls' and boys' names, Denmark, 1677–1986

(fig. 2.4). (Note that the correlation is inverted here because the question is whether *increasing* fashion reflects a *decline* in family size.)

The evidence that shifts in the family (increasing instability, declining size) occur when fashions begin to play an important role in the names given to children is reasonably strong. Insofar as these family measures are linked with the decline of "traditional" family life, this is harmonious with the suggestion that fashion rises as traditional constraints on naming obligations weaken.

Mass Media

Darren, a name unknown in Britain before the American television series *Bewitched* was first shown in 1960. Something about this name made an almost instant appeal to the English public and Darrens immediately began to appear on the scene. By 1971 Darren was the seventh most popular name bestowed on boys, and in 1975 it was still in tenth position.

A great many English parents were obviously willing to take Darren on trust, not bothering about its pedigree. It may well be that the name was thought to be generally popular in the U.S.A. because it was used to name a main character in a series. This was not the case at the time, for amongst the thousands of American students who were born in the 1950s, and whose names I analyzed in 1975, I could find only one Darren. He came from Illinois. [Dunkling 1977, 175, 177]

There is every reason to think that the mass media influences a variety of tastes: clothing, language, lifestyle, toys, sexual practices, smoking, drinking, and, of course, names. The question here, however, is not whether the media influences our choices (for surprising evidence on this matter, see Chapter 8), but, rather, whether the mass media turns naming into a matter of fashion or accelerates the importance of fashion for choices in names. I evaluate this thesis backward from television to movies to radio.

Television Television became an important medium only in the years after World War II. The role of fashion in the naming process was by then both well established and increasing. In our eight countries, there is no reason to assume that television causes the development of fashions in naming. The question, then, is whether the accelerating role of fashion after World War II is greater than it would have been in the absence of television. This is a difficult question to answer under the best of conditions—let alone with data for a few nations. The linkage in Denmark between rates of television ownership and fashion illustrates the problem nicely (fig. 2.5). On one hand, a sharp rise in television

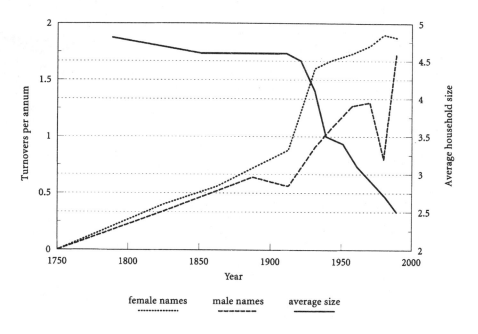

Fig. 2.4b. *Average household size and changes in the top 50 girls' and boys' names, England and Wales, 1750–1989*

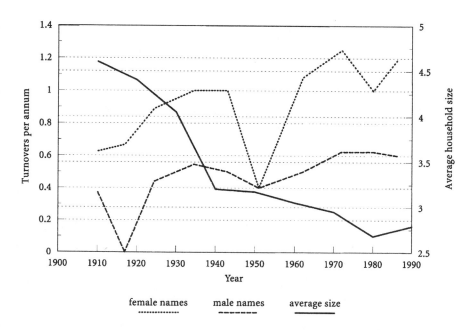

Fig. 2.4c. *Average household size and changes in the top 20 girls' and boys' names, California, 1910–1989*

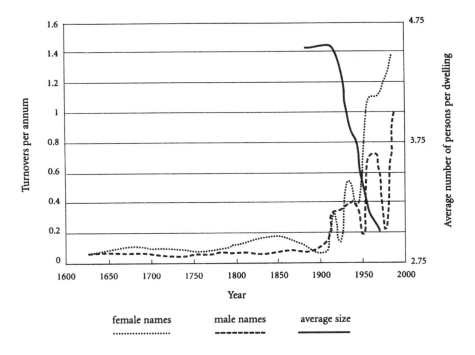

Fig. 2.4d. Average number of persons per dwelling and changes in the top 25 girls' and boys' names, Scotland, 1625–1987

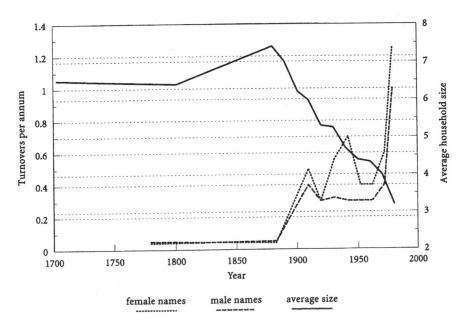

Fig. 2.4e. Average household size and changes in the top 25 girls' and boys' names, Iceland, 1703–1980

Fig. 2.5a. Television licenses per 1,000 inhabitants and changes in the top 20 girls' and boys' names, Denmark, 1677–1986

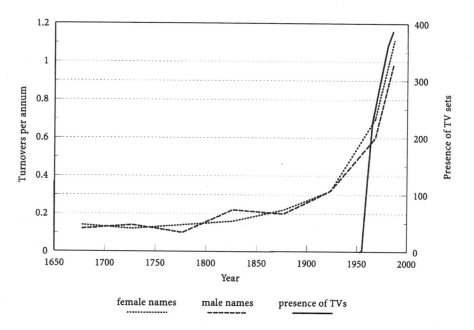

female names   male names   presence of TVs

ownership occurs during a period when the level of turnover in first names accelerates. It would appear that the spread of television led to an increase in the fashion dimension of first names. The curve for accelerating fashion in names until television appears, however, is exponential, suggesting that an acceleration might well have occurred anyway. The level of fashion in names was increasing exponentially in Denmark for decades—beginning with the last quarter of the nineteenth century—so there is no reason to think that the growth of television accounts for the later increase.

A somewhat greater case for the influence of television can be made for England and Wales, California, and France (the only other locations with suitable data). There is no reason to think that television is responsible for an increase in fashion among girls' names in England. For boys, however, the last surge in the level of fashion could be attributed to the role of television—particularly if we allow for a lag between television's growth and its impact on names (something that would occur if the impact is especially strong on children who, of course, in general would not have offspring until some years later). This is not certain, but the growth of television in California is harmonious with

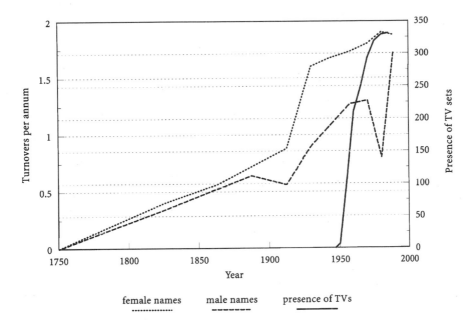

Fig. 2.5b. Television licenses per 1,000 inhabitants and changes in the top 50 girls' and boys' names, England and Wales, 1750–1989

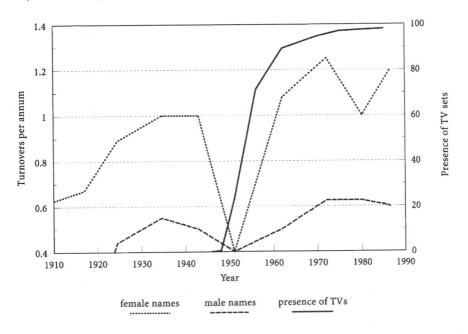

Fig. 2.5c. Television ownership per 1,000 inhabitants and changes in the top 50 girls' and boys' names, California, 1910–1986

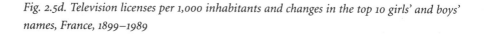

Fig. 2.5d. Television licenses per 1,000 inhabitants and changes in the top 10 girls' and boys' names, France, 1899–1989

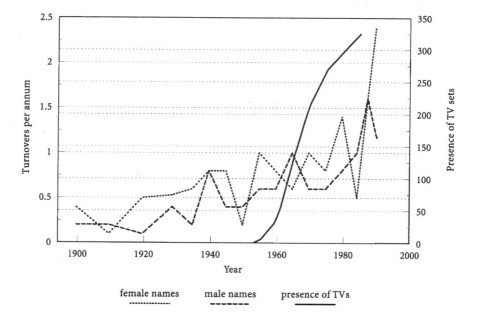

a surge in the turnover of names—particularly in girls—again, if we allow for a lag in the impact of television.[14] Unlike England and Wales, the data for California suggest an analogous impact on boys' names as well, but at a lower absolute level. In France, the surge in fashion among girls' names at least *could* be attributed to the lagged impact of television, though more weakly for boys.

In sum, television is not responsible for the development of fashion in names; fashion in naming preceded the spread of television. If television, then, is not an underlying cause, did it accelerate the increasing role of fashion in naming? In other words, is television a *secondary* external cause, as contrasted with a *primary* external cause? An external influence, one that sets the conditions that lead fashion to develop in a given area, is a primary cause; a secondary influence is one that operates *after* fashion is in play—but does not generate the initial development of fashion. By this standard, television is not a primary cause, but it could be a secondary influence. I will say more about this distinction in later chapters.

Movies When considering the influence of movies on names, we need first to note that movie attendance declines after World War II as television becomes a competitor. Turnover in names, however, does not decline; in fact, its long-term

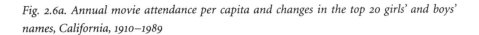

Fig. 2.6a. Annual movie attendance per capita and changes in the top 20 girls' and boys' names, California, 1910–1989

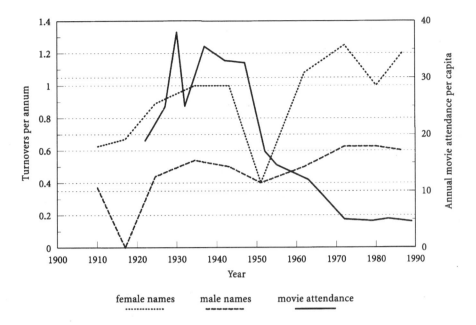

increase continues. It is best, therefore, to concentrate on the potential influence of movies during the years when they were becoming an increasingly popular entertainment. The failure of fashion turnover to drop in the face of declining movie attendance is relevant only if there is reason to expect a symmetrical causal mechanism (Lieberson 1985, chap. 4), such that a decline in movie attendance would drive fashion downward and a rise in movie attendance would drive it up. Moreover, because the popularity of television increases as the importance of movies declines, this may make up for the decline in movies.

Even with these restrictions, movies do not appear to increase the role of fashion in names during the heyday of movie attendance. Although the growth of movie attendance in England and Wales parallels a similar increase in the turnover of names, the increasing importance of fashion for girls' names is not caused by movies because the increase in turnover *precedes* the increase in movie attendance (fig. 2.6). As for boys' names, there is an increase, but it is hardly parallel. In California, the upward movement for both boys' and girls' turnover rates also precedes the increases in movie attendance and certainly slows during the sharpest increase in movie-going.[15] The results are even weaker for France. The situation in Denmark is inconclusive; an upward movement in turnover

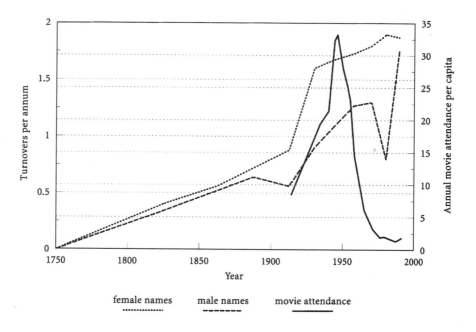

Fig. 2.6b. Annual movie attendance per capita and changes in the top 50 girls' and boys' names, England and Wales, 1750–1991

female names   male names   movie attendance

Fig. 2.6c. Annual movie attendance per capita and changes in the top 10 girls' and boys' names, France, 1899–1991

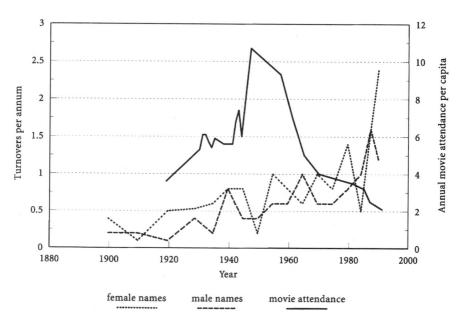

female names   male names   movie attendance

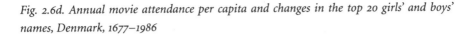

Fig. 2.6d. Annual movie attendance per capita and changes in the top 20 girls' and boys' names, Denmark, 1677–1986

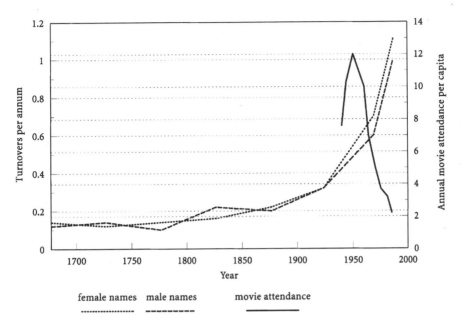

could be caused by the rise in movie attendance—allowing for a lag to operate. But so many other influences show a similar upward movement in that period in Denmark that it is difficult to sort out—let alone to deal with the strong possibility that the fashion curve may well have just been part of a trajectory unaffected by these external events.

Before we leave the movie theater, bear in mind that there is a distinction between whether movies increased the rate of change and whether movies served as an increasingly important *source* of new names. The answer to the first question appears to be negative; the second is addressed in Chapter 8.

Radio The importance of radio should not be viewed from the perspective of those who grew up since the introduction of television. In its heyday, many radio stars and programs with continuing stories could influence naming processes. Even so, the graphs for radio listenership indicate no correlation with turnover in either California or England and Wales for boys' or girls' names (fig. 2.7). In some cases, the lags shift in the wrong direction; in others, the curve for radio ownership and the growth in naming fashions are quite dissimilar. The problem is worse than usual for Denmark. In addition to the difficulty of attributing the

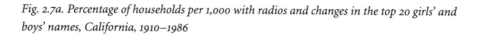

Fig. 2.7a. Percentage of households per 1,000 with radios and changes in the top 20 girls' and boys' names, California, 1910–1986

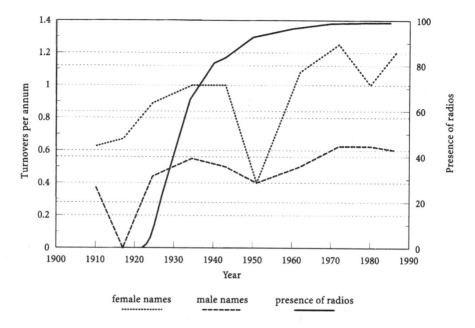

female names   male names   presence of radios

fashion increase to radio listenership, given the exponential growth curve that appears before radio, inspection displays that the radio attendance data take a *convex* shape, whereas the fashion growth is *concave*.[16]

In sum, we can dispense with the mass media. There is no strong evidence that they play any fundamental role in the development of fashion in names, because the trend develops before any of these media became important. Besides, the observed linkages are generally weak, even when we allowing for our small sample of nations. At most, the media may have accelerated a development that was marching forward without them. (This raises an issue that we will consider in Chapter 3—namely, after *basic* or *primary* external forces create a fashion in an area that had previously been a custom, *secondary* forces may begin to influence fashion.)

Still unanswered is the role of the media as a *source* of new fashions. We know that mass media are not a central factor in accounting for the conversion of names from custom to fashion. If names are popularized because they appear in the media, this occurs only because other, more fundamental influences have operated first to make names a matter of taste. This is an understandable error in our thinking: if we observe that a performer's name is widely used for children,

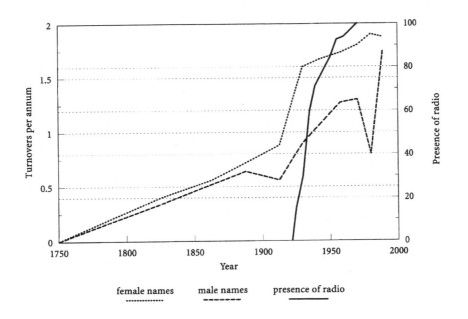

Fig. 2.7b. Percentage of population able to listen to radio and changes in the top 50 girls' and boys' names, England and Wales, 1750–1989

female names ....

male names - - - - - - -

presence of radio ———

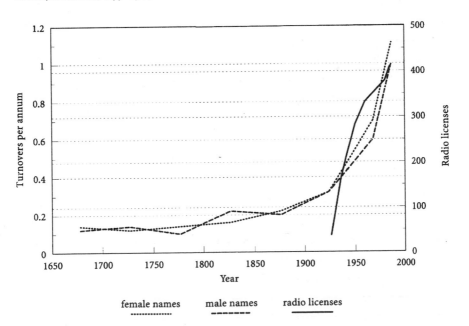

Fig. 2.7c. Radio licenses per 1,000 inhabitants and changes in the top 20 girls' and boys' names, Denmark, 1677–1986

female names ....

male names - - - - - - -

radio licenses ———

it would seem that the media is the "cause." And yes, it is the cause, but it is the cause for the particular taste—not for the fact that names are matters of fashion. More fundamental influences have first made names an aesthetic issue, and—only then—does the media play a role in our specific preferences.

SO, HOW AND WHEN DID NAMES BECOME A FASHION?

It is convenient to discuss fashion as if it is either *present* or *absent*. In fact, as we have seen, fashion falls along a continuum ranging from no change (ruled by custom) to change at an extraordinarily rapid rate (at an extreme, say, no first name is popular for more than a year). The development of fashions in names, such that they are increasingly given to children because of aesthetic matters, is a relatively recent development. Before the twentieth century, fashion had *some* influence on names—witness a small level of change in preceding centuries. Only about a century ago did names develop into matters of taste. Since then, they have been increasingly driven by fashion. The rate of turnover at first was similar for boys' and girls' names, but fashion accelerated earlier for girls, and contemporary rates in most places remain higher for girls. This is in keeping with the recognition of the different emphasis for naming girls and boys, where boys' names in these societies play more of a role of marking continuity with the past and less of a decorative function (see, for example, Rossi 1965). As a consequence, because girls' names respond more rapidly to changing external conditions, there is generally a closer connection between macrosocietal social events and the turnover rates for girls' names.

Given the indisputable evidence of a gradual development of fashion in the choice of children's names, what drives the shift? The linkage between the turnover of popular names and both urbanization and education suggests that these shifts occurred when nations were entering the modern era. At this time the family was also changing in radical ways: divorce increased and household size declined. Contrary to what many assume to be a truism, there is no indication that the mass media introduced fashion into the naming process. The ascent of radio and, later, movies as forms of mass entertainment, as well as the subsequent importance of television, in no way accelerates the increase in the rate of turnover that was already evident in the naming process.

These results are hardly definitive, and they call for clarification. First, a question: Do the causes of changing fashions in names hold up with a more diverse set of countries and more precise measurements? Second, the repertoire of names is sufficiently large to allow for unlimited turnover even before technological developments in mass communication (just consider the enormous number of names found in the Bible alone). The exposure to these new influences could have generated a two-way interaction by increasing the disposition to think of names as a matter of taste rather than custom. At present, however, there is no evidence to indicate that the shifts over time during the rise of television, movies, or radio are exceptional compared to shifts that were developing before this period. Put another way, the evidence supports the conclusion that changing tastes in names started long before the invention of the radio—to say nothing of film and television. Moreover, the turnover rate was increasing before these developments.

In broad terms, we can hypothesize a cluster of factors that would free parents from rules and expectations that had previously determined the names given to children. In many settings, various rules and customs drive the naming of children (using saints' names among Catholics, family obligations, naming children for ancestors). Their decline allowed for a new perspective—to wit, names are viewed as a matter of taste rather than obligation or custom. In other words, naming decisions are increasingly based on whether parents *like* or *dislike* the name. Even the perceived popularity of a name can become part of this aesthetic—where for some parents, to give their child a relatively uncommon name is attractive and for others the opposite holds. The decline in prior influences reflects the rise of individualism in its many forms and the concomitant weakening of various social rules or restrictions on behavior. Particularly important here is the separation of the nuclear family from the controls exercised by an extended family network. A variety of mechanisms operate: a greater spatial separation of family members owing to migration; the decline of agriculture and other activities that generated broad economic interdependencies; and the declining importance of the extended family for the members of each nuclear family—indeed, even the nuclear family itself declines. Especially relevant for names is the shifting position of age: *old* may not be a four-letter word, but it is getting close to it. As the extended family declines, and hence day-to-day contact with the older members of extended families is reduced, the elderly decline from a position of honor to something far less valued. This has consequences on the aesthetics of naming. First names that are associated with the elderly often, by virtue of that fact, appear unattractive to parents contemplating a name for their baby. (This is another matter with names that go back further than, say, the grandparents' generation and hence can become "classics" uncontaminated by usage by actual living old people.)

Of course, *individualism* means less emphasis on the collectivity and a more acute awareness of the separation of individual needs and interests from those of the collectivity. In a collective setting, sharing a name with many other people would appear to be not only acceptable but in fact desirable, whereas in other settings, having exactly the same name as many others would be repulsive.[17]

Last, although the figures I've reported in this chapter are based on concrete evidence, these final comments are matters of conjecture and go way beyond the hard evidence. They are based on heroic extensions of the available data on such topics as education, urbanization, and family stability. Certainly, there are theories suggesting that individualism and personal authority arise from a growth in complex and distinctive social networks (for example, Simmel 1955, 127–195; Coser 1991, 32–33, 91–93). And this is harmonious with the influence of urbanization and education on network expansion (reported in Fischer 1982). Nevertheless, we are dealing with a complex set of interrelated events. As Bonnie Erickson observes in a personal communication: "There were a lot of co-occurring, entangled changes in modernization; hard to tell just *which* strands of this lead to naming changes. And *what* is changing? Feeling free to choose and/or valuing choice-making itself as a pleasure? Part of affluence and commodification has been learning to like making choices (a pleasure once denied to most of the population most of the time). Consider how picking a name has become a prolonged, savored part of pregnancy, with parents discussing names at length with each other and with their networks. It is part of the fun." Obviously, these conclusions will remain speculative until there are better and more direct measures of individualism for long spans of time. An elegant study on naming by Jürgen Gerhards and Rolf Hackenbroch (1997a, 1997b) is relevant here. Employing a shorter time span (1894–1994) and working only with a subarea of Germany, they develop superior data sets that permit the application of relatively rigorous statistical analysis. Some of their results are applicable to the substantive issues under consideration here, although their focus is less on the development from nonfashion to fashion—at least as approached in this chapter. Especially important for our purposes, they report naming features linked to a decline in the role of religion, a decline in the tendency for parents to give their name to their offspring, the development of individuation and a decline in agricultural employment. These may be viewed as yet additional support for the conclusions drawn here.

How the Social Order Influences Names After They Become a Matter of Taste—And How It Doesn't

After the naming process—or any other facet of culture—becomes a matter of choice rather than simply a custom or an obligation, many options open up. Social factors begin to influence the selection of names in ways that formerly were impossible. These external influences are different from the long-term influences that cause names to become the subject of fashion and personal preference. Once that fundamental shift occurs, however, these secondary influences come into play. And, in turn, these secondary influences increase the disposition of parents to regard their child's name as a choice, thereby pushing parents' selections further and further into the realm of fashion.

In the same way as the rings of a fallen tree indicate climatic conditions in years past, so, too, do tastes reflect changes in social conditions. It is as if each social change affects relevant tastes, which then continue until another social change leads to new fashions. The external societal influences are myriad: political, social, economic, normative, technological—to say nothing of wars and domestic conflicts. Movements may also arise within subsets of the population, such as feminism, racial pride, and assimilation—to say nothing about influences from other nations. A second way of interpreting the popularity of tastes focuses on the meaning certain tastes have for individuals and then, in turn, couples these tastes with institutions that seek to manipulate (or create) these associations for their own purposes. In other words, because tastes are often an expression of an individual's identity, organizations will seek to influence these tastes by giving their product an appealing identity. Here, too, these specific tastes and fashions are often linked to external causes because commercial influences are affected by underlying external dispositions of the population at a given time and place. Concerns about sex, identity, and success, feelings of rebellion, and the like are not created by advertisers but are used by them to promote their products. When a sports star, say, a prominent basketball player, promotes athletic footwear, for example, the manufacturer and advertiser are attempting to enhance the shoes by associating them with the imagery conjured by the athlete. Likewise, if teenagers and young adults are especially concerned about how they appeal to others, commercial interests will seek to connect their toothpaste, car, clothing, perfume, beer, underarm deodorant, electric shaver, and shampoo with the response that it will generate among the opposite sex.

Although this popular assumption that changes in taste reflect changes in social conditions ("social" being broadly defined to encompass political, economic, and cultural developments) or commercial influences is true, it is less useful than most observers realize. Some of the most important social developments have at best a minimal impact on tastes. Likewise, the influence of advertisers can be exaggerated (see the numerous failures described by Schudson 1984). Social events are often no help in understanding tastes in terms of either their form or the direction of the change. In this chapter I explore the range of social impacts on fashions in names, providing clear examples where external influences affect tastes and equally clear examples where important external developments have absolutely no influence on the popularity of names.

SOCIAL INFLUENCES THAT AFFECT OUR TASTES

Let us first consider cases where specific tastes in names clearly reflect secondary external influences.

The Association of Tastes with Idiosyncratic Events

External events often influence tastes simply because of the chance association of a name with a significant event. That name then becomes particularly appealing or unappealing, depending on the nature of the event. These influences are readily seen in the political world, although such linkages are by no means confined to this arena of contemporary life. For example, a sudden upward jump in the popularity of *Herbert* corresponds with the election of Herbert Hoover to the presidency in 1928 and is followed by an even faster decline in

Fig. 3.1. Number of children named Franklin or Herbert, 1906–1984

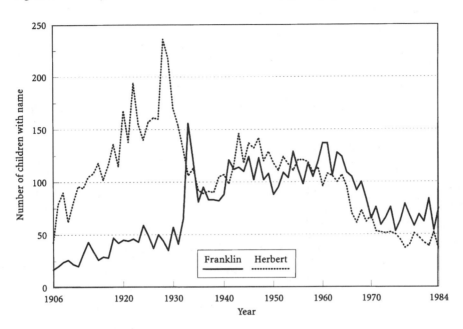

the name's popularity as the United States enters the Great Depression, which started during Hoover's first and only term as president. In turn, the popularity of Franklin D. Roosevelt's first name increases when, after succeeding Hoover as president, he starts to tackle the nation's economic woes. *Franklin* also falls back in fairly short order, though not as far down as before FDR's election. The change in tastes is, in one sense, a matter of chance. The patterns for these names would have been reversed if *Franklin* had been Hoover's first name and if Hoover's successor had been named *Herbert* Delano Roosevelt.[1]

Other examples of a prominent and admired public official inspiring babies' names are easy to find. Warren Harding successfully ran for the presidency in 1920, and we see an increase in the number of baby boys named *Warren* in that year and in his first year in office. After Harding dies in midterm, the succession of Vice President Calvin Coolidge in 1923 leads to an increase in the number of baby *Calvin*s for several years.

The events surrounding Jacqueline Bouvier Kennedy, wife of President John F. Kennedy, illustrate several features of the way taste is influenced by this type of external cause. The name is greatly enhanced in 1961, the first year of JFK's presidency, thanks to both her personal appeal and her prominence. That year

Jacqueline is the 40th most popular name for white girls born in Illinois—a level of popularity that had not been reached since 1944. Just the year before, in 1960, *Jacqueline*'s rank was 69. Whether because the novelty of *Jacqueline* was wearing off or her husband's appeal decreased in office, the name declines in 1962 and 1963 (ranking 48 and 56, respectively), but then it reverses in 1964, when *Jacqueline* moves back up to the rank of 41. This second surge of *Jacqueline* is generated by the president's murder. The First Lady is with her husband in the car when Kennedy is assassinated in late November 1963, is herself immersed in blood, returns to Washington, D.C., and appears with her small children at the funeral. All of these deeply moving events, widely covered on television, contributed to the reversal of *Jacqueline*'s decline in 1964 in the months after her husband's murder.[2] This surge in popularity is a temporary blip, and the position of *Jacqueline* again slips, not reaching as high a level again until 1982.

This is a straightforward illustration of how events that are random (or best treated as random) can enhance the popularity of a name—*Jacqueline* happens to be the name of the young, attractive, glamorous, and polished wife of the new president. After this novelty begins to wear off, there is a new and even greater surge with the shocking assassination of her husband, followed by the bravery and devotion of the young widow to the memory of her husband and the raising of their two children. Some of the appeal of Jacqueline Kennedy, and hence her first name, may of course be a function of the era and the social expectations that then operated for wives. The image of Jacqueline Kennedy might have less appeal in an era where many professional women balance the demands of a career and home and family. Note also the impact of two dramatic events in 1968 on the usage of *Jacqueline*. The murder of her late husband's brother, Robert F. Kennedy, in early June is accompanied by a slight increase in the popularity of *Jacqueline* for a few months. Later that year, a modest drop accompanies her second marriage to Aristotle Onassis in late October. The popularity of *Jacqueline* also appears to weaken when John Kennedy's brother, Senator Edward "Ted" Kennedy of Massachusetts, is involved in the death of a passenger in his car in July 1969, in the event known as Chappaquiddick, which gained great notoriety at the time. Consider the use of *Jacqueline* in the second half of 1969. In the first half of that year, 298 baby girls were named *Jacqueline* in California; in the second half, the number was 230. There then follows years of progressive weakening in the popularity of *Jacqueline* that is not reversed until several years after the death of Jacqueline Kennedy Onassis's second husband and the settling of her claims on his estate in 1977, removing the last linkage with Onassis.[3]

The first names of high-ranking military figures in a war with widespread popular support can also influence naming patterns. In 1942, during World War II, Dwight David Eisenhower, then a relatively unknown officer, became commander of American forces in the European theater. The popularity of *Dwight* enjoyed a striking increase from that year through several postwar years. The name surges again a few years later (in 1948, Eisenhower's war memoir, *Crusade in Europe,* was published and became a best-seller) through 1953 (his first year in the presidency). *Dwight* peaks in 1956, when Eisenhower successfully runs again, and then begins a long decline.

Fundamental Changes in the Social Order

Fundamental changes in the social order often affect the attractiveness of tastes; existing ones lose their appeal and are replaced by newer tastes that more closely fit the bounds set by these new developments. Two significant social changes in recent decades, the feminist movement and the black separatist movement, have each influenced tastes and naming practices in the United States on a variety of dimensions. Both involve an extensive array of taste questions (some of which are considered later in the volume). Here we will look at changing forms of address in the case of women and innovations in the names used by blacks.

From a Man's Wife to Married Woman to Woman: Changing Titles In 1954, the Oakland [California] Junior Chamber of Commerce initiated a "Mother of the Year Walk" in the city's rose garden. Visiting the garden, we find that the first winner is a Mrs. Florence E. Bryant. Others receiving this award in the remainder of the 1950s are: Mrs. Ruth T. Murphy, Mrs. Donald A. Pearce, Mrs. Albert C. Glatze, Mrs. Miles K. Standish, and Mrs. Alfred J. Williams. Not only are all six of the winning mothers identified as married women (by the *Mrs.* title), but four are identified solely through their husband—by using the husband's first name rather than the Mother of the Year's own.

Little changes in the 1960s and 1970s; in the first decade, 6 winners are listed as the wife of their husband (the *Mrs. John Smith* form), 3 of the remainder are also identified as married but with their own first name (the *Mrs. Jane Smith* form), and 1 woman is addressed as a *Dr.,* with her own first name. There are 7 women in the 1970s listed in the *Mrs. John Smith* format, 1 is unknowable because although she is titled as *Mrs.,* only an initial is given for her first name (this form probably uses the husband's first initial rather than hers). Of the remaining 2 mothers, 1 is listed in the *Mrs. Jane Smith* format and—for the first time—a mother is listed without identifying her marital status (as in *Jane Smith*). In the 1980s, only one Mother of the Year in Oakland is identified exclusively as her husband's wife; the rest have the *Mrs.* title, but it is followed by their own first name. Of the 10 winners listed for the 1990s, 2 are in the *Mrs. Jane Smith* format common for the 1980s and the other 8 have no title indicating marital status but are simply in the *Jane Smith* format. Since 1954, Mothers of the Year have gone from being identified by marital status and usually their husband's first name to being listed solely by their own name without indication of marital status. Of course, the latter development might be a way to avoid describing the Mother of the Year as an unmarried woman—but in fact all of the winners were married.[4]

The program notes for each Boston Symphony Orchestra concert provide another example of the way a change in the social order, again the feminist movement, affects naming practices. The program distributed at each concert lists all of the trustees and members of the board of overseers, as well as former members of these bodies (the emeriti trustees and emeriti overseers). Of special interest are the titles used for women who participate in these governing bodies. The symphony is a prestigious organization, and one can be reasonably confident that the members of these governing boards are wealthy and influential in Boston. Participation at this level in the affairs of the symphony is, in turn, a source of prestige.

If we examine the Boston Symphony Orchestra's archives, not until the 1965–1966 season is a woman encountered, a Mrs. James H. Perkins.[5] This situation then changes rather rapidly; checking the first year of each succeeding decade, we see that in the 1970–1971 season, 2 trustees and 12 overseers are women. Without exception, all are identified as their husband's wife, that is, in the form *Mrs. John Smith*. For the affluent, this is a time-honored way for married women to represent the accomplishments of their husbands, much like wearing expensive jewelry or participating in "high society." Ten years later, in 1980–1981, 29 of the overseers and three of the trustees are women. There is virtually no change; all but 1 woman are identified in terms of their husband (the *Mrs. John Smith* format). The exception is a trustee who is identified with her own first name (the *Mrs. Jane Smith* format). In 1990–1991, 9 women are trustees, but there is still no change—all are identified as their husband's wife. (The 5 trustee emeriti are also identified in the same manner—not too surprising, because they are probably older than the active members and are less likely to adopt newer forms of identification.) A modest change, however, is registered among the 32 women who are overseers. (I would guess that the overseers are on the average younger than the trustees, since the board of trustees appears to be an even more prestigious and important group.) Two-thirds of the overseers are still listed in the *Mrs. John Smith* form. Of the remainder, only 1 appears in the *Mrs. Jane Smith* form and the rest are listed without any identification of marital status, that is, simply as *Jane Smith*. There are also now 3 of the 17 overseers emeriti who are similarly listed, with the remainder still *Mrs. John Smith*.

A rapid change takes place in the 1990s. Just three years later, in the 1993–1994 season, there are still 9 women who are trustees, but only 4 have the traditional identification, with an equal number who are simply *Jane Smith* as well as 1 *Mrs. Jane Smith*. The majority of the 33 overseers (presumably younger) are listed in the *Jane Smith* format (19), 2 are *Mrs. Jane Smith,* and 13 cling to the traditional form as their husband's wife. There is also a parallel development among the emeriti. In the 1996–1997 season, the most recent year examined, the number of women on the board of overseers reporting themselves in the *Mrs. John Smith* form declines further from 13 to 9, although female membership increases to 47. By now, of course, this shift may in part reflect the greater participation of unmarried women who occupy the prominent economic positions that men once held almost exclusively.

The Oakland Rose Garden and the Boston Symphony Orchestra leaders are two illustrations of a widespread shift away from the traditional emphasis on designating a woman's marital status and, for those married, substituting their husband's first name for their own. These changes illustrate the influence of external social events which undercut the overwhelming importance attached to identifying women in terms of these roles. I could have used many other examples. Subsets of the women do differ in the disposition to change their identification. Women in the Boston Symphony were slower than the Mother of the Year in Oakland. And, among the former, younger women changed sooner than did older women. Other interesting examples are the titles used by women in the League of Women Voters and the American Association of University Women. Although the figures bounce around from decade to decade, both of these groups adopt the newer identifications earlier than the Oakland mothers and Boston Symphony trustees. By the 1930s, no more than half of the officers and board members of the university women identify themselves through the *Mrs. John Smith* format, and similar shifts are also observed for officers and participants in the league's national conventions. The shift in taste, however, is due to a fundamental shift in the social order, even if it is not reflected throughout the society at the same pace. Subsets of the population differ in their responsiveness to change. In this case, one organization is politically active and socially progressive; the other is geared toward advancing the place of women in higher education. One can emphasize these differences, and they are of course interesting. But this change in taste is indeed a response to a broad and fundamental change in the social order, and this fact should not be overshadowed by differences in the rates of adoption within society.

Unique African-American Names Throughout the twentieth century, black parents were somewhat more disposed than white parents to give their children names they had invented.[6] The gaps, however, were modest. Beginning in the 1960s, there is an unprecedented rise in the use of invented names for African-American children (daughters more than sons). Among African Americans in 1989, for example, 29 percent of girls and 16 percent of boys born in Illinois were given unique names (fig. 3.2; *source:* Lieberson and Mikelson 1995, 930). By contrast, 5 percent of white girls and 3 percent of white boys have such names.[7]

This change in Illinois is not caused by the migration of blacks from south to north. And there is evidence to show that this taste for invented names is not a historic one—at least to this extent.[8] In fact, as we shall see, the timing of this development suggests an influence stemming from the broad and intense social and political changes beginning in the 1960s, a period marked by intensified African-American social protest, the development of the Black Power movement, a renewed emphasis on a distinctive and valued African-American culture, and black separatism (Lieberson and Mikelson 1995).

The interest in African roots and a drift toward Islamic influences, as contrasted with Christian sources, is illustrated by some of the names blacks chose during this period. To mention a few famous examples, in 1964 heavyweight champion Cassius Clay changed his name to Muhammad Ali, in 1971 the basketball star Lew Alcindor became Kareem Abdul-Jabbar, and playwright LeRoi Jones became Imamu Amiri Baraka. Picking up on this interest, publishers printed popular guides to African names to help African-American parents find suitable names for their babies. The impact of Alex Haley's *Roots,* which aired on television in January 1977 and was watched by more people than any other dramatic series, illustrates the attractiveness of names associated with Africa. After the program aired, Kizzy—in *Roots* the American-born daughter of an African who was captured and transported into slavery—ranked as the 17th most popular name given to African-American girls born in Illinois in 1977; in the previous year it was not in the top 200. Likewise, a resurgence of interest in

Fig. 3.2. Standardized percentage of unique names for girls born in Illinois, 1916–1989

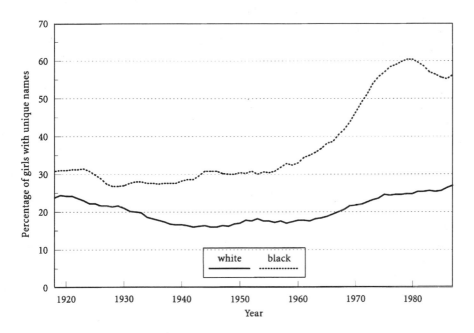

Marcus Garvey, a pre–World War II separatist and nationalist who pushed for a return to Africa, probably inspired the sudden popularity of the name Marcus. The name ranked 164th among names for boys born to blacks in 1956, 98th in 1960, moved up to 13th in 1970, and ranked 5th in 1983 (Lieberson and Mikelson 1995, 940). Much of this change in black tastes is, of course, symbolic. Yet this is exactly the case not only for names but for all other aspects of taste and fashion. Indeed, this symbolic thread runs through much of the nonmaterial culture.

Broad Trends

Tastes often change in a more or less parallel way across a variety of contexts that appear on the surface to be unrelated. Two radically different causes may account for such patterns. One is the influence of a major social change, which affects an array of tastes—such as a catalysmic event or even a change in a social condition that could influence many domains. Examples here might include the influence of television or other forms of mass media on tastes, the development of new sexual mores, or the feminist movement. The other cause for such a sweeping pattern is when a particular taste, influenced by an exogenous condition, in turn affects many other tastes even if there is no substantive linkage. This is a more complicated model, since there are two steps: an initial change that in turn triggers a variety of other taste changes that have no substantive connection to the original external event. In this case, not all changes would be parallel. The question is not easily resolved, but at this point I wish to merely demonstrate the existence of such parallel developments.

Edward Tenner (1989, 22) observes a massive decline in the popularity of men's dress hats (made of felt with some sort of brim around the entire body) in the decades after World War II:

> Not so long ago hats were musts. In scenes of European and American cities before the Second World War the crowd appears as a collective mass of headgear, a hatscape. A man wearing no hat, or an inappropriate out-of-season one, risked street urchins' harassment. Photographs of Depression-era New York bread lines, like engravings of Victorian London homeless shelters, reveal barely an uncovered scalp among the poorest. In the Roaring Twenties, Barnard College women still needed the dean's permission to go hatless on campus. In 1940, editor David McCord '21 wrote in the *Harvard Alumni Bulletin* that a Harvard College sophomore had only a few years earlier solemnly advised a young visiting alumnus of his club that "you'd better put on your hat. Nobody goes without a hat in Cambridge nowadays." . . . Even after the Second World War, a lidless associate in the old-line law firm hazarded partners' reprimands.

Speculating about the cause for the decline in dress hats, Tenner observes that the overt usage of class markers has declined along with the display of authority. Because hats once marked men's place in the social order, this meant their decline as well. How suitable is this explanation? Clearly, informality in material goods and in manners has increased enormously. Parallel developments are numerous. Look at old pictures of sporting events and you are likely to see huge crowds of men, almost all wearing jackets and ties as well as dress hats. Old college photos show men and women in dining halls in suits and dresses, respectively, perhaps a little more dashing than their elders but hardly dressed in the casual manner that is now the standard. Earlier pictures of men and women at home, in what we would view as relatively relaxed circumstances, show them in far more formal wear. Look at advertisements in the popular magazines of the time, and you are likely to see a woman opening the door of her refrigerator wearing a dress and high heels. At present, I am certain to notice a woman in my classroom wearing a dress or a man with a jacket and tie. It is the exception rather than rule—marking a special circumstance such as, perhaps, a job interview—and even then, only for certain kinds of jobs.

Fig. 3.3. Popularity of men's and women's formal wear in Sears, Roebuck catalog, 1920–1990

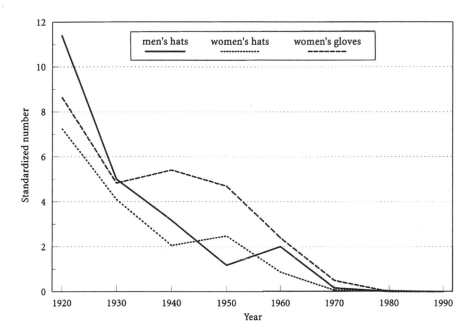

To look at the matter less impressionistically, let us examine the number of men's formal hats, women's dress hats, and women's formal gloves appearing in the Sears, Roebuck spring-summer catalog in each decade from 1920 through 1990. All three items of formal wear decline substantially between 1920 and 1990 (fig. 3.3).[9] Indeed, by 1970, formal hats for either sex, and women's dress gloves, are no longer listed in the catalog.

The decline of formality in clothing is part of a wider shift of tastes in society. Relevant to us here is the comparable growth in the use of nicknames—not as a private matter between friends and family or close workers—but rather in the most public of circumstances.

The public use of nicknames by members of Congress has accelerated in recent decades. Rather than using their given name when dealing with the public, politicians are now far more disposed to call themselves by their nickname. In the late nineteenth century, senators or representatives rarely used nicknames in public (fig. 3.4). A modest shift upward occurred through the first third of the twentieth century, in recent decades the increase has been stunning. By 1992, one-fifth of all senators and one-third of representatives used a nickname instead of their given first name.[10]

Fig. 3.4. Percentage of House of Representatives and Senate members using nicknames, 1888–1992

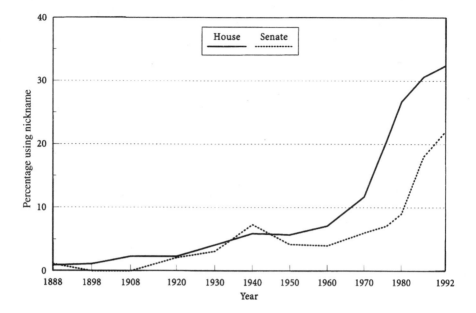

This change occurs within the context of other influences, but a certain convergence appears to be developing. For example, although regional differences in informality still exist, their impact declines in the face of sweeping change toward informality. In 1940, only 1 of 121 members of Congress from the Northeast used a nickname in his or her public listing; by contrast, 13.5 percent of those from the South were so listed. The Midwest and West, too, were more like the Northeast at that time (4.5 and 2.3 percent, respectively). By 1992, 40 percent of southern members of Congress gave their informal names; the West trailed close behind (36 percent), followed by the Midwest (29 percent) and the Northeast (19 percent).

Other features also affect this disposition toward informality. The *Yellow Pages* listings for Boston, Dallas, Los Angeles, and New York allow us to consider differences between occupations and differences among these large cities. Physicians are still disinclined to use a nickname in their listings, with lawyers somewhat more inclined, but neither are as likely as members of Congress. Harmonious with the regional differences noted earlier, professionals in Dallas are far more likely to use nicknames; the lowest rates are in the two Northeastern cities. Looking at the Dallas *Yellow Pages* in earlier years, there is an upward shift from

1927 to 1940 to 1970 to 1993 between physicians and lawyers in their disposition toward using nicknames. Also observed during the same period is the decline of a much more formal practice—namely, the use of initials. Among physicians and lawyers in Dallas this form of address was once common (in 1927, between 40 and 50 percent of doctors and lawyers listed no first name). This form of distancing has virtually disappeared today.

Nicknames of news and sports reporters in four major newspapers, the *Boston Globe, Chicago Tribune, Los Angeles Times,* and *New York Times,* duplicate this pattern. There is a modest upward trend in the disposition to use nicknames in the bylines of the reporters working for these newspapers. News reporters, however, are far less likely to use informal bylines than are reporters writing for the sports section. Although I have not systematically analyzed the reported names of television reporters and anchors, it is my impression that a large number now use nicknames.

Waves of tastes, then, can occur in more or less parallel fashion—witness the shifts toward informality in a variety of domains (clothing, manners, nicknames) at more or less the same time. These common changes may have a substantive meaning. In this case, they could reflect a sweeping shift in the social world in which the overt presentation of power, position, and authority is minimized. And yet a set of parallel changes could simply mean that tastes in one domain influence tastes in other domains: perhaps only the initial shift reflects an external development in society. Later we shall explore how a fashion, once established, may expand outward into other domains on its own. There need not be a deep substantive meaning to these waves of parallel fashion developments. In the commercial world, colors may become popular for a variety of unrelated products at the same time. The automobile industry, for example, uses color consultants to help the manufacturers plan for new exterior and interior colors. Several told me that they copy from each other and look at developments in other fashion areas for clues and ideas: everything from the colors favored for the fabrics of new furniture and to new hot colors in fashion wear.

THE LIMITATIONS OF EXPLANATIONS
BASED ON EXTERNAL INFLUENCES

We have seen a few of the ways changing social conditions can profoundly alter our tastes. By no means are these influences limited to naming practices. It is difficult to think of any arena of taste, ranging from architecture and public monuments to movies to personal items, that are immune from the impact of social change. Many of us probably take this fact for granted. The limitations of this viewpoint are probably less obvious. They entail both an important technical issue and the existence of powerful influences that generate changes in taste even in the absence of change in the social order.

An Important Caution

In accounting for a shift in tastes, people are usually disposed to look for a societal explanation. It takes little imagination to find some plausible social condition that could account for virtually any change in taste. Because the cause is often evaluated in terms of its plausibility rather than through a rigorous test of its validity, it is far easier to find *plausible* ad hoc explanations of tastes than to find *correct* ones.

In describing the decline of men's dress hats, for example, we noted a similar drop in formality over a number of decades and in a variety of domains. From this perspective, the decline in formal hats for men is, rather than an idiosyncratic event, part of this great wave. Suppose, however, in more typical fashion, that all we know is dress hats declined in popularity between different points in time; we know nothing about parallel changes in other tastes or even the decline curve we saw in figure 3.3. Edward Tenner (1989, 25–26) and Michael Schudson (1984, 39–40) both review the ad hoc explanations people have advanced to explain the decline of fedoras. Because these explanations occurred in a vacuum, without knowledge of either other trends or the starting point in the decline of dress hats, they are instructive. The explanations include:

- President John F. Kennedy's hatless style;
- the general trend toward casualness after World War II;
- the move to the suburbs, which meant that people spent more time in cars, and getting in and out of a car while wearing a hat can be awkward;
- again, the increased use of cars, which meant that people spent less time outdoors in winter and hence had less need for a hat;
- the change in men's hairstyles toward longer hair, which made hats harder to wear;
- an increased concern among men about hairstyles that made hats less desirable because they would both conceal the hair and muss up the style;
- a renewed emphasis on the natural, combined with the fact that hats represented the incompleteness of nature;

- the use of hair as a form of self-expression;
- the rejection of hats by younger males because of the association of hats with adulthood and their reaction to the political faults blamed on older generations;
- the association of hatlessness with youth; and
- a reduction in the overt display of authority and power, leading to a decline in hats because of their association with such a display.

Because our earlier empirical results show that declines began at a much earlier period than these interpretations assume—let alone the fact that many other tastes were changing that were not directly affected by these factors—most of these otherwise *plausible* substantive interpretations are false, but without systematic study it is impossible to separate the chaff from the grain. The shift from hats occurs over a long span.[11] Suburbia, John F. Kennedy, the growth in the use of cars after World War II, the new popularity of long hair, and a renewed emphasis on nature are all unlikely explanations for the massive long-term decline in the popularity of dress hats.

This example is important not merely because it illustrates how easy it is for erroneous after-the-fact explanations to be offered for a cultural development. It also shows how easy it is to mistakenly attribute a change in taste to a variety of specific social events, which, we can see, could not have been responsible. In the absence of a rigorous study, the choice among competing explanations rests much more on the rhetorical skills of the proponents and the dispositions of the recipients than on the likely truth of any. If there is a disposition to assume that a change in tastes or fashion must have *social meaning* (in the sense that some minor or major social change must be responsible), then a plausible account will surely be found, particularly if it is not investigated systematically.

Major Events? Yes. Causes? No

Historical events clearly have affected some features of tastes in naming—witness the connection noted earlier between the civil rights movement and the surge in blacks' use of unique invented names for their children (see also Chapter 7). This is not up for debate, although there is a need to guard against the ease of overstating their influence when ad hoc explanations are applied to a specific taste. In fact, some of the most important events of the twentieth century can be shown to have, at most, only modestly influenced essential features of the naming process in the United States. Fundamental features of fashions in naming are unmodified by such major events as two world wars, the Great Depression, the Vietnam protest era, the civil rights movement, and the feminist movement. The influence of these external social developments is nil for both the concentration of names (as measured by the percentage of newborns with the twenty most common names given to infant boys or girls in a year) and the continuity between the names given to children in a given year with those names used five years earlier.

Concentration of Names   The concentration of names reflects the joint influence of cohesion in choices among all subsets of the population as well as the desire to give highly popular names to children. We can see that the concentration of names shifts over time in a rather orderly manner that is barely altered by major events (fig. 3.5). From 1905 until the mid-1940s, there is an upward thrust in the level of concentration of names; after this, there is a downward movement. The level of concentration is unaffected by World War I and is barely influenced in the postwar decade. At about 1920, there is a slight jump for girls, but this level stabilizes in following years. The boys' concentration also jumps slightly, followed by a decade or so of more or less stability, before again rising more rapidly. The Great Depression of the 1930s shows no obvious impact on the concentration of boys' names, which moves upwardly in a rather smooth curve that peaks in the mid-1940s. Not until late in the Depression do we glimpse the possibility that the Depression influenced this feature of girls' names; the concentration dips and is followed by an increase that also peaks in the mid-1940s.

What do we make of the fact that the movement toward greater concentration appears to reverse itself around the end of World War II? We need to bear in mind two things: (1) no such decline appeared at the end of World War I, and (2) the decline that follows is a long-term event that, if anything, later accelerates (in the 1950s for girls and the late 1960s for boys). In any case, the tumultuous 1960s, marked by waves of protest against the war in Vietnam, does not seem to make an obvious mark on the concentration of either girls' or boys' names. As for the feminist movement of the 1970s, the decline is actually more pronounced in the concentration among boys' names, the opposite of what one would expect if a high level of concentration represents a cohesive structure of popular name choices *and* if there is greater turmoil in the tastes for girls' names owing to the social changes wrought during the feminist movement.

As far as concentration trends go for boys' and girls' names, the most one can conclude is that the aftermath of World War II is causally linked to a major shift

Fig. 3.5. Concentration of names, California, 1905–1984

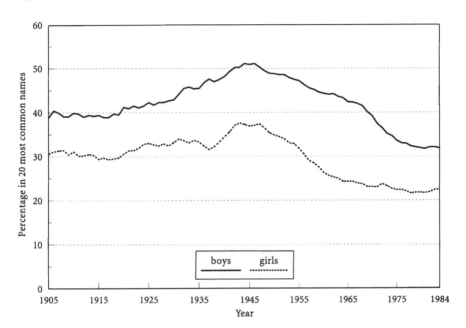

in concentration in the population as a whole, such that either a long-term decline started in the naming cohesion between major subsets of the population (region, religion, socioeconomic status, and so forth) and/or there was increased disposition to avoid picking names once they became very popular and/or there was a rapid turnover in names that reduced the level of concentration. Assuming that this temporal correspondence represents a causal linkage, it is still the case that all of the remaining major events have either no impact or minimal impact on trends in the level of concentration of names.

The results are mixed regarding the impact of the 1960s on African-American naming patterns. For the concentration of boys' names, blacks and whites in Illinois followed very different paths throughout the period.[12] Black concentration started to drift downward in the mid-1940s, long before the political developments of the 1960s (fig. 3.6). Even before then, during the span when white concentration levels were going up, levels for blacks were more or less stable. Of critical importance is that the decline in concentration experienced by blacks in the 1960s and onward parallels the declines experienced by whites. Contrary to the expected influence of the 1960s, there is nothing exceptional about black shifts during that period. Changes in the concentration of the names given to

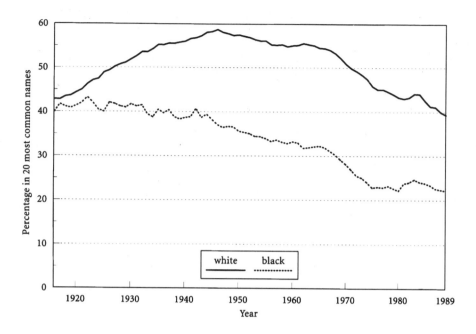

Fig. 3.6. Concentration of names, Illinois, boys, 1916–1989

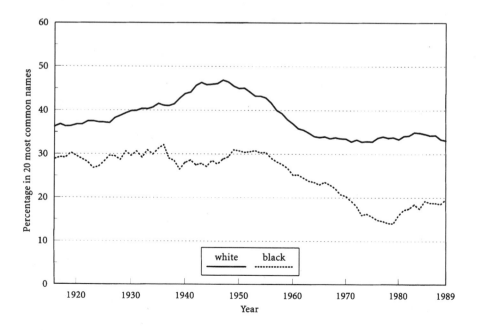

Fig. 3.7. Concentration of names, Illinois, girls, 1916–1989

Fig. 3.8. Spearman correlations with leading names, 5 years earlier, California, 1912–1

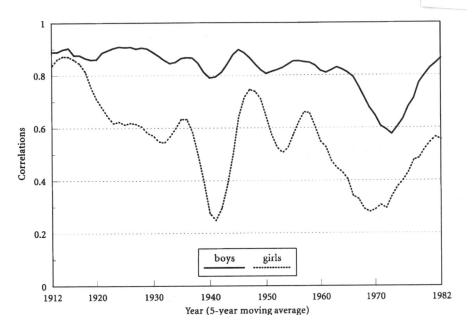

black girls, in contrast, neatly fit the expectation that the 1960s would affect the level of concentration among leading names. For both black and white girls, the concentration index starts to decline in the early 1950s, but it levels off for whites by the early 1960s, whereas the decline accelerates for blacks from the early 1960s all the way through the 1970s (fig. 3.7). Overall, however, shifts in concentration are minimally influenced by major social events.

Change in the Names Unlike the concentration in names, boys and girls differ greatly in the continuity of their names during the time span. Boys' leading names change at about the same rate from 1912 through the mid-1960s (fig. 3.8). Some minor shifts can be related to major social and political events. For example, continuity with names five years earlier declines slightly during World War I. Another small decline occurs late in the Depression, followed by a modest rise during World War II and another modest decline at war's end. These small changes, however, actually underline the minimal influence of these major events.[13] One important shift in the continuity of boys' names *is* associated with a fundamental disruption of the social order. A massive decline in the continuity of boys' names starts in the early 1960s and runs throughout the decade. This is followed by an equally sharp increase in correlations beginning in the early 1970s and onward. The timing of this pattern is harmonious with the proposition that the unrest surrounding Vietnam did increase the discontinuity of boys' names, with the continuity returning as the protest period and the intensity of American involvement in Southeast Asia began to decline.[14]

The correlation between the leading names given to girls each year and those popular five years earlier is far more volatile.[15] From 1916 until the U.S. entrance into World War II, there is a substantial (and largely persistent) drop in the continuity of names. The one noteworthy deviation occurs during the early years of the Depression, but it is difficult to attribute this overall downward trend to any specific event. The reversal of direction in the 1940s appears to be connected to American participation in World War II and in the years immediately afterward. Note, however, that the increase in the level of association with earlier names is exactly the opposite of what would conventionally be attributed to the war. Because of the wartime labor shortage, women began to engage in activities previously restricted to men, such as many kinds of factory work. Yet there was increasing continuity in the names given to daughters born during this span. And when women were forced to give up their newfound opportunities as men returned from the war, continuity declined rather than increased. In general, after World War II, the fluctuations for both sexes are largely parallel, albeit far more substantial for girls. The decline in continuity paralleling the Vietnam period is found for girls, and the reversal afterward also occurs. This reversal is especially meaningful for girls because the feminist movement came to the fore in the 1970s. Again counter to what might be predicted, there is increasing continuity in the leading names given to girls half a decade earlier.

It is possible to create an external interpretation of this by speculating that some parents were less playful with names because they could view the maintenance of earlier names as a mark against new social developments. Whether this is true or not is beside the point here; it does show how easy it can be to explain a change in taste (or absence of a change) in terms of some external development if you are determined to conclude that there *has* to be a cause of that type.

By way of summary, the trends for boys run counter to what we might expect these major events to generate; the only exception is the Vietnam protest era, when the continuity of names given to sons drops off substantially. For girls, f their short-term shifts *are* harmonious with an interpretation that links the social developments discussed above—*some* but hardly all. In many he fluctuations are in the opposite direction from what our substantive

Fig. 3.9. Spearman correlations with leading names, 5 years earlier, Illinois, boys, 1923–1987

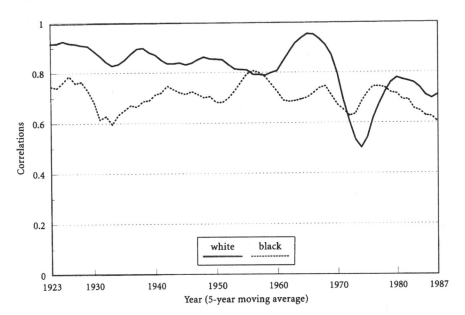

expectation would be. And because of the constant fluctuations in the values during much of the period, it is simply harder to attribute these changes to the social events, even when there appears to be a connection in the expected direction.[16]

During the 1960s among African-American sons and daughters, the correlations fail to change in the expected direction. In spite of intense interracial confrontations, a restatement of black goals and aspirations, and a new emphasis on black culture, whites—not blacks—experience the most dramatic drops in naming continuity during this span. We noted that the influence of Vietnam shows up with a drop in the continuity of names among white sons born in the late 1960s and early 1970s (see fig. 3.8). The drop during that period for the names given to black boys is far less steep (fig. 3.9), and the black protest movement starting in the 1960s does not appear to have any impact at all on this measure until late in the decade (when it is hard to sort it from the influence of Vietnam). Likewise, there are some dramatic fluctuations in the correlations over time for the names given to black girls (fig. 3.10), but they fail to match the substantial decline in the correlations among white girls. Unlike the continuity of names given to boys, among black girls the drop occurs only in the first few years of the decade. In essence, whatever is driving trends in these correlations

Fig. 3.10. Spearman correlations with leading names, 5 years earlier, Illinois, girls, 1923–1987

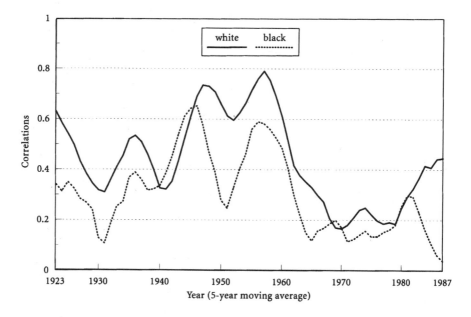

among blacks, it does not seem to be responding to events in the 1960s in the way that one might expect from the importance of the developments in race relations during that span. And these volatile shifts in the continuity of names should not hide the fact that over time the two groups are drifting apart in their tastes.[17]

One last finding should also be mentioned, though it is a side issue and this is not the place for an extensive discussion. The impact of the Vietnam War on naming tastes comes earlier in California than in Illinois—more or less in keeping with the very early and exceptionally intense protest in California.[18]

THE SOCIAL ORDER MATTERS, BUT MORE IS GOING ON

There is clear-cut evidence that even relatively minor fluctuations in the social order will influence tastes—*relatively minor* in the sense that they themselves would not be of sufficient importance to convert a pattern of long-term continuity into practices involving matters of taste. This perspective has limitations, however. It is fairly easy to account for almost any taste in terms of some feature or other of the social order. But ad hoc explanations developed without relatively rigorous criteria are of limited value—witness the various social conditions offered to account for the decline of dress hats.

Also significant is that some of the most important developments of the twentieth century fail to substantially influence tastes in ways that we would expect. To be sure, there are some influences on names, but for the most part the impact of these events is modest. Note that the evidence—particularly for concentration indexes—indicates long-term orderly shifts that in the main do not reflect the kinds of external influences that we would expect. If the levels of concentration in name choices, as well as the degree of continuity in leading names, often display no impact of the broad social influences under consideration, what does affect them? The internal taste mechanisms are the building blocks underlying virtually all changes in taste, and we shall devote the next two chapters to understanding them.

The Ratchet Effect

Internal taste mechanisms (there are a number of them) are the starting point in understanding the nature of tastes and their changes over time. These internal mechanisms are the most fundamental of influences on taste because they do more than move tastes along; they also limit and mold the influence of external, societal, and organizational factors. In this sense, I refer to internal mechanisms as the building blocks of taste; to understand the direction that social influences exert on tastes, we need first to understand how exogenous social influences are channeled and muted by these taste mechanisms.

Fashion is, of course, an internal mechanism that generates changes even in the absence of external shifts. By definition, fashion changes simply for the sake of fashion—a constant stream of new features and designs is a must for many products. This holds not only for clothing; consider also furniture, colors, cars, cuisines, wines, music, and the like. And even though there are organizations with an economic interest in getting us to change—designers, manufacturers, retailers, and advertisers—it is a big mistake to assume that these entities are responsible for the *existence* of fashion. Rather, they take advantage of the fact that a certain subset of the population wants something new simply because it is *new*, or because the old has become boring or merely commonplace. And insofar as this occurs, then we can see how fashion works as an internal mechanism to continuously drive change. Contrary to common assumptions, Fred Davis (1992) and Herbert Blumer (1969) have both demonstrated how fashion-oriented enterprises, rather than dictating new tastes, seek to develop new designs that fashion-oriented customers will find attractive.[1] Of course, there is a secondary feedback such that commercial promotion of fashion in turn intensifies the existing disposition toward change. On this score, names are an excellent example of fashions that change without a "push" from profit-oriented institutions. It is useful to think about fashion in this manner; once established for a given domain, it becomes a mechanism that drives further changes without additional external shifts. Note, however, that the existence of fashion, as a factor for any form of symbolic or material culture, does not by itself explain the nature of the new tastes.

HOW THE RATCHET WORKS

Any new taste would in itself meet the necessity for change. Yet new tastes often follow strikingly orderly patterns. The pioneering empirical studies of changes in women's fashions by Alfred L. Kroeber (1919), and later by Jane Richardson and Kroeber (1940), provide a remarkable historical record of yearly changes in women's fashion, beginning as far back as 1605 and running through 1936. Five-year moving averages between 1787 and 1936 of, respectively, the length of waists and the width of skirts are revealing (figs. 4.1 and 4.2; *source:* Richardson and Krober 1940, 125–27; length of waist is determined by measuring the distance from the woman's mouth to the minimum diameter across the waist, diameter of the skirt is measured in each case at the hem or base).[2]

These fashion changes consist of persistent movements in one direction that are then reversed and followed by a long-term movement in the opposite direction. Figure 4.1, for example, displays a long-term trend toward increasingly narrow waists for women's garments, followed by a reverse movement in the opposite direction, and then back again ad nauseum. Why does this occur? The answer is not immediately obvious because an almost infinite variety of yearly fluctuations would also satisfy the fashion requirement for yearly changes. To explain these orderly changes, I propose an internal change mechanism that I call the "ratchet effect." It is based on the joint operation of two features of taste change. The first is that new tastes are usually based on existing tastes; what is most appealing is a modest variant on existing tastes. This is because new developments are judged in terms of a framework based on the existing practices. Year-to-year shifts, therefore, are usually modest. From the short-term perspective of contemporaries, these small changes are seen not as moderate but rather as noteworthy. Only when we look at the changes from a long-term

Fig. 4.1. Length of waist, 5-year moving average, 1788–1934

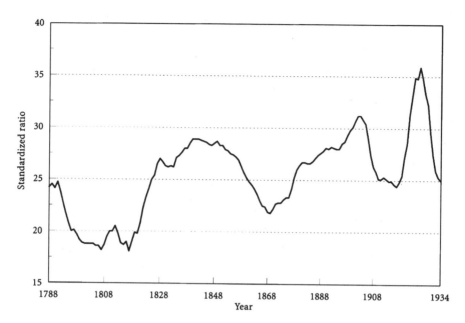

perspective are they visible as modest movements along a long-term path. To take another example, someone contemplating the purchase of a new car will recognize important design differences from cars produced, say, five years ago. Yet if changes in automobile design are examined over a long period, the shifts in most five-year periods appear only as modest changes in a general direction.

This slow movement occurs in many areas of culture. As John Mueller notes in his history of the American symphony orchestra, musical innovations—if they are to succeed—are based largely on an existing set of practices:

> If a composition is actually unique, or as it approximates that description, it is to that extent alien to the stream of human thought, its language is not understood; it would evoke bewilderment rather than curiosity and aesthetic interest. The composer who flouts the current folkways of taste, and disregards the norms of consonance and form prevalent at the time, incurs the same risks of rejection as any other innovator in the political, social and economic, religious, or linguistic world. Not even the greatest innovators who have survived, have been so indiscreet. . . . The early works of Beethoven—with all the isolated points of departure from tradition pointed out by contemporary philistines—bore a sufficient family resemblance to their musical ancestors, to which his hearers were accustomed, that his new works were anticipated with obvious pleasure. [1951, 393]

Fig. 4.2. Width of skirt, 5-year moving average, 1788–1934

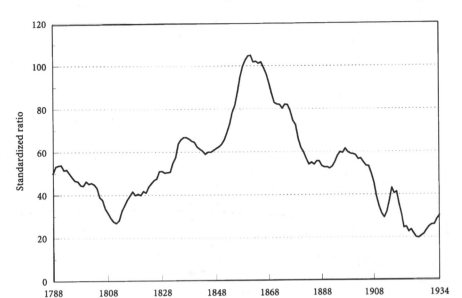

Given this disposition for shifts to be gradual, we can understand the second feature driving the ratchet effect—namely, that fashion must shift fairly persistently in one direction rather than oscillating back and forth. As fashions change, slightly older fashions begin to look out of date, and as time progresses, they look increasingly dated. Were a new fashion to backtrack (say, if the width of the skirt at the hemline had gone from *x* to *y* inches over three years and then reversed back to *x* inches in the next year), then the very newest fashion would be confused with older fashions that had occurred just a few years earlier. This could not work because such a confusion is counter to the point of fashion—to wit, a new taste that is different from recent tastes—thereby setting one off from the others and making them *out of fashion*. Fashions that persistently move from the previous fashions in one direction, however, will not be subject to any confusion. In the case of clothing, people are clearly wearing not old clothes but new ones. There is no confusion, and hence the function of being *in fashion* is not in danger of being mistaken for being *unfashionable*. Consider likewise the consumer response to a new car with styling and color features that are indistinguishable from cars built five years earlier, even if that newer car has all the latest technological innovations.

Other studies confirm that long-term taste shifts do not bounce around randomly but tend to move in one direction and then reverse themselves. In a study of men's fashions in facial hair over more than a century, Dwight Robinson (1976) reports orderly shifts in one direction.[3] The presence of some facial hair progresses upward from the beginning of the period, 1840, through about 1885. After that, there is a steady reduction in facial hair through the end of the period under study, 1972. American presidents exhibit a similar cycle in facial hair. Not one of the first 15 presidents has either a beard or a mustache. Ten of the next 12 presidents, from Abraham Lincoln through William Howard Taft, have a beard or a mustache or both. And no president since then has had facial hair.[4] Agnes Brooks Young, who has examined cycles of fashion for nearly two hundred years beginning with 1760, came to similar general conclusions about the yearly changes in high fashion: the changes are continuous, with no duplications or repetitions of the preceding fashions; the shifts are relatively slow; and they are modifications of previous styles, with no abrupt differences (1937, 205–206).

Just to be absolutely clear, notice how the ratchet effect, like other internal mechanisms, requires the existence of some social conditions (in clothing fashions, for example, sufficient affluence to allow for clothing changes before they are worn out), but the operation of this internal mechanism will then occur without further changes in the external system. As such, the persistent changes in taste do not reflect changes in the social order. For example, while England was at war with Napoleon from 1808 to 1814, there was little communication between England and France. Confident that English fashions during this period were operating independently of Paris and were not affected by copying French developments, Young presents an enlightening report on changes in England: "Fashion continued to change precisely as before. Year by year the variations developed in a wholly normal manner, and the evolution of the cycle type was in no way disturbed" (71). She then observes that the changes in England turned out to be the same as those occurring in France during the same years, with only slight divergences (73–74). In accounting for fashions in men's facial hair, external events also play a relatively modest role, reports Robinson. "The remarkable regularity of our wavelike fluctuations suggests a large measure of independence from outside historical events. . . . but I suspect that they merely reinforce the prevailing style" (1138).

Richardson and Kroeber also consider the influence of broad social events on fashion cycles, in particular, shifts in variability. And although they cannot rule out a variety of explanations, including broad societal ones, they conclude that these broad events are unlikely to account for the fundamental developments of tastes and their cycling. "Generic historic causes tending toward social and cultural instability may produce instability in dress styles also; but their effect on style is expressed in stress upon the existent long-range basic pattern of dress, and the changes effected have meaning only in terms of the term" (1940, 148). So although social events obviously can and do deeply affect shifts in taste, it is all too easy to see the heavy hand of society in every change. As Richardson and Kroeber put it—after writing about claims that women's fashion were influenced by revolution, Napoleon, world wars, communism, fascism, automobiles, and jazz—it is easy to conjecture such influences, but it is difficult to prove them.

Cyclical Reversals in Trends

The reversals in trend shown in figures 4.1 and 4.2 (and observed by Richardson and Kroeber for four other dress diameters) raise an important question about the adequacy of the ratchet effect. The reversal itself is not a problem; any taste must operate within bounds such that a movement in one direction cannot occur indefinitely. Suppose the hemline is moving upward. At some point there has to be a reversal because otherwise the hemline will violate social mores. Or practical constraints may come into play, which can be ignored for a while as extremes are approached—but not indefinitely. Suppose a garment gets longer and longer and eventually begins to trail along the floor. This can work for wedding gowns, a special occasion in which young girls may hold the bride's gown, but it would hardly work for daily wear or even the "usual" special event. These constraints hold for virtually any shift in taste: consider sleeves that get so long that the hand can no longer function, or trends in which automobiles become increasingly long or low.[5]

So, although an eventual reversal is not a problem, the form of the turnabout needs to be considered. In the early stages of the reversal, characteristics are not radically different from those occurring just a few years earlier (see figs. 4.1 and 4.2). This is harmonious with the first assumption of the ratcheting mechanism—namely, that tastes tend to change slowly such that new tastes are only modestly different from the previous ones. But how does the second assumption—namely, that the changes move in a direction that eliminates confusion from very recent tastes—account for the form of these reversals? Even though the values of the reversing attribute are the same as recent ones, there can be no confusion between the new fashion and the one occurring only a few years earlier. This is because of unusually rapid shifts in at least one other fashion attribute. I found that in all but one of twenty-two turning points for six fashion variables, some other feature experienced a rapid change in the direction *away* from its earlier position (based on data reported in Richardson and Kroeber 1940, table 8). Because of this substantial change in at least one other characteristic, the dresses are still visibly different from recently popular ones. Skirt length, for example, reached a low of 91.9 (standardized ratio) in 1814. The index values three years earlier in 1812 are fairly close to the index values in 1817 (three years after the low point). Yet the shift in waist length between 1812 and 1817 was of a magnitude that had previously taken twenty years to occur (from 1792 to 1812).

The second assumption about the ratcheting mechanism, therefore, is not contradicted. When a given characteristic is reversed, at least one other characteristic changes at a relatively rapid level, thereby reducing any confusion (for technical details, see Appendix 1).[6] Incidentally, the length of these long-term cycles provides a clue to the reintroduction of earlier fashions. At some point, old fashions can be reintroduced as new fashions and their reappearance will not be confused with an out-of-date usage. If the popularity of *John* and *Mary*, for example, continues to decline through the years and the people with such names die out, then their reintroduction by parents in some future period will not be confused with their earlier usage and will have a connotation that could not have occurred at that time.

APPLYING THE RATCHET EFFECT TO NAMES

Of what relevance is the ratchet effect to tastes in names? In Western societies parents name their children only once; unlike fashions in clothing, a child's name usually does not continuously change every few years in response to the latest fashion. Yet the ratchet effect has considerable value here, if we avoid too literal an analogy. If a taste changes in a certain direction—rather than always vacillating in a random manner—the ratcheting mechanism suggests that this movement could occur without substantive meaning. Indeed, the influence of a major event is not all-powerful because its impact occurs within the context of, and is enmeshed with, ongoing internal mechanisms. This means that these orderly movements over time are devoid of external meaning. Rather, they largely reflect modifications of the existing tastes owing to the ratchet effect. Names are particularly valuable here because—unlike commercial products—we can avoid the impulse to attribute shifts in their popularity to the influence of organizations with a vested interest in generating a given outcome.

The Sounds of Popular Names in England and Wales

The fifty most common names for children in England and Wales for the years 1700 to 1985, a span of nearly three hundred years, are well documented (table 4.1).[7] Fashions in the sounds of girls' names are easily observed. A full cycle occurs for names with an *a*-ending sound (as in *Laura* or *Sarah*), for example. In 1700 a large number of names have an *a*-ending. This number rises to a peak of twenty-one in 1850 (slightly more than 40 percent of the fifty most common names that year), drops downward to eight by 1900, and then starting another increase through most of the twentieth century.[8] Other endings also experience important long-term shifts in popularity. The *ee*-ending (as in *Emily* or *Katie*) and names ending in an *n*-sound (as in *Helen* or *Katherine*) are examples. There is also a notable decline in the *s*-ending (*Alice* or *Gladys*) in recent decades.

The popularity of sounds at the beginning of names also shifts through the years. Names starting with a vowel increased to seventeen in 1875, then declined, and finally became more or less stable in the second half of the twentieth century.[9] Names beginning with a *J*-sound also fluctuate remarkably in popularity, as do names starting with a hard *K*-sound (such as *Claire* or *Kelly*). Other changes include the recent drop-off in names incorporating a *th* spelling. Shifts in the popularity of different sounds is by no means confined to the English-speaking world; Philippe Besnard and Guy Desplanques report similar results for France (1993, 261–267).

Some of the sounds for boys' names also shift back and forth over time, although change is less common. This is understandable, given that there is less movement in boys' names and hence reduced opportunity for fashions to fluctuate. Nevertheless, we find a substantial increase in the *n*-ending in the second half of the twentieth century, peaking in 1975 at nearly 40 percent of the leading boys names and now moving downward (by 1993, *n*-endings decline to thirteen from the nineteen found in 1975).[10] The *d*-ending for boys also exhibits a full cycle; of modest importance in 1700, the popularity of boys' names ending in *d* rose in the latter half of the nineteenth century and in England and Wales peaked in the first quarter of the twentieth. This was followed by a substantial decline. The *s*-ending for boys' names never exhibited the modest increase observed for girls, but, as with girls' names, it is also unpopular at present. As for beginning sounds, names starting with *H* have essentially disappeared among leading names since 1950.

For both boys and girls, the sounds examined here are found in no more than

Table 4.1. Linguistic characteristics of 50 most common names for children born in England and Wales, 1700–1985

Linguistic characteristic	Number of top 50 names									
	1700	1800	1850	1875	1900	1925	1950	1965	1975	1985
Girls										
Ending sounds										
a	14	13	21	16	8	9	11	15	17	16
ee	13	12	10	11	13	10	8	8	12	16
n	8	8	7	6	7	10	22	18	13	8
s	3	3	3	4	7	4	1	0	0	0
Other sounds										
vowel beginning	11	11	15	17	16	14	6	7	7	9
j beginning	5	6	4	2	2	4	12	8	6	5
k(c) other*	1	1	1	1	0	0	1	2	3	4
th spelling	7	7	5	7	5	5	5	2	3	3
Boys										
Ending sounds										
n	8	8	6	5	5	5	9	16	19	18
d	4	4	4	8	12	13	6	3	2	3
s	4	4	5	3	3	3	2	1	2	2
Other sounds										
h beginning	3	3	5	5	6	4	0	0	0	0

* Other than initial sound

40 percent of the fifty leading names, and usually less. This is important because it suggests a limit to the popularity of a sound before it starts to decline; presumably, newer parents become increasingly disinclined to give names with such linguistic features. Although some parents may consciously decide to avoid such names because of their perceived "overuse," it is likely that the decline also reflects a set of subliminal responses (in the same way that we often know when something is wrong with the structure of a sentence, even if we cannot immediately name the rule that was violated). For example, both whites and blacks in the United States do very well in guessing the gender of children who are given an invented name, even though they have never met the child. They respond to a covert understanding of the associations between gender and sound, just as the

parents do when they use different sound patterns for girls and boys (Lieberson and Mikelson 1995).

Popular Names in the United States

Tastes in name sounds also shift among blacks and whites for much of the twentieth century in Illinois. Among the 50 most common names given to white girls, the number of names ending in *ee* rises from 6 early in the century to 15 in 1977; both the *a*- and *n*-ending increase substantially through the years; likewise, the use of the hard *K*-sound increases both at the beginning of a girl's name and elsewhere (table 4.2). A full cycle occurs for names beginning with a vowel; their popularity declines from 11 to 2 in the post–World War II era and then rises again to 13 in 1987. Interestingly, names ending in *s* exhibit a decline similar to that observed in England and Wales.

The sounds found in popular boys' names change as well, but they are less common and less severe than those for girls. We do see a rise in the *J*-beginning, the *n*- and *ee*-endings, and the usage of a hard *k* inside the name. Two of the declines, the use of names beginning in *H* and ending in *d* are strikingly parallel to the English pattern. *H* disappears in the post–World War II period, and *d* is of minimal popularity by the 1980s.

For many of these sounds, there are parallel changes among blacks (examples are the *J*-beginning and the *ee*-ending for girls, and the *H*- and *J*-beginnings for boys). Indeed, there is only minor divergences in the appeal of various sounds— even in recent years. Blacks and whites may differ in the first names that they favor (Lieberson and Bell 1992; Lieberson and Mikelson 1995), but for the most part these differences are not in the sounds but in the choice of names with these sounds.[11] This fact points to the power of these underlying shifts in the tastes for sounds in the names.

Etymologies

There are also fashions in the sources of popular names. Returning to England and Wales, the etymological cycles are reminiscent of those occurring for diameters of women's dresses. Among girls' names, there are long-term movements for names of French, Greek, Hebrew, and Latin origin (table 4.3). These tastes generally move in one direction and then reverse themselves and move in the opposite way. (When we consider the small number of time points and restriction to the 50 most common names in each period, these movements are remarkably consistent.) Especially noteworthy is the rise in the popularity of Latin

Table 4.2. Linguistic characteristics of 50 most common names for children born in Illinois, 1918–1987

	Number of top 50 names											
	1918		1925		1945		1957		1977		1987	
Linguistic characteristic	White	Black	White	Black	White	Black	White	Black	White	Black	White	Black
Girls												
Ending sounds												
a	7	18	11	14	11	12	15	18	15	28	18	25
ee	6	9	6	9	8	8	10	9	15	12	13	10
n	11	7	14	10	17	16	14	12	12	2	10	3
s	6	3	7	6	3	5	0	2	0	0	0	1
Other sounds												
vowel beginning	11	13	8	11	2	6	2	5	10	9	13	10
k(c) beginning	2	2	1	2	6	3	8	5	11	7	11	8
k(c) other*	0	0	0	0	1	2	2	1	4	9	5	11
Boys												
Ending sounds												
n	6	6	6	6	6	7	7	9	12	12	14	12
ee	3	2	3	7	8	7	9	12	7	8	8	8
d	9	9	10	12	8	10	7	7	5	5	2	5
Other sounds												
j beginning	5	6	6	6	8	9	6	8	11	9	10	9
k(c) other*	3	2	3	2	5	3	6	5	7	6	9	4
h beginning	5	4	5	6	2	2	0	0	0	0	0	0

* Other than beginning

Table 4.3. Etymology of 50 most common names for children born in England and Wales, 1700–1985

Etymology	1700	1800	1850	1875	1900	1925	1950	1965	1975	1985
Girls										
French	6	6	4	5	3	3	8	7	5	5
Greek	8	8	8	3	7	7	9	5	4	4
Hebrew	12	12	9	6	4	2	3	5	8	7
Latin	2	2	7	8	8	7	6	2	4	3
Boys										
Latin	4	4	2	2	4	2	7	7	7	4
Hebrew	20	20	23	11	7	5	6	7	12	13
Greek	11	11	7	7	4	3	6	8	10	8
Old English	4	4	7	6	8	6	4	2	2	3
French	3	3	4	8	8	8	4	3	1	2
Irish	0	0	1	0	1	4	7	5	4	3

names for girls between 1800 and 1850, their popularity for about a hundred years, and then their decline. For their part, names of Hebrew origin decline from being 12 of the top 50 in 1800 to 2 in 1925, before gradually increasing again.

An analogous cycle occurs for Hebrew names for boys—except that their popularity is far greater at their peak. Forty percent of all popular boys names were of Hebrew origin in 1700 and 1800 (20) and even more in 1850 (23). This is followed by a decline to only 5 Hebrew names in 1925, which is then followed by a steady increase. For boys, we can also observe cycles in names of Greek, Latin, Old English, French (including Old Norman), and Irish origin.

These etymological cycles are less obvious in Illinois during the twentieth century. A technical factor may be at work: the etymological cycles occurring in England and Wales move over long spans, and therefore the sixty-nine-year period between 1918 and 1987 in Illinois may be too short to show shifts convincingly. Were the British pattern available only for a similar span of years in the twentieth century, the cycles would be far less apparent. In any case, the British data show the operation of cycles in the etymologies of names that become especially popular. For both boys and girls, these changes are harmonious with the proposition that the ratcheting mechanism operates to move names over a relatively long span in one direction and then in the opposite direction. These changes for etymologies, as well as those observed for sounds, are harmonious with the position that internal mechanisms—independent of shifts in the external environment—are a major influence on the changing tastes in names.[12]

BIBLICAL NAMES: A MORE DEMANDING APPLICATION

The growing popularity of names of Hebrew origin during the twentieth century reflects a new emphasis on biblical names—particularly for boys. Indeed, twentieth-century shifts are remarkably parallel in both Illinois and England and Wales. Since the United States and the United Kingdom both are both Judeo-Christian cultures, is it possible that the twentieth-century resurgence of biblical names—particularly after World War II—is little more than a matter of changing tastes, lacking any deeper meaning? It is especially difficult to think of a rise of popularity in biblical names as void of substantive meaning, driven only by matters of taste and fashion. Scholars have certainly not had difficulty in finding substantive grounds for interpreting the earlier popularity of Old Testament names among Puritans (see Weekley 1939, ch. 6; Withycombe 1977, xxxvii–xl; Stewart 1979, 12–18). And many have linked the rise and decline of saints' names in England to other religious developments.

Because these names are linked to the experiences of characters in the Bible, moreover, symbolism may affect the appeal of names in a specific social context. As noted earlier, Stewart (1979, 226) attributes the popularity of the name *Ruth* in seventeenth-century Boston to the similarity between the situation of women living in the strange New World, more or less certain that they would never again see their families in England, and the story of Ruth in the Bible. By contrast, Stewart argues, the virtual absence of *David* among the Puritan immigrants—despite their considerable disposition toward Old Testament names—can be explained by David's "notorious sins" (93). Specific choices or antipathies of this nature can hardly be attributed to an internal mechanism. But does the recent increase in biblical names correspond to a comparable change in either religious feelings or behavior?

Linguistic Influences on the Choice of Biblical Names

We know that the popularity of sounds varies both over time and in their association with the names given to one sex or another. Starting with a list of 62 male names described as "prominent biblical persons" in either the Old or New Testaments, we can consider whether linguistic characteristics influence the likelihood of their being popular for boys born in the twentieth century.[13] Listed below are the major biblical names associated with the 4 most common endings among the 62 male names: *s, n, l,* and *a.* Also listed separately are the 7 prominent names with the letter *z* occurring somewhere in the name.

s-ending	*n*-ending	*l*-ending	*a*-ending	*z*-anywhere
Annas	Aaron	Abel	Elijah	Ezekiel
Barabbas	Cain	Daniel	Ezra	Ezra
Barnabas	John	Ezekiel	Isaiah	Lazarus
Caiaphas	Jonathan	Gamaliel	Jeremiah	Melchizedek
Cornelius	Nathan	Paul	Jonah	Nebuchadnezzar
Cyrus	Samson	Samuel	Joshua	Zacchaeus
James	Simeon	Saul	Noah	Zerubabel
Judas	Simon	Zerubabel		
Lazarus	Solomon			
Matthias	Stephen			
Moses				
Nicodemus				
Thomas				
Titus				
Zacchaeus				

This is a complicated problem because some of these names refer to men whose role in the Bible is likely to have widespread appeal. We have no difficulty accounting for the appeal of say *John* for Christians or *Moses* for Jews. John is described in the New Testament as Jesus' most trusted disciple; in the Old Testament, Moses receives the Ten Commandments and leads the Jews out of slavery. For other names, their biblical association would make them unattractive. The New Testament describes *Barabbas,* for example, as a convicted thief, seditionist, and murderer. Likewise, *Cain* in the Old Testament murders his brother. For some names, however, it is difficult to decide what the overall disposition would be, based solely on religious reasons; the religious emphasis, moreover, can change over time. Assuming for the moment that there is no association between a name's phonetic characteristics and the potential appeal of the biblical events associated with the name, let us ask a simple question: Is the popularity of a biblical name in the twentieth century influenced by its linguistic structure?

The sounds themselves do indeed affect the choice of names for sons. None of the 7 prominent biblical names with a *z* in it appear among the 50 most common names given to boys (England and Wales, 1700 and 1985; California, 1906 and 1984). This is consistent with the fact that in none of the four periods does a name containing a *z* appear in the top 50. Yet the biblical character of a number of these men are, I would judge, potentially appealing. Names with an *a*-ending are strongly gender-linked in both the United States and England—they are much more common for girls' than boys' names.[14] Again, we see that common practices influence the disposition to use biblical names. The 7 biblical names with *a*-endings rarely make the top 50. *Joshua* is the only one to appear (in England and Wales in 1700 and California in 1984). This is not the place to discuss these names in detail; however, all 7 of the names refer to characters that could, in my estimation, easily appeal to parents if tastes in language were not influencing these choices. Because all 7 of the *a*-ending names are from the Old Testament, one might speculate that their appeal is especially strong for Jews and, in turn, because Jews are a relatively small part of the total population of either England or California, the names do not show up in the top 50. But a quick look at the prominent *a*-ending girls' names dispels that conclusion. Four of these are from the Old Testament, 2 being names that have enjoyed considerable popularity, *Rebecca* and *Sarah*. Clearly, appealing characters with names ending in *a* and from the Old Testament can do quite nicely when their gender is consistent with naming practices. (The other 2, *Bathsheba* and *Delilah*, are involved in events that are probably inherently unattractive.)[15]

By comparison, of the 33 names ending in *s*, *n*, or *l*, 14 are in the top 50 in England in one or both periods and 9 appear in Illinois. These results are harmonious with the view that the linguistic structure of naming practices influences the choice of biblical names—independent of the influence of biblical events associated with the name. Negative stories make it unlikely that a name will be chosen, but the choice of names associated with a favorable biblical character is influenced by its compatibility with existing linguistic practices in society.

The Link Between Religious Practices and the Use of Biblical Names

If shifts in the popularity of biblical names is a product of fashion developments rather than a reflection of religious changes, then it is vital to consider religious developments during the period in question. We can apply two critical tests re-

Fig. 4.3. Biblical names and church attendance, Illinois, white boys, 1918–1987

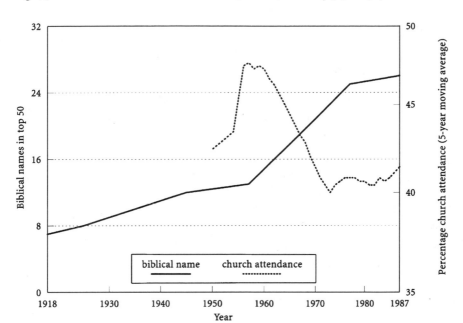

garding the increasing popularity of biblical names: Does their popularity increase when religion is making gains? And with respect to religious beliefs and practices, are parents who give their children biblical names different from those who do not?

First, does the choice of biblical names increase during a period of religious revival? The evidence indicates that the jump in biblical names cannot be explained in this way. Gallup Poll information on church and synagogue attendance in the United States, gathered since 1939, shows a peak in the mid-1950s (49 percent having gone within the past week, compared to 41 percent in 1939), followed by a modest decline back to about the 1939 level, and remaining more or less steady through the 1970s and 1980s.[16] Changes in church attendance, therefore, are not related to the extraordinary rise in biblical names in Illinois (fig. 4.3). Indeed, much of the increase in biblical names occurs *after* church attendance begins to decline.[17]

The information on naming in England and Wales covers a much longer span, so we can consider a full cycle, which begins with a decline in the popularity of biblical names for boys in the nineteenth century, reaches a trough early

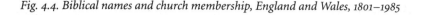

Fig. 4.4. Biblical names and church membership, England and Wales, 1801–1985

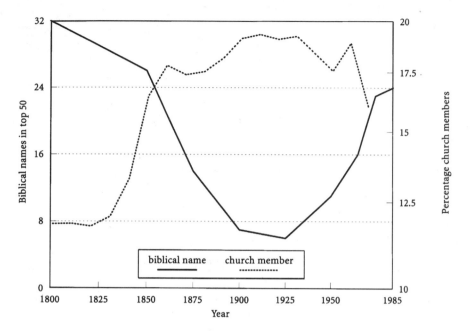

in the twentieth century, and then moves upward for the remainder of the period (fig. 4.4). Unfortunately, information on church attendance for England and Wales begins much later. We can, however, compare this cycle with church membership in Britain from 1800 to 1970.[18] The results are clear: movements in the popularity of biblical names during this span are in no way driven by shifting levels of church membership. Indeed, in England and Wales church membership was going up during much of the period in the nineteenth century when biblical names were declining in popularity. In the twentieth century, fluctuations in church membership are unrelated to the surge in the number of popular boy's biblical names.[19] For both Britain and the United States, changes in religious practices fail to account for shifts in the popularity of biblical names.

From this perspective, the remarkably parallel shift experienced by England and Illinois in the popularity of biblical names during the twentieth century (table 4.4) is a product of mechanisms unrelated to religious intensity. Compared with Britain, the United States has a far greater attachment toward traditional religious beliefs and practices. Fully one-third of the British report no

Table 4.4. *Number of biblical names among 50 most common boys' names, by year of birth*

	1700	1800	1850	1875	1900	1918	1925
England and Wales	32	32	26	14	7	—	6
Illinois (Whites)	—	—	—	—	—	7	8

	1945	1950	1957	1965	1975	1977	1985	1987
England and Wales	—	11	—	16	23	—	24	—
Illinois (Whites)	12	—	13	—	—	25	—	26

— = not available

religious affiliation in 1991, compared with 6 percent in the United States; close to half of Americans pray every day, compared with just 17 percent in Britain; and 71 percent of Americans believe in Hell, compared with 29 percent in Britain.[20] Yet this substantial gap in religious activity and belief has no bearing on the common changes in the popularity of biblical names during this century.

Another way of thinking about this question is to consider whether "religious" parents are more prone to give their children biblical names. Thanks to special arrangements with the National Opinion Research Center of the University of Chicago, the 1994 General Social Survey of the American Population included information on the names given to each respondent's offspring.[21] Accordingly, we can see if the religious practices of adult respondents influence the disposition to give their children biblical names.

Two measures of parental religious intensity are useful here: how often the parents attend a church or synagogue, and the intensity of their religious feelings.[22] Neither the religious practices of parents nor the intensity of their beliefs has a statistically significant influence on the propensity to give their children biblical names (table 4.5). Indeed, in the cases where the results approach significance, it is the least religious parents who seem more likely to give their children biblical names. Obviously, the popularity of biblical names increases in more recent years, but the absence of an association is unaltered by considering when the child was born.[23] Indeed, the only possibly significant result is that parents with no religion are far more disposed to give their daughter's biblical names than are other parents.[24]

Table 4.5. Propensity to give child a biblical name: the influence of parent's religious feelings and behavior

| | Percentage giving child a prominent biblical name | |
	Boys	Girls
Parent's church attendance		
Infrequent	26.4	4.6
Frequent	22.9	4.8
Intensity of parent's religious feeling		
None	27.9	8.9
Moderate	23.4	4.3
Strong	25.1	4.7

In sum, the increasing popularity of biblical names in recent decades is harmonious with the operation of an internal ratcheting mechanism such that tastes gradually move in a specific direction without reflecting any changes in the social order. Moreover, the choice of specific biblical names is itself affected by cultural practices of a nonreligious nature, to wit, the popularity of different sounds in the existing naming practices associated with each sex.

The ratchet effect, as we have seen, accounts for fashion shifts observed over a period of three hundred years.[25] It is one example—albeit an important one—of an internal mechanism that generates taste changes even in the absence of social changes. Moreover, the model postulates movement in a single direction over a long span of time, rather than simply a directionless vacillation. This does not, of course, preclude the operation of causes that fit a more traditional model in which specific social events are considered to account for changes in tastes. Yet even when changing social conditions do operate to change tastes, they are often restricted by the internal mechanisms that still affect the process.

These results leave us with two important challenges. First, although we observe clear patterns of upward and downward movement in the popularity of the sounds used in names and the types of names used (for example, biblical), can we obtain a deeper understanding of what stimulates the initial upward movements in popularity? After all, once they begin, then the ratcheting mechanism makes it relatively easy to understand how they would expand in a certain direction. In addition, are there other internal mechanisms—besides the ratchet effect—that generate taste changes under conditions where external influences are constant? As we shall see in the next chapter, they are related questions.

5 Other Internal Mechanisms

Where do new tastes come from? Many other internal mechanisms, besides the ratchet effect, constantly bring forth *new* tastes. In this chapter I propose and illustrate several other internal mechanisms: the "incremental replacement mechanism," "taste stems," "mutations," "symbolic contamination," and "symbolic enhancement." Although these are by no means the only possible influences on tastes that occur in the absence of changing external social influences, they are especially fruitful to consider here because of their impact on names in particular and because they illustrate different types of internal mechanisms and therefore varied ways changes can occur in the absence of external social processes. Bear in mind that changes due to these influences—as is the case for the ratchet effect—should not be interpreted as reflecting external social changes, but they do require external preconditions.

These internal mechanisms play a role in directing which new tastes will become popular. In the case of names, there are three major sources of "new" tastes. Some are literally new, in the sense that they are inventions due to either novel phonemic combinations or the conversion of existing words into usage as a name. Others are importations from different cultures or subcultures. Last, there are newly important names that are simply revivals of names that have been neglected or barely used. In Western societies, and in others as well, the population is bombarded by events that have the potential for creating new tastes. Whatever the source, one or more internal mechanisms is almost certain to be an influence. These mechanisms affect the likelihood that some tastes will become popular and others won't. They also direct the movement of tastes over time.

THE SOURCES

Why does this bombardment occur? New names are created in a variety of contexts. Without intending to influence the tastes of others, a name is created because it *sounds* right for the purposes at hand. A performer takes a stage name with the intent of appealing to the public, perhaps with a name that seems appropriate for the performer's style. New names may come from a fictional character in a novel, play, or other form of entertainment. Today, of course, we feel the impact of movies and television. This phenomenon is not new; examples of names that first appeared in novels, poems, or plays are *Jessica, Miranda, Amanda, Vanessa,* and *Pamela* (see Chapter 8).

Parents themselves, of course, create names that sometimes become popular. *Florence* owes its usage as a girl's name—in some periods quite common—to Florence Nightingale, a famous English nurse who was named after the Italian city in which she was born (Hanks and Hodges 1990, 121). Another source of innovation results from the expansion in the use of middle names. At one time, in the United Kingdom middle names were confined to the upper classes and were rare in the United States. Of the first 17 U.S. presidents, for example, only 3 have middle names: John Quincy Adams, William Henry Harrison, and James Knox Polk. The remaining 14—from George Washington through Abraham Lincoln and his successor, Andrew Johnson—do not. The great expansion in the use of middle names often meant use of a surname rather than an added first name from the existing inventory of first names. It was a way of honoring the mother's maiden name or tracing back some other familial tie. Such surnames gradually became first names in a two-step adaption process. Surnames with a prestigious past association are more likely to be maintained by a family that traces its link to this name through the female line. In turn, these prestigious middle names (or the surname directly) may become a first name. Some American examples of surnames becoming first names are: *Lowell, Elliot, Cabot, Abbott, Winthrop, Nelson, Aldrich, Morgan, Whitney, Jefferson, Endicott,* and *Lee.*

The increasing interaction between nations and cultures, particularly through the mass media, is now leading to the emergence of an international system in which newly popular tastes can move far more rapidly into other settings. Trends in popular music and clothing are glaring examples. Another culture or location can even be the inspiration for an entire set of new tastes, as in furnishings or clothing. Names, of course, travel easily, and this can lead to an internationalization of tastes.

The *existing* stock of tastes is a major source for *new* tastes. This is because the existing stock is so large that at any given time most older names are dormant (barely used). These unpopular tastes, part of the known repertoire, are names that parents rarely consider for their children. Women's names such as *Lillian, Thelma, Edna, Ethel,* and *Gladys* are probably known to most people in the United States but at present are infrequently considered for daughters (they were all among the twenty most popular names given in California in 1906). Likewise, names such as *Clarence, Harry, Francis, Arthur,* and *Harold* are rarely used for boys at present, although they are undoubtedly widely known (these are among the top 20 boys' names in California in 1906). The repertoire of names is so large that even parents who search through naming books will be unable to seriously consider all possibilities but will probably pass over many names rather casually. Dormant names often remain well known because they are common among older people still alive or are associated with famous figures from the past. Thanks to the historical importance of George Washington, for example, *George* and *Martha* are not likely to disappear from the inventory of American names—even if nobody is given these names for centuries.

When new tastes occur because existing names are rediscovered, the processes leading to rediscovery are largely the same as those that affect invented names. Again, various forms of entertainment and the arts can be a vehicle by which relatively dormant names experience a rebirth of interest. This is not a new process, but the intensity may well be on the increase because of the expansion of the media. Again, these sources are probably especially important for bringing attention to unpopular names in the existing repertoire. Keep in mind that names highlighted in the news also have the potential to affect tastes.

THE INCREMENTAL REPLACEMENT MECHANISM

The ratchet effect involves quantitative changes in fashion; skirts grow longer or shorter, wider or narrower, and so forth. Most fashions, however, consist of both qualitative and quantitative elements. A man's jacket, for example, is characterized by its length, drape, shoulder padding, other facets of the "cut," buttons, quality of construction, pockets, collar, lapels, fabric, colors, and other features. For our purposes, we can view many of these features as either present or not, rather than as matters of degree. We can also visualize a set of qualitative changes in which elements of the initial fashion are gradually replaced. Suppose a blue blazer is popular among men. At some point, the market for blue blazers will be saturated and at least some men will be attracted to something different—but not too different. Manufacturers and retailers will play with variations rather than revolutions. Perhaps consumers will respond to a different color or fabric, or changes in the buttons or a switch from a single-breasted style to a double-breasted style.

New tastes build on existing tastes, and the elements are gradually replaced. Why will the new fashion retain some old elements? Why is a complete change in all elements a rare occurrence? Too massive a change will appear unattractive—even to those seeking a difference—simply because their aesthetic perspective is embedded in the existing fashion, and they cannot avoid judging a new fashion in part through that perspective. The "incremental replacement mechanism" is simultaneously both conservative and radical in its implications: conservative in the sense that newer tastes will tend to incorporate at least some elements of existing tastes, and radical because over a longer span such incremental changes mean that few remnants of the older tastes will remain. Suppose, starting with a taste that includes elements $ABCD$, there is a change such that element E replaces element A, creating $eBCD$ (italic letters in lowercase designate the newly introduced element). In turn $EBCD$ (e is no longer a novelty but becomes part of the convention) may lead to $EfCD$, and so forth until little or nothing remains of $ABCD$. This form of change is far more likely than an immediate shift from $ABCD$ to $efgh$ without these intermediate steps.[1]

Even radical innovations will move closer to existing tastes. This is often seen in cultural borrowing. When, for example, a foreign cuisine is introduced into the United States by recent immigrants from a "new" area, key characteristics of their cuisine will be modified if they clash with American food tastes. Initially, through trial and error, restaurants serving this cuisine will learn that their American customers do not like certain dishes (for example, if the food is hotter than is customary for Americans) or if the ingredients are generally unappealing to Americans (such as dishes made of horse meat, eels, snails, pigeons, and less commonly consumed animal organs). If $CFGH$ are essential elements of a new foreign cuisine, and $ABCD$ are the existing tastes of Americans, then initially the foreign cuisine will tend to take the form $ABCh$. It will include all foreign elements that are shared with existing American tastes along with some—not all—of its distinctive foreign features.

Radical innovation in tastes often occurs without the alteration of many existing conventions. In other words, the dropping of *A* in the *ABCD* cluster of elements is a major shift, but the other elements are not replaced, so that the earliest stage with the absence of *A* looks more like *eBCD* than *efgh*. The initial use of pants by women in Western nations, for example, was a radical change and was greatly opposed for many years. Its initial acceptance in France, in fact, occurred not through a direct confrontation with existing clothing but rather as the special costume appropriate for newly popular sports activities such as bicycle riding (Steele 1988, 167–176).

First Names

First names, of course, are a combination of many elements. Their linguistic dimensions include the phonemes used, the sequence of sounds, the number of syllables, and the accentuation (see Cutler, McQueen, and Robinson 1990). Many names have an etymology and history. It may be French or Celtic; it could be linked to British royalty, the Bible, or the Koran; it could evoke a period in history. It could be a converted surname, an invented name, or a former diminutive (Lieberson and Bell 1992). The name may also have associations or imagery above and beyond those generated by these other features (see, for example, the many references to imagery associated with names in Lawson 1987, 1995).

Once an innovation does occur, it has the possibility of expanding almost indefinitely. If names rarely include element *G*, let us say, then the new popularity of such a name may in turn set off a wave of changes that build on this novel *G* element. What leads to the increasing use of a name containing this *G* element? There is no single answer, but one form is the incremental replacement mechanism. A name with the novel *G* element is introduced only because it also contains a different element that is—at the time—quite popular. Hence the name with a novel *G* element occurs as part of an expansion of other element(s) that are both popular and appealing. After the name is introduced, there is the possibility of an expansion involving *G* that runs independently of the popular element that led to the initial introduction. If the *A* element is especially appealing at a given time, then names with that element will be favored; as the popularity of such names expands, the *A* choices may include relatively unusual elements as well. And so *GA* is introduced, and from that we have the possibility that a new taste expansion will occur, with the previously central elements dropping off as *G* names expand.

Names also exhibit patterns similar to the introduction of new cuisines. Many new first names brought to the United States by slaves, for example, were later altered because African languages do not necessarily mark gender with the same linguistic devices as are found in the United States. When the gender of the name clashes with its linguistic structure (from the point of view of Americans), the name is often modified in its American usage to make the linguistic structure harmonious with the markers found in the United States (see Lieberson and Mikelson 1995). Again, new elements are incorporated within the existing cultural practices or are at least modified in that direction. In similar fashion, even invented names incorporate existing elements of the conventional linguistic structure of names; both the convention to use names to mark gender is still followed, and the usual gender marking devices are carried forward when these names are invented (see Lieberson and Mikelson 1995).

EXPANSION FROM A TASTE STEM

Prefixes of names often serve as "taste stems." In such shifts, a popular name leads to the creation of a variety of other new names sharing a basic element. The innovation then becomes a stem from which a variety of other names also grow. At some point early in the twentieth century, for example, the girl's names *Jane, Jennifer, Carol,* and *Julia* introduced linguistic elements that were not present among other popular names of the time. We can trace the impact of their introduction, seeing how a new taste may in turn expand by generating a set of names with a similar or related linguistic feature. For each of these names, a novel phoneme is introduced that then spreads out through the growing popularity of other names with the same form. A small buildup in a taste results from this development. Eventually, the rate of new additions slows, outstripped by the number of declines, and the use of the sound plateaus or even withers away. This expansion need not involve the creation of new names, although that will happen; rather, the expansion occurs by generating a resurgence of formerly dormant names.

Jane, Jennifer, Carol, and *Julia* do more than merely illustrate the expansion of tastes. They also suggest several specific pathways through which the expansion occurs. Observe how the diminutive form of the initial name becomes part of the expansion. We also see an expansion of spelling forms, though they tend to have shorter lives than the original form. Mass entertainment also plays a role; a performer takes the diminutive, and this increases the name's popularity. (This last point is subtle because the name adopted by a performer is undoubtedly affected by trends and images associated with ongoing developments.) Most interesting, however, are the simple illustrations of how a name, with novel phonemic characteristics when it first appears, leads to a series of other names with the same—or related—phonemes.

Jane

In 1908, among the 100 most common names given to girls born in California, *Jane* is the only name with a *Jan*-spelling, let alone one incorporating the long *a*-sound, as in *Jay* (table 5.1). Even then, *Jane* is not a particularly important name; it is located toward the bottom of the top 100, with the 25 girls who have the name amounting to about one-twentieth of the number named *Mary*. Ten years later, *Jane* is still the only prominent *Jan*-name among girls, with 179 babies receiving this name. From 1915 through 1926, a second *Jan*-name fluctuates in and out of the top 100. It is *Janet,* a diminutive spin-off of *Jane.* Beginning with 1927, *Janet*'s popularity steadily increases for several decades. In 1928, *Janet* is more popular than *Jane*, with *Jane* at a plateau that eventually leads in 1957 to its disappearance from the top 100. The level of popularity *Janet* eventually reaches also illustrates a neglected form of taste feedback. Janet Gaynor was an exceptionally popular actress in the late 1920s and early 1930s. Her name at birth was Laura Gainor, and if we assume that she took her stage name no earlier than 1924, a year before her first movie and the year she turned eighteen, this was when *Janet* was beginning to reach the top 100 in California. *Janet* appeared first in 1920, again in 1923, 1925, and 1927, and consistently for a number of years after that. Janet Gaynor, meanwhile, became a great star after her romantic movie *Seventh Heaven* (1927) and several other major hits.[2] This is an expansionary-feedback process that I call "riding the curve," whereby the stage name taken by a performer is one that is starting to become popular, and the association of the star in turn makes the name even more popular. (As we shall see in Chapter 8, riding the curve is a common event.)

Janice, another derivative from *Jane,* appears on the list by 1938. *Janis,* a spelling variant of *Janice,* in turn is added to the list in 1948. *Janis* and *Jane* are both gone by 1958, and *Janice* fades ten years later. Only *Janet* remains in 1968— and even it disappears from the top 100 names in the following year. However, the *Jay*-sound reappears in a somewhat different form. *Jamie* is among the top 100 in both 1978 and 1988, with another spelling variant, *Jaime,* also popular in 1978. So we come full circle back to the initial *Jay*-sound found in *Jane.*

Table 5.1. Commonly used girls' names beginning with "Jay-Jan"

Name	1908	1918	1928	1938	1948	1958	1968	1978	1988
Jane	x	x	x	x	x				
Janet			x	x	x	x	x		
Janice				x	x	x			
Janis					x				
Jaime								x	
Jamie								x	x

x = Name among the 100 names most frequently given to girls born in the year specified

Jennifer

The name *Jennifer* begins with the sound *Djeh*. In 1908, 3 of the top 100 names begin with a *Djeh*-phoneme: *Genevieve, Jennie,* and *Jessie.* (Here we are interested only in names that begin with *Dj* followed by *eh,* which excludes such names as *Joan* or *Judith.*) All 3 are relatively unimportant, and by 1918 none remains in the top 100 (table 5.2). Some thirty-five years later, in 1952, a *Djeh*-phoneme again shows up among the top 100 names. It is *Jennifer,* a name that enjoys a remarkable streak of popularity. Beginning with 1970, for the next fifteen years it is the most popular name for girls. This would not have been a noteworthy run for a girl's name earlier in the twentieth century, when *Mary* was the most popular girl's name for at least twenty-seven years.[3] Yet the 4 predecessors to *Jennifer*—*Linda, Debra, Susan,* and *Lisa*—occupied first place for ten, three, two, and nine years, respectively.

Some of the considerations about what made *Jennifer* such a popular name are obvious—in particular a striking exposure of the name in the mass media (described in Chapter 8). But the response to that exposure has to be understood within the context of phoneme developments within the society. The rise in the popularity of *Jennifer* does not occur in a vacuum. *Jennifer* appears as a spin-off at a time when many names begin with the *Dj*-prefix. The top 100 in 1908 includes 5 *J*-names and 1 *G*-name all beginning with a *dj*-sound.[4] The number increases steadily, reaching 16 in 1938. There are still 12 other *dj*-names in 1958, when *Jennifer* appears among the most common names. *Jennifer* is simply the first of the *Djeh*-variants to achieve popularity.[5]

The popularity of Jennifer in turn generates interest in 3 other *Djeh*-names,

Table 5.2. Frequently used girls' names beginning with "Jen" or ending with "Er"

	1908	1918	1928	1938	1948	1958	1968	1978	1988
Genevieve	x								
Jennie	x								
Jessie	x								
Jennifer							x	x	x
Jessica								x	x
Jenna									x
Heather							x	x	x
Amber								x	x

x = Name among the 100 names most frequently given to girls born in the year specified

one of which enjoys an enormous success. *Jessica,* which first makes the top 100 in California in 1970, eventually replaces *Jennifer* as the most common name in 1985. Also there is *Jenny,* which appears in the top 100 in 1980 for a rather brief period, and there is *Jenna,* which enters the top 100 in 1984. None of these offshoots are new names: *Jessica* goes back to Shakespeare's *Merchant of Venice* (she was Shylock's daughter); *Jenny* is a short form of *Jennifer;* and *Jenna* is described as a fanciful alteration of *Jenny* (Hanks and Hodges 1990, 175).

The popularity of *Jennifer* also affects the use of names with an *-er*-suffix. For each decade between 1908 and 1938, *Esther* was the only name among the top 100 with such a suffix, and its popularity was not extraordinarily high. Two *-er*-ending names appear after the rise of *Jennifer,* and both become fairly popular: *Heather* in 1968, and then both *Heather* and *Amber* in the next two decades. These are yet further examples of expansion from a taste stem.

Carol

None of the 100 most common names given to girls born in 1908 begin with the C(K)ar phoneme (as in "to *carry*"). *Carol* appears by 1918, and in 1928 it is accompanied by a spin-off, *Carolyn* (table 5.3). Ten years later, *Carol* is the fourth most popular name, given to slightly more than 2 percent of all girls born that year in California. With the addition of *Karen* and *Carole*—the latter being a spelling variant of *Carol*—there are four C(K)ar names in the top 100 in 1938. The rise of *Carole* is another example of a feedback effect between the media and existing tastes. When Jane Peters first appears in a movie using the name Carole

Table 5.3. Frequently used girls' names beginning with "Car" *

	1908	1918	1928	1938	1948	1958	1968	1978	1988
Carol		x	x	x	x	x	x		
Carolyn			x	x	x	x	x		
Carole				x					
Karen				x	x	x	x	x	x
Carrie							x	x	
Karina									x

* As in "carry," not "carton"

x = Name among the 100 names most frequently given to girls born in the year specified

Lombard in 1925 (Quinlan 1981, 290), *Carol* is in the top 100—albeit below the peak reached later. By the mid-1930s Carole Lombard assumed "the unrivaled position as Hollywood's highest-paid artist" (Peary 1978, 32). As with *Janet,* a name's rising popularity influences the choice of a stage name, and this in turn increases the popularity of the name. There is one slight difference, though: *Carole* is a minor spelling variant of the popular form, *Carol.*

Carole drops out by 1948 (the actress had died in a 1942 plane crash), and a long decline in *Carol* is under way by 1948, with *Carolyn* declining ten years later. *Karen,* however, surges so strongly in popularity during this span that the number of baby girls named *Karen* is nearly equal in 1948 to the number named *Carol,* and in 1958 *Karen* is twice as popular as *Carol.* In 1968, *Karen* has begun to decline, *Carrie* appears as a top 100 name, and *Carol* and *Carolyn* are reaching the end of their popularity. Ten years later, by 1978, *Karen* and *Carrie* are among the top 100, but neither is a major name, and this remains the case for the *C(K)ar* names in 1988; *Carrie* is no longer present but has been replaced by *Karina.*

As with *Jan-* and *Djeh-*names, we see an expansion in the tastes for *C(K)ar-*names from none in 1908 until a number appear, including some that are at times among the top 20. Then the taste for this type of name declines, though it was still present in the most recent period examined.[6]

Julia

A similar pattern of expansion and contraction is found in the set of names that begin with the *Joo-*phoneme. Except for 1948, *Julia* is among the 100 most

Table 5.4. Frequently used girls' names beginning with "Joo"

	1908	1918	1928	1938	1948	1958	1968	1978	1988
Julia	x	x	x	x		x	x	x	x
June		x	x	x					
Judith				x	x	x			
Julie					x	x	x	x	x
Judy					x	x			

x = Name among the 100 names most frequently given to girls born in the year specified

common girls' name throughout the century (table 5.4), providing plenty of time for *Julia* to influence the extension of the *Joo*-prefix. *June* first appears in 1928 and remains popular for a couple of decades. The *Joo*-name is joined by *Judith* in 1938 (which is given to 1.5 percent of all girls born in that year). *Judith* is still very popular in 1948, when *Judy* and *Julie* both appear (*Judy* was given to nearly 1 percent of all girls). *Judy,* a nickname for *Judith,* illustrates two processes observed earlier: the expansion of a popular name such that its diminutive also becomes at least moderately popular, and the adoption of an expanding name by a performer whose later success may have increased the adopted name's appeal. The first movie appearance of Frances Gumm under the name Judy Garland is in 1936—four years after *Judith* had entered the top 100. In turn, *Judy* becomes a top 100 name in 1939, when *The Wizard of Oz* propelled Garland to stardom.[7]

By 1958, both *Judy* and *Judith* had peaked (though they were still well into the top 100), but *Julie* appears in the intervening decade and is given to more than 1 percent of girls. *Julie* remains a major name in 1968 and then declines. *Julie* and *Julia* are still among the top 100 in 1988. However, the importance of the *Joo*-prefix has diminished greatly from the point reached several decades before. Indeed, the combined proportion of girls named either *Julie* or *Julia* in 1988 equals the proportion for *Julia* in 1908.

HOW AN INNOVATION ("MUTATION") COMBINES WITH EXISTING PRACTICES TO GENERATE A NEW SET OF TASTES: THE *LA*-PREFIX

The occurrence of a *La*-prefix among popular African-American girls' names is a recent phenomenon. One *Lavera* and one *Larenia* were born in Illinois in 1916. *La Verne,* beginning with 1925 and going through 1960, enjoys a modest level of popularity among black girls.[8] Not until 1967, however, does the *La*-prefix occur among any of the 50 leading names given to black girls (*Latonya*, which ranked 39). For more than a decade, between 1974 and 1986, from 4 to as many as 7 of the 50 most common names given to black girls begin with the *La*-prefix.[9] The high point, 1979, includes *Latoya, Latasha, Lakeisha, Latonya, Latrice, Lakisha,* and *Latisha. Latoya* is especially popular; it is among the 10 names most frequently given to black girls born in each year between 1976 and 1986 (table 5.5). In both 1981 and 1984 the name is second only to *Tiffany* in usage among black girls. The contemporary usage of the *La*-prefix is a distinctively black phenomenon. In 1979, for example, not only are the 7 names absent from the 50 most frequent white names, but not one of these is found even among the 200 most common names for white girls.[10]

How can we account for this development? Let us start by visualizing a model of name innovation and growth analogous to genetic mutation. The stream of mutations is constant, but almost all of them go nowhere because they offer, at the time of their appearance, no advantage for survival. Occasionally, however, a mutation does offer an advantage because of contemporary social conditions, and then it has a greater chance of survival and expansion. In similar fashion, in a society where there are no legal or other formal controls on the names parents may give their children, we can visualize a modest flow of newly invented names (mutations), most of which are not especially appealing to other parents. In short order, then, these innovations go nowhere; others hearing the name do not find it an attractive possibility for their own children. Three major forces would account for this: (1) an antipathy toward giving an invented name to a child; (2) the new sounds are unappealing; and (3) greater pressure on parents to name their child after a relative or friend (hence using a name that already existed). Just as in genetic mutations, there are conditions that would improve the likelihood that a newly created name will appeal to other parents. In particular, the same sounds may be more appealing at a period when it is compatible with general naming trends among the existing inventory of names, or the pressure to name a baby after a relative or friend may weaken, or there is a decline in the resistance to naming innovations. We observe here that the *La*-names begin to "take off" during the period when there is an enormous expansion in the number of black girls given newly invented names (see Lieberson and Mikelson 1995).[11] All of this leads us to expect an increasing number of "mutations" (read "innovations"); again, most will go nowhere, but some will gain a certain level of popularity.

Table 5.5. Popular "La" names and their cognates among black girls

Rank of "La" Names in 50 Most Common Names

Name	1965	'66	'67	'68	'69	'70	'71	'72	'73	'74	'75	'76	'77	'78	'79	'80
Latonya			39	39	20	12	10	9	8	13	14	16	31	28	34	45
Latanya							46			45	30		36			
Latasha								38	12	7	10	8	9	16	9	14
Latoya										17	12	5	6	8	7	7
Latrice										50		50		48	39	30
Lakeisha											38	18	15	13	13	22
Lakisha													34	34	41	
Latisha															47	41

Name	'81	'82	'83	'84	'85	'86	'87	'88	'89
Latonya	34	43	48						
Latanya									
Latasha	18	17	21	24	33	36	35	44	
Latoya	2	3	4	2	6	8	12	14	17
Latrice	29	32	36	38	25	37			
Lakeisha	23	25	25	36	30	30	31	48	40
Lakisha									
Latisha		34							

Invented *La*-names often pop up, but they rarely last long. Typically these names appear in only a small number of years. Between 1930 and 1969, 155 different *La*- names are given to black girls in at least five different years. Of these, 124 are given to fewer than five girls in any year. Indeed, for about half of the names (76), no more than two girls are given the name in any one year. Starting with the year immediately after a given *La*-name first appears, the modal *La*-name is used in fewer than half of the ensuing years through 1969 (42 percent).[12] (Bear in mind that there is an even larger number of names that appear in fewer than five years during this forty-year period.)[13] This suggests that a rather large number of names are independently reinvented during this forty-year span—given that they reappear every now and then. The onomastic structure of the culture leads toward independent reinventions over and over

Table 5.5. Continued

Rank of Cognates in 50 Most Common Names

Name	1965	'66	'67	'68	'69	'70	'71	'72	'73	'74	'75	'76	'77	'78	'79	'80
Tonya	38	29	14	12	14	11	13	12	18	14	35					
Tanya			32	37	23	18	16	19	13	25	21	31				
Tasha							19	10	14	9	15	23	42			
Toya	*Did not reach top 50*															
Trice	*Name barely used in top 200*															
Keisha							41	28	19	18	24	16	18	22	33	
Kisha	*Did not reach top 50*															
Tisha	*Name barely used in top 200*															

Name	'81	'82	'83	'84	'85	'86	'87	'88	'89							
Tonya																
Tanya																
Tasha																
Toya																
Trice																
Keisha	39						47									
Kisha																
Tisha																

again, even though they rarely "take off" in the sense of reaching even a minimal level of popularity (say, given to five or more girls in at least one year) or of being given to at least one child in a majority of the years since it first appears.[14]

This leads us to the second mechanism involved in the rise of *La*-names; the prefix attaches itself to existing tastes and so leads to a new combinatorial popularity. This effect was illustrated earlier in the way ABCD elements would evolve to efgh. Through the years, various *La*-names achieve a modest level of popularity for black girls. *La Verne* was the first to crack the top 100 in the 1920s, and it is the only *La*-name to be among the top 100 until *Latonya* in the 1960s. Beginning with *Latonya* in 1967, a number of *La*-names are found in the top 50 for black girls (see table 5.5). It is striking that in many cases, the name is a combinatorial pooling of *La* with another name, which initially is more popular.

For example, when *Latonya* in 1964 makes the top 100 among black girls in 1964 (just barely, ranking 99), *Tonya* occupies 63d place. Year by year the increasing popularity of *Latonya* is unable to surpass the growth of *Tonya*. When *Latonya* first breaks into the top 50 in 1967, *Tonya* ranks 14. Not until 1971 does *Latonya* bypass *Tonya* and *Tonya* starts to fade. This pattern holds for a number of the major *La*-names, among them *Latanya*, *Latasha*, and *Lakeisha*: they are preceded by a root name of far greater popularity, but the *La*-form eventually bypasses them. *Latoya* is a special case, owing its surge in popularity to the fame of the singer Latoya Jackson. *Toya* is initially more popular than *Latoya*, although neither is very highly ranked. In 1969, when *Latoya* is not yet in the top 200, *Toya* ranks 156. *Latoya* passes *Toya* in 1972 and reaches the top 50 two years later. Then, as these *La*- names gain in popularity, new ones are formed without building on the stem of a popular name. In other words, the taste for *La*-prefixes is sufficiently established that *la*- names can occur on their own. Good examples of this trend are *Latrice*, *Lakisha*, and *Latisha*; these names reach the top 50 for black girls without building on an earlier popularity for *Trice*, *Kisha*, and *Tisha*.

THE CONTAMINATION AND ENHANCEMENT OF SYMBOLS

Tastes usually have a symbolic element. Sometimes this element is relatively obvious, as in a taste that expresses affluence (for example, wearing an expensive wristwatch, such as a Rolex) or esoteric knowledge (meeting someone at a party who is eager to discuss early Ming porcelain) or social-political attitudes (bearded men lacking ties at formal events). Depending on the symbolism, a choice can be appealing or repulsive. A symbolic association may even repel some segments of the population, which then enhances its appeal to others. Symbolic linkages are sometimes weak and may be overridden by other considerations such as cost or social pressures. In other cases, the symbolic image is overwhelming.

The imagery of a cultural artifact will influence the frequency and nature of its adoption and usage, but not always in the same direction. In a discussion of musical tastes, for example, Bethany Bryson (1996) suggests that the association of blacks with some musical genres actually creates a dislike of these forms by whites who hold negative attitudes toward blacks. By contrast, those who are politically tolerant have a greater musical tolerance. Images are not cast in stone but may change over time in ways that alter the nature of the symbolism associated with the entity. These changes could improve or reduce the desirability of a given cultural feature. Indeed, their relative appeal to subsets of the population may actually shift in different directions. For example, as we noted in Chapter 4, beards in the United States were once a sign of conservatism and respectability; now they convey a very different image. Beards would be more appealing for men with one set of dispositions now and more appealing earlier for men with other dispositions.

The association of a taste need not simply involve an individual; it can be enhanced through its linkage with a class or category of people or activities that we find appealing or contaminated in the same way. In fact, this is a widely used device in advertising: a particular brand of coffee is served in the finest restaurants (translate: favored by demanding, affluent, and knowledgeable people); automobiles are not simply automobiles—rather a particular car is favored by young and attractive people, or wealthy people, or people with a certain lifestyle; a beer is linked to people who are having a good time or (for male drinkers) is favored by machos—nerds favor one brand, but attractive people favor another. This is more than an institutionally imposed taste. I find, for example, that virtually all undergraduates in my courses have gone bowling, but they tend not to see this as a recreational activity they will pursue in the future. If you ask why, sooner or later you will encounter a class snobbery—that is, bowling has class and taste associations that some people wish to avoid. It is, in my estimation, not the activity of bowling itself but the class association that in turn contaminates the pastime. Jane and Michael Stern's *Encyclopedia of Bad Taste* (1990) is, I am sure, meant to be enjoyed by the reader as a witty and snobbish product—it is certainly not a technical analysis of tastes. Still we can learn something from it. Consider the following quotations from the Sterns' *Encyclopedia* that are meant to convey why bowling is a bad taste. Bowling is evaluated in terms of neither the skills involved nor the interest of the game, but strictly bowling's association with a particular social class and way of life. Even though, in fact, the origins of bowling are rather "distinguished" in cultural capital terms, observe how the second of the four quotations on bowling turns this into a contamination by its later class association.

> Bowling is the only sport that can be played well while sipping beer from a big waxpaper cup and eating a bratwurst sandwich. Unlike such sports as sailing, tennis, or skiing, all of which demand lean bodies or expensive equipment, bowling requires nothing more than the rental of a pair of used shoes with your size marked on the back.

Although variations of the game had been popular in America since Dutch settlers played ninepins upon arriving in New Amsterdam, it wasn't until 1895, when the American Bowling Congress was founded, that rules about ball size and pin placement were standardized. In the thirties, after Prohibition was repealed, bowling as we know it began to take shape. Big Midwestern breweries such as Blatz, Pabst, and Schlitz sponsored beer teams that toured the country to promote their beverages. Henceforth, beer and bowling were forever linked in the public's mind; and a diversion once the province of pharaohs, kings, and blue bloods became the sport of guys with blue collars and gals with brown stretch pants.

Bowling kingpins have always been distinguished from other athletes by their placid temperament and a quiet kind of concentration that could easily pass for dullness. Being able to relax is the foremost requirement of good bowling, wrote hall-of-famer Don Carter in the book *Bowl Better Using Self-Hypnosis.*

What makes bowling fun, even if you aren't a kegler, is the extravagance of its ornaments, especially the towering wood-look and bronze-like trophies topped with little gold bowlers perfect to display in the window of the local luncheonette or barbershop, next to the taxidermized trout. Nearly anything with a bowling motif is treasured by collectors of Americana and commands a high price at the type of store that sells Fiesta Ware and pink flamingos: decorative balls with built-in clocks, pin-shaped liquor decanters, strike-'n'-spare ashtrays, and lamps that grow out of the backs of hunched-over ceramic bowlers. [1990, 54–56]

Another example of symbolic contamination can be found in synthetic materials such as rayon (made from cellulose) and nylon (a completely artificial material). Polyester fiber appeared after World War II, and Americans in the 1950s embraced polyester fabrics, which kept their shape and didn't need ironing after being washed. The Sterns recount the story of polyester's fate: "The problem was that by the mid-seventies, when the word 'natural' had attained a status of inviolable goodness among many consumers, industrial-sounding 'polyester' connoted the opposite of all that was good. Fabric makers masked it with trade names such as Kodel, Fortrel, Crepesoft, and Golden Touch. But soon there would be no combating the hideous image of double-knit polyester garments, which became so popular in 1974 that manufacturers could not meet the demand for polyester" (237–248).

Polyester clothing was originally associated with informal designs and bright colors; perhaps its culminating moment came when John Travolta appeared in a "shiny white, skin-tight suit (worn with open-collar black shirt) in the movie

Saturday Night Fever, [which] gave polyester a reputation as not merely boorish but downright sleazy" (248). By the early 1980s, as the Sterns put it, "polyester equaled bad taste" (248) and the major manufacturers considered a campaign to change its image. Note how, the negative association of polyester bears relatively little relation to the intrinsic features of the fabric (the exception, which is not a trivial one, being that polyester did not breathe well and led its wearers to perspire). Rather, it is polyester's association with certain kinds of clothing and styles and the fact that it was not a "natural" fabric when that quality again became a desirable feature. (Any renewal in the popularity of polyester would have to be based on a shift from its original role, say, as representing an earlier period that is now in fashion, or as a fabric in its own right rather than an imitation of a natural fiber, or through new forms of weaving it, or through its association with a higher social stratum.)

Age is another example of an attribute that can vary in its appeal depending on cultural elements and other societal developments. The association of a taste with a given age—whether that be old or new (or young)—will sometimes enhance the symbolism and in other contexts detract from it. Incidentally, the relationship is not always a simple linear one. Consider a brand-new automobile, a five-year-old car, a car that is ten years old, and an automobile manufactured sixty years ago. If the antique automobile runs well and is in pristine physical condition (clean body, with its original appearance maintained without updated seat covers, modern wiper blades, horns, lights, wheels, and the like), its value to a limited number of purchasers will be far in excess of almost all new cars, let alone those that are five or ten years old. Age is also an appealing attribute of some institutions. A glance at the program for a performance of the Boston Symphony Orchestra for February 25, 1995, turns up five references to its year of establishment, 1881. Likewise, there is a certain appeal in: a college or university with an early founding date; a store that was established decades ago (all the more so if it is still in the hands of the same family); the oldest church or synagogue in a major metropolitan area or state or region (say, west of the Mississippi or below the Mason-Dixon line or on the Pacific coast).

Being old is not necessarily a symbolic enhancement—more often it probably has a contaminating effect when linked to a taste. One is struck by the warped age distribution in advertisements for soft drinks, clearly geared to teens and young adults. Of course, these groups are especially significant consumers of soft drinks, but that is hardly the only factor. Images of consumer items like this emphasize two qualities: youth and happiness. Youth is used to sell certain cars, forms of new technology and entertainment, and many other products. Some advertisers go so far as to link competing brands with older, stodgier consumers. Ads like these are using age to contaminate the symbolism of a competitor and simultaneously enhance one's own symbolism.

Advertising and other efforts to sell commercial products are not as all-powerful as many believe, however. Many products fail in spite of clever advertising campaigns; it is difficult to persuade consumers to purchase something new.[15]

NAMES AND SYMBOLISM

What does advertising have to do with the symbolism of cultural features that are not driven simply by commercial interests? In particular, what about the mechanisms that enhance or contaminate first names? Just as our tastes for cars, soft drinks, and shampoos are enhanced or contaminated by their association with attractive or unattractive symbols, likewise the attractiveness of a name is affected by shifts in the image associated with it. Here, however, no advertising campaign is seeking to mold the symbolism associated with a product; rather, names are attractive or not based on external forces that affect (in a more or less random way) the symbolism associated with them. In all but the most stable of societies, there is a constant flow of events involving people that alters in each period the symbols associated with some names. External forces account for the individuals who gain prominence or notoriety each year (and thereby affect symbolism associated with their names). We can view these changes as random shifts in the symbolic association of the names, however, and then consider their influence as representing an *internal* mechanism of taste change.[16] We can thereby visualize a mechanism that year after year causes some names to shift toward a more attractive symbolism and other names to become unattractive. Because societies change over time, the meaning of the bases for the symbolic shift may change. Moreover, subsets of the population (whether divided by class, race, ethnicity, religion, values, or other features) will differ in the nature and degree of enhancement or contamination that a given association will have on the symbolism.

Declines in symbolic favor—though sometimes difficult to document, let alone understand—are still more readily analyzed than favorable shifts in usage. Put another way, the forces leading to symbolic enhancement are not mirror images of the forces that contaminate a symbol. A variety of factors beyond imagery can affect an increase in a name's popularity. For example, Humphrey

Bogart was a popular actor for many years, but we need not assume that the failure of *Humphrey* to become a popular name for boys has anything to do with the imagery associated with Humphrey Bogart; it could merely represent the linguistic characteristics of the name. By contrast, a sudden decline in a name is unlikely to reflect a massive phonetic shift (because such shifts are not rapid), and so it is easier to search for a symbolic reason for this shift. We will start, then, with the somewhat less complicated questions pertaining to events in which cultural elements decline because they become associated with less favorable imagery: the "contamination effect."

The Symbolic Contamination of Names

Donald Donald provides an example of how a popular name can decline after it is contaminated by a shift in its symbolic association. In the early twentieth century, *Donald* is given to an increasing number of boys in California, moving up steadily from 0.6 percent to 3.8 percent between 1905 and 1933. The name then declines from 1934 through 1984. What leads to this drop? Sooner or later, of course, a name peaks and then starts to drop in popularity—so this curve per se is not unique. Yet the peculiar timing of the event suggests a contamination of *Donald*. In 1934, the cartoon character Donald Duck first appears in a Walt Disney cartoon (Daniel 1989, 665). The animated duck is an immediate success— Donald Duck appears as a Disney toy as early as 1936 (O'Brien 1990, 140). The instant popularity of Donald Duck as a cartoon character very likely generated the beginning of a long-term decline in the name.

Ebenezer Names can be contaminated by their association with an unattractive fictional character. *Ebenezer* was once a popular name among Puritan colonists, particularly in New England. Although the decline of *Ebenezer* is part of the general decline of Old Testament names in the nineteenth century, there is reason to think that the name suffered because of its association with Charles Dickens's character Ebenezer Scrooge in *A Christmas Carol,* published in 1843 (Stewart 1979, 103–104; Hanks and Hodges 1990, 94).

Adolph The disappearance of *Adolph* in 1932 from the list of 200 names most frequently given to white boys in Illinois can be linked to the rise to power of Adolf Hitler in Germany (table 5.6). *Adolph* falls below the 200 mark briefly in 1928 and then permanently beginning in 1932—as Hitler gains increasing control

Fig. 5.1. Donald, *1905–1984*

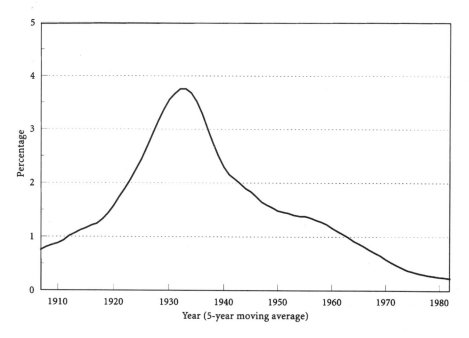

Year (5-year moving average)

of the German government (becoming chancellor in January 1933). Whether the decline of *Adolph* would have occurred as rapidly in the absence of Hitler is not entirely clear. The name loses popularity in a period of declining immigration from Germany and elsewhere in central Europe. Yet there is little doubt that eventually the name is profoundly contaminated by Hitler's regime. *The Chronicle of the Twentieth Century* (Daniel 1987, 415–427) summarizes Hitler's swift and brutal transformation of Germany into a dictatorship in 1933:

January: Hitler is named German Chancellor.

February: Hitler wins dissolution of Reichstag; Hitler places curbs on leftist opposition; Reich begins press censorship; fire destroys Reichstag.

March: German police arrest hundreds as Hitler intensifies drive on left; Hitler and Nationalist allies win Reichstag majority; Hindenberg drops German flag, orders swastika and empire banner to be flown side-by-side; American Jewish Committee demands Washington act on Hitler; Reichstag gives Hitler power to rule by decree; 55,000 stage Anti-Hitler protest in New York; Nazis open first concentration camp; Nazis order ban against Jews in business, professions, and schools; Film director Fritz Lang quits Germany, refusing collaboration with Nazis.

April: Nazis support boycott of Jewish merchants; Nazis seize Einstein funds in Ger-

Table 5.6. Rank of Adolph *among white boys*

Year	Rank	Year	Rank
1916	126	1927	177
1917	131	1928	
1918	146	1929	180
1919	138	1930	180
1920	173	1931	195
1921	143	1932	
1922	161	1933	
1923	140	1934	
1924	173	1935	
1925	181	1940	
1926	184	1945	

Note: Rank shown only when among the top 200 names in year specified

man bank; Foreigners barred from leaving Germany without police permit; Nazis seize church of German state.

May: Nazis make bonfire of banned books; Nazis confiscate all property of Communist party; Hitler breaks up all trade unions.

June: Nazis outlaw the Social Democratic Party, are now Germany's only political party.

July: Nazis begin evicting Jews from civil service; Hitler decrees NSDAP sole legal party in Germany; Nazis round up 300 Jews in Nuremberg, while 50,000 Londoners march against Anti-Semitism; Nazis pass law to purify German race.

August: Nazis send Jews to prison camps.

October: Hitler leaves League of Nations, demands equality.

November: Nazis take over Ullstein Press, largest in German Reich.

December: Nazi storm troops become official organ of Reich; 400,000 Germans to be sterilized, Pope condemns program.

The focus on Adolf Hitler's activities in 1933—coupled with events in the following decade and revelations after the war—leads to a massive contamination effect.

Oscar The changing popularity of *Oscar* shows not only how chance external events can first enhance and then contaminate the symbolic nature of a name but also how and why the same symbolic process can be muted in one setting while operating in another.[17] *Oscar* is an old Anglo-Saxon name that disappeared after the Norman Conquest. Several chance factors led to the name's resurrection and later popularity. *Oscar* first reappears in the eighteenth century in poems James Macpherson claimed to have translated from the Gaelic poet Ossian. Napoleon Bonaparte, who admired these poems, named his godson *Oscar*, and this boy later became King Oscar I of Sweden. Years later, Oscar II is treated by an eye surgeon named Wilde, who in turn gives the name *Oscar* to his son, attributed in one account as "a special kind of name-dropping" (Dunkling 1977, 91). The popular ascent of the Irish writer Oscar Wilde increases the name's use in Britain and the United States—with the name added in the United States also thanks to substantial immigration from areas of Europe where *Oscar* had become popular because of its usage as a king's name. Then the symbolism associated with *Oscar* becomes contaminated after Oscar Wilde faces criminal charges in 1895 for homosexual sodomy, undergoes a sensational and widely publicized trial, and is eventually jailed. The contamination of homosexuality in the Victorian era led parents to avoid naming newborn sons *Oscar*. The name withers away accordingly: *Oscar,* is the 30th most popular male name in the United States in 1875, but by 1900 (the year of Wilde's death) it is no longer in the top 50, and it had not reappeared through 1975.[18] Likewise in England and Wales, *Oscar* is not popular during the twentieth century; about 2 boys per 10,000 (0.02 percent) were given this name in the period from 1900 to about 1935, with less than 1 per 10,000 later on, followed by a modest recovery in more recent decades (6 per 10,000 in 1990).[19]

What makes *Oscar* more than merely another example of how external events may alternatively enhance and then contaminate a name is the continued popularity of *Oscar* during this period in Scandinavia. For here the existing symbolic association with Swedish royalty prevents the name from being contaminated by the Oscar Wilde scandal. The difference between Scandinavia and the two English-speaking nations raises an additional consideration in thinking about the contamination and enhancement processes. The popularity of *Oscar* depends heavily on Oscar Wilde in Britain and the United States; in Scandinavia it does not. If the appealing association of *Oscar* with royalty is predominant in Scandinavia, then it is less likely that the name will be contaminated by the events surrounding Oscar Wilde. In the same fashion, one would speculate that unattractive events surrounding King Oscar would have greater symbolic contamination of *Oscar* in Scandinavia than in either the British Isles or the United

States. In effect, if the imagery surrounding *Oscar* is anchored in two different sources, then the contamination of one source is less likely to influence the imagery that is derived primarily from another source. This of course requires a more careful look based on similar situations.

One other feature of symbolism merits further consideration. If a taste is widely used, would any new association of the name with an appealing or unappealing person have only a minor effect? We might think of this as reflecting the following principle: the impact of a new symbolic development on tastes will tend to be greatest for infrequently used names and least for widely used names. The influence of John Wayne (a very popular actor), Richard Nixon (a disgraced president), Michael Jordan (an exceptionally popular and skilled basketball player), and Michael Tyson (a boxer found guilty of rape) are likely to be of minimal impact on the popularity of their first names. By contrast, Michael Jordan's popularity could easily have a substantial influence on the usage of *Jordan* as a first name.

This view of course holds constant the intensity of the new event—whether positive or negative in the response associated with it. Also, we can see that the association of a given first name with public figures will vary—witness *Oscar* in Scandinavia compared with *Oscar* in the United States. On that basis, we would also expect to find that symbolic associations based on the attributes of a real or fictional person with a given name will tend to diminish over time. *Adolph*, for example, was (and is) intensely contaminated. The intensity of feelings and awareness of Hitler is such that even a half-century after World War II the name is still very much associated with Hitler and naming a son *Adolph* would almost certainly remind many of Hitler and would likely be viewed as some sort of endorsement of him—at least in the United States and probably in many other nations. Compare this with the diminished likelihood of a similar negative association with a child named *Michael*. As time progresses, however, the potential for a favorable symbolic association with *Adolph* will eventually increase—not because Hitler will be reevaluated (highly unlikely), but because the automatic association of *Adolph* with Hitler will weaken. Under those circumstances, at some point the appearance of a man with characteristics that are exceptionally appealing and who is named *Adolph* could alter the current intense contamination of the name. The appeal of the new *Adolph* character would be affected by when it appears. With increasing distance over time, there will be a decline in the minimal appeal necessary to generate interest in the name. Likewise, a name

Table 5.7. Rank of Lee *among white boys*

Year	Rank	Year	Rank
1960	112	1966	113
1961	114	1967	96
1962	112	1968	117
1963	113	1969	120
1964	115	1970	125
1965	115		

Note: Rank shown in years preceding and following the
Kennedy assassination

such as *Nelson* could readily have a strong impact on naming practices—at least
in the short run—thanks to the relative infrequency of the name's usage and the
enormous admiration of the South African leader Nelson Mandela.

Harmonious with this view is the revival of *Oscar* that occurs years after the
Oscar Wilde scandal. After 1908, *Oscar* disappears from the 100 most frequently
used names for boys born in California until 1973 (sixty-five years later). It
remains in the top 100 for a number of years since then. The modest resurgence
(it is not among the leading names within the top 100) is helped by the remote-
ness of the events surrounding the earlier scandal, and hence a decline in the
immediate association of the name *Oscar* with Wilde. Perhaps, too, homopho-
bia was beginning to ebb a tad. In any case, bright new *Oscars* appear on the
scene. Among the characters in the exceptionally popular, long-running children's television show *Sesame Street* is Oscar the Grouch.[20] Also there is Oscar
Robertson, an outstanding basketball star in both college and professional basketball throughout the 1960s and early 1970s, and elected to the Basketball Hall
of Fame in 1979 (Hollander and Sachare 1989, 354–355, 661).

Lee The analysis of *Oscar* raises—but does not resolve—complicated questions about how symbolic changes enhance and contaminate the popularity of
names. *Lee* ranks as the 112th most common name given to white boys in 1960,
the year that John F. Kennedy is elected president. Its popularity remains reasonably stable during the next few years (table 5.7). There is a brief decline in late
1963, right after Lee Harvey Oswald assassinates Kennedy. (Because the assassination occurred in November of that year, 1963 as a whole shows no precipitous

drop in the popularity of *Lee*.) In the following years, the propensity to use *Lee* for a boy's name does not decline. Indeed, the name enjoys a favorable jump in popularity in 1967, ranking 96 in that year. The popularity of *Lee,* counter to the enormous outpouring of sympathy after the murder of John Kennedy, and counter to all expectations that the popularity of the name would be contaminated for a significant number of years, holds its own. One possibility here is that the symbolic contamination due to Lee Harvey Oswald is countered during the 1970s by the popularity of another *Lee,* the actor Lee Marvin, who wins the Academy Award for best leading actor in 1965.

The Symbolic Enhancement of Names

In Chapter 3, we saw how the name *Jacqueline* was enhanced through its symbolic association with Jacqueline Kennedy as well as how various presidents have influenced the popularity of first names, and in Chapter 8 we shall explore the role of entertainment on the appeal of names. The following examples of symbolic enhancement, however, reveal internal mechanisms we have not yet explored.

Beverly The steps that lead *Beverly* to become a popular female name in the United States illustrate a more complex example of symbolic enhancement. In this case, the process of symbolic enhancement moves the name from its original use for boys in England to its use for girls in the United States. (The reference to "Beverly Farms" in the quotation below refers to a location in Massachusetts just off the Atlantic coast, used by President Taft as a summer White House in the days before air conditioning.)

> Beverley was in fact the original spelling of a place name in Yorkshire, England, but in making the journey to the U.S.A. it dropped the last "e." The next stage in the name's development occurred at the turn of the century. At that time it was widely reported in the press that President Taft had been spending some time at Beverly Farms. This seems to have been enough to convert Beverly overnight into a "high class" name, similar to Ritz, say, or Savoy. It was therefore borrowed as a name for many other places, including the Los Angeles suburb of Beverly Hills.
>
> The association of Beverly Hills with movie stars probably suggested the use of the name to Beverly Baine, a star of silent movie days. Either she, or more likely, the general aura of luxury that quickly became associated with Beverly Hills, commended the name to others. By 1925 Beverly had become one of the top fifty American first names. It was to remain so throughout the next twenty-five years. [Dunkling 1977, 20–22]

We see several steps: first, a president's link to a community enhances the name; in turn, this leads developers of a new community to use the name; in turn, an actress takes the name, thanks to the new community's glamorous association; and finally, many parents choose the name used by the star actress, Beverly Baine. *Tiffany* is a more current version of a name that is adopted from its connection with something popularly seen as "high class"—to wit, an expensive jewelry store.

English Names in Denmark   Another example of symbolic enhancement stems from the use of English-language names in the Danish town of Aarhus between 1800 and 1950 (Kisbye 1981). It provides a good example of how different subsets may find very different symbolic meaning in the same taste, such that its usage is simultaneously unappealing to one set and attractive to another. In 1800 there is virtually no use of English names, but their popularity later increases as Shakespeare (introduced to the Danes through German translations) and then Dickens (whose great popularity among the Danes peaks toward the end of the nineteenth century) become widely read. Other English authors also influence the giving of names through the end of the century and on through the first few decades of the twentieth century. Torben Kisbye argues that this trend reflects the discovery of English literature by those of high social status, who then give their children names found in these works. When English-language writings later become available to the "masses," and often entail pulp fiction to boot, the working class begins to use these names and the higher strata accordingly cease giving their children English names (recall the description in Chapter 1 of the class imitation mechanism; it is discussed more extensively in Chapter 6).

Symbolism and Subsets of the Population   There is no question that the tastes of one group may affect the tastes of another group. If group *A* is associated with a given taste, then the imagery associated with *A* could contaminate the taste for the *B* population or it could enhance the taste—it all depends on the relations between the two groups. Subgroup differences in taste can also be driven by other influences; subsets of the population often resonate to different symbolic ideals and, therefore, in turn choose different tastes. Tastes may, for example, reflect historical differences rather than contemporary processes. Likewise, groups may employ tastes to set themselves apart from others for reasons other than simple socioeconomic status. It is all too easy to forget these other factors and think solely of lower-income groups chasing after the tastes of the higher strata and the wealthy classes, in turn, using distinct tastes to maintain their distance. After all, differences in wealth often affect material matters; in addition to the example of the mobile home mentioned earlier, think of standards of home repair and car maintenance, concern about cost when choosing a restaurant, sending a child to college, or going to an orthodontist, and so forth. Beyond this, however, subgroup differences in tastes may simply reflect varying attitudes toward the symbolism involved.

Monetary factors obviously do not affect the ability to give a child a particular name. Yet taste differences will often occur regardless of the enhancement or contamination of a name due to the choices of another class. Rather, differences in taste can reflect varied responses to what the name symbolizes. Or classes may share a common symbolic association with a name but differ in how attractive they find that symbol for a child's name. A mother's educational level clearly influences the names she gives to her children, and the differences are especially pronounced for daughters.[21] A look at a number of the leading names given to white daughters born in New York State points up this pattern (table 5.8). In the case of *Emily*, we see that about 0.3 percent (3 per 1,000) of girls born to women with some high school (but not graduates) are named *Emily*.[22] The disposition toward *Emily* moves upward with mothers' education such that, among women with a post-college education, 1.4 percent (14 per 1,000) are named *Emily*. The disposition toward *Allison, Lauren, Megan, Catherine, Elizabeth*, and other names listed at the top of table 5.8 also tends to increase with the level of the mother's education. By contrast, other names are more likely to be favored by mothers with less education. In the case of *Crystal*, for example, 1.36 percent of daughters born to mothers with some high school—but not graduates—are given this name. The disposition diminished such that virtually no daughters of mothers in the highest level of education are given this name. Other names at the bottom of the table, such as *Tammy, Maria,* and *Angela*, are also given to daughters more frequently by less educated mothers.

Almost all names have images attached to them. Some names evoke strength, while others convey weakness; on a continuum within each sex, some names are seen as more masculine, while others are less so. Of significance here is the link between the images of a name and class differences in the disposition to use that name. Highly educated mothers tend to use girls' names that connote strength, activity, sincerity, and goodness. Mothers with lower educational levels

Table 5.8. Names given to white girls, by education of mother, New York, 1973–1985

Name	Net difference index	Percentage receiving name by number of years of school completed by mother				
		9–11	12	13–15	16	17+
Emily	.39	.27	.22	.76	1.17	1.43
Allison	.33	.11	.56	1.05	1.55	1.65
Lauren	.32	.13	.64	.99	1.49	2.07
Megan	.32	.12	.66	1.57	1.94	1.33
Catherine	.21	.56	.76	1.25	1.93	1.67
Elizabeth	.20	.79	.96	1.47	2.19	2.67
Sarah	.20	.82	1.52	2.23	2.91	3.32
Laura	.18	.47	.76	1.24	1.52	1.47
Erin	.17	.27	.76	1.22	1.38	.86
Rachel	.15	.55	.77	.98	1.55	1.49
Rebecca	.13	.67	.80	1.11	1.54	1.51
Amy	.01	1.13	1.29	1.46	1.45	1.57
Christine	−.02	2.29	3.48	3.44	3.28	2.73
Amanda	−.02	1.08	1.10	1.09	1.25	1.27
Stephanie	−.02	.99	1.25	1.27	1.28	1.07
Kelly	−.03	.67	1.33	1.42	.84	.72
Erica	−.04	.77	.76	.72	.81	.86
Heather	−.04	.97	1.40	1.49	1.23	.80
Danielle	−.04	.74	1.29	1.17	.77	.99
Kimberly	−.06	1.08	1.19	1.33	1.12	.68
Jessica	−.07	2.73	2.26	2.44	2.16	2.31
Jennifer	−.07	3.86	4.78	4.21	3.80	3.42
Jamie	−.07	.76	.89	.83	.74	.60
Stacy	−.08	.64	.92	.73	.61	.60
Lisa	−.09	1.10	1.58	1.13	.91	1.15
Nicole	−.10	1.56	2.17	2.06	1.17	1.07
Melissa	−.11	2.18	2.15	2.04	1.55	1.29
Michelle	−.11	1.67	2.28	2.06	1.06	1.09
Angela	−.27	.79	.69	.49	.19	.10
Maria	−.27	1.01	.65	.36	.36	.28
Tammy	−.45	.84	.37	.18	.06	.06
Crystal	−.47	1.36	.51	.32	.07	.00
Valid *N*		10,330	31,557	12,695	6,900	5,027

Source: Lieberson and Bell 1992, 525

are relatively less likely to favor such names. By contrast, for boys, names with an image of strength are more likely to be chosen by mothers with less education. This does not mean that highly educated mothers want weak sons or that less educated mothers want inactive daughters. Rather, it means that some images are more important to one educational subgroup and other images are more important to another. The point of this is that taste differences in the choice of names can operate simply if parents differ in what characteristics are most important to them—and it need not reflect processes of class contamination or enhancement or that the parents differ in their images of the name (though neither can be ruled out automatically).

It is not possible to predict when events will alter the symbolism attached to a name and, in turn, when the symbolic changes will affect tastes (whether it be names or tastes generally). For one, there is always the possibility that the observed outcome was caused by a different condition. The very rough link between the decline in the popularity of *Adolph* and the rise of Hitler makes it difficult to say whether a causal connection exists. In a way, this is a blessing of riches—worse is the situation when the popularity of a taste either does not change at· all or is in the opposite direction. We saw, for example, that the disposition to name a son *Lee* drops only briefly after Lee Harvey Oswald kills President Kennedy. What does this mean? Because the most we can conclude is a probabilistic principle—namely, that some conditions will *tend* to enhance and others will *tend* to contaminate a taste—any specific contrary outcome fails to negate the proposition. We would like to know more about this, if at all possible.[23] Of course, some other influence—symbolic or otherwise—could be operating to nullify the symbolic influence under consideration (as we speculated in the case of *Lee*). The extensive information on popular performers and fictional characters (described in Chapter 8) provides an opportunity to address this question of when apparent enhancement or contamination actually operates to change a taste and when it does not. In any case, even at this point, the results on symbolic enhancement and contamination are sufficiently strong to make it clear that this is a significant internal mechanism by which tastes are changed. To be sure, the symbolic approach depends on external events (which is more or less a constant flow in most nations) that then set off an internal mechanism that leads to symbolic enhancement and contamination of tastes. These alter the imagery associated with a taste and in turn affect the likelihood that the taste will expand or contract in popularity. Sometimes these symbolic changes *do* reflect substantial shifts in the social order (if, for example, a nation is at war, the symbols associated with the enemy will be contaminated), but this should not be confused with the fact that these symbolic changes occur even when there are no changes in the social order. Rather, there is a continuous flow of what are best viewed as chance associations between names and conditions that may alter the symbolic attractiveness of names.

6 Models of the Fashion Process

Fashions are rarely the product of external forces or internal mechanisms alone. Both are always present, though their influence may differ. So far, for problem-solving purposes, we have considered settings in which the influence is primarily external or internal. We now move on more complex influences on taste, wherein both internal and external forces play important roles and it is impossible to view one factor as the predominant influence. In this chapter, I approach fashion as the joint product of both external conditions and a hitherto unexplored internal mechanism: collective behavior.

COLLECTIVE BEHAVIOR

By definition fashion involves change, specifically, change that occurs for its own sake, as opposed to change of a "functional" nature such as can result from new technology. Of course, fashion also has a "function"—to be different from what was—but it is difference simply for the sake of difference.[1] In fact, fashion is a form of collective behavior, sharing three general properties with other forms of collective behavior, as James Coleman notes in *Foundations of Social Theory:*

- They [that is, forms of collective behavior] involve a number of people carrying out the same or similar actions at the same time.
- The behavior exhibited is transient or continually changing, not in an equilibrium state.

- There is some kind of dependency among the actions: individuals are not acting independently. [1990, 198]

Of particular interest here is the last of Coleman's points, specifically the existence of a feedback system whereby each person makes choices that are constantly affected by the behavior of others who are, in turn, also influenced in the same manner.[2] If choices are affected by what others are doing, then outcomes become complicated and not necessarily what anyone intended. The appeal of a given taste is, in this regard, dependent on the behavior of others. This leads to constant shifts in the relative attractiveness of a given taste. More on this shortly.

In spite of the usual association of the term *model* with mathematical formalizations, the models I describe here are formulated in largely nonmathematical ways. After noting the special difficulties when modeling feedback systems in collective behavior, Coleman concludes that "it is necessary to develop and apply models and theories that are less mathematically elegant and parsimonious but accord more with reality" (902). At this point, moreover, I am more comfortable attempting to describe and analyze fashion processes, leaving the mathematical modeling to others more skilled in such efforts.

CLASS IMITATION AND AVERSION

The class imitation model of changing fashions in women's clothing, proposed by Georg Simmel in 1904 and Bernard Barber and Lyle Lobel in 1953 and described in Chapter 1, is an excellent starting point for thinking about fashion models. It is straightforward, appears to apply to a variety of tastes, and entails a type of collective behavior. Before proposing a new collective behavior model of internal change, we need first to consider the suitability of class imitation as an internal mechanism accounting for changes in tastes. In a nutshell, the higher classes adopt new fashions that set them off from everyone else. In turn, the strata below are attracted to these fashions *because* they are associated with higher status. This trend continues downward until the classes at the bottom eventually imitate the fashions favored by those of higher status. At some point, the higher classes again adopt newer fashions to set themselves off from others, and in turn lower strata imitate these new fashions, and so on.

This model is especially appealing because it suggests a collective process that generates outcomes unintended by the participants but that occur because of the behavior of others. We can appreciate it as a model of a collective fashion process in which stability can never occur because each change creates the seeds of its own destruction. Those of the higher strata who adopt a new fashion are able to enjoy it for only a limited time before its very function—as a marker of status—is contaminated by others who adopt it. The function, then, is destroyed for the initial adopters and also for those who imitated it when the lower classes realize that it is no longer the fashion of the higher strata.

How valid is this proposition? It is of undoubted value in accounting for various facets of fashion behavior—both past and present—particularly as the bourgeoisie attains sufficient affluence to permit imitation of the highest strata. There is evidence that class imitation plays a role in the naming process. Rex Taylor (1974) reports a shift over time in the use of the *Jr.* suffix for the naming of boys, which he interprets with exactly these mechanisms. For much of the nineteenth century and the first part of the twentieth, writes Taylor, the suffix was used to mark the status of middle- and upper-class American families. Examining data on Richmond, Virginia, he observes that *Jr.* was at one time "virtually confined to the white population, and more specifically, the white-collar and property-owning classes" (19). Later in the twentieth century, however, Taylor finds an increasing disposition for the working class to use the *Jr.* form for their first son and, in turn, a decline in the practice among the higher strata.[3]

Other reports of class imitation influencing names are many: the use of middle names in both the United Kingdom and the United States stems from imitating the practices of the British aristocracy (Weekley 1939, 4; Withycombe 1977, xliii–xliv; Stewart 1979, 30), and in England, the United States, and France, names initially favored by higher strata have been shown in turn to have been copied by other classes (Williams 1956, 230*n*13; Taylor 1974; Dunkling 1977, 174–177; Lieberson and Bell 1992, 541–544; Besnard and Desplanques, 1993, 271–286). Careful inspection of the evidence of a class-based recycling of tastes in the *contemporary* period, however, is less than fully convincing.

First of all, little is gained by providing *examples* of names adopted first by higher strata and later by lower strata. Nothing can be made of these examples if the reverse order of adoption occurs with about as many other names. Moreover, even if high-to-low movements are somewhat more frequent than those in the opposite direction, many names are adopted more or less simultaneously by multiple classes. Further, a second part of the proposition must also hold if the model is valid: not only should high-to-low adoptions be substantially more common than low-to-high adoptions, but the decline of the name ought to occur sooner for the higher strata, because the model—if valid—would predict that the higher classes are first to give up a name after the lower strata begin to use it. If the higher strata adopt certain names earlier but show no greater propensity to give them up, then a key part of the model is invalid, and there is thus no reason to rule out a simple process of diffusion.

This two-step recycling model, based on class imitation followed by class aversion, may well be true for earlier periods in history and it may well be true for other fashions—say, for clothing—in at least some time periods. But the available evidence suggests that it does not go very far in explaining changing tastes in names. Eleanor Bell and I (1992) have found that patterns in New York State are in the *form* that a class imitation model would predict: new adoptions of names by highly educated mothers often precede adoptions by less educated mothers, with adoptions in the opposite direction being far less common. Yet the lags are so brief (a name typically goes from high to low in just a few years) that imitation is unlikely to be the cause. As we observe:

> In the case of Justin . . . the adoption process spans only four years. The name first makes the top 20 in 1977; by 1980 it has made the top 20 for all five [educational] groups. Now by the standards of, say, clothing this would be reasonable to understand through copying from a single initial model. But for clothing there is a set of mechanisms for such a diffusion: print media devoted to fashions, stores that promote new fashions, television and movies to carry forward fashion messages. However, it is not entirely clear how rapidly one class would learn of the names adopted by another class. In some cases, the explosion is so rapid that we speculate that it is really differential rates of adoption from a single source rather than a chain of diffusion per se based on an appeal driven by the impression that higher-strata persons are using this name for their children. Ashley, for example, first becomes a top-20 name in 1983 for two classes (some college and post-college), then for two more a year later (high school graduates, college graduates) and makes the top 20 in 1985 for the 9–11 group. There is imitation or copying, to be sure, but it may come from a single stimulus that subsets of the population are differentially exposed to, say, the use of a name inspired by an upscale woman's clothing chain that is more popular with one subset than another. [543–544]

Philippe Besnard (1995) argues that French naming data provide strong evidence of a downward diffusion of names in recent years, but closer inspection reveals otherwise. Careful analysis of French naming patterns in recent decades (between 1945–1949 and 1980–1981) actually indicates the absence of a class imitation process for both boys' and girls' names. Leading names among the working class often appear without ever being used by the higher levels of society, other leading names appear simultaneously among the working class and higher classes, and leading names often remain popular among the higher classes long after they decline among the working class (Lieberson 1995, 1322–1323).

Texas

Information for every fifth year from 1965 through 1990 on names given to white children born in Texas provides an excellent opportunity to evaluate the appropriateness of the class imitation model for naming practices. Unlike previous analyses of specific first names, class influences on both when a name becomes popular *and* when it loses popularity can be measured. Let us look at the 20 most common names given to white girls of both low and high socioeconomic status (SES) born in Texas between 1965 and 1990 (table 6.1).[4] With these data, we can determine if mothers of higher socioeconomic status generally precede mothers of lower socioeconomic status in adopting popular names and, in turn, if those mothers then drop the names before the mother of lower SES do. The first pattern would be expected if the mothers of lower SES are imitating the tastes of the mothers of higher SES; the second pattern would be expected if a name loses its appeal to high SES mothers when it becomes popular among mothers of lower SES. *Cynthia* and *Deborah* are among the names already popular at the beginning of the period, 1965, and cannot be included in the adoption analysis because we do not know who adopted the name first (although we can look at differences in who first gives up the name). Likewise, names remaining popular among both classes at the end of the period, 1990, obviously cannot be analyzed in terms of which socioeconomic group first gives up the name.

The imitation model is at best modestly successful in explaining the popularity cycle. Of the 29 low SES girls' names that first become popular in 1970 or later, 17 were also adopted in the same period for the daughters of high SES mothers (compare columns 1 and 2 for *Amanda, Amber,* and *Amy*); 4 were not popular among high SES mothers (table 6.1a); and 8 had previously reached popularity among high SES mothers (for example, *Ashley* and *Emily*). In other words, one-fourth of the 29 girls' names reaching popularity among the low socioeconomic group after 1965 fit the class imitation model—that is, they were already in use for the high socioeconomic group.[5] This means that three-fourths of lower SES girls' names became popular *without* imitation of the higher socioeconomic group.

Turning to the 26 girls' names that were dropped by at least one class after

Table 6.1. *Popular white girls' names, Texas, by mother's socioeconomic status (SES), 1965–1990*

Name	Year first appearing in top 20 by SES of mother		Most recent year in top 20, by SES of mother		Class model fits for:	
	Low (1)	High (2)	Low (3)	High (4)	Appearance (5)	Disappearance (6)
Amanda	75	75	90	90		
Amber	80	80	90	85		Y
Amy	70	70	85	85		
Angela	65	65	80	80		
Ashley	85	80	90	90	Y	
Brittany	85	85	90	90		
Chelsea	90	90	90	90		
Christina	75	75	85	85		
Courtney	90	90	90	90		
Crystal	80	80	85	80		Y
Cynthia	65	65	70	65		Y
Deborah	65	65	65	65		
Donna	65	65	70	65		Y
Elizabeth	65	65	90	90		
Emily	90	85	90	90	Y	
Heather	75	70	90	85	Y	Y
Jennifer	70	65	90	90	Y	
Jessica	80	80	90	90		
Julie	70	65	75	75	Y	
Karen	65	65	70	70		
Kimberly	65	65	85	85		
Laura	65	65	75	85		
Lauren	85	80	90	90	Y	
Lisa	65	65	80	75		Y
Mary	65	65	75	75		
Megan	85	85	90	90		
Melissa	65	65	85	85		
Michelle	70	70	80	80		
Misty	75	75	80	75		Y
Pamela	65	65	65	65		
Patricia	65	65	65	65		
Rachel	85	80	90	90	Y	
Rebecca	65	65	90	90		

Table 6.1. Continued

	Year first appearing in top 20 by SES of mother		Most recent year in top 20, by SES of mother		Class model fits for:	
	Low	High	Low	High	Appearance	Disappearance
Name	(1)	(2)	(3)	(4)	(5)	(6)
Rhonda	65	65	65	65		
Samantha	90	90	90	90		
Sarah	80	75	90	90	Y	
Shannon	70	70	70	75		
Stephanie	70	70	90	90		
Susan	65	65	65	70		
Tammy	65	65	75	70		Y
Tiffany	80	80	90	80		Y
Tracy	70	70	70	70		

Note: Unable to determine correctness of theory when columns 1 and 2 are both "65" or columns 3 and 4 are both "90"

Table 6.1a. Names found only in top 20 of low SES girls

Name	Appear	Disappear
April	75	80
Brandy	75	75
Kayla	90	90
Linda	65	65
Sandra	65	65
Teresa	65	65
Tina	70	70

being popular among both classes: 14 were dropped by both groups in the same period; 3 were dropped first by mothers of lower SES, and 9 were first dropped by mothers of higher SES.[6] Here, 35 percent of the names fit the theory in which higher strata are the first to drop commonly shared tastes, but the remaining 65 percent of names are either given up by both groups at the same time or are abandoned even earlier by mothers of lower SES. Popular girls' names, therefore, overwhelmingly do not operate in accordance with either side of the class

Table 6.1b. Names found only in top 20 of high SES girls

Name	Appear	Disappear
Erin	80	80
Hannah	90	90
Katherine	90	90
Kelly	70	75
Kelsey	90	90
Lindsey	85	85
Lori	65	65
Stacy	70	70
Taylor	90	90

imitation theory. In fact, of the 11 girls' names that undergo a full cycle of popularity during this period, only one, *Heather,* fits *both* components, being picked up by lower SES mothers after having become popular with the higher SES mothers, and in turn being dropped first by higher SES mothers.

The greater stability commonly found among boys' names means that there is less turnover to study. Again, the vast majority of newly popular names do not follow the class imitation model. Of the 18 names becoming popular for boys of lower SES since 1965, 12 become popular at the same period for both groups; 3 achieve popularity only among mothers of low SES; and 3 boys' names occur among mothers of lower SES only after they become popular among mothers of high SES (table 6.2). Just 17 percent of popular boys' names, therefore, are adopted by parents of low SES in the manner predicted by the imitation model— a very weak result. As for declines, of the 17 that were dropped by one or both groups, 4 left in the same period, 3 were first dropped by the mothers of lower SES, and 10 names are first dropped by mothers of high SES. Thus 10 of 17, or 59 percent, of the boys' names declining in popularity among the mothers of low SES meet the condition expected by the imitation model.

Although an impressive number of boys' names first decline among mothers of high SES, this is not totally convincing support for this model. First, the adoptions of boys' names by mothers of lower SES do not appear to follow the pattern expected by the imitation model—indeed, popularity among the high socioeconomic group follows popularity among the low socioeconomic group as often as the opposite sequence implied by the theory (3 in each case). Again, as

Table 6.2. Popular white boys' names, Texas, by mother's socioeconomic status (SES), 1965–1990

| Name | Year first appearing in top 20 by SES of Mother | | Most recent year in top 20, by SES of mother | | Class model fits for: | |
| | Low | High | Low | High | Appearance | Disappearance |
	(1)	(2)	(3)	(4)	(5)	(6)
Andrew	85	85	90	90		
Brandon	80	80	90	85		Y
Brian	70	70	80	85		
Charles	65	65	80	75		Y
Christopher	65	65	90	90		
Cody	85	85	90	90		
Daniel	75	75	90	90		
David	65	65	90	90		
Eric	80	75	80	75	Y	Y
Jacob	90	90	90	90		
James	65	65	90	90		
Jason	70	70	85	85		
Jeffrey	65	65	75	80		
Jeremy	75	75	80	80		
John	65	65	90	90		
Jonathan	80	80	90	90		
Joseph	75	80	90	85		Y
Joshua	75	80	90	90		
Justin	80	80	90	90		
Kenneth	65	65	70	65		Y
Kevin	65	65	85	80		Y
Mark	65	65	70	75		
Matthew	75	75	90	90		
Michael	65	65	90	90		
Paul	65	65	70	70		
Richard	65	65	80	75		Y
Robert	65	65	90	90		
Ryan	85	80	90	90	Y	
Stephen	70	65	70	70	Y	
Steven	65	65	85	75		Y
Thomas	65	65	75	70		Y
Timothy	65	65	70	65		Y
William	65	65	90	90		
Zachary	90	90	90	90		

Note: Unable to determine correctness of theory when columns 1 and 2 are both "65" or columns 3 and 4 are both "90"

Table 6.2a. Names found only in top 20 of low SES *boys*

Name	Appear	Disappear
Aaron	90	90
Donald	65	65
Gary	65	65
Ronald	65	65

Table 6.2b. Names found only in top 20 of high SES *boys*

Name	Appear	Disappear
Chad	75	75
Gregory	65	70
Kyle	85	90
Scott	65	70
Travis	90	90
Tyler	90	90

for girls' names, we also see the rarity of a sequence in which a name is both first chosen and first dropped by mothers of higher SES (1 of the 7 names experiencing a full cycle of popularity). And we are again reminded that the gaps between the class adoptions is extremely brief, meaning that one class is highly unlikely to be learning the behavior of another class before either adopting or dropping a name. As table 6.2 indicates, a number of the names that are popular among both socioeconomic groups in 1965 remain popular among both in 1990, hardly strong evidence of an aversion by the higher socioeconomic group to use names popular among people of lower SES. In fact, there is stunning evidence that most of the leading names in 1965 remain quite popular for boys, and with essentially no obvious difference in the disposition of higher status parents to give up on these names. *James,* for example, is the most popular name for boys in 1965; twenty-five years later, in 1990, it is the 6th most popular name among both groups (table 6.3). Although many of these names experience a decline during this period, there is simply no indication that parents of higher SES are fleeing from these names because they are popular among other socioeconomic groups.[7]

In short, the Texas results are largely consistent with the surprising conclusion

Table 6.3. Changing popularity of white boys' names in the top 20 for both high and low socioeonomic status (SES) parents in Texas, 1965

Name	SES	1965	1970	1975	1980	1985	1990
					Rank by year		
James	H	1	2	4	4	5	6
	L	1	2	4	4	4	6
John	H	2	3	5	6	6	5
	L	3	3	6	6	5	7
Michael	H	3	1	1	1	2	1
	L	2	1	1	1	3	1
David	H	4	4	6	9	10	13
	L	4	4	7	8	10	12
Robert	H	5	5	7	10	8	11
	L	5	5	5	7	8	9
William	H	6	7	8	11	9	9
	L	6	6	8	10	11	10
Richard	H	7	11	19	*	*	*
	L	7	9	13	20	*	*
Mark	H	8	13	18	*	*	*
	L	8	15	*	*	*	*
Charles	H	9	12	14	*	*	*
	L	9	10	11	18	*	*
Jeffrey	H	10	9	11	19	*	*
	L	11	13	16	*	*	*
Steven	H	11	14	16	*	*	*
	L	15	11	14	*	19	*
Christopher	H	12	6	3	2	1	2
	L	17	7	3	2	1	2
Kevin	H	13	10	12	20	*	*
	L	10	12	18	*	20	*
Thomas	H	14	17	*	*	*	*
	L	12	16	19	*	*	*
Kenneth	H	15	*	*	*	*	*
	L	14	17	*	*	*	*
Timothy	H	16	*	*	*	*	*
	L	13	19	*	*	*	*
Paul	H	19	20	*	*	*	*
	L	20	20	*	*	*	*

* No longer in top 20 for the SES category

drawn from naming patterns in France summarized above (see Lieberson 1995, 1321–1323). In both cases, class imitation does not play a major role in either the introduction or the disappearance of popular names in recent years. The names that are popular among different classes by and large reach popularity everywhere at the same time—or within such a short gap that the imitation theory cannot apply. At most, the only conceivable support for the class imitation model is the tendency for boys' names to decline earlier among sons of high SES. This is not the only pattern, but it does raise a question that requires further consideration. And yet, even if the class imitation pattern occurs more often than the opposite tendency, it is clear that the model does not go very far in helping us understand the naming process among either boys or girls.

A GENERAL COLLECTIVE MODEL

A better model, the collective behavior model, incorporates some of the aesthetic appeal of the class imitation model in a more general and less constrained form. For this model, we can postulate the following ten conditions, which apply to fashions more generally as well as to names in particular:

1. At any given time, an individual makes a choice unaware of exactly what the entire population is doing at that time, let alone what it will do at a later time.
2. Because the individual's choice is made in part in ignorance of the decisions being made by all others, a later awareness of what others were choosing at the same time may alter the initial appeal of the choice made.
3. Likewise, because most people are unable to judge what the choices will be in the future—let alone what the response will be to the current choice being made—these developments in the future may well clash with the initial appeal of the current choice.
4. In both cases, the behavior of the entire population influences the individual's satisfaction with the choice that is made. This has two dimensions: the behavior of others at the same time as the choice is made, and the choices made by others at a later time. For example, someone who selects a name that is relatively uncommon because that feature makes it appealing will not be pleased to discover later that many other parents were making this choice at the same time or that a few years later the name becomes very popular. By the same token, someone selecting a name in part because it *is* popular will not be happy to learn in the future that it is no longer popular.

5. Put another way, an instability occurs if the choices made by others are not harmonious with the behavioral conditions each individual assumes are in operation (implicitly more often than explicitly).

6. The response to this instability is, of course, a function of how important the discrepancy is from the ideal. (The behavior of others cannot help but have some influence, but it may be relatively minor.) If a girl is named after her maternal grandmother, for example, this choice may well tolerate a wider range of levels of popularity than would a choice in which popularity is a central factor in the decision.

7. The response to this discrepancy is different for material and immaterial forms of taste. For material forms, the response will follow what I propose to call the "durability-cost principle": to wit, the likelihood of replacement is inversely related to both its cost and its durability. An item that is both expensive and durable, such as a house, will have a low probability of being replaced if its fashion is no longer appealing because of collective processes. An item that is both cheap and relatively perishable, such as a pair of shoes, will change far more rapidly when the collective instabilities occur. Of course, the influence of the durability-cost principle will vary inversely with an individual's income and wealth.

8. The response to forms of taste that are not of a material nature and are purely symbolic (such as names), are, of course, not influenced by durability and expense. The response is affected by the cultural and organizational practices with respect to the durability of the symbol involved. In the case of first names, at least in the United States and most Western nations, they do not often change in the course of a lifetime. Hence, we would not expect this type of fashion to shift as the collective fashion patterns change.[8]

9. For these types of symbols, as well as for durable and expensive material items, we would expect changes to occur differently from the way people replace their clothing as fashions change. For more durable goods and symbolic culture, more of the change occurs through new waves of the population entering the relevant age cohorts. Changing fashions here have to be viewed not in terms of changes by the same person (as would be the case for replacing one's wardrobe) but in terms of changes in the choices made by the same *type* of people in each succeeding cohort (as well as to changes in the dispositions of individuals in each cohort). To be sure, choices of a house, dining room furniture, bone china, sterling silver cutlery, and the like can change through the years—particularly if income goes

up or if needs (as distinct from fashions) change. And of course, all of this is relative and a matter of frequency: some wealthy people can (and do) redecorate their house whenever they choose to respond to shifts in furniture design fashion or buy a fancy new car every couple of years (and hence respond to changes in the popularity of car colors and design changes). On the whole, however, durable and expensive items are less likely to be changed rapidly within a person's lifespan, and hence relatively more of the change occurs between age cohorts.

10. The location of a fashion on the durability-cost continuums affects the nature of the feedback to collective behavior. As we move toward fashions that are easily replaced because they are inexpensive or are not durable and so need frequent replacement anyway, then the main focus is on individuals responding to their earlier choices with new choices.[9] As we move toward material fashions that are not easily replaced or symbolic goods that are hard to replace because of the culture or structure in which they are embedded, individual behavior is approached in a more subtle way. It is less about a person's changing choices and more about changes through cohorts replacing earlier cohorts. In the case of names, for example, new waves of young adults reach childbearing age and of course name their children, earlier parents drop out as they pass childbearing age, and so on through time ad infinitum. We can think of these changes as involving people with new tastes, and this is undoubtedly correct. If, however, one is willing to make a counterfactual assumption, it is also appropriate to think that if the earlier wave of parents were to reappear, they, too, would make different choices because the collective position of their earlier choices are now different and thus in many cases will be less appealing than other choices. Each new wave, in other words, will be different not only because its dispositions are different but also because the same dispositions will have different outcomes owing to the changing position of each name (or other fashion).

POPULARITY DISPOSITIONS REMAIN STABLE
EVEN AS THE NAMES CHANGE

It is easy to see how the collective conditions in this model will lead to disequilibriums in naming preferences. Although the number of parents who discuss names in terms of their perceived popularity is an empirical question, I believe that this perception plays a role in the decisions made by most parents. If we consider those parents with a taste toward the rare or uncommon name, two forces can upset the assumptions implicit at the time of their child's birth. First, parents do not know what choices other parents are making at the same time (or even in the years immediately preceding their choice). Accordingly, other parents—with the same disposition—may "independently" arrive at the same choice of name. This name is, of course, not a truly independent choice but can represent a natural extension of existing tastes (see the discussion of *Rebecca* in Chapter 8) that appeals to parents, or it could be a response to a new development in popular culture, the arts, politics, and the like. Mass communication can cause many parents to make the same choice at the same time. The second source of instability occurs because parents differ in how the popularity of a name affects their taste.

In this respect, the outcome is somewhat counterintuitive: the appeal of specific names will shift even if the disposition of parents along the continuum from favoring rare to very popular names is constant. Names will change in their level of popularity—sometimes increasing, other times decreasing—even though parental dispositions for different levels of popularity remain unchanged. What happens is that a set of parents with one type of disposition is replaced by another set of parents with a different disposition. Suppose, for example, a specific name has an appeal to parents favoring unusual names. Their adoption of that name, however, may now make the name too popular for later parents with the same inclination toward rarity. In contrast, the name could generate a following among new parents who find a mildly popular level just right. And this can progress upward, with a new set of parents, with different dispositions, replacing earlier parents. At some point even the appeal of a popular name will decline for parents who are attracted to such names. There is a limit to the level of popularity that even they will accept. How many parents at present would knowingly give their child a name that is also used by 10 percent of all children? There will be a decline in a name's popularity if those parents who find such a number acceptable are less than those for whom 10 percent is too large. This implies that a taste for popularity will affect the concentration of children in the most common names, even as these names themselves change radically.

If we return to the illustrations in Chapter 3 of the concentration in names for boys and girls born in Illinois since 1916 (see fig. 3.2), we can now interpret these results from a somewhat different perspective. In the face of major external social events, we observe a strikingly stable level of concentration. This constancy occurs, moreover, amid enormous changes in the most common names.

Changes in concentration are slow and gradual even though almost none of the initial top 20 names remains there for very long. Most parents responsible for children' names in a given period were not parents a few decades earlier. Yet the level of concentration for the new leading names changes only modestly. The taste for fashion and popularity, I submit, affects the distribution of names even when the taste for specific names leads to an almost complete turnover in the most common names. Names change much more rapidly than does the set of tastes that lead to the distribution of popularity. *The popularity distribution, in effect, has a certain permanent quality in the short run—even though there is an enormous turnover in the names themselves.*

CYCLES

Once a name wanes from popularity, it does not reach great popularity again for a long time. For example, among girls' names that drop out of the top 20 between 1907 and 1919—*Ethel, Gladys, Lillian, Grace, Edith, Edna, Eleanor,* and *Anna*—none have reappeared by 1989 (the last year considered), for an average (median) of slightly more than seventy-five years. If we look at every name that is among the 20 most popular in California for girls and boys for the vast part of the twentieth century (tables 6.4 and 6.5), a strong pattern emerges (the maximum possible length of time out of the limelight is of course shorter for names that appear more recently). Very few names reappear, and these are mainly statistical flukes. The girl's name *Frances,* for example, dropped just below the top 20 in 1930, remaining there for a few years, and then again just made the top 20 for three more years before declining. As of 1989, it had not reappeared. Similar short-term fluctuations are shown for several other names, but *Catherine, Elizabeth, Christina,* and *Maria* are the only significant exceptions. These are names that are out of the top 20 for eleven to twenty-nine years before returning.

The popularity of boys' names is, as usual, more stable. Yet the same conclusion holds: names that drop out tend to stay out for many years. Again statistical blips involve several names that drop out and then briefly reappear in the top 20 a few years later before dropping out for a long span. *Joseph, Kevin,* and *Jose* are the only names that are out for a number of years before reappearing (forty-three, fourteen, and forty-two years, respectively).

Why do popular names remain in decline for such long periods after they drop out as a leading name? Because the number of names to choose from is almost infinite, many once-popular names are inevitably doomed to remain

Table 6.4. *Recycling of girls' names in the top 20, California, 1906–1989*

Name	First year in top 20	First year gone	Years gone from top 20*	Years before reappearance
Ethel	1906	1909	81	
Gladys	1906	1910	80	
Lillian	1907	1910	80	
Grace	1906	1913	77	
Edith	1906	1914	76	
Edna	1906	1914	76	
Eleanor	1914	1918	72	
Anna	1906	1919	71	
Florence	1906	1920	70	
Mildred	1906	1922	68	
June	1921	1922	68	
Catherine	1906	1924	—	24
Catherine	1948	1967	23	
Evelyn	1906	1925	65	
Marian	1906	1926	64	
Marie	1906	1927	63	
Marjorie	1910	1928	62	
Jean	1918	1929	61	
Lois	1924	1929	61	
Doris	1918	1930	60	
Frances	1906	1930	—	3
Frances	1933	1936	54	
Ruth	1906	1932	58	
Alice	1906	1933	57	
Dolores	1928	1935	55	
Janet	1934	1935	—	3
Janet	1938	1939	—	3
Janet	1942	1956	34	
Gloria	1925	1937	53	
Helen	1906	1938	52	
Dorothy	1906	1940	50	
Beverly	1926	1940	50	
Marilyn	1930	1942	48	
Joyce	1931	1942	48	
Betty	1919	1943	47	
Virginia	1909	1944	46	

Table 6.4. Continued

Name	First year in top 20	First year gone	Years gone from top 20*	Years before reappearance
Joan	1929	1944	46	
Shirley	1923	1945	45	
Carolyn	1939	1947	43	
Cheryl	1944	1949	—	4
Cheryl	1953	1962	28	
Judith	1937	1950	40	
Margaret	1906	1951	39	
Janice	1945	1952	38	
Carol	1932	1958	32	
Sharon	1937	1958	32	
Barbara	1914	1959	31	
Diane	1937	1959	31	
Nancy	1930	1960	30	
Donna	1931	1961	29	
Pamela	1944	1963	27	
Lori	1959	1964	26	
Kathleen	1942	1965	25	
Linda	1938	1966	24	
Mary	1906	1969	21	
Susan	1940	1969	21	
Karen	1941	1969	21	
Tina	1968	1969	21	
Sandra	1938	1970	20	
Teresa	1953	1971	19	
Kelly	1963	1971	—	6
Kelly	1977	1979	11	
Patricia	1922	1972	18	
Deborah	1949	1972	18	
Tracy	1965	1973	17	
Cynthia	1951	1974	16	
Julie	1957	1975	15	
Laura	1958	1976	14	
Shannon	1969	1977	13	
Monica	1977	1978	12	
Angela	1970	1980	10	
Jamie	1976	1980	10	

Table 6.4. Continued

Name	First year in top 20	First year gone	Years gone from top 20*	Years before reappearance
Kimberly	1960	1981	9	
Veronica	1973	1981	9	
Lisa	1958	1982	8	
Tiffany	1980	1983	—	5
Tiffany	1988	1989	1	
Amy	1971	1984	6	
Rebecca	1972	1984	6	
Crystal	1981	1987	3	
Heather	1970	1989	1	
Amber	1979	1989	1	

* Through 1989

Table 6.4a. Names in top 20 after comeback

Name	First year in top 20	First year gone*	Years before reappearance
Elizabeth	1906	1934	24
	1957		
Maria	1907	1937	29
	1965		
Christina	1947	1953	11
	1963		

* Through 1989

unpopular for many centuries. But why some names and not others? Several influences operate. Many once popular names are later unattractive because their phonemic structure is no longer in vogue. Others are associated with imagery that is no longer appealing. Flower names and other names associated with "traditional" roles, for example, have lost favor for daughters. And some names owe their initial popularity to a figure who is no longer popular or admired. Unless the name has been in use for so long that it gains, so to speak, a life of its own, and thus no longer depends on the initial source of its appeal, it is likely to suffer as the "source" declines. These are not the only factors that keep

Table 6.4b. Names still in top 20

Name	First year in top 20
Michelle	1960
Jennifer	1965
Stephanie	1967
Melissa	1971
Nicole	1972
Sarah	1973
Jessica	1974
Amanda	1979
Vanessa	1982
Ashley	1983
Megan	1983
Danielle	1984
Rachel	1985
Brittany	1986
Lauren	1986
Samantha	1987

names from recycling fairly soon. After all, not all previously popular names clash with the sound patterns currently in vogue, and not all carry images that are unacceptable to contemporary parents. Yet, with few exceptions, names that drop from popularity stay out of the top 20 for extremely long periods.

What else is operating here? We can view age itself as a valence that makes features attractive or unattractive. Many old and traditional features of Western society were at one time attractive or admired simply because they were *old*. This is still true in some cases; Harvard University is unlikely to downplay its age or traditions because it enjoys a certain cachet by being old university. In similar fashion, antique objects gain attractiveness and great value by virtue of their age if they are in good repair. If they are not in good repair or are not salvageable, then they are as likely as not to be called *junk*. As Western societies have changed, I would speculate that the widespread positive association with age has in many instances reversed into a negative connotation. In the case of names, an association with older people and out-of-date fashions undercuts its appeal—at least under the current conditions where they appear as both unfashionable and therefore unattractive.[10] As it happens, then, a name long out of use can

Table 6.5. Recycling of boys' names in the top 20, California, 1906–1989

Boys	First year top 20	First year gone	Years gone from top 20*	Years before reappearance
Clarence	1906	1907	83	
Frederick	1906	1911	—	3
Frederick	1914	1915	75	
Francis	1906	1916	74	
Henry	1906	1922	68	
Harry	1906	1924	66	
Walter	1906	1926	—	3
Walter	1929	1930	60	
Albert	1906	1927	—	4
Albert	1931	1932	58	
Arthur	1906	1929	—	3
Arthur	1932	1933	57	
Harold	1906	1931	59	
Jack	1916	1935	55	
Raymond	1906	1939	51	
Frank	1906	1940	50	
Gerald	1931	1943	47	
Edward	1906	1946	44	
George	1906	1950	40	
Larry	1940	1953	37	
Dennis	1939	1954	36	
Gary	1935	1959	31	
Donald	1912	1960	30	
Paul	1907	1960	—	4
Paul	1964	1969	21	
Charles	1906	1961	29	
Ronald	1930	1964	26	
Gregory	1947	1964	26	
Kenneth	1924	1966	24	
Timothy	1955	1969	21	
Thomas	1906	1970	20	
Scott	1962	1973	17	
Mark	1949	1976	14	
William	1906	1977	13	
Jeffrey	1953	1980	10	
Richard	1907	1981	9	
Brandon	1985	1987	3	
Jason	1969	1987	3	
Brian	1959	1988	2	

* Through 1989

Table 6.5a. Boys' names in top 20 after comeback

Name	First year in top 20	First year gone*	Years before reappearance
Jose	1927	1931	42
	1973		
Joseph	1906	1949	5
	1954	1955	5
	1960		
Kevin	1960	1966	4
	1970	1972	14
	1986		

* Through 1989

Table 6.5b. Boys' names still in top 20

Name	First year in top 20
John	1906
James	1906
Robert	1906
David	1922
Michael	1936
Steven	1940
Daniel	1946
Christopher	1961
Eric	1965
Anthony	1966
Matthew	1970
Joshua	1974
Ryan	1975
Nicholas	1979
Justin	1980
Jonathon	1981
Andrew	1983

reappear when nobody can think that the parent is simply out of fashion. The earlier wave of people who carried the name has died out, and so the association with *old* changes from real live persons—aunts and uncles, grandfathers and grandmothers—to historical names that no longer have that negative association with the elderly. Indeed, these are the right names for use if there is a thrust toward "earlier" names.[11]

This process is related to the phenomenon that underlies the ratchet effect. At some point, an old-fashioned name becomes so remote from recent tastes that confusion with out-of-fashion names is no longer possible and the fashion for that name can thus reappear. This is clearly the case for fashion revivals, in which clothing of several decades past—witness the late 1990s revival of 1970s-style platform shoes and bell bottoms among teenagers—can gain a new playful appeal because the fashion is now immune from misunderstanding. Because of the length of the human lifespan, names generally do not have such relatively short recycling possibilities, and so the damaging association with old people lasts for a longer span. Eventually for names, the confounding disappears. To name a boy *Ezekiel* or a girl *Millicent* today connotes an earlier name, but with a different image than it would have ten or twenty years after these names first faded.

Keep in mind, too, that cycles in the popularity of specific names involve asymmetrical causal processes that I've described elsewhere (Lieberson 1985, ch. 4). Namely, the cause(s) of the name's increase in popularity do not explain what leads the name eventually to decline in popularity. It is true, by definition, that fashion requires change. But the specific influences that lead to an increase are very different from the influences that cause a decrease.

DIFFUSION

Any model of fashion must take into account how tastes move within society. Something is obviously occurring when an initially uncommon name becomes popular. Diffusion can occur in two central ways. One involves mass communication (largely from the realm of popular entertainment, but also through an awareness of social and political developments in one's country and elsewhere in the world). The other, social interaction, incorporates a slow and uncertain growth in the awareness of a name that may take a much longer time to spread and that does not depend—at least initially—on mass media for its expansion.

Mass Communication

Mass communication can influence naming tastes in three ways:

1. Mass media remind people of a name that they know but rarely consider when naming their children. In essence, a name from the vast pool of relatively neglected names receives attention when it appears in the media.

2. The imagery of a name is revised because of a new linkage introduced in the media; a name gains a new image because an appealing performer or fictional character has this first name. In any case, there is the possibility for an alteration through a new association of the name. This is a tricky and complicated matter; the novelist, for example, or the actor taking a stage name, will at least implicitly be influenced by their image of the name's impact on the audience. A writer is not likely to use a name that clashes with the character's personality, social position, and the like; likewise a performer will be affected by the kind of roles he or she envisions.

3. The media may also present an unknown name to a large public: a name used in a foreign culture, an invented name, or one that is simply not widely known. An example is *Lilith*, the name of a character on the popular 1980s television show *Cheers*. A little-known Assyrian and Babylonian name meaning "of the night," *Lilith* is the figure in rabbinic legend who was Adam's first wife, before she was supplanted by Eve and became an evil spirit (Kolatch 1984, 360).

Through these mechanisms, a large segment of the population is simultaneously made aware of a name, and rapid popularity can ensue. Certain segments of the populations, such as teenagers and preteens, are populations with distinctive links to the media. A hit song, children's program, or performer who appeals to a narrow age group can have a delayed effect on naming, influencing name choice only when these youngsters reach childbearing age. The opposite also holds; entertainment that reaches an audience that is largely past childbearing age will have a minimal effect on names. Older parents, of course, may resonate to a name that has less appeal to those who are younger. In all cases, we are talking about a development in taste that can operate without intermediate parties (such as opinion leaders or validators of the information). The name goes directly to a population of current or future parents who may respond even though their exposure is a byproduct of other interests that lead them to learn of the name. Not everyone is aware of the name this way because not everyone reads the story in which it appears, sees the movie or television program, knows the sports star, political figure, or performer, and so forth. So even in this context a secondary diffusion occurs as others become aware of the name through contact with others who are using it. This generates an exceedingly rich and interesting question because those who learn of the name in this secondary manner will be unaware of the imagery created by the fictional character or performer. One would predict, as a consequence, a much lower usage of the name by those who are in the secondary diffusion stage—particularly for names with an image that was enhanced or created by its association with the media.

Social Interaction

A second form of diffusion starts without any assistance from the media—at least in the early stages. Social interaction is a slower process that starts with a small number of parents giving their child an invented name or a name that is rarely used. If those in contact with a child having such a name find it appealing and are stimulated to use it, this can expand its use, which in turn increases the likelihood that even more new parents will become aware of the name, and so forth, at a progressively faster rate. The potential exposure of the name early on is unpredictable because it depends heavily on its appeal for the relatively small number of people in contact with the child's name. As we saw in the case of *La*-prefix names in Chapter 5, most invented names die off without any impact. Likewise, the inventory of standard names is enormous, with the vast majority being given to at most a handful of children. These names, both standard and invented, come and go mainly without any impact. If those using the name continues to expand, then at a later stage, *awareness* of it will reach the vast majority of new parents. Note that I say *awareness*, not necessarily *use*. The name's use depends on a variety of other qualities such as how it fits into the existing linguistic forms of names, any image association that has developed, and the like.

Ignoring matters of the name's "appeal"—such as how its sounds fit with prevailing trends, its imagery, and other conditions of this nature—the specific patterns of interaction will affect the chances for expansion. A high level of residential segregation among people with similar dispositions will increase the chances of initial growth, as will a high level of social interaction among people who share common taste dispositions. In these cases, those exposed to the name are more likely to resonate to it. The intensity of interaction among parents from a similar social milieu and with a similar outlook will thus help an innovation along in its early stages, when it depends on expansion of the few children who bear the name. Racial, ethnic, and class segregation factors can play a role in serving as a hothouse for the name's initial development. This hothouse stage is a necessary prerequisite, but whether it will then cross into the larger society and achieve great popularity is by no means certain. Suppose, for example, a child is named after a renowned violinist or conductor. If the family and child interact with others who have a relatively higher probability of knowing of the musical figure and appreciating the accomplishment, then this interaction could increase the likelihood of the name being picked up within this narrow subset of the population. Likewise, if a certain group has a greater disposition toward giving children unique or unconventional names, then exposure to this population (through social or spatial factors, or both) will increase the chances that the name will expand in use. By contrast, an invented name given to a child in a milieu that is not as receptive to such naming practices will be less likely to expand.

In either form of diffusion, *awareness* is a necessary but insufficient condition for *use*. Ultimately, the name has to appeal to parents, and we have observed a number of mechanisms that can influence this response. Names appearing in the mass media have the advantage of being exposed to many people at once. Names starting off without mass exposure are less likely to expand unless they have an inherent potential appeal, because only an extremely small number of new parents will learn of the name when it is introduced. In this scenario, more of a chance factor is operating—"chance" in the sense that a name might be likely to gain popularity if it becomes known to many parents. But there is also the added issue of whether the name will even begin to grow because it is dependent on a small number of responses. An interesting feature here—one that will become very clear in Chapter 8 when we consider the influence of the entertainment industry on names—is that a hybrid diffusion process can also operate—namely, after a name begins to gain a modest number of users, it is picked up in the mass media, which then accelerates the name's growth. An analogous process operates in other areas of fashion: trends in clothing, cuisine, music, and slang often develop slowly within a subpopulation and then, in turn, gain attention when mainstream clothing manufacturers, restaurants, musical groups, entertainers, and the like accelerate the diffusion to the population at large. In clothing fashions, for example, there are stores catering to those customers who want novel and unusual fashions. A popular item in this subset of stores may then be marketed in other stores catering to those with an adventurous taste and eventually gets picked up in mainstream stores.

Status

One can easily understand the temptation to speculate about how taste in names follows a diffusion process from high- to low-status groups—even though the empirical evidence in recent decades fails to support such a proposition. It is, however, vital to understand a basic distinction between *diffusion* and *imitation*. If there is imitation, then there is diffusion, but there can be diffusion in the absence of imitation (see Lieberson 1995). The existence of diffusion hence is not evidence that imitation is the cause. Imitation implies that one subset copies the choices made by another because of that subset's special characteristics (as in the class diffusion proposition discussed earlier). Diffusion also occurs for reasons other than imitation; in the case of fashion, it may simply reflect an awareness of new tastes—regardless of their origins. Put another way, music and clothing are excellent examples of mainstream tastes that are often initiated in smaller subsets of the population that themselves are not necessarily attractive to the mainstream. If social class, for example, plays a role, it may be through the imagery associated with a particular name or some other fashion, rather than through its actual use by a higher-status group. *Tiffany* is a good example. The name is derived from a fancy and expensive image, but its usage is not predicated on its occurrence as a name for higher-status girls: *Tiffany* is "originally a name given to girls born on the Epiphany (January 6), but it became almost obsolete until the 1960s. The film *Breakfast at Tiffany's* (1961) made the name of the fashionable New York jeweler's widely known, and managed to associate the name with Audrey Hepburn, and with luxury. Parents quickly responded and by the late 1970s it was being especially well used by black American families, often in variant forms" (Dunkling and Gosling 1983, 274).

A further implication of the diffusion process is that the mass media can spread a new taste more rapidly. This is an empirical question that merits additional study, but it also implies that the growth curve for names not spread through the mass media will peak later. In practice, this is a sticky matter to study, because the response to an initial media source may not be immediate—if the population most affected has not yet reached childbearing age (say, the effect of a name used on a popular Saturday morning television show directed toward young children).

One critical feature of fashion impels change above and beyond the basic requirement that tastes change. The model of fashion developed here entails unintended consequences that operate because of incomplete information available in the world of fashion. Adopters of different tastes end up with fashions (or in this case, children's names) that they might not have chosen were they fully aware of the choices going on around them at the time *and* able to know what choices would later be made. This lack of full information is a very powerful consideration. To take a nonfashion example, suppose I am in a city where there is an unmet demand for a luxury hotel. I decide to build such a hotel. Now consider the ramifications of information. After concluding that an unmet need exists that could be profitable, I learn that six other high-quality hotels are under construction. I will have second thoughts—this was a good idea if certain conditions were met, but now the market will be flooded and there will be more supply than demand for the foreseeable future. If I had not found out about these other projects, I might well have gone forward with my construction and suffered a loss. Also, even if I know that there are no current projects in the pipeline, I am vulnerable to the acts of builders in later years that again may undercut my demand-supply assumptions.

The hotel construction example is somewhat analogous to a taste choice—but the problems in making a fashion choice are greater. When one buys clothing, it is much harder to scope out what others are buying at the same time than it would be to determine upcoming hotel construction projects. And, of course, it is even harder to know what names are being used for children born at the same time, let alone what future parents will be doing. (I have encountered numerous parents who, at the time they named their child, were unaware that a relatively large number of other parents were choosing the very same name.) At a later time, of course, the name given at birth will be so much a part of the child that parents are unlikely to find it unattractive and change it. Yet the point remains: the choices would be different—depending on the disposition of parents on the popular-unpopular continuum—if parents *had* fully known about developments at the time of choice and in the near future. A certain instability is thus inherent in fashion because of the "errors" this collective process generates. Change will occur just because some people will want new fashions worn by virtually no one else and likewise some parents will want novel names for their children—or at least names that are not too common. And, of course, the collective process leads to consequences that may later be unattractive to people who made the choices they made, and the ensuing readjustments can in turn hasten further changes in fashion.

The *succession* process reflects this lack of complete information at the time a choice is made, which in turn means that a given taste choice can easily turn out—in its social context—to be different from what one imagined. A name chosen because it is relatively uncommon could prove to be very popular; likewise, a popular name could turn out to be either more popular or less popular than one imagined. Names are not discarded like out-of-date clothes. The special feature of names is that change occurs primarily through shifts in the choices made by successive cohorts coming from the same subpopulations of society. The tastes in names change not only because some dispositions expand in the society and other dispositions decline (an important factor in the long-term) but also because parents with the same dispositions as those in an earlier cohort will make choices that differ from their predecessors' choices. Unlike the hotel construction problem, or the analogous problem for the purchaser of stock who seeks to anticipate its future value, tastes in names do not incorporate the same effort to make a "rational" decision based on what the future is likely to bring. Tastes of this sort are not matters of "strategy" or "negotiation," but they have an implicit element of a similar quality. Namely, a name's appeal will be affected by the decisions of others, and these are unknown and probably less likely to be estimated or estimated correctly. As a consequence, once tradition loses its control over the choice of names—that is, once names become a matter for taste considerations—the influence of collective processes on tastes becomes powerful and ignorance about the choices being made will generate highly volatile shifts.

One final point. Although I have been describing this collective model in terms of how a single preference of individuals (the desired *popularity* of a name) is transformed into outcomes that are often not the desired one, tastes are obviously a function of other dispositions that can be included in the general collective model. If, for example, names connote certain images, the distribution of names may overload the imagery and make them unattractive. Likewise, the etymology of names can be overloaded (if, say, an enormous number of girls are given French names or Old Testament names, and so forth). Or the sounds of names can change in appeal, depending on how popular or unpopular they become. In all of these cases, not specific names themselves but a collective attribute of names is being favored or rejected.

7 Ethnic and Racial Groups

Ethnic and racial groups in the United States, with their diverse histories, provide rich opportunities to observe macrosocietal conditions interacting with internal mechanisms to generate distinctive tastes.[1] The naming behavior of blacks, Southeast Asians, Mexicans, Jews, and other ethnic and racial groups in the United States allows us to view the way tastes reflect symbolic considerations, assimilation, segregation, generation, religion, and historical practices before immigration. African Americans, of course, have a long and tumultuous history; arriving under slavery and going through a postbellum era in which merger and assimilation were key thrusts, before undergoing periods of vigorous confrontation in the assertion of civil rights and a distinctive culture. Black Americans' turn toward their African roots and the unique nature of their experience in the United States both affect their tastes. Americans of Chinese, Japanese, and Korean ancestry share the common handicaps faced by Americans whose origins are not "white," but their histories are distinctive in important ways that make it fruitful to avoid the gross tendency to pool them under the undifferentiated rubric, "Asians." Americans of Mexican descent vary widely in the recency of their location in the United States. Many are migrants; others are American-born descendants from earlier immigration streams; and still others are not migrants at all—their ancestors lived in territories that were annexed into the United States through conquest or purchase. Jews are interesting for other reasons. Although the usual assimilation issues faced by non-

Hispanic whites in the United States also influence Jewish tastes, the group is influenced by religious issues that are more distinctive than those confronted by the vast majority of European migrants to the United States, who are of Christian background (even though their specific denomination has a bearing on naming tastes). It is especially interesting, however, to see how name choices reflect both these macrosocietal influences *and* the simple movement of tastes that occurs regardless of special circumstances.

THE JOINT RELEVANCE OF INTERNAL MECHANISMS
AND EXTERNAL INFLUENCES

Symbolic association can be a far more subtle and nuanced mechanism than simply the enhancement or contamination of a name throughout a population. Even among assimilating groups, symbolic meanings are not uniform. The symbolic enhancement or contamination of taste, in this case a name, may not be the same for all subsets of the population—indeed, the symbol may be attractive to one and unattractive to the other (or at least neutral for one). A less extreme feature is that the symbolic attachment mechanism for a given taste is stronger for one subset than another. The tastes of white ethnic groups in recent years illustrates this mechanism. In some instances, the groups find a particular name appealing—but not equally so—because its symbolic meaning varies among them. Occasionally, a name shows up that is radically enhanced for only one group. All of this occurs in the context of a broad movement of specific white ethnic groups becoming more like each other in their major naming preferences.

Another mechanism that is operating here—again in the context of assimilation—is the impact of existing tastes on later tastes. The mechanism whereby tastes usually change gradually and are influenced by existing forms is nicely illustrated in the case of the names Mexican-American parents (born in the United States) choose for their daughters. The strong linguistic connection among Mexicans, between gender and the linguistic character of names, actually influences which popular Anglo names Mexican-Americans adopt in the United States. Even as members of this group move away from Spanish names and toward those employed in the larger society, existing Mexican tastes still drive their choices.

The same mechanism, whereby the appeal of new tastes reflects earlier tastes, also affects the names created by African Americans. In this case, the thrust is not toward similarity with dominant white tastes but away from conventional preferences. Even so, the influence of earlier tastes on new names also operates; witness the way these names reflect features of existing practices (in this case, particularly referring to the delineation of gender). In earlier periods of history, however, there is a symbolic influence on the names white slaveowners chose to give blacks and, in turn, a symbolic contamination of these names among blacks after emancipation.

The desire of Chinese, Japanese, and Korean immigrants to adopt names favored by whites influences their choices. The rapidity of this adoption is noteworthy. Again, background cultural features affect the relative appeal of names widely used in the United States. Korean choices, particularly in the names immigrants give their American-born children, reflect a distinctive cultural feature—namely, that many Koreans are practicing Christians. A pre-migration disposition toward many biblical names thus affects the choices after migration. Again, there is the tendency for new tastes to reflect existing ones—even when changes in taste are under way. The influence of the imitation mechanism is noteworthy for immigrants because they are often disconnected from current developments in the newly adopted society. For this reason, earlier popular names affect their choices—thereby generating a lag in tastes. American-born parents of Chinese, Korean, and Japanese origin have a closer link to general taste developments in the United States—since they are part of that society—and the imitative source for their tastes largely disappears. In addition, there is a shift in the biblical name choices made by second-generation Korean parents.

Jewish naming choices exhibit several different mechanisms, again operating in the context of an initially strong shift away from many names favored in Europe. Earlier, some names used by the dominant society were so appealing to Jews that they eventually become associated with Jews. This then generates a symbolic contamination for non-Jews, such that they avoid the names; in turn, the very strong Jewish association makes them less appealing to Jews as well. Examples are of this process are *Seymour, Stanley, Sheldon,* and *Morton.* The influence of Judaism and Christianity on choices is a clear example of a symbolic association. For Jews, the Bible consists of the Old Testament; for Christians, there is the New Testament as well. Accordingly, names associated with either part of the Christian Bible can appeal to Christians, whereas historically among Jews, not only is the New Testament an unacceptable source for names, but names associated with the New Testament as such are symbolically contaminated. This shifts through the years, as some Jews become increasingly assimilated and lose touch with conventional Jewish religious practices. A striking pattern occurs in recent years where Jews are as likely as non-Jews to use names derived from the New Testament, albeit favoring Old Testament names over others. A more complicated set of mechanisms, suggestive of imitation influencing a long-term trend, is also uncovered in the more recent resurgence of Old Testament names for Jews and non-Jews alike. This is an imitation process operating within a broader, long-term change.

This brief summary does not fully explain the internal mechanisms affecting the naming choices of various ethnic and racial groups in the United States. As we shall see, each of these cultural groups exhibits far more complex patterns of collective behavior in choosing their children's names.

ASSIMILATION

Given the strong thrust toward assimilation among most groups that migrate to the United States, the names immigrants give to their American-born children often differ from those preferred in the homeland. Many traditional old-country names may be difficult for Americans to pronounce (if they are not from an English-speaking nation), or they may simply have a set of morphemic features that sound "alien" to Americans. As assimilation occurs through a variety of processes, these names decline in use among succeeding generations. Traditional old-country names are simplified to meet American speech standards, are simply changed by children who were given them, or are supplemented by added "American" names. Indeed, migrants themselves sometimes drop their original name, replacing it with an "American" one.

"American naming practices" are nothing more than the names in use by the descendants of all of the immigrants who have preceded the latest migration wave. (With the exception of American Indian names, as well as invented names first occurring in the United States, names in the United States are adaptations of names that can be traced to foreign sources.) Many names appear in a variety of languages but differ in their pronunciation or spelling. Some of these are biblical and are part of the inventory known to many Christian groups, as well as to Muslims and Jews. *A Dictionary of First Names,* for example, lists cognates for *John* in Irish, Scottish, Welsh, French, Breton, Italian, Spanish, Catalan, Galician, Portuguese, Basque, Romanian, German, Low German, Dutch, Danish, Norwegian, Swedish, Polish, Czech, Russian, Hungarian, and Finnish (Hanks and Hodges 1990, 180). One common form of shift simply involves using the English

vhen immigrant parents name their American-born children (or even
__ng this change for their own names), as when *John* is used instead of *Juan*,
Jean, *Ivan*, *Jens*, *Johann*, *János*, or *Giovanni*. *John* is exceptional; the number of
cognates and the breadth of its usage is not typical. Yet the shift toward the
English form frequently occurs, even though some parents still favor a non-
English form, such as *Maria*, a form of the English *Mary* that appears in many
languages (Hanks and Hodges 1990, 223–224, 228–229). Obviously, immigrants
from Christian, Muslim, and Jewish sources are almost certain to share various
biblical names—even if they are spelled and pronounced differently. But this
commonality applies to a far greater range of names. The non-English equivalents of *Margaret*, *William*, and *Richard*, for example, decline after migration to
the United States. Even when the immigrant names are easily pronounced in
English and their phonemes are attractive in terms of currently favored English
sounds, they rarely catch on—at least at first. Very likely the association of these
names with immigrant groups—and possibly groups regarded as inferior or
possessing unattractive characteristics—keeps them from spreading. This can
and does change, particularly as the group gains social standing and their image
improves. At a later point the name may also catch on through a different source
(as, say, through its use by a performer or as the name of an attractive fictional
character).

The net result is that many of the names, widely used in the immigrant
homelands, quickly lose favor in the United States. In *The American Language*,
H. L. Mencken provides numerous examples of immigrant names that experience a rapid loss of popularity in the United States (1963, 632–642). *Johann*,
Hans, *Conrad*, *Caspar*, and *Gottfried* were once common names among German
immigrants. Likewise, *Kunigunde*, *Waldburgia*, *Irmingard*, and *Sielinde* were
common female names among German immigrants that slid into oblivion in
short order after emigration to the United States. Popular Norwegian names
that lost ground include *Anders*, *Fritjof*, *Halvor*, *Leif*, *Nils*, and *Thorvald* for boys
and *Astrid*, *Ragna*, *Sigrid*, and *Solveig* for girls. Mencken also describes the
decline of previously popular names among Spanish, Portuguese, Romanian,
Italian, Finnish, Jewish, Polish, Irish, Ukrainian, Russian, Czech, Bohemian,
Greek, Armenian, Syrian, Hungarian, Chinese, and Japanese sources. In some
instances, names are converted to an existing English name, such as *Franz* into
Frank and *Ludwig* into *Lewis*. *Eric(k)*, *Carl*, *Karen*, and *Dolores* are rare cases of a
distinctive immigrant name becoming popular in the United States.

White Ethnic Groups in Illinois

Of all the groups entering the United States through the centuries, none epito-mizes the assimilation model more than the descendants of Europeans who migrated to the United States during the heyday of immigration, from the inception of the nation through the great cut-off of the mid-1920s. A variety of economic, cultural, and social criteria all point to the merger of these groups (see Lieberson and Waters 1988; Lieberson 1996). Tastes in names among nine major white ethnic groups in Illinois are no exception.

In each group the prominent names given to boys and girls overlap substan-tially with those favored by other whites (table 7.1).[2] This overlap is particularly high for boys. Nineteen of the 20 names most commonly chosen for the sons of British, German, or Scandinavian origin are also among the top 20 for the remaining whites—almost a complete match in prominent tastes.[3] At the very least, in the case of sons of Irish or Mexican ancestry, 15 of their top 20 overlap with the choices among all other whites. The overlap is not as great for girls' names (ranging from 18 for German and 17 for both French and Scandinavian), but with the exception of Mexican girls (10), at least 15 of the top 20 are also prominent for the daughters of other whites.

Symbolic Dimensions The merger of tastes among white ethnic groups is con-sistent with H. L. Mencken's examples from past years. Yet an important ethnic influence continues to operate, even though it is muted and secondary to the union of tastes across ethnic lines. First, a certain symbolic statement of attrac-tion to—or pride in—the individual's ethnic group does show up. Although Mencken is undoubtedly correct in observing an earlier decline in the use of dis-tinctive names—particularly among groups from non-English-speaking coun-tries—at present names may again be used precisely because they are ethnic markers and so gain a new appeal. This is concurrent with an increase in the favorable image of these groups through the years, as well as with an ethnic revival stimulated by the African-American cultural movement (see Fuchs 1990, 337). Even in earlier periods, ethnic naming choices occur as a way of displaying pride in periods of both conflict and calm. Louis Adamic (1942, 131–134) asserts that the visit to the United States of Crown Princess Ingrid of Denmark in 1939 made her name quite popular in the Northwest, presumably due to the strong Danish presence there. He likewise observes a revival of Finnish first names as these immigrants developed pride in their origins in response to the 1939–1940

Table 7.1. Overlap in white naming preferences, by ethnic origin of mother, Illinois, 1985–1988

	Overlap in top-20 choices with all other whites	
Ethnic origin of mother	Sons	Daughters
American	16	16
British	19	15
French	18	17
German	19	18
Irish	15	15
Italian	16	15
Mexican	15	10
Polish	17	16
Scandinavian	19	17

Note: Data are for children of American-born mothers of the ethnic ancestry specified; the "American" ethnic response refers to mothers specifying this category for the ethnic entry

Russo-Finnish War, a conflict that which generated widespread admiration for Finland among Americans. He also mentions that many Japanese Americans imprisoned in detention centers during World War II switched back to their Japanese given names.

Consider a present-day example, Irish tastes. Irish-American parents are far more likely to give their children names with an Irish connection than other parents. *Ryan, Kevin, Patrick, Brian, Sean,* and *Timothy* all rank higher for Irish sons than other sons (table 7.2). *Kevin,* for example, was the 6th most popular name given to Irish sons during a period when the name ranks 25th for the white sons of all other groups.[4] *Michael* is an exception; the name does have a long history in Ireland—indeed, *Mick,* one of the pet forms, evolved into a slur word for referring to the Irish (Coghlan 1979, 88). Yet this name enjoys such widespread popularity that it is the top name not only for Irish sons but for all other white groups during this period. A similar Irish tilt shows up among the names given to daughters: *Catherine, Kelly, Caitlin, Erin,* and *Kathleen* are especially popular with Irish parents (table 7.3). Although *Megan* is actually a Welsh nickname for *Margaret,* apparently many Americans incorrectly attribute its origins to Ireland (Dunkling and Gosling 1983, 190–191). Accordingly, its use for Irish daughters also merits inclusion here as another example of the preference

Table 7.2. *Prominent names of sons, by ethnic origin of mother, Illinois, 1985–1988*

Rank	British	French	German	Irish	Italian	Mexican	Polish	Scandinavian
1	Michael	Michael	Michael	Michael	Michael	Michael	Michael	Michael
2	Matthew	Matthew	Matthew	Matthew	Anthony	Daniel	Matthew	Matthew
3	Christopher	Christopher	Daniel	Daniel	Joseph	David	Daniel	Eric
4	Andrew	Daniel	Christopher	Ryan	Nicholas	Anthony	Joseph	Andrew
5	Ryan	Andrew	Ryan	John	Matthew	Jose	Christopher	Daniel
6	Daniel	Ryan	Andrew	Kevin	Daniel	Christopher	Brian	Ryan
7	John	Robert	Brian	Patrick	Christopher	Joseph	Nicholas	Christopher
8	David	Nicholas	David	Brian	John	Nicholas	Steven	Brian
9	Brian	Joseph	Nicholas	Christopher	James	Eric	David	Steven
10	James	Brian	Eric	James	Ryan	Juan	Ryan	John
11	Nicholas	John	Steven	Sean	David	Matthew	John	John
12	Steven	Steven	Joseph	Joseph	Steven	Robert	Andrew	David
13	Robert	James	John	Timothy	Robert	Steven	Robert	Kyle
14	Kyle	Eric	Kyle	Thomas	Brian	Andrew	James	Nicholas
15	William	David	Robert	Robert	Andrew	Joshua	Kevin	Robert
16	Eric	Justin	James	Andrew	Thomas	Adam	Eric	James
17	Joshua	Kyle	Joshua	David	Mark	Jonathan	Thomas	Joshua
18	Joseph	Adam	Kevin	Steven	Jonathan	Carlos	Jonathan	Kevin
19	Jonathan	Thomas	Adam	Nicholas	Kevin	John	Timothy	Joseph
20	Kevin	Jonathan	Timothy	Kyle	Jason	Alexander	Adam	Timothy

Note: Data are for children of American-born mothers of the ethnic ancestry specified

Table 7.3. Prominent names of daughters, by ethnic origin of mother, Illinois, 1985–1988

Rank	British	French	German	Irish	Italian	Mexican	Polish	Scandinavian
1	Sarah	Ashley	Sarah	Megan	Nicole	Jessica	Amanda	Sarah
2	Catherine	Jessica	Ashley	Catherine	Ashley	Amanda	Jennifer	Ashley
3	Ashley	Amanda	Jessica	Sarah	Jessica	Christina	Sarah	Catherine
4	Elizabeth	Sarah	Amanda	Ashley	Amanda	Vanessa	Jessica	Jessica
5	Jessica	Jennifer	Jennifer	Kelly	Jennifer	Jennifer	Ashley	Amanda
6	Amanda	Catherine	Catherine	Jennifer	Christina	Crystal	Catherine	Jennifer
7	Megan	Nicole	Megan	Jessica	Lauren	Melissa	Lauren	Megan
8	Jennifer	Lauren	Nicole	Caitlin	Sarah	Sarah	Stephanie	Emily
9	Rachel	Elizabeth	Elizabeth	Amanda	Catherine	Erica	Nicole	Nicole
10	Lauren	Brittany	Stephanie	Elizabeth	Stephanie	Ashley	Kristin	Elizabeth
11	Emily	Stephanie	Lauren	Erin	Danielle	Stephanie	Megan	Kristin
12	Laura	Megan	Brittany	Nicole	Samantha	Nicole	Elizabeth	Amy
13	Stephanie	Emily	Rachel	Lauren	Megan	Elizabeth	Samantha	Brittany
14	Kelly	Amy	Kristin	Stephanie	Elizabeth	Maria	Michelle	Stephanie
15	Brittany	Rachel	Amy	Kathleen	Michelle	Samantha	Melissa	Lauren
16	Lindsay	Samantha	Emily	Brittany	Brittany	Veronica	Amy	Kelly
17	Amy	Danielle	Kelly	Mary	Kristin	Jacqueline	Kelly	Rachel
18	Nicole	Heather	Laura	Samantha	Gina	Monica	Laura	Laura
19	Allison	Christina	Samantha	Kristin	Melissa	Victoria	Christina	Lindsay
20	Rebecca	Michelle	Melissa	Amy	Angela	Michelle	Kimberly	Melissa

Note: Data are for children of American-born mothers of the ethnic ancestry specified for Irish names. The opposite symbolic influence also operates: names with an English association do less well among the Irish—an antipathy that doubtless reflects longstanding conflicts over Ireland. *Andrew,* probably associated with the English—thanks to its use by Britain's royal family—is less popular with the Irish. The name ranks 16th among the Irish—lower than among any other group—particularly when compared to sons of British, French, German, or Scandinavian ancestry. *Ashley* and *Heather,* both names of English origin, are less popular among the Irish. The lesser popularity of *Brittany* among Irish daughters may also be explained in these terms; the name is linked not only to an area of France but also to *Britannia,* the island of Great Britain.

Religious factors also influence Irish tastes. *David, Joshua, Jonathan,* and *Adam*—leading Old Testament names among whites during this period—are less popular among the Irish. The only exception is *Daniel*—which is an Old Testament name of long-standing use in Ireland (Coghlan 1979, 36). By contrast, the names of some major New Testament figures are more popular among the Irish: *John, James,* and *Thomas.*[5] There are not too many major biblical names in the top 20 for girls, but there is the same tendency as for sons: *Sarah,* an Old Testament name, is equally popular among Irish and other whites, but *Rachel* is more in favor among other whites. *Mary,* by contrast, still occupies a fairly prominent position with the Irish, despite its decline elsewhere.

In varying degrees the other ethnic groups also respond differently to the leading names—if only in the level of attachment to them. *Andrew, John, James, Robert, Kyle,* and *William* are favored by British parents. These names have a contemporary or historical tie to Britain. The set of distinctive British preferences for daughters does not display an obvious pattern. German naming preferences, for both boys and girls, are remarkably similar to those exhibited by other whites. Because of the unpopularity of many German symbols in the United States, due to the two world wars, one may speculate that German symbolic ties are minimized. *Eric* and *Kristin* are frequently given to the offspring of German parents, and these are names that have German links. Their popularity among German parents, however, may be abetted by their non-controversial ties with Scandinavia.

Compared to the German ethnic group, parents of Scandinavian origin are probably less likely to feel an inhibition to use a name associated with their European roots. As a consequence, their preference for *Eric* is much stronger (it is the third most popular name for the sons of Scandinavians) and at least modestly stronger for *Kristin* (the 11th most popular name for daughters). The basis of other differences are not always neatly pinned down. *Steven*, for example, ranks higher for Scandinavian boys. One possibility is the transformation among immigrants of the name *Sven* into *Steven* reported by Mencken (1963, 633). The influence of French ethnic origin on parental choices shows up in their greater preference for several girls' names of French origin: *Amy, Danielle*, and— to a lesser extent—*Nicole* and *Michelle*. *Robert*, long in use by the British and Americans, is originally a French name. In turn, it remains especially popular for sons of French ancestry in Illinois.

Americans of Italian ancestry favor several names with an historic link to their European origin—indeed to an exceptional degree for some names. *Anthony*, the second most popular boys' name for Italian sons, ranks 34th for other whites. *Giuseppe* is a very popular boys' name in Italy. Its English form, *Joseph*, ranks third for Italian sons, compared with 15th for others. Likewise, *Marco* was once a very popular name in Italy (see Yonge 1884, 134–135), and this in turn generates greater use by Italian Americans of an English form, *Mark*. Two Italian names, *Gina* and *Angela*, rank 18th and 20th, respectively, among Italians, but 120th and 45th for others. For reasons that are not obvious, two French names are especially popular among Italian Americans, *Danielle* and *Michelle*, as is the *Nic*-prefix, *Nicole* for daughters and *Nicholas* for sons. Ethnic preferences may thus reflect more than simply the appeal of names that symbolize group membership. The groups will also differ in such characteristics as social class, generational distance from the time of immigration, attitudes towards the group (and therefore the desire to emphasize or deemphasize group membership), and other tastes that in turn affect name choices. It is, of course, easier to interpret preferences that reflect a clear link to the group such as use of a traditional name (say, *Anthony*), or a name that can represent or symbolize group membership even if it is not a traditional first name (say, *Kelly*).

Parents of Polish origin also have some special preferences and antipathies, different from other white Europeans, but I am hard pressed to account for such preferences as Steven, Lauren, Kristin, Michelle, and Kimberly. Predominantly Catholic groups are less likely to favor Old Testament names. This is true here for *Rachel* and *Joshua*, but it is not so for *Sarah* or *Jonathan*, *David* or *Daniel*. (Many Jews in the United States descend from Polish-born immigrants, so it is possible that this category reflects the divergent tastes of Polish Catholics and Jews.) Mexican naming preferences display a tendency to retain the Spanish form of names that have popular English versions. This is unusual, compared to the leading choices among the other ethnic groups, where continuity occurs through use of the English version of the name or the Old World version if it is the same as the English form. Here we see that *Jose, Juan,* and *Carlos* (in English, respectively, *Joseph, John,* and *Charles*) are popular for the sons of Mexican-American parents—as is *Maria* for girls. Mexican Americans and other whites exhibit other taste differences as well.

Fashions in Ethnic Names

White ethnic groups, as we can see, mainly favor the same prominent names. Still, an ethnic influence remains—some preferences are either historically grounded in the group's distinctive history or serve as a contemporary symbolic representation of the parents' ethnic origins. The ethnic group itself can become fashionable in the naming process, such that names suggesting a particular group may appeal to a far larger segment of the population. "Irish" names are a good example of this trend. The popularity of Irish names for both boys and girls grows tremendously in Illinois between 1916 and 1989.[6] Many of these "Irish" names are not popular in Ireland—indeed, many are not conventional Irish names. Rather, some were recently adopted as first names outside Ireland in a setting where their Irish association appeals to many parents. *Kelly* and *Ryan,* for example, are Irish surnames converted to first names; *Shannon* derives either from its use as a surname or the name of the river; *Erin* is a Gaelic word that for centuries was a poetic name for Ireland, though not a first name (Hanks and Hodges 1997, 82, 224). For reasons discussed earlier, I also include *Megan* here. Although Irish Americans especially favor these names, the names appeal to other white ethnic groups, though not so strongly (see tables 7.2 and 7.3). Consider, for example, the use of boys' names among blacks during this period. There may be a modest lag, and *Patrick* does not catch on as well, but overall a similar pattern is visible. In 1989, the same 5 names occur in the top 50 for both black and white boys born in Illinois. (There is not a comparable black preference for girls' names.) These results are another fine example of the taste cycle mechanism discussed in Chapter 6, in which a given name starts slowly and increasingly expands as parents begin to look around for related tastes.

In brief, the world turns upside-down for groups that are of low regard when they first migrate to the United States and who are mainly not at all eager to continue using their Old World names (particularly if they were from a non-English-speaking source). Although tastes among white groups strongly merge, some descendants now use names that are or were associated with their ethnic ancestry. As social conditions change through the decades, groups may begin to

Table 7.4. Popularity of "Irish" names in Illinois by year of birth and race, 1916–1989

Sons

Whites

No names in top 50: 1916–1940

1945	Patrick				
1950	Patrick	Kevin			
1955	Patrick	Kevin	Brian		
1960	Patrick	Kevin	Brian		
1965	Patrick	Kevin	Brian	Darren	
1970	Patrick	Kevin	Brian	Sean	
1975	Patrick	Kevin	Brian	Sean	Ryan
1980	Patrick	Kevin	Brian	Sean	Ryan
1985	Patrick	Kevin	Brian	Sean	Ryan
1989	Patrick	Kevin	Brian	Sean	Ryan

Blacks

No names in top 50: 1916–1950

1955		Kevin			
1960		Kevin	Brian		
1965	Patrick	Kevin	Brian	Darren	
1970	Patrick	Kevin	Brian	Sean	
1975	Patrick	Kevin	Brian	Sean	
1980	Patrick	Kevin	Brian	Sean	
1985	Patrick	Kevin	Brian	Sean	
1989	Patrick	Kevin	Brian	Sean	Ryan

Daughters

Whites

No names in top 50: 1916–1935

1940	Kathleen					
1945	Kathleen					
1950	Kathleen					
1955	Kathleen					
1960	Kathleen	Kelly				
1965	Kathleen	Kelly				
1970	Kathleen	Kelly	Shannon			
1975	Kathleen	Kelly	Shannon	Erin	Megan	
1980	Kathleen	Kelly	Shannon	Erin	Megan	
1985	Kathleen	Kelly	Shannon	Erin	Megan	Caitlin
1989	Kathleen	Kelly	Shannon	Erin	Megan	Caitlin

Blacks

No names in top 50: 1916–1965

1970		Kelly				
1975		Kelly				
1980		Kelly				
1985		Kelly				
1989					Megan	

Notes: Names shown in years when they are among the 50 most common names for the specific race. Names examined for each period are: *Sons:* Barry, Brendan, Brian, Darren, Kelly, Kevin, Neil, Patrick, Ryan, Sean; *Daughters:* Caitlin, Colleen, Doreen, Erin, Kathleen, Kelly, Maureen, Megan, Mona, Shannon.

appeal to others. The positive imagery associated with their names now becomes appealing to others, too. In effect, these European groups have assimilated to the tastes of the larger society, but others have also assimilated to these groups. It is what I call the "pizza effect": just as this initially foreign food is also operationally now an American food, so some "foreign" naming tastes have become American naming tastes. As such, *Kelly* is not a distinctive marker of Irish ancestry. Certainly, it is the 5th most popular name for girls of Irish descent in Illinois in the years 1982–1986—higher than for any of the other groups. But *Kelly* is also among the top 20 names for daughters of British (14th), Scandinavian (16th), Polish (17th), and German (17th) parents. *Kelly* may be a somewhat greater identifier for Irish daughters, but it is not a sharp identifier of Irish ancestry—just as eating pizza is hardly a marker of Italian origin.

MEXICAN AMERICANS IN TEXAS

The tastes of Mexican Americans in Texas provide a remarkable example of how shifts in taste owing to external influences (migration to the United States) are molded and modified by existing tastes stemming from traditional (in this case, Spanish) naming processes. This gives us a chance to observe the joint influence of both external forces and internal mechanisms of taste.

One way to examine these trends is to look at, for every fifth year from 1965 through 1990, the names given by two subsets of the Mexican population living in Texas: Mexican immigrants (foreign-born persons of Mexican origin living in Texas at the time of their child's birth) and Mexican Americans (American-born parents of Mexican origin living in Texas at the time of their child's birth). We can then compare these naming tastes with the names popular among Anglo parents (non-Hispanic whites born in the United States and living in Texas) and black parents in Texas (table 7.5).[7]

Between 1965 and 1990, the preferences of immigrant Mexican parents have little in common with those of Anglo parents.[8] Of the 20 most popular names given to sons of immigrant parents from Mexico, as few as 2—and no more than 5—are favored by Anglo parents (col. 1). The overlap is somewhat greater for daughters' names (from 4 to 7 of the 20 most common names are shared by Anglos and Mexican immigrants). Mexican immigrants tend to maintain traditional names for sons while being more likely to use fashionable—hence changeable—names for daughters (see Rossi 1965 for another example).

The power of assimilation shows up in the names that Mexican-American

Table 7.5. Twenty most popular names: overlap between Blacks, Mexicans, and Anglos in Texas, 1965–1990

	Number of top 20 names shared				
	Mex-FB and Anglos	Mex-U.S. and Anglos	Mex-FB and Mex-U.S.	Blacks and Mex-U.S.	Blacks and Anglos
Year	(1)	(2)	(3)	(4)	(5)
Sons					
1965	4	10	11	4	7
1970	2	10	9	5	7
1975	2	10	8	6	8
1980	2	11	8	8	10
1985	2	13	7	10	12
1990	5	15	8	10	10
Daughters					
1965	6	10	14	8	10
1970	5	12	11	3	6
1975	4	15	9	4	5
1980	5	14	9	6	7
1985	7	11	12	7	8
1990	7	14	8	5	4

Notes: Mex-FB = Mexican children born in Texas whose mothers are foreign-born Mexicans

Mex-U.S. = Mexican children born in Texas whose mothers are Mexicans born in the United States

mothers give their children (col. 2). Without exception, the overlap with Anglo tastes is far greater than it is among Mexican immigrants. The naming tastes of Anglos and American-born parents of Mexican origin are still different from one another, but merger in their naming tastes is impressive. In fact, Mexican Americans largely overlap more with Anglos than with Mexican immigrants (cols. 2 and 3).

Mexicans and Blacks

Is the bond between groups that are popularly referred to as "people of color" in the United States stronger than the bonds they have with American whites?

This issue commonly crops up in discussions of contemporary race and ethnic relations in the United States. Obviously, children's names are a small part of broader questions about socioeconomic gaps, residence, political matters, and alliances among groups. But first names do measure actual cultural behavior rather than mere ideology or attitudinal preferences. Texas provides us with an opportunity to look at the similarity between Mexican Americans and blacks, as contrasted with each group's overlap with whites. Throughout, Mexican-American tastes overlap more with Anglo choices than with black preferences (compare cols. 2 and 4). In some years, the gaps are modest (girls in 1965 and boys in 1985), but they are persistently in the same direction. Moreover, the overlap that does exist between Mexican-American and black tastes only reflects the dominant impact of Anglo naming preferences. Names that are popular among blacks but not Anglos are almost never among the 20 most commonly used names for Mexicans; by contrast, a number of the names that are popular for Anglos—but not blacks—are also favored by Mexicans. In effect, if a name is favored by blacks (or Mexicans) but not Anglos, then it will not be favored by the other non-Anglo group. The overlap in names favored by both blacks and Mexican Americans—though small—reflects the fact that these names are popular in the Anglo world. If a name is not popular among Anglos, then it is extremely unlikely to be favored by *both* black and Mexican parents—one or the other may favor it, but not both. By contrast, names that are used by Anglo parents may also be chosen by either black or Mexican-American parents without being chosen by the other minority group.

An example based on the leading names given to daughters in 1985 illustrates these points. Seven names are among the 20 most frequent choices made by both black mothers and Mexican-American mothers. These are: *Ashley, Christina, C/Krystal, Erica, Jennifer, Jessica,* and *Stephanie.* All 7 are also among the 20 leading choices for Anglo daughters. Not one name shared by Mexicans and blacks is absent from the Anglo top 20. And yet, Mexicans share an additional 4 names with Anglo daughters that do not make the list of leading black names in 1985 (*Amanda, Elizabeth, Laura,* and *Melissa*), and similarly, blacks and Anglos both favor *Brittany,* although Mexicans do not. The dominant society is an Anglo society, and their culture is a culture that affects other groups. Blacks and Mexicans each have their own subcultures, but they are entwined in both the Anglo culture and their own. Rarely, however, do blacks and Mexicans in Texas share a common taste for names unless that taste is also held by Anglos.

The Influence of Existing Practices

As observed earlier, new tastes do not occur in a vacuum; rather, existing tastes influence new tastes. Although changes occur in the direction of the dominant host society, these shifts are also influenced by the tastes existing among Mexicans at the time of their immigration. Comparisons between Mexican immigrants and the dominant Anglo culture involve three sets of tastes: those in the United States but not commonly followed in Mexico; those in Mexico but not commonly followed in the United States; and those common to both settings. The third is of minimal interest to us, because they facilitate assimilation without special adjustment. The impact of the first two on Mexican choices in the United States, however, helps us to see how existing tastes influence new tastes—even when there is a movement toward assimilation.

The decline in the use of *Jesus* among Mexicans in Texas illustrates how tastes common to the migrants' homeland adjust to practices in the receiving society. *Jesus* is widely used in the Hispanic world, "where it is regularly bestowed as a token of Christian faith" (Hanks and Hodges 1990, 177). By contrast, *Jesus* (or its equivalent in other languages) is not used in many other cultures, and it is certainly avoided in the American tradition, regardless of the parents' beliefs. Because there is a laissez-faire policy in the United States (unlike such nations as France and Germany) parents are free to choose any first name they wish. Only Anglo cultural norms restrain Mexican-American parents from naming their son *Jesus*. *Jesus,* a very popular and admired name used by Mexican immigrants for their sons born in Texas, exhibits a clear and substantial decline in favor among American-born parents of Mexican descent—and this is exactly in keeping with the naming norms found in the English-speaking world. *Jesus* is the third most popular name given to the sons of immigrant mothers born in Texas between 1965 and 1990 (between 2.5 and 3.5 percent of sons born after migration to Texas). By contrast, among the sons of American-born mothers of Mexican ancestry (hence at least second generation) from 1 to about 1.5 percent are named *Jesus*. In 1985 and 1990, the name declines in rank such that it is the 19th and 18th most popular name given to the sons of these American-born mothers.[9] Of course, we would expect other common Mexican names to decline if they rarely occur among Anglos—regardless of whether they violate an Anglo naming taboo. *Jose* and *Juan* (the first and second ranking boys' names used by immigrants in Texas), for example, also decline among the sons of American-born parents of Mexican descent. The decline in *Jesus,* however, is steeper.[10] The antipathy toward giving a son this name is learned by the descendants of Mexican immigrants and accelerates its decline (in effect, becoming another example of the contamination effect described earlier).

Were our concern simply to view naming choices as an indicator of cultural assimilation, then we have accomplished our task.[11] This itself is an important matter; naming data provide an opportunity to study one facet of cultural change in a relatively rigorous manner, much as we can examine socioeconomic features. A group's movement toward cultural assimilation, however, involves more than dropping features that are unattractive to the receiving society. Not all the names popular among immigrant parents disappear among the American-born generations. Likewise, American-born parents of Mexican origin do not favor *all* of the most common names used by Anglo parents for their children. Are there mechanisms that help us understand the specific names that Mexican-American parents favor? Premigration tastes also impact on the adoption of the host society's tastes—in this case, their names. Again, this follows from a simple principle proposed earlier, that existing tastes influence new tastes.

The names of Mexican-American daughters are a good example of this general principle. The *a*-suffix is a strong gender marker in Spanish: among the 225 names from Spain and South America (excluding Brazil) listed by Connie Lockhart Ellefson in her popular book *The Melting Pot Book of Baby Names,* fully 80 percent have *a*-endings (1987, 178–183). By contrast, this ending occurs only once among the listing of Spanish boys' names (181–183). Among Mexican immigrants, a similar *a*-ending pattern occurs for children born in Texas. Of the 20 names most frequently given by immigrants to their sons born in Texas, not one ends in *a*. Among the 20 most common girls' name in each period, however, the number with *a*-endings ranges from 15 to 18 (table 7.6, col. 1). Observe that there is only a modest decline in the frequency of *a*-endings among the daughters born to second- and later generation mothers of Mexican origin (col. 2). Keep in mind, however, that *a* is a rather common ending for females in many other cultures (see, for example, Lieberson and Mikelson 1995). Between 1965 and 1990 from 10 to 13 of the top names used for daughters of Anglo parents in Texas also have names ending in *a* (col. 3)—although the preponderance is less overwhelming. If the mechanism under consideration here (namely, that the development of new tastes is deeply influenced by the existing tastes) helps us understand how parents pick the names of their children, then this leads to a specific expectation: Mexican Americans are more favorable disposed toward

Table 7.6. Occurrence of a*-endings in the 20 most popular names given to Mexican and Anglo daughters, Texas, 1965–1990*

| Year | Number with *a*-endings | | | Influence of endings on the new names adopted by Mex-U.S. mothers Percentage adopted | |
| | Mex-FB | Mex-U.S. | Anglos | *a*-ending | Other ending |
	(1)	(2)	(3)	(4)	(5)
1965	17	17	13	56 (9)	0 (5)
1970	18	15	12	50 (8)	43 (7)
1975	18	14	11	75 (8)	63 (8)
1980	18	15	10	71 (7)	50 (8)
1985	16	14	10	33 (6)	29 (7)
1990	15	14	10	86 (7)	33 (6)

Note: In columns 4 and 5, number of relevant Anglo names indicated in parentheses

using Anglo names for their daughters if the name ends in an *a*-sound and are less inclined to use names without an *a*-ending.

The *a*-ending among popular Anglo names for girls does indeed influence its appeal to second-generation Mexican-American parents.[12] Of leading girl's names that are popular for Anglos but not for immigrants, those that end in *a* are more likely to be adopted by second-generation Mexican Americans than are other popular Anglo names that do not end in *a*. The differences are sometimes modest, but they are consistently in this direction—no minor matter considering the size of the overlap (compare cols. 4 and 5). Compared with Mexican immigrants having children in Texas, second- or later generation mothers of Mexican origin are more likely to favor the names that Anglos give their daughters. The influence of past tastes still operates: the suffix so exceptionally common for female names in Spanish—and certainly a gender marker among names popular in the United States—affects the chances that Mexicans will copy a name from Anglos. Names closer to the premigration dispositions of Mexicans have greater appeal when they switch to the practices in the receiving society.

Because Spanish has no male gender-linked suffix as ubiquitous as the *a*-ending among girls, an analogous analysis for sons is not possible. The antipathy of Mexicans in the United States toward *Joshua,* however, is at least consistent with the general conclusion. Neither *Joshua* (the only Anglo boys' name with an *a*-ending in the top 20 during this period) nor any other *a*-ending male name appears in the 20 most frequent names Mexican immigrants give their sons. This is expected, for cultural assimilation of immigrant groups is usually only partial, and, in addition, relatively few *a*-ending names are even remotely popular for boys in any case. The naming behavior of second-generation parents is of interest, however. *Joshua* becomes a popular name for their sons, but at a slower pace and in a less pronounced fashion than among Anglos. *Joshua* ranks 13th in 1975 among Anglo sons, 5th in 1980, and third in both 1985 and 1990. Mexican-American parents lag far behind; *Joshua* does not become a top 20 name for their sons until 1985, and it ranks 9th at a time when it is third among Anglos. It approaches the Anglo level five years later, ranking 4th among the sons of the second generation when it is still in third place among Anglos. Just as Anglo girls' names with *a*-endings are favored because they are closer to the existing tastes among Mexicans, likewise the limited evidence for the only major *a*-ending boy's name used by Anglos in this period suggests a resistance to using that name—although eventually *Joshua* gets used by Mexican-American parents.

The Texas experience is by no means novel. Danish choices of Shakespearean names tend to favor names "that are not totally alien in pronunciation and structure to traditional Danish nomenclature" (Kisbye 1978, 601). More generally, it is reasonable to speculate that migrants are more likely to use names in the host society that have sounds that also occur in their country of origin. By contrast, names with sounds that are uncommon in the migrants' homeland and are difficult for them to pronounce (for example, the English "th" for native speakers of French) or with a letter that has a radically different pronunciation in the two languages (the initial letter *J* in English and Spanish) are not going to be adopted by newcomers when they begin to shift to names commonly used in the United States. The opposite process probably also occurs; names with sounds that are difficult for many Americans to pronounce (for example, the guttural *ch* in German) are probably going to decline even more rapidly than other names that were part of the migrants standard repertoire of names.

ASIAN AMERICANS IN CALIFORNIA

Unlike migrants from many other sources (such as Latin America, Europe, and some of the Commonwealth nations), Chinese, Japanese, and Korean immigrants speak languages that are not even vaguely related to English. Even the character-based form of their written languages is radically different.[13] On top of this, the naming rules are different. Given these conditions, what names do Asian immigrants to the United States use for children who are born *after* they have immigrated? Three issues are pertinent: one is simply ascertaining the level of shift toward American choices and away from homeland names. Second, because assimilation involves not merely a shift in names but also a choice of names that are synchronous with other subsets of American society, what are the new choices when migrants drop Old World practices? Third, in contrast with the names given by immigrant parents to their American-born children, what is the level of assimilation in names when we consider the tastes of later generations, namely Asian-American parents born in the United States?

Assimilation

All of these Asian groups adopt "American" names—particularly for sons—at a stunningly rapid pace. Many of the names most commonly given to white children in the mid-1980s in California are also popular among the children of Asian immigrants (table 7.7).[14] Among the 20 names most frequently given to the American-born sons of Chinese, Japanese, and Korean immigrants, 12, 16, and 12, respectively, overlap with those most commonly given to whites. As with Mexicans in Texas, the parents' generation is an important influence. Naming practices among American-born parents of Asian descent are even closer to those of whites; between 15 and 16 of the 20 most common names are the same as occur for the sons of white Americans in California. The shift toward the girls' names common among whites is less pronounced; between 7 and 9 of the whites' top 20 also appear for daughters of immigrants. But this gender gap disappears in the girls' names favored by Asian-American parents; there the overlap with whites is as large as it is for boys. The similarity between the preferences of Asian-American parents and whites is reasonably comparable to the level of overlap found among white ethnic groups in Illinois. Because on average most of the white ethnic groups have probably been in the United States for more generations, the commonality of this shift is impressive.[15]

Density

The influence of residence on naming underscores the strength of the Asian thrust toward the tastes of white Americans and the role played by the parents' generation. In this analysis, all Chinese mothers are divided into those living in an area with either a *high* or *low* density of Chinese residents (based on compilations

Table 7.7. Overlap in the 20 most common names given by white and Asian parents to children born in California, 1982–1986

| | Overlap with whites, by parents' nativity | | | | | |
| | Chinese | | Japanese | | Korean | |
	Immigrant	U.S.-born	Immigrant	U.S.-born	Immigrant	U.S.-born
Sons	12	15	16	15	12	16
Daughters	7	16	7	13	9	17

Note: Asian mothers are classified by their birthplace; white mothers are non-Hispanic and born in the United States; only children born in California are included

from information provided on California birth certificates).[16] A priori, one expects ethnic residential density to play a role in naming practices. Chinese mothers living in dense Chinese areas are more isolated from tastes in the larger society; parents will be more exposed to the practices of other Americans if they live in areas where relatively few Chinese are present.[17] Moreover, selectivity also plays a role because presumably those living in dense areas are less disposed toward assimilation.[18] In fact, segregation is only a modest influence on the leading names chosen by immigrant parents, albeit in the expected direction. Among immigrant Chinese mothers, those living in high-density areas give their children names that are slightly more dissimilar from white choices (table 7.8). Location has no impact on the names American-born mothers of Chinese descent give their sons; at first glance, it seems to have a substantial impact on daughters' names. (I do not believe that too much should be made of this apparent deviation from the general conclusion, however. Because the number of cases of highly segregated American-born Chinese mothers is modest and there is more dispersion in girls' names, very small numbers are influencing these comparisons.)[19] Based on the data, *generation* is *by far* the more important factor, even for offspring of highly segregated parents (especially if unmeasured selectivity biases the data toward a greater causal influence of segregation). Assimilation is rapid—at least on this dimension—and both American-born parents and Asian immigrants strongly favor "American" names for their children. Immigrants do, however, have a weaker connection to popular culture, and that occurs almost as much among those who do not reside in a more *segregated* location.

This somewhat surprising result appears on the face of it to be contradicted

Table 7.8. Influence of residence v. generation on the overlap between prominent names chosen by whites and Chinese, California, 1982–1986

| | Overlap by mother's birthplace and gender of child | | | |
| | Sons | | Daughters | |
Density of Chinese settlement	Foreign	U.S.	Foreign	U.S.
Low	13	15	7	16
High	11	15	6	12

Note: Asian mothers are classified by their birthplace; white mothers are non-Hispanic and born in the United States; only children born in California are included

by conclusions reported by Susan Cotts Watkins and Andrew S. London (1994), who consider a somewhat related question about name-changing among Italian and Jewish immigrants after arrival in the United States early in the twentieth century. They hypothesize that social interaction with outsiders influences the shift toward "American names." I believe, however, that a careful examination of their evidence and reasoning will show that their results fail to support such a conclusion and, in fact, that their results are actually harmonious with the opposite conclusion. (See the Appendix for a more extensive discussion.)

A Broader Merger: A Look at Different Groups

If various ethnic groups all respond to the same set of dominant white tastes, by definition they will have many names in common. This principle is nicely illustrated when we compare each of the three Asian groups in California with the choices made by Mexicans in Texas. Ethnic differences in taste drop rapidly.[20] Only 2 of the leading names that Mexican immigrants give their sons are also popular for the sons of each of the three Asian groups. By contrast, American-born parents of Mexican origin have far more overlap with the names chosen by American-born parents of Asian origin (9, 8, and 11, respectively, for Chinese, Japanese, and Koreans compared with Mexicans). The overlap increases for daughters, too. Between 4 and 5 of the girls' names favored by Mexican immigrants are the same as those chosen by immigrants from the three Asian cultures. The analogous overlap between American-born parents of Mexican and Asian extraction ranges between 7 and 9. Because of the common orientation toward the choices of non-Hispanic whites, groups migrating from radically different cultures share an increasingly common set of leading first names. Note, however, that the overlap is by no means complete.

It is common to encounter discussions of Asians as if they were somehow different from other Americans. Compared with the immigrant generations, the naming choices of American-born parents from these three different countries also show an increased overlap with the choices made by one another. The average overlap among American-born parents of Asian descent, however, is the same as each has with native whites.[21] This means that the shared tastes of the different Asian groups is simply a byproduct of their rapid assimilation to prevailing white tastes. This is the same process that operates in Texas—except that there is a more limited overlap between blacks and Mexicans.

Dated Choices: A Look at the Specific Names

Let us look at the 20 most common names given to the daughters of immigrant Asian mothers born in California between 1982 and 1986 (table 7.9, cols. 1, 2, and 3). At first glance, these names appear unremarkable. In comparison with the preferences of Mexican immigrants in Texas, the choices among mothers from China, Japan, and Korea are quickly moving into the white mainstream.[22] For all three groups of daughters, *Jennifer* is the most popular name—as it is for California whites (col. 7). Most of the other names, moreover, will be familiar to readers acquainted with American culture. There are some exceptions, of course. Four of the popular names given to Japanese daughters are clearly of Japanese origin: *Mariko, Mari, Megumi,* and *Emi.* In addition, a relatively uncommon name for whites in California, *Naomi,* has a certain international appeal because it works in both Japanese and English. There is a plausible explanation for these uncommon choices: not all of these Japanese mothers are permanent immigrants to the United States. Many Japanese families are living temporarily in the United States either as Japanese nationals on assignment to a Japanese company's American operations or as college and graduate students at American universities. Under these circumstances, some foreign-born Japanese parents would prefer either a distinctly Japanese name or one that will serve in both American and Japanese cultures. Notwithstanding these exceptions, all three groups have a strong disposition to adopt "American" names—a conclusion that is all the more obvious if we consider the dominant names in their countries of origin.

Table 7.9. Names most frequently given to daughters born in California, by ethnic origin and generation, 1982–1986

Rank	Immigrants			American-born			
	Chinese (1)	Japanese (2)	Korean (3)	Chinese (4)	Japanese (5)	Korean (6)	Whites (7)
1	Jennifer	Jennifer	Jennifer	Jennifer	Jennifer	Jessica	Jennifer
2	Stephanie	Michelle	Grace	Stephanie	Kristin	Jennifer	Sarah
3	Jessica	Lisa	Christine	Kimberly	Lauren	Nicole	Jessica
4	Tiffany	Stephanie	Jane	Jessica	Nicole	Kristin	Ashley
5	Christina	Christina	Sarah	Michelle	Stephanie	Ashley	Amanda
6	Michelle	Christine	Esther	Lauren	Jessica	Michelle	Nicole
7	Christine	Sarah	Christina	Christina	Ashley	Kimberly	Megan
8	Catherine	Jessica	Michelle	Kristin	Allison	Melissa	Catherine
9	Karen	Erica	Jessica	Catherine	Michelle	Amanda	Heather
10	Amy	Amy	Catherine	Nicole	Kelly	Lindsay	Stephanie
11	Jennie	Mariko	Susan	Allison	Sarah	Christina	Christina
12	Diana	Naomi	Diana	Tiffany	Erin	Catherine	Melissa
13	Linda	Catherine	Hannah	Melissa	Melissa	Stephanie	Rachel
14	Angela	Nicole	Jennie	Ashley	Kimberly	Lauren	Michelle
15	Nancy	Emily	Elizabeth	Kelly	Amy	Heather	Elizabeth
16	Annie	Melissa	Stephanie	Sarah	Christina	Megan	Kristin
17	Lisa	Mari	Janet	Megan	Catherine	Sarah	Crystal
18	Melissa	Megumi	Angela	Elizabeth	Stacy	Elizabeth	Amber
19	Kimberly	Emi	Sharon	Rachel	Amanda	Laura	Lindsay
20	Alice	Tiffany	Eunice	Lindsay	Lindsay	Rachel	Kelly

Taking a closer look at the list of names in table 7.9, we can see that many of the choices lag behind those in the dominant white culture. They are not "strange" or "odd" names—rather, some *were* once prominent names among whites. *Michelle*, for example, is more popular among the daughters of all three Asian immigrant groups than among whites. This name first reached popularity (the top 20 for all races combined) in 1964—about twenty years earlier than the period under consideration here. Although still a popular name, it was in gradual decline beginning in 1975. Mothers migrating from Japan and China favor *Stephanie*, a name that first become popular some years earlier (reaching the top 20 in 1967) and had peaked in 1972. *Naomi, Amy, Erika,* and *Lisa* are also "dated." This is the case—although perhaps less obvious—for names such as *Lisa*, peaked much earlier for whites in California. Among the Chinese, *Stephanie* enjoys a far more favorable position than the name has ever held among whites. *Jennie, Diana, Linda, Nancy, Annie, Lisa,* and *Alice* are all familiar names, but they are nowhere as popular in the 1980s for whites, nor were they for at least several decades before.[23] The California-born daughters of Korean immigrant women display a similar pattern. *Grace, Jane, Esther, Susan, Diana, Jennie, Janet, Sharon,* and *Eunice* are all names that had peaked much earlier for daughters of native white mothers. In the 1980s, they are far more popular among Korean immigrants than whites.

Boys' names show a pattern of similar lags among the names chosen by immigrants for their sons (table 7.10). Among the sons of immigrant Chinese, for example, the top 20 includes *Alan* and *Henry,* names that peaked far earlier for native whites. Likewise, names in decline among whites—such as *Eric* and *Jeffrey*—enjoy far greater favor among Chinese in 1982–1986. The same may be said about the positions of *Steven* and *Mark* among the sons of Japanese immigrants. Of the 20 most frequent names given by Korean immigrants to their sons, many fare less well among sons of native whites: *James, John, Paul, Edward,* and *Peter.*

This temporal gap from white tastes largely disappears among the choices of Asian parents who were themselves born in the United States. This is suggested by even a cursory survey of the leading names given to the daughters of American-born mothers of Chinese, Japanese, and Korean descent (cols. 4, 5, and 6). As is the case for daughters, the boys' names in favor among American-born Asian mothers have less obvious lags from the names popular among American-born white parents during this period.[24]

Table 7.10. Names most frequently given to sons born in California, by ethnic origin and mother's generation, 1982–1986

	Immigrants			American-born			
Rank	Chinese (1)	Japanese (2)	Korean (3)	Chinese (4)	Japanese (5)	Korean (6)	Whites (7)
1	Jonathan	Christopher	Daniel	Christopher	Michael	Christopher	Michael
2	David	Michael	David	Michael	Christopher	Michael	Christopher
3	Michael	David	James	Matthew	Matthew	Matthew	Matthew
4	Christopher	Jason	Michael	Brian	Brian	David	Ryan
5	Kevin	Brian	Brian	Ryan	Ryan	Jason	Daniel
6	Eric	John	Andrew	Jonathan	Kyle	Daniel	David
7	Jason	Steven	John	Jason	David	Joseph	Joshua
8	Steven	Matthew	Christopher	Kevin	Brandon	Eric	Brian
9	Andrew	Daniel	Jason	Steven	Kevin	Brian	Robert
10	Jeffrey	Andrew	Paul	Brandon	Eric	Jonathan	James
11	Brian	Sean	Joseph	David	Daniel	Richard	Steven
12	Alan	James	Edward	Eric	Jeffrey	Justin	Nicholas
13	William	Ryan	Eric	Daniel	Jason	Brandon	Andrew
14	Daniel	Jonathan	Jonathan	Justin	Robert	James	John
15	James	Kevin	Steven	Nicholas	Sean	Timothy	Jason
16	Alexander	Robert	Peter	Andrew	Jonathan	Nicholas	Sean
17	John	Jeffrey	Richard	Jeffrey	Steven	Ryan	Justin
18	Richard	Mark	Eugene	Derek	Nicholas	Andrew	Jonathan
19	Henry	Eric	Samuel	Robert	Scott	Kevin	Joseph
20	Matthew	Nicholas	William	Aaron	Justin	Joshua	Brandon

Accounting for These Lags

The three Asian immigrant groups clearly favor some names that are no longer as popular among native whites. Three plausible interpretations could account for both the large initial gap and its decline in later generations. One is linguistic. Because languages vary in the set of sounds employed, native speakers of each language will have some difficulties in producing certain sounds that are standard in another language. In turn, this will make some names that are popular in English less appealing to native speakers of a different language and thus reduce their use of these names for their children. Parents, then, will consider a wider array of names simply because they encounter difficulties in pronunciation. This aversion will disappear in short order as their American-born descendants become fluent in English. A second factor is that Asian immigrant groups—like all such groups—are not fully connected with contemporary developments in the larger white culture and inadvertently use dated names (obtained perhaps from older movies, popular music, white coworkers, older people with prestige, and the like). Even the stereotypes held by immigrant Asians of popular American names may be dated. (Consider, for example, the names that Americans might think are common in France—say, *Pierre* or *Jacques*—or in Germany—*Hans* and *Heinrich*.) These could be terribly poor choices for migrants who want to give their son a name that blends in with current tastes.

The third factor is particularly applicable to Korean choices. This relates to the influence of different subcultural tastes that may lead immigrant parents to use names from any period that meets this disposition. A relatively large proportion of Koreans are Christian and therefore may choose biblical names because of their special appeal—and these are not necessarily the same biblical names that are in fashion among American-born whites.[25] Hence, such dated names as *Grace, Esther,* and *Eunice* could be popular not because Korean immigrants' knowledge and "feel" for contemporary culture is limited but simply because these names have a special cultural appeal to Koreans. However, there is clear evidence of a lag here as well. Most of the biblical names occurring in the top 20 for the sons of Korean immigrants are less popular among whites than are the biblical names chosen by American-born parents of Korean ancestry. *Daniel, David, James, John, Paul, Peter,* and *Samuel* are all more popular among Korean immigrants than native whites in the years 1982–1986. Fitting the lag interpretation, their use declines among the generation of American-born parents.[26] Migrants, unfamiliar with the receiving culture and yet desiring to shift to the symbols of the receiving society, will make "mistakes" in their estimates of these symbols—particularly when they are themselves part of a constantly changing cultural process. By definition, as assimilation progresses there will be both a greater desire to use these symbols and a better reading of them owing to greater immersion in the cultural system.

AFRICAN-AMERICAN NAMES: CHANGING TASTES

The link between black and white naming tastes reflects relations between blacks and whites in the United States in many ways. There is, however, no simple one-to-one connection. External developments are not free to play out to their fullest—as if operating in a social vacuum. Rather, they are modified by other social forces as well as by the internal taste processes themselves. Existing social influences (as, for example, those linked to gender relations) and internal taste mechanisms (as in the tendency for new tastes to evolve from current ones) combine to restrain and mold the thrusts generated by sociopolitical changes in race relations. As such, African-American names are an amalgam of external events that also simultaneously reflect these other influences.

Slavery

Thanks to Newbell Niles Puckett's remarkable collection of black names (1975, chap. 1), we can consider the 10 most popular names of slave and free black men and women in the 1700s. In effect, this is a comparison between names whites favor for their slaves and the names former slaves take during the same period (table 7.11). Many of the prominent slave names for men are fairly common, but notice that the slaves have the diminutive form rather than the standard name itself: *Jack, Tom, Harry, Sam, Will, Dick,* and *Robin.*[27] *Peter* and *John* are the only two ordinary names that are prominent in their formal version (we will deal shortly with *Caesar*). Freed blacks favor more formal names. *Sam* and *Dick* still occupy the same ranks, but *Jack* and *Tom* decline in popularity, and *Harry, Will, Robin* drop out of the top 10 chosen by free blacks in the South. *John* moves from 9 to 1; *James, George, William* (as contrasted with *Will* among slaves), and *Jacob* are also in the top 10 list for free men. Moreover, no new diminutives appear among the top 10 slave names.

The patterns among black women are similar, albeit less dramatic. Among the 10 most common slave names 5 are pet names: *Bet* and *Betty* (both diminutive forms of *Elizabeth*), *Nan, Peg,* and *Sary*. Only 2 of these diminutives remain

Table 7.11. Leading names of blacks, slave and nonslave, 1700–1800

Rank	Men		Women	
	Slave	Freed	Slave	Freed
1	Jack	John	Bet	Sarah
2	Tom	James	Mary	Hannah
3	Harry	George	Jane	Rachel
4	Sam	Sam	Hannah	Bet(t)
5	Will	William	Betty	Mary
6	Caesar	Peter	Sarah	Phillis
7	Dick	Dick	Phillis	Jane
8	Peter	Jacob	Nan	Ann
9	John	Jack	Peg	Elizabeth
10	Robin	Tom	Sary	Nancy

Source: Puckett 1975, 8–9; based on his collection of 2,883 black names in the eighteenth century

among the top 10 names for freed blacks. Of the remaining 2, *Bet* drops in rank and *Peg* is in a three-way tie for 10th place. By contrast, not one of the 5 standard names popular among slaves disappears from the leading choices of freed blacks. In addition, *Rachael, Ann, Elizabeth,* and *Nancy* now appear. As is the case for men, no new diminutives show up among the manumitted women. There is a shift away from the diminutive version of the formal name (witness *Elizabeth* and *Nancy*).

The names favored by freed blacks in this period were not in opposition to the naming tastes of whites—rather, whites were in opposition to viewing slaves' names in the same way as the names they gave themselves. This is clear when we compare these black names with those popular among whites in Georgia.[28] Four of the top 10 slave names for women are also prominent for whites, compared with 7 of the most common names taken by free black women in the South. In all cases, none of the diminutive black names occurs among whites. There is a similar, though less dramatic, movement for males. Only one of the leading slave names, *John,* overlaps with leading white names; 4 of the freed black names overlap with whites (*John, James, George,* and *William*). As Puckett observes, "The free Southern Black employed his freedom in adopting a name that offered him more dignity and individuality while, at the same time, reflecting an English tradition" (11).[29]

White dispositions toward black men are also revealed in two other features of slave names. During slavery, writes Puckett, white masters often gave their slaves the kinds of names they gave their farm animals.

> The attitude of the master toward the slave was less that of a parent toward his child than that of an owner toward his property. Probate records reveal a tendency to personalize and identify accurately by name all livestock, human or otherwise; mules and cows are often listed by name, and are distinguished from slaves mainly in terms of appraised value. To furnish an interesting comparison, 235 names of mules were abstracted from Lowndes County, Mississippi, Probate Records for 1858. Of this number, 197, or 84 per cent, occur also as slave names, including not only such common names as *Bet, Eliza, Jinny* and *Tobe,* but also such classical names as *Cato, Dianna, Hector* and *Pompey.* [10–11]

Second, as is revealed in the preceding quotation, owners often favored classical names for their male slaves, with *Caesar* being the most common (13). The use of classical and literary names for slaves, I would speculate, reflects irony that implicitly reminds everyone of who the people so named are not—in the same way as a dog named *Prince* or *King* is certain not to be mistaken as occupying a high position in society. Harmonious with this speculation, we observe a relative absence of these classical names among whites.

In some locations at least, there is evidence that black slaves gave themselves other—secret—names unknown to their owners and that this practice continued after the demise of slavery (Turner 1949; Obermiller 1993). Generally, however, African names disappeared. Puckett estimates that nearly 10 percent of male slave names in the eighteenth century may be of African origin. By contrast, less than 0.5 percent of black names are of African origin by the mid-nineteenth century (347). Of interest is how these names are subtly altered in the United States to mesh with the tastes and practices of colonists from English-speaking sources. An *a*-ending is fairly common for male names in the areas of Africa from which slaves came; in the United States, however, this ending has a strong association with female names and is relatively uncommon for males. An examination of Puckett's data shows that about half of male names with an *a*-ending lose the ending in the United States. By contrast, one-third of female names that lack an *a*-ending in Africa gain it in the United States.[30] This is evidence of an internal taste mechanism that modifies the adaptation of African names. Because the African names are new to whites, there is a tendency to make them consistent with American gender markers. This is, of course, not a problem for names known in the Western tradition—nobody in the United States, for example, would think that *Joshua* is a female name.

The Postbellum South

The inclination of freed blacks to use names that are favored among whites continues in the early postbellum era. Overall, London and Morgan (1994) find only modest naming differences between blacks and whites residing in Mississippi in 1910. Their more detailed analysis shows, however, that the racial gap in names increases with each succeeding birth cohort. It is not blacks who are changing: their cohort changes are minimal. (This is not surprising because many blacks favored assimilation during this period.) Instead, write London and Morgan, the increasing gap is due largely to changes among whites attempting to distance themselves from blacks—a need that becomes pronounced after black emancipation and whites seek to reconstruct previously institutionalized barriers. The development of Jim Crow after the Civil War adds weight to this interpretation.

The nature of these gaps (as well as the inspection of how African names are modified in the United States) again raises the view of tastes as the product of external influences combined with internal mechanisms. Naming tastes in the postbellum era overall were changing much more slowly than they do today. Because there was minimal shift among blacks, white changes had to accelerate to pull away from black tastes. As a consequence, this occurs not through the adoption of previously unpopular names—a process that would have been much slower in that era—but rather through a shift toward those prominent white names that were already less popular among blacks.

Popular Names in the North

The names of black and white children in America today differ enormously. These gaps are relatively new, reflecting the influence of profound sociopolitical forces. The outcome, however, is more than the product of these external developments. The process inferred for Mississippi around the turn of the twentieth century contrasts sharply with African Americans' efforts in recent decades to mark themselves off from whites and emphasize their distinctive culture. In this case, the gap does not expand simply because of a shift toward those long-popular black names that were already less favored by whites. Because of the rapid turnover in tastes and the emphasis on rejecting older tastes, these shifts

Table 7.12. Top 20 names for baby girls born in Illinois by race, 1989, 1940, 1920

1989		1940		1920	
Shared by blacks and whites		*Shared by blacks and whites*		*Shared by blacks and whites*	
Ashley	Jessica	Barbara	Joyce	Alice	Helen
Brittany	Michelle	Beverly	Margaret	Anna	Margaret
Christina	Nicole	Carol	Mary	Catherine	Marie
		Dorothy	Patricia	Dorothy	Mary
		Joan	Sandra	Elizabeth	Mildred
			Shirley	Evelyn	Ruth
				Frances	Virginia
White only	*Black only*	*White only*	*Black only*	*White only*	*Black only*
Amanda	Alicia	Carolyn	Betty	Betty	Ethel
Caitlin	Amber	Donna	Brenda	Eleanor	Gladys
Catherine	Ariel	Janet	Dolores	Florence	Lillian
Elizabeth	Bianca	Judith	Gloria	Lorraine	Louise
Emily	Candace	Karen	Gwendolyn	Marion	Lucille
Jennifer	Crystal	Linda	Helen	Marjorie	Thelma
Kelly	Danielle	Marilyn	Jacqueline		
Lauren	Dominique	Nancy	Loretta		
Megan	Ebony	Sharon	Yvonne		
Rachel	Erica				
Rebecca	Jasmine				
Samantha	Kiara				
Sarah	Latoya				
Stephanie	Tiffany				

involve the introduction of novel or rarely used names that rapidly become popular.

The overlap between the prominent girls' names preferred by black and white parents in 1989 in Illinois is small. The lists of the top 20 black and white names have only 6 names in common: *Ashley, Brittany, Christina, Jessica, Michelle,* and *Nicole;* 14 of each group's leading 20 are different (table 7.12). I suspect that most American readers—whether black or white—could easily guess in advance which group favored each of these names. These racial differences are by no means explained by gaps in socioeconomic status. The divergence between white and black mothers with the same education is far greater than the divergence between black mothers of greater and lesser education (Lieberson and Bell 1992, 523–524).

This racial split is absent earlier in the century, when racial gaps in education were even wider. In 1940, the groups had 11 names in common, and many of the other names are not notably "black" or "white."[31] Some striking differences do exist: blacks favor French and other Latin names more than whites do (a taste that still occurs). *Dolores, Jacqueline,* and *Yvonne* are in the black top 20, although in fact whites actually favor *Linda.* Going back to Illinois births in 1920, each group's top 20 includes 14 common names, and the others appear to reflect modest differences in preference—indeed, the names that remain names are relatively important in the group even if not in the top 20.

There is an analogous decline in common tastes for sons, but it is not as dramatic as for daughters. The races share 14 of their top 20 boys' names in 1920, 13 in 1940, and 10 in 1989. Not only do blacks and whites overlap more for sons, but the remaining names in the black top 20 are also less often marked as "black" names because many are also fairly popular among whites. In 1989, for example, of the 10 popular black first names absent from the white top-20 list, 8 are more or less in the top 50 among whites.[32] The only exceptions are: *Darius* (it does not rank among the top 200 names for whites) and *Marcus* (which ranks 129th). By contrast, the racial discrepancies are far greater among the girls' names. Fourteen of the 20 names most commonly used for black daughters are not among the top 20 for whites. Five of the 14 prominent black names do make the top 50 among whites: *Danielle* (24), *Amber* (26), *Erica* (34), *Tiffany* (36), and *Crystal* (42). And *Alicia* and *Jasmine* rank 57th and 76th, respectively, among whites. But the 7 remaining names are infrequently given to whites (*Dominique, Ebony, Kiara,* and *Latoya* do not rank in the top 200 names for white girls) or at best are of minimal significance (*Bianca,* 123; *Ariel,* 125; *Candace,* 130).

Black and white tastes thus clearly diverge during the twentieth century. In addition, there is more "play" in names given to daughters of either race. Girls' names are less traditional and more fashionable (that is, they change more frequently), and they are often not drawn from the existing inventory. Changes in boys' names are less severe, reflecting the role of sons as bearers of tradition. Among black, the more conservative naming trends for boys holds for newly invented names as well; blacks are more inclined to be inventive in choosing names for their daughters than for their sons.

Distinctive Names

In Chapter 3, I described the spectacular increase in the use of newly invented names for African-American children beginning in the 1960s. Even if we assume that this reflects the influence of major external causes, an internal mechanism exerts a dramatic influence on the specific tastes. Strictly speaking, the creation of a new name is limited only by the parents' imagination. In practice, the existing naming practices in the society affect the choices. Because in the United States (and most other societies) names mark the infant's gender, parents who invent names still follow the linguistic connections between gender and naming that exist among the very same set of major names that they are passing over. For example, many of the most popular names given to black and white girls end with an *a*-sound. By contrast, this ending is rarely found among popular boys' names (*Joshua* is the only exception during the period studied). This is the most obvious gender-associated ending, but there are many more. For example, 7 of the 100 most popular names given to black sons end in *d,* as do 9 of the popular names given to white sons, but not one of the leading names given to black or white daughters has this ending (for other examples, see Lieberson and Mikelson 1995, 935–940). Interestingly, those linguistic features occurring in popular names are also employed to identify gender among invented names: subjects who look at samples of actual names parents give their children can guess quite well which names given to sons and daughters (Lieberson and Mikelson 1995). Existing tastes still operate to mold and modify a radically different approach to names.

Name as "Place"

There existed in the South, during much of the twentieth century, what sociologists and others have labeled "the etiquette of race relations." The irony of that phrase is intentional, because it refers to whites' notions about "proper" black behavior. These practices, imposed on blacks, maintained racial differentials in status. In a nutshell, this etiquette meant deference to whites in all incidental forms of contact: blacks having to step out of the way of whites on the sidewalk; whites being served first in a store, even if blacks were ahead of them; blacks being required to give up their seats on buses for whites; black men being punished if their behavior gave even the slightest hint of a sexual interest in a white woman; separate toilets and water fountains; and blacks being required to enter a white person's home through the back door—to name just a few.

It is not surprising that part of this etiquette also included forms of address between the races. Best known, perhaps, was the requirement that blacks address whites by their last name (in the form of Mr. Smith, Mrs. Smith, etc.) and, conversely, that whites used first names to address blacks. As historian Eugene Genovese observes (1972, 445), it was very difficult for a white in the South to call any black man "Mr." The practice of using "boy" to address (or refer to) an adult black man was to become a major issue early in the Civil Rights era—no differently than did the once widespread application of "girl" to adult women subordinates (white or black).

Consider the possible impact of this "etiquette" on the naming process for women living in Augusta, Georgia, in 1937 (when this racial etiquette was in full bloom in the South—the city directory labeled each entry by race).[33] Seventeen of the 20 most common names given black females in Augusta end in a vowel sound (the only exceptions are Louise, Elizabeth, and Alice). These were (in declining frequency): Mary, Annie, Mattie, Carrie, Rosa, Lillie, Emma, Mamie, Hattie, Sarah, Fanny, Louise, Elizabeth, Ella, Julia, Lula, Lizzie, Marie, Susie, Alice, and Janie. White names from the same period start with the same top 2, Mary and Annie, but half end in consonant sounds: Margaret, Elizabeth, Louise, C[K]atharine, Ruth, Frances, Helen, Alice, Lucille, and Ethel.

A variety of interpretations are possible for this gap, not the least being that blacks are simply more likely than whites to report nicknames—therefore, these differences are not true reflections of what appears on their birth certificates. But another possibility stems from the fact that names with vowel endings, particularly nicknames ending in *ee*, are often less assertive and carry a childlike connotation. The language we use with children often adds an unnecessary *ee*-ending, for example, doggie, piggy, kitty cat, bunny rabbit, mommy and daddy (instead of mom and dad), teeny weeny, Mikey (instead of Mike), and so forth. There is also some evidence that nicknames are more common in younger ages and that they indicate intimacy and hence lower social distance (see Skipper 1984, p. 29). In a place and period where there must have been a strong emphasis by whites on keeping blacks in their "place" and when "uppityness" would be punished, it is not totally farfetched to speculate that this pattern reflects an emphasis on their subordination. These racial differences underline the fact that African-American naming practices through the centuries have reflected the changing nature of race relations, both *actual* and *ideological*, from the earliest forced migration under slavery through today.

JEWS

Religions differ in the appeal (and relevance) that various names have for their adherents. An ethnic group's religious affiliation thus often fosters distinctive name preferences. This connection, however, is by no means precise: the strength of individual religious attachments, the popularity of names for the society as a whole (and therefore the attraction of the names for reasons of fashion, rather than religion), the importance that a religion attaches to the names parents choose for their children, and the religion's position in the society will all affect the appeal of particular names. Like the other groups considered in this chapter, Jews comprise an ethnic group. However, they also have a distinctive religion. It is "distinctive" in two ways. First, although the overlap between religion and ethnicity is not total (there are more ethnic Jews than observant Jews), the religion–ethnic origin overlap is far greater than for most ethnic groups in the United States. The vast majority of Mexican-Americans, for example, are Roman Catholics, but they are not the only ethnic group that is predominantly Catholic. The potential influence of Catholicism on naming practices is therefore not unique to one ethnic group. Second, the New Testament is irrelevant to Judaism, creating a gap from Christians that is, by definition, far greater than those among Christian groups.

Three European Examples

The combined impact of ethnic origin and religion can vary widely in ways that are probably linked to currents in ethnic and religious relations from society to society. France in the seventeenth century, Poland during the late nineteenth century and post–World War I era, and Germany during World War I, illustrate some of these variations.

France French culture has traditionally placed a strong emphasis on the commonality of being French, and this emphasis is coupled with a common language that is shared in varying degrees by both Jews and Christians. The gaps that do exist tend to be in the outer reaches of France and derive primarily from regional and linguistic issues. Jacques Houdaille's study (1996) of differences in Protestant and Catholic first names in seventeenth-century France shows how religion can influence naming preferences. *Jean, Pierre,* and *Jacques* are the three most common names given to Protestant boys. Among Catholics, *Jacques* is less popular, but the other two are consistently in the top three. By contrast, Old

Testament names such as *Isaac, Daniel, Samuel,* and *Abraham* show up among the ten leading names on at least one of three Protestant lists, but are not similarly favored by Catholics. Girls' names also show some overlap by Protestants and Catholics. *Marie* ranks very high for both; *Jeanne* sometimes appears among the three most common names in some Protestant and Catholic lists. But *Suzanne,* which is always among the top three for Protestants, is never among the top 10 for Catholics. One possible explanation for this discrepancy is that the Old Testament story about *Suzanne* fits well with a Protestant thematic emphasis about virtue. Another Old Testament name, *Sarah,* is also popular among Protestants but not Catholics. Religious differences thus affect tastes even in a relatively homogeneous society. Faiths are almost certain to differ in both the symbolic meaning they associate with names and in how they evaluate that meaning.

Bialystok Bialystok is located in what is today the northeastern corner of Poland, not too far from Belarus.[34] Before the Holocaust, it was home to a substantial Jewish population, and it is probably reasonably representative of the areas in Eastern Europe from which large numbers of Jews migrated to the United States in the late nineteenth century and early twentieth century. The naming practices here raise two interesting questions: what names did Jews use before migration, and how different were they from names used by other local populations? Using data collected and analyzed from the Bialystok Registar's Office in an outstanding study by Zofia Abramowicz (1993), and translated into English for this project by Edyta Bojanowska (at the time a student at Harvard), we can consider these questions for a period when Bialystok was under Russian rule (1885–1905) and the years of Polish independence between the two world wars.[35]

In 1885–1905, there were three major religious groups in Bialystok: Roman Catholics, Evangelicals (mainly people of German ancestry), and Jews. To a stunning degree, each group goes its own way, with very little overlap in names (and indeed in language). Among the 25 most popular names given by each religious group to their sons and daughters, only a few are held in common:

1885–1905	Boys	Girls
Catholics and Evangelicals	4	5
Catholics and Jews	1	0
Evangelicals and Jews	0	0

Of the 25 most popular names given to Jewish daughters, none are similarly prominent for the daughters born either to Catholics or to Evangelicals, and there is only one overlap between Catholic and Jewish sons (different forms of *Joseph*—a name prominent in both Old and New Testaments). Again, there is no overlap between Jews and Evangelicals. The duplication in tastes between Catholics and Evangelicals is also small.

Poland achieved independence after World War I, bringing with it a new pressure on the population to conform to Polish as the official language. The overlap in names between Catholics and Evangelicals increases, and the data now available for the Russian Orthodox shows their overlap with Catholics to be comparable to the level for Evangelicals. Religious divisions (along with related ethnic and linguistic characteristics) continue to leave the people of Bialystok deeply divided in their choice of names. And yet, Jews remain exceptionally different from the other groups, with the only overlap among the top 25 boys' or girls' names again being the common use of *Joseph* among Jews, Catholics, and the Orthodox.

1919–1939	Boys	Girls
Catholics and Evangelicals	7	8
Catholics and Jews	1	0
Evangelicals and Jews	0	0
Catholics and Orthodox	8	8
Evangelicals and Orthodox	3	6
Orthodox and Jews	1	0

In this setting, ethnic origin and religion overlap strongly for each group—not just Jews. Catholics are Poles, Evangelicals are Germans, and the Orthodox are Russians. Tastes in names are intensely linked to the ethno-religious membership of the population. There is massive segregation.

These two European examples are *examples*—no more and no less. They do not describe the effects of religion on naming practices throughout Europe, but they indicate a level of ethno-religious difference in name use that is relatively uncommon in the United States. Polish society lacked the assimilating forces of U.S. culture, the power of religion was great, and there were pronounced language differences between the groups.[36] Unlike Jews in Western Europe, those living in Poland and in other areas of Eastern and Central Europe were more likely to maintain Yiddish as their mother tongue—even though they learned the language(s) in use by Gentiles. Likewise, their children's names often employed the Yiddish language form. This is itself important because the same name—if used differently—is operationally an unshared name. *Maria* and *Mary*, for example, or *José* and *Joseph* may refer to the same biblical figure, but they are pronounced differently (spelling variations alone, as in *Crystal* versus *Krystal*, would be another matter). Of course, this principle applies to more than biblical names: witness *William*, *Wilhelm*, and *Guillermo* or *Catherine*, *Katinka*, and *Caterina*.

A Brief Comparison with Danzig On display in the Jewish Museum in New York is a memorial plaque salvaged from the Great Synagogue of Danzig. The plaque lists fifty-six Jews "who died for their Fatherland during World War I." The Fatherland, of course, is Germany, for Danzig was a German city until the end of World War I. And yet any visitor who wasn't aware of this fact would have no difficulty determining Danzig's location; nearly all the first names on the plaque are obviously German: Adolf, Artur, Benno, Bruno, Carl, Curt, David, Eduard, Egon, Erich, Ernst, Fritz, Georg, Gustav, Hans, Heinrich, Hermann, Hugo, Julius, Justus, Leo, Louis, Max, Nathan, Oskar, Philipp, Sally, Siegfried, Theodor, Victor, Walter, Wilhelm, and Willy. The contrast with Jews' choice of names in Poland is stark; Danzig Jews are assimilated into the larger society, at least in their choice of names; in Poland, by contrast, they are almost completely segregated in tastes. In general, it would seem, Jews in Western Europe were assimilating rapidly toward the tastes of the larger society. The far more isolated position of Jews in much of Eastern Europe, coupled with their far more intense Orthodox Judaism and the prestige enjoyed by Western Europe, affects naming behavior. (Of course, I cannot fully compare Bialystok and Danzig here in terms of the influence of city size or differences in the Jewish percentage of the population.) The extraordinarily distinctive tastes of Jews in Poland, when compared with those of Germany or the United States (as we shall see below), remind us that internal taste mechanisms are predicated on the external conditions that generate assimilation. On the other hand, the specific names that are chosen from the inventory of popular names hinge on these mechanisms.[37]

California

The differences between the names of Jewish children born in California between 1905 and 1915 and those born in Bialystok not too many years earlier are dramatic.[38] In California the names preferred by Jews and other whites overlap to a far greater degree.[39] Yet this tells only part of the story. At least 14 of the 20 most common Jewish boys' names and 11 or so of the girls' names in Bialystok are from the Old Testament (table 7.13, cols. 2 and 6). Moreover, for both biblical and nonbiblical names, Yiddish is the predominant source of Jewish names in Poland. Although *Leib* and *Iosif* have German and Russian roots, respectively, the Polish influence on names is minimal. As we have seen in many other settings, the smaller number of biblical names among Jewish daughters in Poland can be attributed to the tendency for "play" or "fancy" with girls' names, as in the use of Yiddish or Hebrew names whose English equivalents are *Beautiful, Love, Queen, Rose,* and *Joy.* Columns 1 and 5 of table 7.13 permit a comparison with the names given to Catholic sons and daughters in Bialystok during that period.

Assimilation is far more pronounced in the United States. Even when they use a name popular in the Old World, Jewish parents choose "American" versions rather than Yiddish or Hebrew forms for their children. This is clear among the top 20 Jewish names in California (table 7.13, cols. 3 and 7). Yiddish and Hebrew names fall out owing to a strong intergenerational thrust toward English. To be sure, many parents did not immediately abandon their native language: Old World names could be maintained either without formal inclusion on the birth certificate or as a middle name (as Asians often did).

The Jewish preference for Old Testament names carries over into the United States, though it is distinctly weaker than in Bialystok. Six of the top 20 boys' names and 5 of the top 20 girls' names are from the Old Testament. In each case, this is roughly half the number in Bialystok. One interesting twist on these tastes is similar to the *a*-ending preference of Mexican-Americans: the choice of biblical names among Jews is affected by practices among other Californians. *Joseph,* the only top 20 Old Testament boys' name in use among non-Jews (ranking 7th), becomes the most popular name among Jews born in California. Similarly, *Ruth* is the most popular name given to Jewish daughters. *Ruth* is not a high-ranking name in Bialystok; it is, however, the highest-ranking Old Testament name among non-Jews (ranking 5th). *Elizabeth,* the 7th-ranking female name for non-Jews, is also in the top 20 for Jewish girls.[40] As with *Ruth,* when an Old Testament name is popular among other Americans it can be especially appealing for Jews because it is simultaneously traditional and American. *Mary,* the most popular name for daughters of non-Jews during this period, is also popular for Jewish daughters, though it does not rank as high. On its face, *Mary* seems a surprising choice for Jews—given the general resistance toward New Testament names and Mary's central role in Christianity. Two explanations are plausible: one is that some proportion of Jewish parents were knowingly giving their daughters a popular Christian name simply as an assimilative act; the other is that they confused *Mary* with *Miriam*, the sister of Moses and a traditional name among Jews. *Mary* and *Miriam* are forms of the same name—the difference lies in the sources used to translate the New and Old Testaments. As George Stewart observes about *Mary* in *American Given Names:*

> The name arose from an unusual development of the same name that is elsewhere given as Miriam, occurring in the early Hebrew texts at M-R-Y-M. The Greeks (e.g., in the Septuaguint) rendered this as Mariam. Speakers of Latin, however, apparently took the final *m* as the sign of accusative case, and then assumed a nominative, Maria.
>
> The Vulgate followed this course, inconsistently rendering the name of the mother of Jesus (and of those others of the New Testament) as Maria and the name of the sister of Moses as Miriam. The tremendous authority of the Vulgate assured the adoption of that usage in the languages of western Europe. In English the accent shifted to the first syllable, in accordance with the usual practice in that language.

Because Jews in the United States were rapidly turning to the English forms of the biblical names, they may have not recognized the consequences of naming their daughter *Mary*. It is not possible to evaluate these interpretations, let alone to deal with the possibility that both are operating.

Something of a Puzzle

Because of Jews' rapid shift to English-language names and the fair level of overlap early in the twentieth century between their name choices and those of non-Jews, later developments are surprising. There is no simple progression toward increased commonality in the names favored by Jews and non-Jews over the next eighty years.[41] The highest level of overlap for Jewish daughters is 16, and that is certainly reasonably comparable (albeit unexceptional) with what we see for white ethnic groups in Illinois in the mid-1980s (see table 7.1). That level, however, occurs in the early 1940s, during World War II; it is never reached again through 1984. Indeed, with the exception of Mexican-Americans in Illinois, the overlap for daughters' names is lower than for any of the ethnic groups in Illinois.[42]

The experience for Jewish sons is similar, though less dramatic. In two comparisons, 1954–1955 and 1970–1971, 16 of the most common names for sons are the same for both Jews and non-Jews. This is comparable to the overlap

Table 7.13. *Comparison between names given to Jewish and other children in Bialystok, 1885–1905, and California, 1905–1915*

| | Sons | | | | Daughters | | | |
| | Bialystok | | California | | Bialystok | | California | |
Rank	Catholic (1)	Jewish (2)	Jewish (3)	non-Jewish[a] (4)	Catholic (5)	Jewish (6)	Jewish (7)	non-Jewish[a] (8)
1	Iosif[1]	Abram	Joseph	John	Mariyanna[8]	Khaya	Ruth	Mary
2	Anton[2]	Moisey	William	William	Mariya	Khana	Helen	Dorothy
3	Stanislav	Yakov	David	George	Anna	Sora	Esther	Helen
4	Vladyslav[3]	Khaim	Morris	Robert	Yadviga	Ester	Dorothy	Margaret
5	Ioann[4]	Isaak	Harold	Charles	Bronislava	Sheĭna	Frances	Ruth
6	Aleksandr	Gersh	Harry	James	Gelena[9]	Liba	Lillian	Catherine
7	Frantsisk[5]	Iosif	Charles	Joseph	Stefaniya	Malka	Rose	Elizabeth
8	Kazimir	David	Abraham	Edward	Leokadiya	Rivka	Sarah	Frances
9	Zygmund[6]	Samuil	George	Frank	Iozefa[10]	Sara	Ida	Alice
10	Bronislav	Leib	Albert	Walter	Zofiya[11]	Leya	Anna	Evelyn
11	Mikhail	Izrail'	Henry	Harold	Aleksandra	Rakhel'	Gertrude	Florence
12	Konstantin	Salomon	Robert	Albert	Yanina	Beĭlya	Alice	Virginia
13	Vachlav	Meer	Jacob	Richard	Stanislava	Masha	Jeanette	Mildred
14	Petr	Aron	Samuel	Thomas	Antonina	Dvora	Mildred	Marie
15	Boleslav	Berel'	Jack	Arthur	Apoleniya[12]	Reĭzel'	Bessie	Anna

16	Edvard[7]	Yudel'	John	Henry	Kazimira	Feĭla	Mary	Maria
17	Vikentiĭ	Shmuel'	Arthur	Harry	Viktoriya	Freĭda	Rosie	Marion
18	Feliks	Mordkhaĭ	Benjamin	Francis	Veronika	Pesha	Edith	Eleanor
19	Pavel	Lev	Alfred	Raymond	Felitsiya	Lea	Elizabeth	Edith
20	Adol'f	Movsha	Sidney	Donald	Frantsiska	Ginda	Gladys	Marjorie

Source: Polish data transliterated from original source, Abramowicz 1993, chap. 1

[a] Children of a non-Hispanic white parent who was born in the United States

Notes: [1] Also includes Osip, Yuzef

[2] Also includes Antonii

[3] Also includes Vladislav

[4] Also includes Ivan, Yan

[5] Also includes Frants

[6] Also includes Sigizmund

[7] Also includes Eduard

[8] Also includes Marianna

[9] Also includes Elena

[10] Also includes Yuzefa

[11] Also includes Sofiya

[12] Also includes Apoloniya, Apolloniya

occurring among four of the ethnic groups in Illinois later in the mid-1980s (Irish, Italian, Mexican, and American). Beginning with 1972–1973 and continuing through 1984, however, the overlap of Jewish sons with other white ethnic groups is lower than for any of the nine white groups in Illinois.[43] Of course, we know more about Jewish naming patterns over time than about the other white groups, for which there is only one "snapshot" in the mid-1980s. Moreover, because the Jewish estimates are based on small numbers of cases, they are less stable.[44]

These gaps are "real" in the sense that they reflect more than merely technical factors, but they are not solely due to what might naively be labeled "differences in taste." Jews and non-Jews are responding to similar tastes in names more than the level of overlap would suggest. In fact, part of the difference in their children's popular names results from the *timing* of their choices. In recent decades, names that ultimately become popular for both Jews and non-Jews tend to reach the top 20 earlier among Jews (table 7.14). Thus at any given time there will be some names among the top 20 for Jews that are not yet so frequent for non-Jews but will later reach that point.

The striking difference in timing for newly popular daughters' names is a more recent event—it was not present in the first half of the twentieth century. Among girls' names that become popular between 1905 and 1959 for both Jews and non-Jews, each group is equally likely to be the first to favor the name (reaching the top 20).[45] A radical change occurs from 1960 through 1984 (see table 7.14). Of the 19 names that are newly popular for Jewish and non-Jewish daughters, only 4 reach the group's top 20 at the same time, 3 are initially popular among non-Jews, and 12 names first reach the top 20 for Jewish daughters. Since 1960, when there is a difference in timing for non-Jews and Jews in usage, nearly always it is the Jews who are first (12 of 15 names).[46]

Indeed, the changing popularity of Old Testament boys' names and the lag of non-Jews behind Jews clearly show how external and internal processes interact to create the smaller overlap between Jews and non-Jews and the greater tendency for non-Jews to follow Jewish tastes in recent decades. The only problem is that we need *three* hands to describe what is going on. On one hand, among Jews, Old Testament boys' names initially decline over time, representing a shift from giving boys traditional names to giving sons names that are more popular with other Americans. Ironically, Jews so favored some of the replacement names for their sons that these names in turn developed the same association with Jews (examples are *Irving, Seymour,* and *Stanley*). On the other hand,

Table 7.14. *Priority of names popular among both Jews and non-Jews, California,*
1905–1984

Daughters		Sons	
Jews precede	*non-Jews precede*	*Jews precede*	*non-Jews precede*
1959 or earlier	*1959 or earlier*	*1959 or earlier*	*1959 or earlier*
Janet	Catherine	Andrew	Donald
Janice	Cynthia	Daniel	Edward
Joyce	Donna	David	James
Judith	. Doris	Eric	Kenneth
Julie	Eleanor	Gerald	Paul
Laura	Evelyn	Jack	Richard
Lisa	Florence	Jeffrey	
Lori	Jean	Lawrence	
Marilyn	Margret	Mark	
Michelle	Marion	Scott	
Sandra	Marjorie		
Sherry	Nancy		
Shirley	Pamela		
Susan	Patricia		
1960 or later	*1960 or later*	*1960 or later*	*1960 or later*
Amy	Ashley	Jason	Christopher
Danielle	Kelly	Jonathon	Gregory
Erica	Kimberly	Joshua	Kevin
Jennifer		Matthew	Sean
Jessica		Steven	
Melissa			
Rachel			
Rebecca			
Sarah			
Stacy			
Stephanie			
Tracy			

Note: Year heading refers to when the name first reached top 20 for the group specified

Table 7.15. Old Testament names popular among Jewish and non-Jewish Sons, California, 1905–1984

	Years when name ranks 21–50	Years when name ranks in top 20
David		
Jews	—	Every Period
non-Jews	1905–25	1926–84
Joseph		
Jews	1936–75, 1978–79, 1984	1905–35,1976–77, 1980–83
non-Jews	1948–53, 1956–59	1905–47, 1954–55, 1960–84
Samuel[a]		
Jews	1916–40, 1964–65, 1970–71, 1974–83	1905–25, 1984
non-Jews	—	—
Benjamin		
Jews	1968–71	1905–15, 1972–84
non-Jews	1974–84	—
Jacob		
Jews	1916–30, 1974–79, 1982–83	1905–15, 1980–81, 1984
non-Jews	1980–84	—
Abraham		
Jews	—	1905–15
non-Jews	—	—
Daniel		
Jews	1926–35, 1941–43	1944–84
non-Jews	1905–45	1946–84
Jonathan		
Jews	1948–65, 1970–73	1966–69, 1974–84
non-Jews	1968–79	1980–84
Joshua		
Jews	1958–59, 1964–67	1968–84
non-Jews	1972–73	1974–84
Adam		
Jews	1960–61, 1964–67	1962–63, 1968–69, 1972–84
non-Jews	1974–84	—
Aaron		
Jews	1958–59, 1962–69	1970–84
non-Jews	1968–84	—
Nathan		
Jews	1905–15, 1972–73, 1976–79, 1982–84	—
non-Jews	1976–81	—

Table 7.15. Continued

	Years when name ranks 21–50	Years when name ranks in top 20
Noah		
Jews	1970–71, 1974–75, 1978–84	—
non-Jews	—	—
Joel		
Jews	1974–83	—
non-Jews	—	—
Seth		
Jews	1970–71, 1974–81	—
non-Jews	—	—
Jared		
Jews	1976–77, 1980–84	—
non-Jews	—	—

Notes: Data are for children of a non-Hispanic white parent who was born in the United States; see text for details

[a] "Sam" in the period 1916–25

there is a subsequent resurgence of interest among Jews in Old Testament boys' names. (There is a similar surge for daughters—*Rachel, Rebecca,* and *Sarah*—but the number of leading names is smaller.) This resurgence first becomes obvious late in the 1950s, roughly when African-Americans were beginning to emphasize their own distinctive culture with pride. And on the third hand, the Jewish preference for these biblical names precedes a similar, though less pronounced, shift among non-Jews.

In an earlier chapter, we observed that the New Testament is an important source of major names given to sons but that the overall popularity of New Testament names is fairly steady (even if the popularity of specific names changes). In fact, the cyclical increase in biblical names for sons is due primarily to the rise in Old Testament names. In turn, Jews and non-Jews differ dramatically in the use of these names for their sons such that Jews again precede non-Jews. The pattern is striking: Jews increasingly use Old Testament names for their sons and then these names also become popular among non-Jews (table 7.15).[47] The Old Testament is the source for 6 of the 20 most common names given to Jewish sons born between 1905 and 1915 (*David, Joseph, Samuel, Benjamin, Jacob,* and *Abraham*). The flourish of Old Testament names subsides early in the twentieth century (probably owing to a high emphasis on assimilation); for decades there is little difference between non-Jewish and Jewish boys. *David* is popular among other whites through almost the entire period, and *Joseph* is also popular much of the time (because Joseph is an important name in both testaments, its meaning here is ambiguous). The resurgence of these names starts with *Daniel,* which reaches the top 20 among Jews (1944–1945) just before it does among non-Jews (1946–1947). *David* and *Daniel* are the only Old Testament names that occur among Jews until the early 1960s, when the movement toward such names begins to affect the top 20 for Jews. Now *Adam, Jonathan, Joshua, Aaron, Joseph, Jacob,* and *Samuel* appear among the 20 most popular names for Jewish sons. (The development is slow at first and then quickens.) Also shortening is the time it takes for a name entering the second tier of popularity (ranking between 21 and 50) to reach the top 20. *Jonathan,* in the second tier starting in 1948, does not reach the top 20 until nearly twenty years go by. This period progressively shortens as the appeal of Old Testament names solidifies and expands.

The Issue Among girls, there is clearly a lag; if a name reaches a great popularity among both non-Jewish and Jewish daughters, in recent decades Jews almost always precede non-Jews. This lag is sometimes only a matter of a few years, but at other times it is more substantial. What leads these lags to occur in one direction? There are several possible causes. One is that Jews are generally of higher socioeconomic status than non-Jews and hence more likely to precede others if an imitation mechanism is operating. Yet a rough effort to take socioeconomic status into account provides no support for class imitation. Bearing in mind that many of the lags are of relatively few years, another possibility is that Jews may simply be responding to the same social developments somewhat earlier. The apparent lag then is caused not by imitation but rather by diffusion from the same central source. Yet another nonimitation mechanism could cause this lag: many of the newly popular names for daughters stem from some facet of the entertainment industry. Jews are heavily represented in this industry, and so their tastes in names may influence the names used in the industry for performers and fictional characters. This would be a two-step development: from Jewish tastes *to* popular entertainment, then from popular entertainment *to* diffusion into society at large.

Boys' names follow a different pattern. There is no lag to speak of between Jews and non-Jews in either direction; one group does not precede the other in the same disproportionate manner. However, Jews lead the way in the growing popularity of Old Testament names for sons, adopting more of these names than non-Jews, and, moreover, they also lead the way when both groups end up favoring such a name. Here is how this might come about. Old Testament names have a greater attraction for Jews than others simply because of their symbolic association with Jewish heritage, much as "Irish" names are more popular among those of Irish heritage than among other groups. As Jews feel increasingly free to assert their ethnicity through social changes (temporal—the creation of Israel—as well as generational), Jewish naming fashions change. The earlier adoption of Old Testament names by Jews may actually also reflect these factors. The greater appeal of these names for Jews means that they respond more favorably and more rapidly to additional Old Testament names. Again, we need not think of this as a matter of imitation of one group by another.

These are *plausible* accounts. Yet unless our account is empirically grounded, then it is simply a circular argument—a trap we saw earlier in the interpretations of the decline in the popularity of men's dress hats. It is not possible, with the limited data available here, to perform a more demanding evaluation. In the next chapter, however, we shall analyze the popularity of *Rebecca* with more rigor.

There is little doubt that the naming preferences of various ethnic groups in the United States reflect important external influences. Disposition toward assimilation, nationalism, opposition toward the larger society, symbolism, recency of arrival, and group history are among the external influences on ethnic tastes in names. On one hand, it is extremely difficult for groups to avoid the influence of the larger society on their tastes. It is not impossible, but it would require massive isolation from the dominant society at a level far greater than exists between black and white populations in the United States—to say nothing of the lesser isolation of most other groups at present. It would depend on virtually no interchange between the groups other than exchanges that are void of virtually any social component. The influence of mass media, literacy, and mobility aspirations requiring entry into the dominant society (or at least more than purely asocial forms of interaction) will all undermine efforts to have a set of tastes that are uninfluenced by the dominant society. It would be interesting to see if populations such as the Amish or Hasidic Jews, with their isolation and distinctive customs that appear to reject the practices of the larger society (for example, clothing), are able to avoid the constant shift in popular first names in the larger society. (Such an intergenerational examination would help us locate more precisely the strength of various barriers.)

And yet, we can observe the operation of a number of internal mechanisms. Crucially, old tastes influence new tastes, creating a gradual shift. Those who try to alter their earlier tastes to copy the receiving society's practices are still affected by their old tastes. An exceptionally clear example of this is how Spanish naming customs affect Mexican-Americans' choices when they give "American" names to their daughters. In one form or another, this also influences the naming tastes of Asian Americans, Jews, and—for that matter—African Americans in earlier periods. On the opposite end, African Americans' shifts from existing practices are still affected by these earlier tastes such that newly invented names reflect the phonemic linkages with gender. These outcomes display a process whereby external influences are modified and altered by the earlier tastes of the group. Ethnic tastes in names reflect the conjoint set of external and internal influences.

8
Entertainment and Entertainers

Mass entertainment, though not responsible for the existence of naming fashions, does influence some specific naming practices. In this chapter, we'll consider the impact of names in the movies (both performers and fictional characters), along with the historical influence of novelists. Other important forms of mass entertainment, such as popular music, contemporary fiction, sports, theater, and television, also of course affect naming tastes, and it is generally assumed that the influence of mass media on society's tastes is enormous. One researcher into this phenomenon, Heidi Vandebosch, has reviewed the evidence and conducted her own study. Her conclusions are worth noting here:

> [The] media not only present names to the public, they also make them meaningful. If names are known to prospective parents, and if they evoke positive images, they will be diffused. Often these positive images are based upon an association of the name with one or more well known media personalities, which leads to an increasingly widespread practice of naming children after actors or actresses, sports personalities and the like. Much of the time parents, either deliberately or unconsciously, choose these names in order to induce wished-for qualities into their children (Seeman 1983). Thus, name associations, and often name stereotypes as well, can be influenced by the image of a single famous person bearing the name. It is, however, also possible that namers are affected by the picture of a range of standardized media characters bearing a particular name. Television drama in particular is seen to stereotype names to the extent that they become type names, easily recognizable by their audience.
>
> While positive name associations encourage the selection of names, negative name

associations may lead to a reduction in their use and even to their exclusion; unfavorably evaluated personalities or types can cause this reaction on a scale such that some names can quickly lose their popularity. [1998, 258–259]

A number of Vandebosch's points are excellent. But as we explore this topic we need to keep in mind her observation that claims about the media's role in naming fashions often draw on anecdotal and inconclusive evidence.[1]

STORIES AND NAMES

For a fictional story to *work*—in other words, for it to engage the audience and create the intended impact—the audience generally needs to respond as if what they are reading (or seeing) is real (even though deep down they know it is not). In the performing arts, the audience must put aside the knowledge that they are watching a performer pretend to be someone else.

A fictional character's name is no different than such other attributes as height, weight, age, facial features, diction, hair, clothing, and manners. It is merely one of the devices writers use to create a believable character. Whether that character is the hero or heroine, a villain, teenager, school principal, automobile salesman, detective, grandparent, or any other major or minor part—the name is meant to be plausible for such a character. In other words, the name is part of the imagery that is to be conveyed. It is successful if it helps to make the story work so that the character is believable and the audience (or the reader) responds in the way the creator intends. As Emile Zola wrote in *Dr. Pascal*, "I always judge a young author by the names which he bestows upon his characters. If the names seem to be weak or to be unsuitable to the people who bear them, I put the author down as a man of little talent, and am no further interested in the book" (quoted in Dunkling 1993, 132).

We know that the name given to a fictional character (whether invented or—more often—drawn from the existing inventory of names) may easily affect the popularity of a name (and not always favorably). Likewise, a performer's stage name (whether the birth name, an invented name, or a name drawn from the repertoire) can also affect name preferences. Imagery is associated with all existing names; indeed, even invented names have connotations that are driven by their sounds and associations with other names (Lieberson and Mikelson 1995). For these reasons, the name can advance the character's believability. It can be relatively innocuous, or it can clash with the character and behavior being portrayed. A two-way interaction can ensue when the existing imagery associated with a name is reinforced by the portrayal of the attributes of a fictional character with that name. If the fictional usage has its intended impact, this adds substance to the imagery, reinforcing the stereotypes of the name.

If there is minimal opportunity for characterization—say, in a short story, or a television commercial, or a minor character in a longer story—then stereotypes will be used to convey the intended character (or at least not clash with it). All possible stereotypes—such as those associated with age, physical features, gender, clothing, race, facial features, diction, and the like—are employed to signify the character at a glance. If a dentist's spouse, for example, is to endorse a particular brand of toothpaste in a thirty-second television commercial, then it is vital that every feature of the production instantly lead the viewer to think of the character on the screen as a spouse—rather than as a performer *playing* a part. Nothing can clash with what the audience will instantly accept as a dentist's spouse. It is like looking at an artist's sketch that conveys a picture with a few broad strokes.[2] In a full-length movie, there is less need to employ stereotypes (name being one of them) to ensure the desired response to a character. Even then, a name that goes against stereotype means more work to counter the viewer's initial impression (unless it is meant for the *true* character to be revealed later in the story) and most full-length movies work with stereotypes. In comedies, of course, humor can be drawn when a name is intentionally used to develop a strong clash between the character and the stereotype associated with the name. Think of a "redneck" sheriff in the South whose first name is *Irving* or a gangster named *Percy,* an Ivy League professor nicknamed *Kitty* or the cook in a greasy diner named *Elizabeth.* These hypothetical examples prove the rule. The character's status and the imagery of the name are incongruous, and therefore may be employed for comic purposes or to startle the audience or generate curiosity. Because authors are trying to flesh out a character, however, and they use the imagery associated with names (both first and last) as ways to do this, fictional names by and large are not startling because they are part of the illusion.

Some Types of Names That Writers Use

A writer can use a name to further the portrayal of a fictional character in several ways. Each has the potential of influencing tastes. Before we turn to these, it is important to distinguish between the image intended and the image conveyed. The choice of a given name may be brilliantly successful (as in many of the invented names found in the novels of Charles Dickens) or it may fail to convey the intended imagery. Writers, after all, may or may not be successful in gauging what name will help to generate the desired response (note that I say *help*, not *cause*, because many elements can be used to build a character and the needed response).

Invented Names The novelty of the name may itself be used to convey something about the bearer, such as a lack of conventionality. The sounds used for the name are undoubtedly meant to also convey—or at least be harmonious with—other features of the fictional person. (Phonemes, even when not part of an existing word, still convey images.) Invented names may also resonate with viewers. If the name is linked to an appealing character and the choice of phonemes is appealing, then parents may later give the name to a child.

Names from a Foreign Culture Foreign novels or plays, when translated for a new audience, typically retain the characters' names as in the original or modify them only slightly. It is also almost mandatory that a foreign character have a name associated with his or her homeland. Incidentally, imagery issues play a role here, too. For one, the audience needs to recognize the name as used in the character's homeland. (On this score, it is unlikely that an American writer will name a French male character *Kevin* or *Thomas* even though these names were the two most popular names for boys born in France between 1990 and 1992; Besnard and Desplanques 1993, 21). Second, if the foreign name is well known, the audience may hold stereotypes about it that—ideally—fit the character. With all of this, adoption of the name for children is deeply affected by the disposition toward the particular culture or society. Those that are unattractive to the audience are likely to have names that are thereby unattractive as well, and vice versa.

Relatively Neglected or Unpopular Names In some cases, the author can use the name because imagery is still associated with it (consider *Wanda, Thelma,* and *Lillian* or *Walter, Harold,* and *Francis*). This use draws attention to the name and creates the potential for renewed interest in it. In other cases, a neglected name also has neglected imagery and so provides a shell for the author to develop the fictional character in complicated ways without getting tangled up with existing imagery. A name used in this way can benefit from the association with a newly introduced character and blossom accordingly.

Popular Names A popular name may be used for a character because the name's image is harmonious with the fictional person's status (say, a name favored by working-class parents or a name associated with a region, occupation, or personality trait such as "manly" or "smart"). A popular name may be selected simply because it *is* popular and that fits in with the desired impact. Although the imagery of all names can be affected by the fictional character bearing the name, it is least likely to occur for popular names because the existing imagery is probably more robust and less influenced by one example or another of a character with the name in a story. By definition, of course, popular names have a certain appeal to begin with. So for these names it is as much a question of whether a negative association with a character can weaken its popularity as it is of whether the name's appeal can expand even further.

The impact of a television show or a motion picture on a name can be both massive and rapid. Compare the potential impact of an invented name when it is given to a character in a television show as opposed to a real child in a real family. For the fictional character, the exposure is both massive and simultaneous. For the real child, diffusion would begin with a single source and—without an assist along the way from some form of mass media—has at best the potential for slow diffusion at first, with rapid growth only much later. Even if only a modest number of parents use the invented name occurring in a television show, the children bearing this name become multiple stimuli for its later adoption. Not only do the media differ from an individual's choice in the rapidity of potential diffusion, but there is also a profound difference in the likelihood of the name ever reaching any given level of popularity. In the early stages, there is a far greater chance that the invented name used by one family for their child will, as it were, *abort*—namely, it will never be picked up by anyone else and will therefore disappear. In an earlier chapter we saw this in the case of names with a common phoneme that were invented by African Americans: few of these names eventually reach a level of significant popularity, but many more are dropped. It is not impossible for a name to become popular without the benefit of the media, but it is far less probable. One caution is in order: it is a mistake to automatically interpret minimal usage of an uncommon name appearing in the media as being caused by either the character's failure to be appealing (for the purposes of naming a child) or antipathy toward the name's phonemic structure. Rather, an influence can be delayed *if* the movie or television show appeals only to the audience that is young and not yet in the child-bearing ages. Likewise, a name used initially for a relatively small number of children can expand much later through the contact of these offspring with others. By contrast, a television show or motion picture favored by viewers in their late teens and early twenties can have an almost instant impact if they resonate to the name.

An Old Story

The influence of fictional forms of entertainment on tastes is not a modern phenomenon; it predates television and motion pictures by centuries. The concerns of early writers were no different than those of today's authors: to use names that further the story, to make the characters and situations believable, and to gain the desired response from the audience. Many names owe their initial popularity—or even invention—to novels, plays, and poetry. I will cite examples in no systematic way, but rather to simply exhibit their influence.

Shakespeare was responsible for the popularity of such female names as *Rosalind, Olivia, Portia, Jessica,* and *Juliet.* When writing his book *American Given Names* in 1979, George Stewart found minimal use of *Jessica* in the United States. This he attributes to the name's lack of appeal for Jews (understandable, given its association with the *Merchant of Venice* as the name of Shylock's daughter); and yet, its Jewish connotations at that time lowered its appeal to non-Jews. (Keep this interpretation in mind; it is relevant for a speculation about the changing popularity of *Rebecca* later in this chapter.) *Vivien* owes its popularity as a girl's name to Alfred, Lord Tennyson. Likewise, *Ida* was revived in the nineteenth century as the name of the heroine in Tennyson's *The Princes,* and *Maud's* popularity increased after Tennyson wrote a poem of the same name (Hanks and Hodges 1997, 116, 170, 251).

Many names invented by writers have become popular through the initial story or even a later one. *Pamela* was invented by the sixteenth-century poet Sir Philip Sidney, but it achieved popularity almost two centuries later when Samuel Richardson chose the name for novel his novel of 1742, *Pamela* (Hanks and Hodges 1997, ix). *Ethel* originated in either a novel by William Makepeace Thackeray or one by Charlotte Yonge in the mid-nineteenth century and, in any case, was popularized by these novels (Withycombe 1977, 108). *Wendy* was invented by J. M. Barrie for his play *Peter Pan* in 1904. *Amelia* is also an invented name, being the heroine in a 1751 novel by Fielding (Hanks and Hodges 1997, 10, 254). *Myra* is probably an invented name, stemming back to Fulke Greville, Lord Brooke, a poet who lived between 1554 and 1628 (Withycombe 1977, 225). *Thelma* and *Lorna,* both invented names, are the heroines of Victorian novels: *Thelma: A Society Novel,* by Marie Corelli, and *Lorna Doone,* by R. D. Blackmore.[3]

According to Alfred Kolatch's *Name Dictionary* (1967, 355), *Gay* was invented by Alexander Pope and *Vanessa* by Jonathan Swift. *Miranda* owes its origin to Shakespeare's character in *The Tempest* (Crystal 1995, 150). And although Shakespeare popularized *Rosalind,* the name was invented by Edmund Spenser (Weekley 1939, 133). Sir Walter Scott invented *Cedric* for a character in *Ivanhoe,* and the name later became popular after it appeared in Frances Hodgson Burnett's children's novel *Little Lord Fauntleroy* (Withycombe 1977, 61).

Decisions about the names of fictional characters are influenced by the writer's milieu. If the connotations associated with names vary at different times, then their potential impact will also be altered. Even the choice of sounds for invented names will be influenced by existing tastes for popular conventional names: invented names usually follow gender marking conventions. Moreover, as we have seen, the popularity of various phonemes waxes and wanes over time in orderly ways. Other influences on the impact of names include changes in the social order. Relations with different cultures and societies shift over time, in turn altering the appeal of a name and its meaning. Attitudes toward age likewise change, affecting the literary function of a character whose name is associated, for example, with the elderly. Names associated with authority or "the establishment" may have positive connotations in some periods and negative ones at other times. All of these influences illustrate how writers throughout time have used different names for the same type of character *and,* by contrast, the same name for different characters.

As an example, here are some of the ways that Mark Twain uses names to convey imagery and generate the desired responses among his readers, as observed by George Stewart:

> Huckleberry itself is obviously fanciful, but its common abbreviation, Huck, may be explained as a diminutive of Hugh. The other hero, however, bears a name—Tom— already, for centuries, typically English. With this name, we can only expect him to be a "good guy."
>
> On the other hand, his sneaky little brother is Sid—that is, Sidney—one of the recently introduced snobbish names of English aristocracy, which Twain disliked.
>
> Twain seems to be considering his fictional St. Petersburg as an American village of his own time, that is, of the middle 1840's. Indeed, he was seeing the life of that time through the rosy-tinted glasses of nostalgia. The names which he gives to the schoolchildren project this idea. The boys are Ben and Bennie, Billie, Johnny, Jeff, Jim, Bob, Joe. The girls are Becky, Mary, Gracie, Sally, and Susie.
>
> Though the bearers of such names may occasionally lapse from virtue, they in general maintain the old American tradition. In fact, in this mythical St. Petersburg an unusual name signals aberrant behavior. The hated model boy, for instance being opposed to Bill or Billy—is Willie, a name that had come to suggest something of a

namby-pamby. There is also an Alfred, from whose name we can obviously expect little that is good. Actually, he turns out to be the unsympathetic smartie from St. Louis.

Huckleberry Finn leaving the village behind and entering somewhat into the larger world shows a comparable enrichment of its names. With Harney Shephardson we have an example of the new custom of using a family name. The six Graingerford children display an interesting split. The boys are named in the long-established tradition—Tom, Bob, and Buck (this last, probably, a nickname). The girls, however, echo the Romantic names—Emmaline, Charlotte, and Sophia.

The names of slaves, as Twain presents them, offer no distinction from those of the general population—Jim, Betsy, Elizabeth, Johnny, and Nat. Only Balum (for Balaam) is unusual, but there is no reason why one of the masters should not also have borne that Old Testament name. [1979, 36–37]

THE INFLUENCE OF MOVIES AND STARS ON NAMES: A COMPLEX STORY

To avoid unnecessary confusion, before proceeding we should recognize that *some* movie star names indeed do influence parents' choices of names for their children. A few extremely popular names, moreover, can be traced back to a particular performer. But common assumptions about the impact of performers on the popularity of names are often unsupported by solid long-term information on the timing of the increase in usage. When people observe that a name that is popular at a certain time is also the name of a star they often infer— incorrectly—that the star is the source of the name's popularity.

Many prominent performers have names that are popular in society as a whole. This fact matches the common expectation that stars have an enormous impact on popular tastes in names. In fact, however, the observed connection does not reflect the influence of stars on children's names. The vast majority of prominent star names scarcely affect naming practices, in part simply because there are so many new stars each year in a variety of media—among them popular music, movies, television, and sports, as well as popular models, writers, and and other personalities. Character names also pop up constantly in new television programs, movies, popular songs, novels, and the like. And, of course, the inventory of existing names for parents to consider is huge. Under these circumstances, it is almost impossible that many movie names will become popular names for children.

Cause and effect, in fact, are often reversed from what one expects: many movie stars themselves have names that are either already popular or are increasing in use. This is what I call "riding the curve." Whether a performer's name is already well established or is showing signs of growth, it is easy for a retrospective look at names (without, of course, the suitable statistics) to conclude that the star is the cause of the name's popularity. When Norma Jeane Baker made her debut in 1948 as Marilyn Monroe and became a star two years later, the name *Marilyn* had long enjoyed considerable popularity. Indeed, *Marilyn* had peaked in 1935—more than ten years earlier—when it was the 7th most popular name for white girls born in Illinois. The name was still popular when Monroe became a star, but it was clearly over the hill (*Marilyn* ranks 18th by 1943, 23d in 1948, and 26th by 1950) and continued to move downward (47th in 1955).

The Influence of Movie Stars and Characters

The influence of stars or major characters on naming practices is not easy to ascertain. Some names must be left out of the analysis because they are already important at the time of the star's debut or character's appearance. Because *John* was the most common boy's name when the actor Marion Morrison adopted that name, it is difficult to determine whether John Wayne's popularity influences the name's later use. In recent decades, another name. *Jennifer,* has been exceptionally popular for girls; at its peak, slightly more than 1 of every 20 white girls born in Illinois between 1972 and 1974 received the name. Because the most popular movie of 1970, *Love Story,* centers on an attractive young woman named *Jenny,* a diminutive for *Jennifer,* it is tempting to attribute the name's growing popularity as reflecting this movie. And at first glance, the numbers appear to support this conclusion (fig. 8.1). However, if we look more closely, we see that *Jennifer* was rapidly rising before the release of *Love Story:* it was given to 1 percent of all white girls born in 1965; by 1969—the year before the movie— 2.6 percent were given this name. It is thus difficult to credit the movie with increases in the popularity of the name *Jennifer* during the early 1970s. There is nothing abrupt about the form of the curve to suggest any deviation in the name's growth after the motion picture. On the other hand, there is nothing to show that the movie did not cause the last part of the rise. We would need a very strong model of what the increase in *Jennifer* would have been in the absence of the movie.[4]

The popular child star Shirley Temple (her original name) is another example of someone with an established name at the time of her professional debut. *Shirley* was the 5th most common name for girls in 1928, the year of Temple's

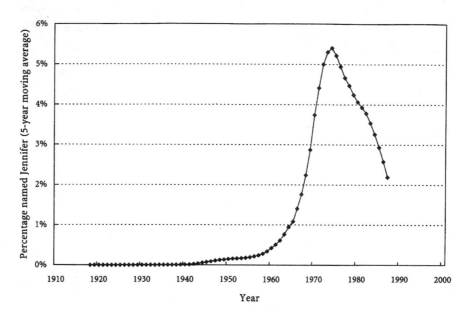

Fig. 8.1. Popularity of Jennifer *among white daughters, by year of birth, Illinois, 1918–1987*

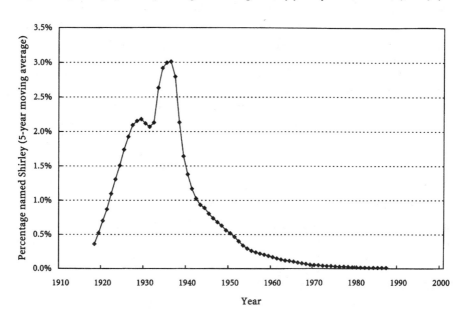

Fig. 8.2. Popularity of Shirley *among white daughters, by year of birth, Illinois, 1918–1987*

Fig. 8.3. Popularity of Jessica *among white daughters, by year of birth, Illinois, 1918–1987*

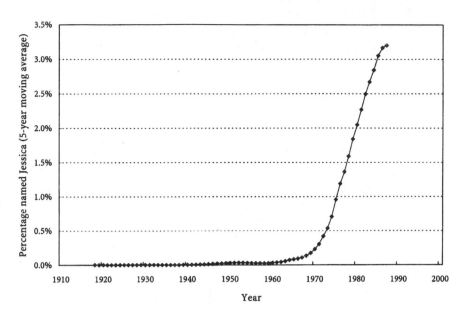

birth. Although still very popular, the name *Shirley* had started to decline in 1933, the year before the child actress became a major star. Starting with 1934, when Shirley Temple received a special Oscar for her contributions to screen entertainment, the decline in the popularity of *Shirley* was reversed (fig. 8.2). *Shirley* climbs to 4th, and in the following year becomes second only to *Mary*. The reign was brief, however: *Shirley* drops to 15th in 1940 and down to 24th in 1945. This brief upward reversal is evidence of Temple's impact on the popularity of *Shirley,* though not enough to reverse for very long the downward trend that had been developing. In spite of her popularity and the name's popularity, it would be a big mistake to attribute any causal connection other than that Temple's parents gave their daughter a popular name.

The actress Jessica Lange provides another interesting example of the confluence of movie stars and names (fig. 8.3). When Lange was born in 1949, *Jessica* was not among the 200 most commonly given names for white girls. As late as 1964, it still was not in the top 200. It slowly began to rise, however. With 67 white girls in Illinois named *Jessica* in 1965, it ranked 166th. It popularity then increased more rapidly, to 152d in 1968, 99th in 1970, 48th in 1973, and 28th in 1975. One year later, in 1976, Jessica Lange made her film debut in *King Kong*. Though the critics panned the movie, it was the third most popular film of the year. *Jessica* ranks 20th in 1976 and continues upward in the following years, in 1986 replacing *Jennifer* as the most popular name for girl babies. Does the Oscar-winning actress Jessica Lange play a role in the popularity of *Jessica?* Given the name's rapid rise before Lange's debut, it is hard to say. What we can say with certainty is Lange is riding the curve, using a name that is rapidly gaining in popularity at the time of her screen debut.[5]

NEW MOVIE STARS

These conclusions about *Jennifer, Shirley,* and *Jessica* are based on impressions obtained by looking at the form of the curve before and after the name becomes prominent. The results are much clearer when the star or character has an uncommon name. A sudden surge in the use of a name after it is a prominent character in a popular movie or the name of a new movie star leaves little doubt about the cause. Likewise, there is clearly no movie influence when a name is barely used both before and after a star or character appears bearing that name. (As noted earlier, uncommon names are likely to the greatest impact anyway, because a character or star with a common name will probably do *relatively* less to focus attention on a name or alter its imagery.) In order to analyze the relative influence of popular culture on babies' names, we can combine a list of movie stars (Peary 1978) with the five top-grossing movies in each year (Sackett 1990) and the best films of each decade (the Citadel Film Series). In this compilation, for every performer nominated for the Academy Award for best leading or supporting actor or actress, I include the name of both the performer and the performer's character. The resulting influence on parents' name choices can then be seen by looking at the names given annually to white boys and girls born in Illinois between 1916 and 1989. Stars and characters who are known by a diminutive, such as Debbie Reynolds and Eddie Murphy, are examined for both the diminutive and full forms of the name (in these cases, *Deborah* and *Edward*).

Stars' and characters' names are then included if, during the first year in which a name appears, no more than 10 children are given that name, and if there is a comparison group of at least 50 other names that first appears in Illinois with the same frequency as the "media" name. We can compare the growth in the popularity of the "movie" name with the growth in these nonmovie names, using the same initial level of popularity as our starting point. Of special interest are the level of a name's popularity at the time of the star's debut (indicating the name's growth before the star's influence) and its level when stardom is reached.[6] In turn, we can consider the popularity of the name both five and ten years after stardom. (The process is similar for gauging the influence of a character's name, although there is no analogue for the debut period.) This procedure allows us to compare changes in the use of stars' or characters' names for children with a relatively large number of other names that are similarly popular.[7]

Stars' Names

When we look at actresses' names in comparison with at least 50 other girls' names with the same initial level of popularity, there is no question that the performers' names became far more popular in ensuing years (table 8.1). Five years after stardom is reached, all but 2 of 28 actresses have names that exceed more than 90 percent of the comparison names (that is, names that start at the same initial level as the star's). The same can be said for male actors; again, the vast majority of their names also exceed the level attained by 90 percent or more of the comparison names. Frequently, however, much of the gain has already occurred when the performer debuts. The growth in a name's popularity that appears to reflect the star's influence is actually caused by a performer using a name that is already popular. This makes sense if we assume that performers take names (or keep their given names) because they think that they will appeal to audiences. The result? A spurious connection due to a choice of either a popular name or one that is in the process of becoming popular (riding the curve).

Many of the stars' names, in fact, are not much more popular than the comparison names. Of actresses' names, 19 of 28 are given to 50 or fewer daughters at the time of their debut (table 8.2). This is the same number at the time when stardom is reached, and it is close to this number (14) five years later. At the other end of the spectrum, considering actresses whose names are extremely popular, the number of daughters with these names five years after stardom is similar to the number at the time of their debut. The most impressive shift is the jump from one to three names that are given to at least 1,000 daughters in a year.

The case is even stronger when we look at the impact of male actors on the popularity of boys' names. In the debut year, the year of stardom, and five years later, 25, 25, and 23 actors, respectively, have names that are given to 50 or fewer sons. A single name given to at least 2,000 boys is present at the debut year and the star year, but none are at this level five years after stardom. All in all, the names of these actors have modest consequences for the names parents give to their sons.

Table 8.1. Popularity of stars' names compared with other names starting at the same level

	Year of debut	Year of stardom	Five years later	Ten years later
Number of actresses				
*Percentage**				
95–100	14	18	22	20
90–94	3	2	1	2
10–89	2	2	2	1
0–10	9	6	2	2
Total number	28	28	27[a]	25[a]
Number of actors				
*Percentage**				
95–100	16	19	20	17
90–94	6	7	3	4
10–89	3	2	4	5
0–10	6	3	3	2
Total number	31	31	30[a]	28[a]

Notes: * Percentage of comparison names that the star name exceeds in popularity
[a] Some star names excluded because data not available on them for the 5- or 10-year period after stardom

With these results, we must question whether such a phenomenon as the stardom effect even exists. Because many of the names that become popular do so in the period before the stars with those names first appear in a movie, it is difficult to conclude that stardom is responsible for the modest gains of ensuing years: later gains could well simply reflect existing conditions. Keep in mind that most names that are uncommon at the time of a star's popularity generate only a minor subsequent increase. Claudette Colbert, Greta Garbo, Lana Turner, Ingrid Bergman, and Racquel Welch, for example, are all major stars, and a modest bump can be traced to each actress's popularity. *Claudette* goes from no daughters in the year of Colbert's debut to 33 girls at stardom, but remains at 33 five years later and is down to 20 girls after another five years. No daughters were named *Greta* in the year of Garbo's debut, but there are only 7 when she first reaches stardom, and 18 and 9 the five and ten years afterward. And before turning downward *Lana* peaks at fewer than 90 daughters, *Ingrid* barely reaches 50 girls, and *Racquel* rises to 80.

Table 8.2. Number of children with stars' names

Number given stars' names	Number of actresses				Number of actors			
	Year of debut	Year of stardom	Five years later	Ten years later	Year of debut	Year of stardom	Five years later	Ten years later
2000+	0	0	0	0	1	1	0	0
1001–2000	1	1	3	2	0	1	1	3
601–1000	1	1	0	1	1	0	1	1
501–600	0	0	1	0	0	0	1	1
401–500	1	1	1	0	0	0	1	0
301–400	1	0	1	0	0	1	0	0
201–300	1	2	1	5	1	1	0	0
101–200	4	4	4	2	1	2	2	2
51–100	0	0	2	3	2	0	1	0
11–50	1	7	5	4	4	5	7	7
0–10	18	12	9	8	21	20	16	14
Total number	28	28	27[a]	25[a]	31	31	30[a]	28[a]

[a] Some star names excluded because data not available on them for the 5- or 10-year period after stardom

Several actresses do, however, set in motion substantial long-term increases in a name's popularity. *Jennifer* owes its popularity to the actress Jennifer Jones, who was born Phyllis Isley and earned the Academy Award for best actress in 1943 at age 24. *Marlene* owes its popularity to Marlene Dietrich (born Marie Magdalene Dietrich in Germany). *Shelley*—a name that attains modest success—clearly rises in popularity due to the actress Shelley Winters (Shirley Schrift).[8]

So we can't really attribute too much to movie stars. Are the names of performers often names that become popular in society? Yes. Are these names usually ones that were either extremely popular by the time that the performer appears or, at the very least, names that were exhibiting a popularity curve showing an unmistakable upward thrust by the time the performer debuts? Again the answer is yes. It is not too surprising that an actress making her debut in 1957 might take the stage name Sandra Dee (who was born Alexandria Zuck in 1944), considering that 1,400 white girls born in Illinois that year were given the name *Sandra*. Likewise, *Rita* is the 43d most popular name in 1926 when Rita Hayworth (born Margarita Carmen Cansino in 1918) debuted uncredited as a dancing child. In other words, causality often runs in the opposite direction: performers are born with—or adopt—popular names.

Although the names of most male actors do better than other names of comparable initial size, here, too, many of these stars' names have a minimal impact on naming practices. Bing Crosby (Harry Lillis Crosby), Boris Karloff (William Henry Pratt), Charlton Heston (John Charlton Carter), Elvis Presley, Humphrey Bogart, Montgomery Clift (Edward Montgomery Clift), Rock Hudson (Roy Harold Scherer, Jr.), Tab Hunter (Arthur Gelien), and Woody Allen (Allan Stewart Konigsberg) are all examples of important stars whose first names were initially given to a handful of white boys in Illinois—or at most two handfuls. No more than 10 boys have any of these names in the year of the star's debut. And no more than 10 are given the name when they become stars, as well as both five and ten years after stardom is achieved. In other words, these names may do better than average with such a small start, but stardom has little impact on their use by others. Cary Grant (Archibald Alexander Leach), Marlon Brando, and Tyrone Power are among the names with a slightly greater impact, but barely so (peaking at 27, 32, and 37 boys in Illinois, respectively). This modest impact is also the case for names that were initially given to more than 10 baby boys when the actor became a star. All in all, only 6 of the 31 names are ever given to at least 500 boys in a given year. Of these, only the popularity of *Gary* is clearly generated by the appearance of an actor bearing this name (Gary Cooper, born Frank James Cooper). The growth of *Jeffrey* precedes the popularity of the actor Jeff Bridges, as do the names *Kevin* (Kevin Costner) and *Jonathan* (from Jon Voight). Two Irish names, *Ryan* and *Sean,* do attain considerable popularity in the period following the debut of Ryan O'Neal (Patrick Ryan O'Neal) and Sean Connery (Thomas Sean Connery). However, given the general movement toward Irish first names in this period, as well as the prior upward movement in both names when these actors made their debut, it is difficult to determine if the exceptional popularity of either name is linked to the performers' success. (The evidence is somewhat stronger for *Ryan:* there is a striking increase in the name's popularity five years after Ryan O'Neal achieves stardom.) Of the men considered, it is only *Gary* that reaches great popularity in a way that is clearly attributable to an actor's name.

Characters' Names

The names of leading characters in movies also have minimal impact on parents' name choices. Of the 119 women's names appearing as an important character in a movie, 69 were already more popular than at least 90 percent of their comparison names (table 8.3). At the other extreme, 36 are no more popular than the comparison names (or even less so). The name's prominence in a movie has a minimal impact; five and ten years later, respectively, 32 and 34 of them still exceed none of their controls. At the other extreme, the number of characters' names exceeding 90 percent of their comparison names is 68 five years later and 65 after ten years. The same pattern occurs for male characters: the percentage of the names that exceed most of the comparisons is uninfluenced by the name's appearance as an important character. There is some decline in the percentage of names exceeding at least 90 percent of the comparison names. On the other hand, there is a slight decline in character names that barely exceed any of the control names.[9]

The modest impact of characters' names also shows up in the absolute numbers of children with these names. Observe that a small number of these names are very important, being given to 1,000 or more white children in Illinois at the time of their appearance (table 8.4). Again, there is generally no strong upward movement in the years following (an exception is the name given to 1,000 girls). Also observe the large number of characters given to 10 or fewer infants both five and ten years after a major character appears with the name. The numbers change somewhat from the year when the character appears, but overall the

Table 8.3. Popularity of characters' names compared with other names starting at the same level

	Character first appears	Character five years later	Character ten years later
Number of female characters			
*Percentage**			
95–100	60	61	60
90–94	9	7	5
10–89	14	15	10
0–10	36	32	34
Total number	119	115[a]	109[a]
Number of male characters			
*Percentage**			
95–100	34	35	28
90–94	14	10	10
10–89	19	19	16
0–10	62	59	56
Total number	129	123[a]	110[a]

Notes: * Percentage of comparison names that the character name exceeds in popularity
[a] Some character names excluded because data not available on them for the 5- or 10-year period after initial appearance

influence on naming is minimal. There is an increase at the lower levels, but the stability is extremely high in terms of names given to more than 200 boys or girls.

Why is the net effect of the characters' names so weak, with virtually no increase in the ensuing years? Several factors are clear: some of these names had previously received attention because the movie draws on a play or a popular novel or well-known historical figures. Also, as noted earlier, writers themselves use names to convey certain qualities for their characters. On this score, writers are often *followers* of the existing imagery associated with names rather than *creators* of imagery. Also, many names are attached to unattractive characters and therefore may become contaminated. There are exceptions, of course; sometimes writers invent names or pick names that are barely known. The key word here is "sometimes." As is the case with movie stars' names, the influence of characters' names on parents' naming decisions is minimal.

Table 8.4. Number of children with characters' names

Number given characters' names	Number of female characters			Number of male characters		
	Character first appears	Character five years later	Ten years later	Character first appears	Character five years later	Character ten years later
2000+	1	1	0	0	0	0
1001–2000	2	3	5	1	1	1
601–1000	2	2	1	1	1	1
501–600	1	0	0	0	1	1
401–500	2	1	2	0	0	0
301–400	2	3	3	1	2	1
201–300	3	3	3	2	0	3
101–200	5	8	10	2	3	2
51–100	7	13	10	3	4	2
11–50	20	16	19	10	6	7
0–10	74	65	56	109	105	92
Total number	119	115[a]	109[a]	129	123[a]	110[a]

[a] Some character names excluded because data not available on them for the 5- or 10-year period after initial appearance

REBECCA BECOMES POPULAR: A CONFLUENCE OF INFLUENCES

We have seen how easy it is to overestimate the influence of media on naming tastes and probably other tastes as well. Without precise information on the history of a name's popularity through the years, it is easy for the casual observer to err by reversing the *cause* from the *effect*. This is easily corrected when one examines the name's changing popularity against the actual timing of the media event.

This is not a trivial lesson, yet there is more to consider. Even when the name of a fictional character or a new star clearly precedes popular use of a name, this fails to provide a full understanding of the causal process. Because most movie names do not appeal to a sizable number of parents, we have to ask what features, if any, distinguish those names that do influence parents from the larger number that do not? It would be naive to think that every case can be explained: the influence of random factors must be considerable; moreover, not all possible causal influences can be examined.[11]

We turn here to the media influence on the popularity of one name, *Rebecca*. This is an example, and is intended as such. It is not meant to be generalized across the board. It does provide a detailed illustration of a taste that reflects a complex set of causes involving both the media and internal mechanisms.

Through the centuries, *Rebecca* has enjoyed periods of considerable popularity among English-speaking parents on both sides of the Atlantic. Its prominence is rooted in the Old Testament, for Rebecca was the wife of Isaac and the mother of Jacob (and Esau). *Rebecca* was one of the most common names among the early immigrants to the American colonies, particularly among the Puritans of New England (Hanks and Hodges 1997, 206; Stewart 1979, 219), and it was popular elsewhere in the British colonies (Fischer 1989, 308, 506). The name earlier had been favored by Christians in England during the Reformation, when Old Testament names were in vogue. It was also an important name for Jewish daughters, though of course Jews were a relatively small component of the population in either the United States or the United Kingdom.

By the start of the twentieth century, *Rebecca*'s popularity had waned, though it was still in use. In England and Wales, it was tied as the 14th most popular name for girls in 1700 and was 18th in 1800, then it moved down to 49th in 1850, and by 1900 it was below the top 50, remaining there until some time between 1965 and 1975, when its popularity in England rose dramatically. *Rebecca* ranked 9th in 1975, and was the most popular name for daughters in 1993 (based on

Fig. 8.4. Popularity of Rebecca *among white daughters, by year of birth, Illinois, 1918–1987*

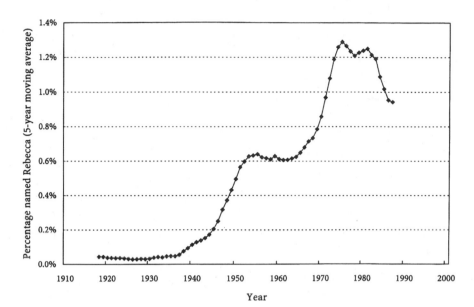

Dunkling 1993, 50–51). The long-term data are not anywhere as good for the United States, but we do know that *Rebecca* was unimportant during the first forty years of the twentieth century. This is clear for white girls born in Illinois,[12] where between 1916 and 1938, *Rebecca* is—by any standard—an unimportant name. In 1933 and 1934 the name first appears in the top 200 (and barely so). Between 1935 and 1938, *Rebecca* falls back below the top 200. Beginning in the late 1930s, the name begins to gain in popularity (fig. 8.4). By 1945, *Rebecca* ranks as the 92d most common name for baby girls (the first time it is among the top 100). For many years, the name is part of the *active* inventory of names. There is a steady upward movement through 1953, when the name reaches the rank of 29. The name plateaus during the remainder of the 1950s and through-out the 1960s. A new surge in popularity early in the 1970s made *Rebecca* a top-20 name in 1972.

The influence of the media on the popularity of *Rebecca* must be understood in terms of its harmony with cultural trends in general and internal taste mecha-nisms in particular. As we shall see, internal mechanisms provide us a deeper understanding of how the influence of motion pictures or other mass media is embedded in these mechanisms.

The Replacement Effect

Visualize a given taste disposition held by part of the population. For clothing, it might mean a preference for conservative fashions or unusual styles, or it might mean choosing whatever appears to be in fashion at the moment. Such dispositions occur for almost all matters of taste (even if they are also affected by social class, race, region, political attitudes, and the like). Because the population is gradually replaced through the aging process, constancy in the different dispositions will occur only if the younger cohorts have the same overall distribution of attitudes as those they are replacing.[13] Obviously, change will occur if the dispositions are different among younger people—if, say, a smaller proportion of the younger cohorts is disposed toward classic clothing or a larger segment is disposed toward unusual clothing, and so forth. Even if we assume that the disposition will remain constant over a long time span, choices will change, as we saw in Chapter 6. Suppose that a given name is chosen by some parents because it is rarely used. Later it is picked up by other parents who become attracted to the name because they sometimes encounter it *and* the name is not widely used. Later parents who favor uncommon names will no longer find the same name appealing because it is—from their perspective—too popular. If the name later gains an appeal for parents favoring widely used names, the second set of parents will no longer consider the name for their child. Even parents who incline toward popular names still have an implicit limit on the maximum acceptable level of popularity. When this limit is reached, they, too, will reject the name. This feedback on a constant disposition will also operate for more than simple matters of popularity. And here we get back to understanding how the popularity of *Rebecca* reflects the influence of a fairly constant taste disposition that later expands because of a shift in tastes.

Through the years, there has been a steady disposition toward the use of Old Testament names for daughters. In 1916, 1920, 1925, and 1930, *Ruth* is one of the 20 most favored names for white daughters in Illinois. By 1935, *Ruth* drops slightly below this level, and there is no Old Testament replacement.[14] By 1940, another Old Testament name appears in the top 20. *Judith* is extremely popular, ranking as the second most popular name for daughters. *Judith* remains among the top 20 in both 1945 and 1950 (ranking 4th and 16th, respectively). And in 1950 a second Old Testament name, *Deborah*, appears among the top 20. This name has a long run: occupying first place in 1955 (*Judith* has fallen out of the top 20 by then), second place in 1960, third in 1965, and 15th in 1970. Throughout this span, it is the only Old Testament name among the top 20 for daughters. *Deborah* falls out in 1975, but Old Testament names for girls are beginning to reflect the expansion of such names for boys (see Chapter 7). Both *Sarah* and *Rebecca* are among the top 20 in 1975 and 1980; *Rebecca* fades somewhat in 1985, but now *Rachel* and *Sarah* are among the top 20.[15] In 1989, 3 of the top 20 are Old Testament names (*Sarah* in third place, *Rachel* in 17th, and *Rebecca* just making it back at 20th).

Whatever else, the popularity of *Rebecca* is influenced by a modest but persistent parental inclination toward using an Old Testament name for their daughters. The subset of parents with this disposition is not massive, but it is enough to put one of these names usually in the top 20.[16] This gives us a clue as to why *some* Old Testament name will be favored and—given the biblical trend among boys' names during this same period—why this taste may expand to more than one girls' name. But it does not provide us with any clues as to why *Rebecca,* and not another name, is favored. For that, we need to consider another internal mechanism we have encountered earlier.

The *A*-Ending, Once Again

Between 1916 and 1989, an important shift occurs in the disposition to use girls' names that end in an *a*-sound (a schwa). In 1916, 2 of the 20 most common names for white daughters in Illinois end in an *a: Anna* and *Virginia*. This is the case in 1920 and 1925. By 1930, there are 3 additional names: *Patricia, Barbara,* and *Norma*. The total declines to 4 by 1935 but is back to 5 in 1940.[17] We see that *Rebecca* first makes the top 200 after an increase in the popularity of *a*-ending names had begun. The number of top-20 names with a schwa ending remains at 5 in 1945. In 1950, however, it rises to 7 (*Linda, Patricia, Barbara, Deborah, Sandra, Donna,* and *Pamela*). It is 8 in 1955, with the addition of *Cynthia*. By 1960, 11 of the top 20 end in an *a*-sound, thanks to the popularity of *Laura, Theresa,* and *Lisa*. This declines to 7 in 1965 and 5 in 1970 before moving up to 7 in 1975 (now including *Sarah* and *Rebecca*) and 8 in 1980 (again including *Sarah* and *Rebecca*), then dropping again to 6 in 1985 and 1989.[18] Although *Rebecca* reaches the top 20 after the schwa ending has peaked in the top 20, its upward movement was greatly facilitated by this internal taste shift. Indeed, the popularity of *Rebecca* is reminiscent of the schwa influence on the Anglo girls' names favored by Mexican-American parents in Texas (see Chapter 7).

Table 8.5. *Popularity of Old Testament names for white daughters born in Illinois, 1916–1989*

| | Name's rank (1 = most common), by year of birth | | | | | | | | | | | | | | | | |
	1916	1920	1925	1930	1935	1940	1945	1950	1955	1960	1965	1970	1975	1980	1985	1988	1989
Ruth	6	5	6	13	22	24	30	49	71	76	108	135	200	179	174	—	—
Esther	25	32	47	68	84	123	177	182	—	—	—	—	—	—	—	—	—
Sarah	38	65	69	74	73	70	86	83	82	80	58	41	8	2	5	3	3
Rachel	159	174	—	—	189	—	—	—	189	185	147	54	29	24	13	15	17
Miriam	180	157	166	—	187	—	—	—	—	—	—	—	—	—	—	—	—
Naomi	185	173	182	143	158	160	—	—	—	—	—	—	—	—	—	—	—
Judith				135	27	2	4	16	28	37	70	125	155	—	—	—	—
Rebecca						117	94	50	33	40	41	34	12	17	23	24	20
Deborah						174	110	9	1	2	3	15	50	94	129	167	157
Becky								147	144	145	150						
Debbie									109	116	164						
Leah											154	137	114	79	85	88	88
Abigail															102	—	—
Hannah															118	59	50

Note: — = name was not one of the 200 most common names in the year

One More Fact

It is also helpful to look at the naming events that take place through the years until *Rebecca* becomes a major name. At each point in time, even when there is only one top-20 Old Testament name, other biblical names have appeal for a smaller number of parents. In 1916, there are 5 names besides *Ruth* (table 8.5). They are all in decline: *Esther, Rachel,* and *Naomi* eventually disappearing from the top 200 (although Rachel later returns and becomes a major name); *Miriam* bounces around for a few years at a low rank and then also leaves the top 200. *Sarah* is declining but never disappears from view before reaching a high level of popularity decades later. Not until 1930 does another Old Testament name, *Judith* (ranking 135), appear. As noted earlier, the name moves very rapidly; by 1935, as *Ruth* starts its long decline, *Judith* ranks 27th. In 1940 there are two new names in the pool, *Rebecca* and *Deborah.*[19] Tracing the names through the years, we find some Old Testament names rising slowly to the top and others moving rapidly upward. *Rebecca* is not one of rapid risers, as comparisons with *Judith, Deborah,* and even *Sarah* make clear. Rebecca is, however, now "in play," ranking 117. *Rebecca* moves up in 1945, 1950, and 1955 but stalls by 1960. It receives a new boost in the late 1960s and early 1970s, finally making the top 20 in 1972.

Summing It Up

Independent of motion pictures, the popularity of *Rebecca* is influenced by important internal mechanisms. Through much of the period, a fairly steady segment of parents is attracted to giving daughters an Old Testament name. Parents come and go, and the popularity of the specific name changes, but one of the top-20 names is usually from the Old Testament. As long as such a disposition remains in force, *Rebecca* and other Old Testament names are possible choices. In the decades after World War II, Old Testament names for boys gradually became increasingly attractive (Chapter 7) and this then expands to daughters.

None of this helps us understand why *Rebecca* is one of the new choices. On that score, a broad taste movement is found such that names with an *a*-ending are increasingly favored for daughters. This preference begins to decline by the time *Rebecca* reaches the top 20, but by then *Rebecca* is among the contenders because it has become fairly popular. This subset, as table 8.5 makes clear, consists of two types of lesser names: previous top-20 names that are still in use but on the decline, and names that are moving upward from a lower level of use.

It is difficult to predict if a name in the second category will eventually reach the top 20 or stall before then.

Back to the Movies

For *Rebecca* (or any other name) an upsurge during the second half of the twentieth century leads us to consider the influence of mass media. *Rebecca* appears prominently in several important novels and a variety of movies (some of which are based on these novels). This survey, though not exhaustive, proves rewarding.

Kate Douglas Wiggin's *Rebecca of Sunnybrook Farm,* first published in 1903, was a perennially popular children's book, with a special appeal to girls. Three movie versions were made: a silent film starring Mary Pickford, a talkie in 1932, and a revamped version in 1938 starring Shirley Temple. This last movie combined an appealing story with an actress at the peak of her career. In 1934, 1.5 million Shirley Temple dolls were sold, and they continued to sell well throughout the Depression (O'Brien 1990, 142). The child star was also successfully linked to an enormous array of other products for girls (Cross 1997, 117). The year after Temple's starred in *Rebecca of Sunnybrook Farm, Rebecca* reappears, ranking 140 (the name had barely made the top 200 in 1933 and 1934 but again falls below this level from 1935 to 1938).

Rebecca is also the title of a Daphne du Maurier novel that was a best-seller in 1938 and 1939 and became an Alfred Hitchcock film (with the same title, starring Joan Fontaine and Laurence Olivier), winning the Academy Award for best picture in 1940. It is hard to evaluate the potential impact of this popular novel and movie, for the title character is Maxim de Winter's beautiful deceased first wife, who at the end is revealed as both faithless and malicious, despised by her husband. Despite these negative associations, the movie certainly calls the name to the attention of a vast audience.

More speculative is the co-occurrence earlier in the 1930s between *Rebecca's* initial appearance and several movies featuring a character named *Becky,* the diminutive form of *Rebecca*. Becky Sharp, the heroine of Thackeray's *Vanity Fair,* is described by Leslie Dunkling (1983, 232) as one of the most famous female characters in English literature, and although her character, too, is not an attractive one, again it calls attention to *Rebecca*.[20] After four earlier silent versions, *Vanity Fair* was made into a sound movie in 1932. Although this last film was not a great success (Walker 1995, 1141–42), all of these versions would have increased the name's visibility. *Becky Sharp,* another movie derived from the novel, appeared in Technicolor three years later (Elley 1992, 42). More influential for the name *Becky* is the character Becky Thatcher in Mark Twain's *Tom Sawyer*. As the girl who holds a special appeal for Tom, Becky Thatcher benefits from the novel's conversion into a movie in 1930 (Elley 1992, 5, 624).[21] A couple of decades later, two other important movies appear to have influenced the popularity of *Rebecca*. The beautiful Jewish woman Rebecca is an important character in Sir Walter Scott's classic novel *Ivanhoe* (1819). In 1952 the tale was made into an acclaimed movie in which Elizabeth Taylor, an actress of extraordinary beauty, plays Rebecca opposite Robert Taylor's Ivanhoe. The movie received three Academy Award nominations, including one for best picture. In 1972, Rebecca is again the name of a leading character, in the critical and box-office success *Sounder*, a moving tale about black sharecroppers in Louisiana that appealed to both black and white audiences. Cicely Tyson was nominated for the Academy Award as best actress for her portrayal of Rebecca (Bogle 1988, 199–200).

The appearance of *Ivanhoe* corresponds roughly with a plateau in the popularity of *Rebecca* (see fig. 8.4). One speculative causal connection is that the name's association with actress Elizabeth Taylor dampens its attractiveness for parents who might otherwise have been inclined to favor the name. This would reflect Taylor's public image as "a heroine/villain named Liz on a grand scale of wealth and seduction—ever-present bared shoulders, décolletage, and full-skirted evening gown overflowing with sensual promise" (Peary 1978, 84). Or perhaps the name plateaus because the *Rebecca* in *Ivanhoe* is Jewish, a sharp contrast with earlier movies where the *Rebecca* character is not portrayed as Jewish. It is not possible to determine whether either or both of these associations would have minimized the name's appeal for parents. The abrupt end of *Rebecca*'s increasing popularity does suggest, however, that something happened at about that time to stop the name's spread.

Rebecca's resurgence may be connected with the appearance of *Sounder* in 1972. In Illinois, the name's popularity among white girls had started to increase a few years earlier. Noteworthy is the rise in the name's popularity in 1971—the year *before Sounder* was released. This rise, by itself, suggests an influence with a source other than the movie. Keeping in mind both the observation (in Chapter 7) that Jewish parents favor Old Testament boys' name somewhat earlier than non-Jews—as well as the speculation about *Ivanhoe*—it is helpful to compare Jewish and non-Jewish parents in the timing of the name's popularity. Because this cannot be done for Illinois, I turn to estimates for California (based on surnames). We see above that the surge in the popularity of *Rebecca* starts earlier

Table 8.6. Popularity of Rebecca *among Jews and non-Jews, and the influence of* Sounder

| Illinois | | California | | |
Year	Rank	Year	Rank Jews	Rank non-Jews
1966	36	1966–1967	33	33
1967	37			
1968	35	1968–1969	20	32
1969	31			
1970	34	1970–1971	12	33
1971	24			
1972	18	1972–1973	8	14
1973	10			

for Jews. In 1970–1971, *Rebecca* ranks 12th for Jews but remains at 33 for non-Jews. Indeed, the preference among non-Jews was stable until the appearance of *Sounder*. A striking change occurs for non-Jews after the appearance of *Sounder:* the name's rank among non-Jews rises sharply from 33 to 14 in 1972–1973.

Granted the striking correspondence between the increase of *Rebecca* among non-Jews and the appearance of this movie, one still might ask how it can be that the association of *Rebecca* with a black woman would increase the name's popularity among whites. Yet the black characters had great appeal to whites, and as Donald Bogle observes, not only is the heroine Rebecca admirable and strong but the movie is not threatening to whites:

> It has to be admitted that *Sounder's* portrait of black Americans harked back to the past. The characters are safely distanced in the Depression and they are without the outright rebelliousness and rage of the then contemporary urban figures of such films as *Shaft* and *Sweet Sweetback's Baadasssss Song*. Often they seem passive and submissive. They are both—but only within the bounds of survival. *Sounder's* protagonists do not lie to themselves or their viewers. They don't parade a chic *rhetorical* radicalism. Instead they live by and cope with everyday realities, determined to find in life whatever pleasures and triumphs are available. [Bogle 1988, 201]

Moreover, although parents could easily be reminded of the historical association of *Rebecca* with Jews, I speculate that a movie in which a black woman has this name will not generate an analogous association with blacks. And in fact, such a link does not occur. In 1972, when *Sounder* was released, *Rebecca* ranked 181 for black daughters. At the peak of Rebecca's popularity among whites in 1973 and 1974 in Illinois (when it ranked 10th), its rank among blacks was still only 155 and 156. Accordingly, a black character who possesses many admirable characteristics may be able to open the name up to greater popularity for whites while at the same time having virtually no effect on black tastes.

In sum, several influences were driving the final surge of *Rebecca*. The leading Old Testament name, *Deborah*, was fading rapidly and no longer in the top 20. This provided an opportunity for a replacement—given that the number of parents favorably disposed to Old Testament girl's names was at the very least holding its own. (It had probably expanded, because more than one Old Testament girl's name now becomes popular at the same time and an even greater expansion occurs among boys.) *Rebecca* was by then in the pool of modestly popular Old Testament names (arriving there because of the combined influence of the mechanisms and earlier motion picture events described above). Old Testament names were especially appealing to Jews, and the timing and magnitude of their popularity for non-Jews lagged (as we saw in the discussion of boys' names in Chapter 8). The enormity of the popularity among Jews was of some consequence for the overall rank of *Rebecca* in the state, but because Jews are a small part of the Illinois (and California) population, an increase in the non-Jewish disposition toward *Rebecca* is critical for the name's reaching the top 20. Given the correspondence in timing of the movie *Sounder* and the timing of this non-Jewish jump in popularity, the movie is the likely cause.

A Nontrivial Technical Consideration

Last, the reader should bear in mind that analyzing the influence of media events on tastes is often difficult because of four special complications: there can be lags in the media impact on the name's usage; in some periods it is hard to determine whether the impact is due to only one movie and—if so—which one; there are no strong models of what the form of the curve would take had the movie(s) not appeared; since names can (and sometimes do) reflect the influence of many other media forms, certainty is more difficult than usual. For example, any or all of three events in 1938—the publication of the novel *Rebecca*, yet another *Tom Sawyer* movie, and the Shirley Temple version of *Rebecca of Sunnybrook Farm*— could be responsible for the thrust in the name's popularity the next year. And lags are definitely possible: the impact on children seeing either the Shirley Temple film or *Tom Sawyer*, for example, would show up only years later when the children reached child-bearing age.[22]

Consider the difficulty in analyzing any possible influence on *Rebecca* from the English novelist Cicily Isabel Fairfield, who became Rebecca West in 1911. She was a feminist, and her books featured strong, unconventional heroines (Parker 1994, 721). West also wrote for the left-wing press and made a name for herself as a fighter for women's suffrage. Her social and cultural writings have attracted more attention than her novels. It would be extremely difficult—barring exceptionally detailed information—to ascertain any influence, but it is certainly possible that West's first name might have generated some appeal among mothers inspired by her feminist views.

THE LESSON AND THE PROBLEM

The impact of movies on names is, as we have seen, far more limited than is widely believed. This chapter is not the final word on the connection between mass entertainment and names—let alone the influence of the media on other fashions and cultural practices.[23] And, of course, even less is known with certainty about the role of mass entertainment in other domains of culture. But the surprising results here—counter to widely held views—make such investigations all the more necessary. There are lessons to be learned, whether it be for media influences on naming or for other practices.

Timing

If a cultural change appears to be correlated with its appearance in some form of mass entertainment, this is inadequate evidence for concluding that a causal connection exists. Because the media are geared to reflecting existing dispositions and tastes, the first step is to analyze the timing of the two events. For names, the timing is often not what we think it is without the benefit of data. The periods when *Marilyn* was a popular name for daughters and when Marilyn Monroe was a movie star do overlap. Yet on examination we see that the name was popular far earlier than the actress—indeed, the name had already begun its decline when Monroe appears (and continued to do so after her stardom). In the absence of reliable data, it is just too easy to make this type of mistake.

An article by Cleveland Evans examining naming tastes in Washtenaw County, Michigan (which includes Ann Arbor, the home of the University of Michigan), remarks on the popularity of *Linda* for girls born there in 1951. "Ann Arbor was full of veterans going to school on the G.I. Bill. The war had been the most important thing in the lives of these young parents, and they were proud of their .

role in it. So when the 1945 movie *The Story of G.I. Joe* featured a smash song called 'Linda,' thousands of Joes responded by giving the name to their daughters. Linda was the big fad of the early Baby Boom; in 1951 over 5% of the girls born in Washtenaw County received the name" (Evans 1983, 51). The facts are correct; there was such a song, and *Linda* was the most popular name for girls in 1951. But I cite this account by Evans, a superb scholar who deals with first names and their connection with cultural events, to illustrate how studies of a name's popularity over time can help us evaluate a given interpretation—in this case the role of the 1945 movie—and also to illustrate a valuable mechanism that affects the impact of the media on our tastes.

First of all, *Linda* was a popular name long before *The Story of G.I. Joe*. By 1939, the name ranks 17th for white girls born in Illinois, moves up rapidly to 7th in 1944, the year before the song, and becomes the most popular name for daughters in 1947. Under the circumstances, it is hard to allocate too much influence to the movie. Whether the appearance of the movie jolted its popularity upward is difficult to say. On one hand, *Linda* was in 7th place for two years in a row before climbing to 5th in 1945 and upward. On the other hand, there is no evidence of a decline in popularity before the song became a hit. Moreover, this explanation fails to take into account the possible influence of Linda Darnell, an actress who "was among Hollywood's most popular stars in the 40s" (Katz 1990, 305).[24]

Influence from Within: The Context of Existing Practices and Changes

My primary purpose in discussing *Linda* is to illustrate a central internal mechanism for understanding whether mass media are likely to affect a fashion or culture more generally. I refer to the state of existing tastes *and* ongoing changes in those tastes. In the case of names, if the media uses one that is either in harmony with the existing direction of change or has characteristics that reflect stable practices, then its adoption is more likely. If it either diverges substantially or is in the opposite direction, then I hypothesize a minimal impact. (On the rare occasion when mass entertainment triggers a divergence from existing trends, then there is a fashion or cultural revolution.) Some of these comments may, I fear, appear platitudinous. But they are not—witness the propensity in cultural analysis to attribute external causes to cultural events as if there is no need to consider the direction and thrust of what I have been calling internal mechanisms.

Returning to *Linda,* we note that the song "Linda" from a popular 1945 movie became a hit. Although we cannot know how the song got its name, it seems reasonable to assume that the lyricist thought it would be appealing. If so, then what is actually operating is a feedback mechanism in which the song reflects the appeal of the name and this, in turn, may increase parents' decisions to name their daughters *Linda*. In addition, as we have observed elsewhere, the name has two phonemic qualities that strengthen its appeal. The *a*-ending was gaining in popularity during this period. This is reflected in the popularity of names like *Rebecca,* in its use in invented names for daughters, and in the tendency among Mexican Americans to favor such the *a*-ending for their daughters' Anglo names. (This last example also illustrates how the context of existing tastes affects dispositions toward other tastes.) Also, during this period the *-lyn* phoneme has great appeal for girls' names. In 1939, when *Linda* first enters the top 20, *Marilyn* and *Carolyn* are already there, and a similar phoneme (albeit with a different spelling) occurs for a name that ranks between 21 and 29, *Catherine*.

Granted, this is an ad hoc explanation, but if there is a media influence, its impact has to be understood within the context of *Linda* fitting into an existing taste. Our culture is saturated with hit songs, television shows, movies, novels, and star performers. Yet one factor that we know influences parents' choices is the phonemic appeal of a name, and this means that: those phonemic qualities are probably more likely to be among those in the current panorama of tastes.

In an earlier chapter I commented on the appeal of *Darren* in Britain, thanks to the showing of the American television series "Bewitched." Of interest to us here is how it came about that an invented name did so well among the British. Without using circular reasoning, we can assume that the character did not irritate British audiences. Yet if we consider the phonemic nature of this invented name, some clues come forward that fit nicely with the mechanism discussed above. Of the 50 most common boys' names in England and Wales in 1975—a year when *Darren* ranks 10th—19 end in an *n*-sound. This compares with 10 in 1950 and 4 in 1925. Although it is hard to make a simple causal argument, one can say that the adoption of *Darren* occurs when there has been a remarkable surge in tastes for boys' names with an *n*-ending.

This pattern involves more than phonemes, but it can be generalized into a variety of taste trends to explain the presence or absence of a media effect on the population. Other movements include the changing disposition toward Old Testament names and the rise in the preference for Irish names. As we move outward to other fashions as well as to culture more generally, phonemes are obviously not a consideration, but the principle still holds. Those tastes—or cultural features—exhibited in the media are more likely to be followed in the larger society if they fit into existing trends. First, notions of what will be appealing affect the likelihood that certain tastes will appear in the media. Second, the response of audiences will reflect ongoing developments in various mechanisms. Whether it be the type of home, interior decoration, family relations, vacations, or behavior at work, the influence will be found within that context. The media tend to fit their products into what their audience is likely to accept and find appealing. Any movie made today about the president of the United States—whether a real historical figure or a purely fictional creation—is almost certain to portray a leader with many warts for the simple reason that a president without warts would not be believable. In an earlier era and culture, just the opposite would hold.

The Persona

A broad and sometimes subtle set of characteristics is also likely to affect the strength of any media influence on popular naming tastes—what we might call "the persona." This persona includes everything from the performer's or character's physical features (I would speculate, for example, that the names of men who are "pretty" would not be appealing today, nor would those of women who are conspicuously "sexy"). It will also be influenced by the character's behavior in the story—to say nothing of clothing, occupation, social class, age, and ethnic and racial origin. Many behavioral features are probably relevant. Is this a performer who communicates (and represents) an attitude that strikes a responsive chord in the audience (not a mystical idea but, rather, behavior that represents a disposition that has not yet come to the fore)? For example, does an actress play roles in which she refuses to be pushed around by men, maintaining her independence? Such behavior may have had more appeal in an era when many women could only fantasize such behavior. The effects of such qualities are likely to be hard to gauge. For example, decades ago women's eyebrows were severely plucked into an artificial shape. At some point, actresses must have appeared with more natural-looking eyebrows or with more natural-looking makeup or with less of an interest in appearing as a sexual icon for men. Likewise, among men, there must be shifts in actors' public images or the roles they play so that some characters are portrayed in a less intensely "macho" manner than might have appealed to audiences in an earlier era.

The problem with the persona is not that it is a false direction for understanding the likelihood of a character affecting cultural tastes. Rather, it requires a rigorous set of tools and measurements of these features—lacking these, we cannot have faith in the validity of the conclusions we draw. Moreover, the key appeal of the persona will vary over time and—within a period—to different audiences. Visualize, for example, differences between Eleanor Roosevelt, Jacqueline Kennedy, Nancy Reagan, and Hillary Rodham Clinton in their behavior and the images they evoke. In turn, consider how their first names might attract or repel different subsets of the population. Such an analysis is useful in accounting for class differences not only in naming preferences but in other tastes. (Cultural capital is important, but class differences are driven by far more than cultural capital.)

Ascertaining how features of the persona connect with ongoing shifts in the disposition of the population (or, more likely, a subset of the society) is difficult to ascertain. It requires rigorous and imaginative ways of converting relevant attitudinal features and behavior into measurable entities. And, in turn, if circular reasoning is to be avoided, it takes precision in ascertaining shifts and dispositions in the population. This question, we must remember, is best viewed as probabilistic. It is all the more difficult because we are only addressing a probability that the set of persona with one particular feature will increase or decrease the usage of their name. It would be a mistake to expect an accounting for every single star name that does—or does not—strike the fancy of parents. Why, for example, did the appearance of Gary Cooper lead to *Gary* becoming an enormously popular name, whereas Humphrey Bogart, Clark Gable, Bing Crosby, and Cary Grant (other major stars of about the same period) had minimal effect? What limited the naming appeal of Hedy Lamarr, Lana Turner, Ingrid Bergman, and Vivien Leigh? Movie buffs and those who are familiar with these performers will undoubtedly have answers for most or all of them. Yet it illustrates well how much needs to be done to provide rigorous answers.

Going beyond names, the persona can help us understand media influences on other tastes as well. However, the same performer or character may influence one fashion more than another. A popular actress's clothing, for example, may affect fashion styles, yet her name might have no influence on popular names. With every taste or trend, we must first trace the cultural development before it appears in the mass media and, if we discover grounds for attributing the change to a media effect, then we must ascertain the likely reason.

Broader Issues: The Cultural Surface and Cultural Change

What can we say, in the end, about how tastes change? Fashions of all kinds—not just first names—also reflect the influence of mechanisms that can persistently spew out new tastes even when external conditions are fixed. And, we have seen that even when external developments are important, internal mechanisms will still modify and mold their impact. The details may differ for specific fashions, particularly in the presence of far different external conditions (such as when organizations seek to influence tastes). Yet the basic principles hold: even commercial influences are restricted by the broader internal mechanisms of taste.

The perspective I have developed for analyzing names—emphasizing how internal mechanisms can generate change in the absence of external social change—is related to other recent efforts in cultural studies that point in multiple ways to the internal dynamics of culture.[1] My concern in this chapter forms part of this effort: using a theoretical approach to names as a way of understanding the complicated nature of cultural change that involves domains far removed from what we traditionally call fashion. Here, too, I illustrate how mechanisms used for names can be applied to this broader question and suggest special mechanisms that I believe hold promise for our eventual understanding of dimensions of what I call the "cultural surface."

THE CULTURAL SURFACE

It is difficult at best to make sense of the diverse set of cultural elements that make up a society. The combination is impossible to understand if we expect the elements to consist of interrelated parts that in some way form a holistic pattern. This is because in all but the most stationary of societies, present-day culture consists of elements that appeared at different times for varied reasons. Moreover, not all of the earlier elements survive until the present; other influences cause some to remain and others to disappear. From this perspective, the ongoing culture that we experience is best thought of as a "cultural surface," representing a diverse set of births, a variety of causes responsible for the continued appearance of existing elements, and additional conditions that have caused other elements to disappear.

I do not wish to overstate my thesis; some elements of the cultural surface are of course related, if only because later features spin off from earlier features and certain fundamental social conditions do not shift rapidly. So patterns *do* exist. But the point is that our present cultural surface comprises elements that are survivors of earlier developments. Not all elements survive, even if they were created at the same period by the same causes. And this means that the factors leading some elements to survive are different from those that first led to their appearance. A society's culture, in this regard, is not simply a set of interrelated parts, and it is best to think of culture as a surface consisting of many parts, some of which are related but many of which are unrelated or linked only remotely. An accounting for the cultural surface at a given time requires consideration of three *types* of causes (of which much is not immediately visible): the initial occurrence and growth of each element; its continuation in the likely event that the initial causes no longer operate; and the forces that cause other earlier elements to decline or disappear.

Tastes in names or even other fashions are relatively simple compared to the task of accounting for the enormously complex processes that underlie the cultural surface. But I believe that the cultural surface also involves the operation of a wide set of internal cultural mechanisms that affect these steps, granted that external societal forces also play a role. I do not propose a full system but rather will suggest mechanisms that can help us answer each step, providing illustrations that will help us see the possibilities offered by this view.

Girls' Names in California: The Cultural Surface Illustrated

The 25 most popular names for girls born in California in a recent year (table 9.1) vividly illustrates both the cultural surface and how the approach to names

Table 9.1. Most popular girls' names, California, 1997

Rank	Name	Rank	Name
1	Jessica	14	Melissa
2	Jennifer	15	Hannah
3	Ashley	16	Kimberly
4	Emily	17	Victoria
5	Samantha	18	Taylor
6	Stephanie	19	Amanda
7	Sarah	20	Lauren
8	Vanessa	21	Natalie
9	Elizabeth	22	Madison
10	Alexis	23	Michelle
11	Maria	24	Megan
12	Jasmine	25	Diana
13	Alyssa		

is relevant for understanding cultural developments in general. The names on the list have no simple explanation. Some are only recently popular (*Madison*, *Taylor*, and *Jasmine*); others, such as *Michelle* and *Megan*, are fading from the top 25—let alone the exceptionally popular level they once reached within that category. *Elizabeth* and *Sarah* have been popular for long spans and continue so. *Mary*, by contrast, the most popular name for girls during much of the twentieth century, has long since faded. Several androgynous names appear in the list— *Alexis, Taylor,* and *Lauren* (and a case could be made for *Ashley*)—but none are in the top 25 for boys. It is hard to say that the cause for the initial popularity of these names matches what drives their popularity at present (Lieberson, Dumais, and Baumann 2000). No longer is the same daring androgyny associated with giving daughters these names as there was when they were actively given to boys. *Jennifer* continues to enjoy a remarkably long span of exceptional popularity for daughters. If we think back to the initial stimulation for the name's popularity, it is improbable that many of the parents choosing this name in recent decades are even vaguely aware of the once-popular actress Jennifer Jones (see Chapter 8). *Jennifer*'s continued popularity, then, is another example of how a cultural element continues to survive long after its causal origin disappears. *Mary*, by contrast, illustrates how we must also consider the causal mechanisms (as well as external influences) that lead other cultural elements to decline. No single influence—whether external or internal—will help us account for the names that appear on this list and highly popular names in earlier decades that are no longer popular. This is easy to see for names, but it is an equally powerful consideration for culture more generally. When we look at the elements, we see only the surface and not the variety of causal influences that create it. The display of names at a given time is the product of diverse, separate influences.[2]

Geographic Names

Geographic names provide a simple way of viewing the cultural surface as the product of changing causes.[3] Place names in the Midwestern state of Iowa reflect a variety of sources operating in different periods. *Iowa* is an Indian name, as are many such others as *Pottawattamie, Poweshiek, Tama,* and *Chickasaw* Counties—to say nothing of the *Mississippi* River. French names such as *Des Moines* and *Dubuque* reflect the influence of early French explorers and traders. Other Iowa names reflect an earlier propensity to honor American political leaders and patriots: *Washington, Webster, Madison, Marion, Franklin,* and *Hamilton* Counties are just a few.[4] There are even some Spanish names in Iowa, as in *Palo Alto, Buena Vista,* and *Cerro Gordo* Counties, and of course many place names stemming from nature, among them the *Beaver* and *Raccoon* Rivers and *Council Bluffs*.[5] And, of course, all of these names intermingled, representing a mix of originating causes over a long span of time. If we are to fully understand the cultural surface, then we must next consider that these current names are not all of the names that have ever been used; many Indian, French, and Spanish names, for example, are no longer in use. With this perspective we could see the present cultural surface as the product of other influences that lead some to be replaced and others to be maintained.

BEFORE TURNING TO CULTURE: RELEVANT CONCLUSIONS FROM THE ANALYSIS OF NAMES

In addition to the role of internal mechanisms for understanding the cultural surface, three important features of names are useful to consider in this broader context: the operation of a *causal hierarchy*; the erroneous disposition to interpret the creation of a new taste (and cultural elements more generally) and the simultaneous decline of an old taste as simply the product of the same causal influence; and, last, what I call the "iceberg fallacy," which we can understand through questions about the influence Monica Lewinsky's affair with President Bill Clinton has had on the popularity of *Monica*.

A Causal Hierarchy

As I have observed elsewhere, "Not all causal influences operate in the same way. . . . [It is] frequently useful to think of causal factors as hierarchically organized such that some set the preconditions for others to operate and that the latter, in turn, regulate what further factors come into play" (Lieberson 1997, 375). Names illustrate a hierarchical causal structure such that some social conditions are necessary preconditions before other social conditions will begin to influence choice of names; in turn, this second level serves as a necessary precondition for other conditions, and so on. Names were not always primarily a matter of taste. As we saw in Chapter 2, in many countries there was minimal change in the roster of commonly used names until late in the nineteenth century or early in the twentieth (with change starting slowly and then increasing ever more rapidly). Although many influences affect fashion at present, not all influences are equal. The external conditions responsible for the initial development of a taste dimension to naming also set in motion influences that could otherwise not play a role. Simply stated, a wide variety of internal mechanisms develop. In turn, additional internal and external influences appear that are dependent on this second set, and so forth.

This view of a causal hierarchy is appropriate for other dimensions of culture. The failure of a causal factor to influence culture at a given time and place has relatively little meaning for general questions about the factor's influence on the phenomenon under consideration.[6] Influences on culture need to be analyzed in some sequential form such that earlier influences are the necessary preconditions for the occurrence of later influences. This idea is hardly novel. In his book *Outsiders*, Howard Becker (1963, chap. 2) makes good use of a sequential model in explaining his view of how deviance develops. For those acquainted with plant ecology, a similar model is the succession process in areas completely burned by forest fire, in which a long chain of events leads once again to a stable forest. Regrowth occurs not because all of the previous plants spring up at the same time; rather, there are usually early plants that are necessary preconditions for later plants, and so forth through a full cycle.[7] Thinking of culture as entailing a causal hierarchy does not mean that we must begin with Adam and Eve— rather, one can start with the cultural patterns existing at any given time and analyze developments in a period that follows.

Birth and Death Are Not the Same

The cause or causes of the decline of an existing cultural element must be distinguished from those that lead to the appearance of a new one. They may overlap, but the overlap is unlikely to be total. This distinction, although it may appear self-evident, can be counterintuitive. When we observe the decline of a name that occurs at more or less the same time as its replacement by another, it is all too easy to attribute a simple causal connection between the two events. In practice, there is no reason to expect the explanation for the decline of a cultural feature to provide a fully satisfactory explanation for its replacement. Suppose, for example, that the feminist movement is responsible for a decline in the popularity of flower names for daughters (*Lily, Rose, Violet, Daisy,* and the like). Because all daughters are given names, we know that a void exists that must be filled. The reason for the decline in flower names does set some limits on the likely replacements: names with a similar connotation are unlikely to be chosen. Yet we are still at a loss to say which of many possible names are will become take their place. One possibility is an increase in the use of names that are already popular; another is the appearance of "new" names; perhaps older and unpopular names will return to popularity. And of course, more than one of these outcomes is possible. Knowledge of the decline's cause, in this example, is insufficient to account for the replacement—other than setting a broad constraint on what will be acceptable to these parents. We must look further to understand the causes of the replacement. Consider the analysis of Old Testament names for daughters in Chapter 7. (This is a good example, incidentally, of how taste mechanisms affect replacements even though—in this case—the decline is a product of an external social development.)

A different taste process shows further how the decline in a taste does not pinpoint the replacements. In circumstances where the class diffusion–class replacement model operates, we can understand why a taste adopted by higher strata loses its appeal to them after other strata copy it. And, in turn, we understand why the high strata would seek to set themselves off again with a fashion that is different from the one favored by lower-ranking strata. So far, so good. Which one will be picked? All we know from the cause of the decline is that the new fashion must be one that enables the higher strata to set themselves apart again. The specific characteristics of this fashion are not determined by the cause of the decline. All that is necessary, say in a matter of clothing, is an exclusivity that will permit this marking function to operate again. Is the specific fashion chosen for marking the boundary a matter of chance? This is unlikely, although chance factors may play a role. Rather, we need to look at other conditions that set bounds on the new taste: it will probably be affected by existing taste processes (witness our earlier discussion of the ratchet mechanism) and other mechanisms that move tastes in a certain direction. In this regard, observe that the same proposition may be applied to Pierre Bourdieu's argument in Chapter 1 with respect to cultural capital. If we take Bourdieu's contention that the higher strata employ cultural knowledge to maintain their position and subordinate other strata, then we may still ask what forms of cultural capital will be emphasized—the arts, technology, manners, or the like.

Monica

As I was writing this book, public interest was turned toward a sexual liaison between President Bill Clinton and an intern, Monica Lewinsky. A sociologist asked what I thought would be the consequences for the name *Monica*: would *Monica* become more or less popular because of the scandal? This question struck me as interesting because it reveals how the necessary basis for making a prediction is more complicated than it might appear. It also displays how easy it is to misinterpret the eventual answer—no matter what that answer is. Because my goal is to develop principles to help us understand culture, I look at the question here in the abstract, approaching it from several angles. (The necessary data I describe are not available yet for *Monica* trends in the years immediately preceding the affair, so I cannot follow my own procedure. However, whatever disappointment you may have, the logic below should help you understand the mechanisms involved in both addressing and interpreting this type of question.)

To answer the question in a meaningful way, we first need to know the popularity trends of the name before the affair. Visualize four possibilities: (1) the name was dormant—that is, few girls were being named *Monica* in the years immediately preceding the scandal; (2) the name was gaining in popularity in the preceding years; (3) the name was declining in popularity; and (4) the name enjoyed a modicum of stable popularity. In each situation, we could predict what to expect were there no Lewinsky affair or—more accurately—had the affair not become public. In each case, our best expectation would be more of the same. If the name was dormant, our best guess would be continuation of the dormancy. If *Monica* was mildly popular but showing no trend, then again more of the same. If the name was gaining or losing over the years, we would predict that either of these trends would continue. (In all four cases, we recognize that in some small proportion of the time we would be wrong. Each year most dormant names remain dormant, but a few do not; likewise each year most declining names—or increasing or stable ones—continue on the same path, but a few do not.)

So what can cause something to *happen* that differs from these expectations? In fact, it doesn't take much. The greatest chance for derailment occurs with dormant names. Here we start with a condition in which parents are ignoring the name *Monica*. Because of this highly publicized event, it is more or less impossible for them to ignore the name in the same way. If many parents find the name even less attractive because of the scandal (the contamination process), we can expect the dormancy to continue. But here's the catch. If a small proportion of parents use the name because of the focus on Monica Lewinsky or because the name *Monica* seems enhanced, then the name will gain in popularity *even if the same events contaminate the name for the vast majority of parents*. So, if we start with the simple assumption that almost no parents would otherwise be using the name in the next few years, then even a small minority starting to name their daughters *Monica* will slightly increase the name's popularity. Yet this rise says nothing about the response of the overwhelming majority of parents.

Suppose instead that *Monica* has been moving along at some fairly stable level in the years preceding the affair. The analysis is not radically different. We could say that a modest proportion of parents, m, had been using the name *Monica* and that a far larger proportion, o, had been using some other name. If we can assume that the new set of parents in the year following the scandal had identical dispositions, then the net movement of *Monica* is the product of two transitions: what number of the m population are now turned away from the name and what number of the o population are now turned toward the name. The difference between the two will mean that *Monica* gains or loses in popularity. Again, because we start with so many more people initially disposed not to use *Monica*, it takes only a small proportion of the o parents to switch for the name to gain in popularity even if the vast number of m are no longer attracted to the name.

This analysis holds whether the name is gaining or losing in the years before the affair. If the name is rising in popularity, we would expect that m would go up in the absence of the affair, yet the vast majority of parents would still remain in the o population. Therefore, we are again concerned with the impact of the Lewinsky scandal on the much larger set of parents who would have been disposed to use another name (*o*) and the pull in the opposite direction from those who would initially have been disposed to use the name but who reverse as a consequence of the affair. (The analysis in the case of a declining name is fairly similar, but the trends are in the opposite direction.)

The impact of a dramatic event on the popularity of the taste is a function of its pull on those initially not disposed to that taste versus its push away from the taste among those who would otherwise have been attracted to it. When tastes are highly fragmented—as is the case with names—the impact on those initially disposed against the taste can overwhelm any reversals. This is because there are so many more possibilities in the first category. Because subsets of the population differ in their dispositions, a change in the name's pathway may also reflect a new symbolic connotation of the name that appeals to a different subset of parents. So, to answer the question about *Monica,* we also need to know the numbers associated with each disposition.

Now we get to the interpretation of the raw results. What does it mean if *Monica* gains in popularity? declines in popularity? or does not change much at all? First, is this movement very different from what might have been expected based on the simple trajectory before the scandal? If it does not appear very different, then the initial answer has to be that there is no effect. (At the risk of being overly preachy, notice that this conclusion can occur only if we have some information on what was occurring in prior years.) But there is a second step: the effect of the event might appear to be nil because two subsets balance each other out. If this is the case, then we would need information on the parents choosing the name in the period immediately before and immediately after the event (in this case, the publicity over the affair). Is there a sharp social class shift or ethnic-racial or political disposition, or some other difference between parents now and a few years ago?

So where does that leave us in terms of the analysis of culture? We get to what I call the "iceberg fallacy," a difficulty that occurs in interpreting many features of culture. Given the fact that a cultural development can become quite noteworthy, in either its growth or its decline, without involving the overwhelming majority of the population, it is easy to attach more significance to the event than it merits—"significance" in the sense of viewing the change as telling us more about the society than can be justified. First of all, this type of taste experiences remarkable movement even though the vast majority are unaffected by the event. *Jessica,* the most popular name for girls born in California in 1997, was given to a little more than 1 percent of daughters. The 25th most popular name for that year, *Diana* was given to 0.5 percent. These are not trivial figures, but it is easy to overstate the population's magnitude.

The movement may simply reflect the dispositions of one small subsegment of the population. We have to be certain that not too much is being read into these events. Is the change in some other cultural element simply the product of a relatively small segment of the population, or does it represent merely the visible surface of a much deeper and more profound disposition in the society? If the answer is the latter, we are looking at an iceberg, with a lot more going on than the behavior of a small subset of the population suggests. At the other extreme, by contrast, if the cultural event is the product only of the visible component of the population, then to see more into it is to commit the iceberg fallacy. This is the danger when practitioners of cultural "analysis" use a cultural element that in fact occurs among only a modest subset of the population to indicate some profound feature of the larger society.

This viewpoint, incidentally, is also helpful for highly charged events. A small number of people may be responsible for acts that are extremely disturbing— say, racially motivated shootings or other criminal acts or symbolic offenses. It is hard to avoid wondering if such events represent phenomena that are not yet visible. Are we looking at the tip of an iceberg, or is what we see largely what there is?

NEW CULTURAL DEVELOPMENTS

External influences obviously play an important role in the creation of culture, and these external influences must be studied in themselves. Yet internal mechanisms play an important role here, even when we are considering matters far removed from traditional "fashion." As we have seen, many domains that are traditionally not viewed as related to tastes have a fashion dimension. In fact, there are aesthetic elements in matters removed from what we traditionally think of as aesthetic topics. In the same way that we find some names appealing whereas those favored earlier are less so, mechanisms likewise influence these other dimensions of culture.

Existing cultural elements are a crucial building block for new cultural developments; indeed, what is "new" is often a novel combination of the old with some additional input (Barnett 1953). As William Ogburn observes, "By definition, to invent is to contrive something new. But in trying to describe the particular new thing about an invented object, it is seen that the new is sometimes quantitatively inconspicuous in comparison with the amount of old in such a newly invented object" (1950, 88). This cultural feature fits in very well with the internal mechanisms I've developed in this volume—witness the naming expansions that spread from one element to another and so forth, as in the expansion from a core innovation. Of course, an extension to culture more generally will entail the development of additional mechanisms that are not relevant for names.

AFTER THE ORIGINAL CAUSE DISAPPEARS: MECHANISMS THAT MAINTAIN CONTINUITY

The connection between past cause and present condition is not simple. The initial causal conditions may have long since disappeared, but this need not mean that the cultural element also goes away. Some examples are in order:

- The location of the letters on the standard *QWERTY* keyboard, which was patented in 1878, is far from ideal and could be much more efficient, but it remains the almost universal design long after widespread recognition of this fact.
- The origin of terms may disappear, but the words themselves will live on.[8] A few examples: *jersey* is a fabric originally produced on the Channel island of Jersey; *charlatan* derives from an Italian word referring to natives of Cerreto, famous for its quacks and frauds; a *Philadelphia lawyer* refers to lawyers from that city in the colonial period who were exceptionally skilled in their knowledge of the law's intricacies. In all three cases, the original source is irrelevant to the use of the terms; a jersey need not be from the island, nor are charlatans confined to a town in Italy, and Philadelphia lawyers live everywhere.
- Rules of the road, such as everyone in a country driving on either the right-hand or left-hand side of the road, smoothes the flow of traffic and prevents collisions. Such rules have been in existence since long before the invention of the automobile. Once established, however, these rules generally persist without any particular reference to any of the reasons (if there were any) for the initial favoring of the right-hand or left-hand side of the road (Kincaid 1986).
- English contains many Latin words referring to education: *alma mater, campus, curriculum, cum laude, diploma, emeritus, graduate, magna cum laude, summa cum laude,* and *valedictorian.* Knowledge of Latin was once a primary

marker of the educated classes. Yet although few people today study Latin, these words remain.

- The arbitrary division of an hour into sixty minutes and the division, in turn, of a minute into sixty seconds are remnants of the ancient Babylonian base-sixty numerical system (Hoffman 1998, 31–32).
- *St. Petersburg,* Florida, is named after the Russian city that was the birthplace of one of the original developers. That was many years ago: the developer is long dead; the city is no longer simply a product of the initial development; and there have been many other important prominent people in the city since then. However *St. Petersburg* is still called *St. Petersburg.*

These examples illustrate cultural features that remain after the initial cause fades. What influences help to maintain a cultural element in these circumstances? The answer lies in a simple social fact: many events have "lives of their own," continuing on long after the initial cause disappears. Put another way, many causal links are partially or entirely asymmetrical. The asymmetry refers to the fact that a shift in causal condition may lead to an outcome that will not reverse itself when the causal condition moves back to its initial status.[9] These are points I have discussed elsewhere in considerable detail (Lieberson 1982; Lieberson 1985, chap 4).

This asymmetrical causal pattern occurs when the change itself generates new conditions that make the initial cause irrelevant. An example of this is a lingua franca. Once a language is established as the international language of communication (the situation presently served by English in much of the world; earlier occupied by French in the Western world and, before that, by Latin), the tongue will not automatically disappear when the initial conditions that led to its prominence are no longer operational. This is because a variety of new support elements maintain it, for example, groups that have learned a language because it serves as a lingua franca will in turn have an interest in that language continuing as the lingua franca even if they were initially indifferent (Lieberson 1982, 56–60).[10]

The age of a cultural feature is another asymmetrical maintenance process that maintains a cultural feature after the original cause disappears. When an element of either nonmaterial or material culture exists for a long time, it can gain a symbolic enhancement simply by virtue of its longevity. A geographic name in use for centuries, say, usually gains a certain positive attraction by virtue of its history and may continue long after the initial reason for using the name has disappeared. The practices that a family follows during holidays—although perhaps arbitrary or due to "chance" when first established—will gain an attraction simply because they have always been practiced. Were it possible to start the holiday celebration all over, then some other practice might enjoy a similar attraction through the years.[11]

Patriotic and religious celebrations tend to have this quality: the very age of the practice (often described in terms of "tradition" or "history") gives the practice a certain appeal that may be totally unrelated to the causes of its origin. In the United States, the Constitution has this quality. Its durability over centuries makes the document all the more sacred such that antipathy toward breaking from the tradition increases with the document's age. We can speculate about those parts of the Constitution that were adopted (or excluded) by only a narrow margin: had the outcome been in the opposite direction, then in most instances those provisions would now be viewed as sacred—and any change would be approached with great reluctance.

For some cultural elements, the perceived short-term cost of a change outweighs the long-term benefits that would follow. This is probably behind the resistance to changing the typewriter keyboard, or the resistance in the United States toward the use of other scales, as in the case of miles versus kilometers or Fahrenheit versus Celsius. (Of course, in terms of measurements, additional influences might include the symbolic implications of change or their long-standing use in the United States.) In any case, resistance to changing, for example, in either direction between left- and right-handed rules of the road probably involves short-term costs that exceed any relative long-term benefits.

Last, we should consider the "cultural lag hypothesis" (Ogburn 1950, part 4). Briefly, the hypothesis is that different parts of culture have different rates of change. When material culture changes, slower to respond is the nonmaterial culture that was adapted to the previous material conditions. This generates a lag between the two that "may last for varying lengths of time, sometimes indeed, for many years" (203). Ogburn saw the resulting lag as often generating social problems because various symbolic features, such as laws, mores, and the like, were not synchronous with changing material conditions. This hypothesis generated considerable attention, as well as extensive criticism, when it was proposed in 1922, and it is largely dormant at present. Part of the objection stemmed from the critics' tendency to state theories in a deterministic manner and, in turn, their expectation, if a theory is valid, that there should be no deviations from the predicted outcome. Hence, any uncertainty or incompleteness is taken as enough evidence to sink a theory. Unfortunately, this tendency is present even now. It is an unjustified standard for several reasons, two of which are important for our purposes. First, because we live in a probabilistic world, it is unrealistic to expect that a theory will always "work" in all contexts. Second, the demand that a theory always hold if it is valid involves an implicit assumption that a valid theory will have consequences that always occur regardless of any other conditions that may be pushing the outcome in another direction (Lieberson 1998, 184). This may hold for gravity, but it is not likely to hold for social processes—if only because it is so difficult to eliminate all other possible influences—especially in nonexperimental settings.

I mention Ogburn's cultural lag hypothesis here because it is an outstanding model of the kind of mechanisms that can be developed to account for the continuation of a cultural element after the initial cause is removed. There are probably a number of other mechanisms (I've described some in this section) that will encompass many different concrete accounts of why cultural elements do not change after their initial cause has faded.

MECHANISMS THAT LEAD TO THE
DECLINE OF CULTURAL ELEMENTS

A suitable explanation of the cultural surface needs to account for the decline of cultural elements. This erosion can be subdivided into two radically different contexts: declines that take place after the initial cause disappears, and those that occur even though the initial causal conditions continue to be present.

Starting with the first situation, in which the initial causal conditions fade away, it strikes me that some of the same mechanisms that maintain culture absent the original causes are—in other circumstances—relevant as forces influencing a cultural element's decline. Understandably, using the same mechanism to explain both cultural maintenance *and* disappearance would appear to be sophistry or, at best, nothing more than a bad case of illogical circular reasoning. In practice, the same mechanism can operate in either direction, but the question is which direction will be switched on and for how long.

It is a mistake to interpret the cultural lag hypothesis to mean that nonmaterial culture remains forever even when material conditions change and the nonmaterial culture is no longer adaptive. Rather, there is a *lag*. On this score, the cultural lag hypothesis is really a perspective leading us to think about the speed of change—and the causes of these changes—when the initial causal conditions are no longer present. To make it a tighter concept for our purposes at hand, it will be necessary to ascertain the conditions affecting the dissolution rate of nonmaterial elements when material changes eliminate their adaptive utility (of course, this will also require some standards for determining what we mean by "nonadaptive").

Another mechanism, with a similar feature of helping to account for maintenance or decline, is the notion of "symbolic contamination and enhancement." If, for example, we continue to use Latin terms for many educational matters in the United States, it is probably because the prestige of Britain in the colonial period—rather than the forced imposition of English practices and standards— avoided the symbolic contamination that might have changed these cultural elements after American independence. By contrast, the outcome after independence for cultural elements imposed on a conquered people is less certain. There are two pulls: contamination as a reminder of foreign imposition, and enhancement owing to the prestige associated with the foreign practices. Because we know that both occur, the task for understanding a cultural element's persistence or disappearance after the initial conditions have eroded is not to apply the appropriate label in the situation at hand but, rather, to figure out the conditions under which the mechanism will go in one direction as opposed to the other.

Especially challenging is the second situation, when a cultural element declines even though its initial causal condition remains unchanged. Certainly, it is not difficult to envision a variety of *external* changes that could minimize the initial influence. This is an important possibility, and undoubtedly it is often a central factor. Among the external changes that could undercut the existing cultural element—even though its initial cause is still present—are political events, social movements, contact with other societies and cultures, economic issues, changes in other cultural facets, and intellectual developments. These and other sweeping changes can lead existing cultural elements to wither.

Changes in the rules of the road illustrate some of these complexities (this discussion draws on the excellent study of this topic by Kincaid 1986). Countries with left-hand rules before the invention of the automobile have progressively reversed the direction in the ensuing years. Left-hand rules covered one-third of the world in 1919 but applied to only one-sixth by the late 1970s and early 1980s. Reviewing the changes in both directions, Kincaid found the following influences: military occupation, conformity with neighbors, the influence of powerful states, national unity, the trend to world uniformity, the availability of cars, and politics (17–20). Most of the remaining area with left-hand rules by the late 1970s were former British colonies or dominions: India, Australia, South Africa, Pakistan, Ireland, and others. Canada, however, is not among them. It is easy to understand why Canada would be relatively early to shift to right-handed rules (indeed, Canadian changes in the 1920s are first in this direction since Italy's shift in the late nineteenth century).[12] In fact, Canada began with split practices; the initial French influence (based on French right-hand rules) ruled in Quebec, Ontario, and the prairie provinces. The remaining provinces and Newfoundland were initially governed by British laws and therefore incorporated the left-hand rule. In the 1920s, the "British" provinces progressively shifted to the right-hand rule in order to facilitate travel between provinces, to make these provinces more appealing to tourists driving from the United States, and to facilitate travel to the United States by Canadian drivers.[13]

We must be careful about such accounts—certainly, we learned that moral when we considered the external events offered to explain the decline of men's hats (Chapter 3). Under any circumstance, the influence of internal mechanisms is relevant here. In what follows, I sketch out a few examples of how a cultural element may change even though its initial cause remains and new external developments are absent.

Many cultural characteristics have bounds, whether implicit or explicit. When the cultural element reaches a certain extreme level, the initial cause of the characteristic is no longer central, and other conditions (already present) are brought into play. Consider the cost of medical care. As technology and costs grow, medical care reaches a point at which an ever-present force—cost—begins to play a progressively more important role, and it is one that pushes in a different direction. The rising costs to employers who pay for employee health care lead them to look for new alternatives to rein in their expenses. This in turn makes group plans attractive because of their promise to provide more economical forms of medical care. Eventually these group plans experience pressures to hold down costs—in part because of their desire for profits and in part because the organizations compete among themselves for employer contracts—and this brings about practices that are increasingly unacceptable to many patients, and so new changes must occur. Changes of this nature will probably continue indefinitely unless a more stable solution is reached that provides the health care that people want in an economic context that is satisfactory to both employers and patients.

We can think of many cultural elements as implicitly existing within a set of bounds. The restraints are there, but they are not triggered unless a threshold is reached, and then they become increasingly powerful. Cultural elements, then, can exist so long as they do not go beyond a certain range, or they can exist if they do not occur among too many people within the society. When the bounds are reached, other existing elements, previously dormant, are brought into play.

There is, to put it another way, the potential for cultural elements to self-destruct. The development of a cultural feature can set into motion its own decline. This is obviously the case for fashions (in names and otherwise), in which overpopularity becomes the seed for the fashion's destruction. It is obviously the case for movements that reach an extreme and ultimately generate a strong counterreaction. These mechanisms of cultural decline have a quantitative dimension; the extreme limit of the cultural element or the magnitude of its influence sets into opposition the previously dormant elements of society.

IN BRIEF: INTERNAL MECHANISMS, TASTES, AND THE CULTURAL SURFACE

The usual assumptions about names in particular, and fashions in general, are questionable. When approached correctly, tastes exhibit orderly processes and understandable movements over time that, I confess, are an aesthetic joy. Fashions are less influenced by external events than is commonly assumed, often changing because of internal mechanisms that—once established—operate independently of society. These internal mechanisms force changes in tastes even if the social order itself is constant. I remind readers of the contrast between this perspective and the almost automatic disposition at present to assume that an external change must account for a new taste or the decline of an older one. Social commentators make more of "reflection theory"—the notion that cultural events reflect the social order—than is justified. And their reliance on this theory leads to the search for substantive significance behind each new fashion ("substantive" in the sense that each new fashion is thought to reflect a particular development in society). Although broad social developments do affect fashion and taste, their influence is neither as common nor as overwhelming as these commentators would have us believe. Reflection theory ignores the role of internal mechanisms and therefore the fact that changes will occur even when external social conditions remain constant. Cultural analysts today generally use far less extensive evidence than is available for names, with the result that seemingly plausible speculations based on reflection theory are rarely challenged.

I have no difficulty when an interpretation based on reflection theory is evaluated with rigorous evidence. Unfortunately, this is rarely the case; and the problem is that today one can always find some post-hoc broad social event to account for either the emergence of a new fashion or the decline of an older one. New themes and developments are constantly occurring in the political, technological, economic, cultural, ethical, and international planes—let alone in the media and arts. I am reminded of the significance Freud could always find in almost any number that a patient might mention in a free association. Whether that number is 7, 93, 412, 6, or 81, an imaginative listener who knows enough about the speaker can certainly find profound significance in the choice. In the same manner, a social commentator can always come up with some external change to explain any fashion development. If one assumes that external changes in the social order explain these cultural features, then almost certainly at least one external change in the society can be found to provide a plausible explanation.

Explanations employing reflection theory may sometimes be true, but typically the evidence is so weak that a variety of other plausible accounts cannot be ruled out. In *Fermat's Last Theorem*, Amir Aczel (1996, 103) illustrates a technical point made by the mathematician André Weil regarding the validity of a theorem: Suppose, on observing seven men and seven women in a room, one conjectures that these are seven married couples. There is no obvious reason to argue against this inference, since the number of men equals the number of women. But there is no reason to accept this conjecture either, since there are many other plausible conditions—for example, they could all be single, some could be married and others not, and so forth. The evidence is weak: although the conclusion is harmonious with what is observed, the explanation could easily be false.

The approach I have developed here for names can be employed in culture more generally. The cultural surface, along with the three critical sources of change—creation, maintenance, and disappearance—gives a way of thinking about culture as a process. At each of the three sources of change, as is the case for names and fashion, internal mechanisms are operating that can affect the outcome even in the absence of new social developments; at the very least, they interact and modify these social changes. Why would we expect to find mechanisms enabling us to understand the great array of cultural features, many of which are nonmaterial and symbolic? The answer turns us back to where we started. *If such matters as tastes in names—and fashion more generally—operate under orderly processes, then there is every reason to expect that the same reasoning (indeed some of the same internal mechanisms) will help us understand the entire cultural surface.* This is a natural extension of the approach toward first names developed in this volume. I hope it will not be the last word.

Appendix 1 • Sources for Graphs in Chapter 2

CALIFORNIA

First Names

Unpublished data obtained from State of California, Department of Health Services, Health Demographics Section, Sacramento

Divorce Per Inhabitants

United States Bureau of the Census (*Marriage and Divorce* 1925, 12; 1932, 16); United States Bureau of the Census (*Statistical Abstract* 1952, 80; 1962, 70; 1972, 64; 1982, 84–85; 1992, 89; 1993, 102–103)

Household Size

United States Bureau of the Census (*Statistical Abstract* 1922, 55; 1932, 44; 1952, 49; 1962, 44; 1972, 40; 1982, 48; 1993, 58)

Urban Population

Dodd (1993, 11)

Education

National Center for Education Statistics (1992, 17, 49)

Cinema Attendance

Jarvie (1986, 95); UNESCO (1964, 426; 1968, 455; 1973, 827; 1982, VI-18; 1987, 9–12, 9–13; 1991, 8–12)

Radio Licenses

United States Bureau of the Census (*Historical Statistics* 1975, 2: 796); United States Bureau of the Census (*Statistical Abstract* 1986, 545)

Television Licenses

United States Bureau of the Census (*Historical Statistics* 1975, 2: 796); United States Bureau of the Census (*Statistical Abstract* 1986, 545)

DENMARK

First Names

Hornby (1978); Pedersen (1990, 13–23, 136); Meldgaard (1990); Meldgaard (1993)

Divorce Per Marriages

Flora (1987, 2:170–172); United Nations (1949, 192; 1958, 326–327, 468–469; 1969, 466–467, 682–683; 1976, 468–469, 650–651; 1992a, 508–509, 524–525, 748–749, 754–755)

Household Size

Andersen (1977, 71); Johansen (1975, 146–147); United Nations (1988, 1034–1035)

Urban Population

Andersen (1977, 80); Andersen (1979, 120); United Nations (1992, 180)

Education

Andersen (1977, 73–74)

Cinema Attendance

Danmarks Statistik (1952, 391); UNESCO (1964, 428–429; 1993, 8–14, 8–15)

Radio Licenses

Danmarks Statistik (1925, 90; 1929, 88; 1937, 100; 1942, 109; 1946, 110; 1952, 298, 391); UNESCO (1993, 9–7)

Television Licenses

UNESCO (1964, 460–461; 1971, 750–751; 1993, 9–14, 9–15)

ENGLAND AND WALES

First Names

Dunkling (1977, 186–195; 1993, 46–47, 50–51)

Divorce Per Marriages

Dennis (1994, 21, 23); Flora (1987, 2:205–207); United Nations (1958, 470–471; 1969, 682–683; 1977, 650–651; 1992a, 510–511, 524–525, 748–749, 756–757)

Household Size

Coleman and Salt (1992, 221–223); Flora (1987, 2:324–326)

Urban Population

Coleman and Salt (1992, 41); Dennis (1994, 4, 6–9, 14); Mitchell (1978, 52); United Nations (1983, 199)

Education

Dennis (1994, 8); Flora (1983, 1:623–626); Mitchell (1978, 52–55)

Cinema Attendance

Corrigan (1983, 30); Dennis (1994); Mitchell (1978); UNESCO (1964, 429; 1968, 457; 1971, 719; 1972, 803; 1977, 986; 1989, 9–16, 9–17; 1993, 8–14, 8–15)

Radio Licenses

Pegg (1983, 7); Dennis (1994); Mitchell (1978); UNESCO (1964, 452–453; 1971, 736–737; 1993, 9–8)

Television Licenses

Corrigan (1983, 30); Dennis (1994); Mitchell (1978); UNESCO (1964, 460–461; 1971, 750–751; 1993, 9–15)

FRANCE

First Names

Michaëlsson (1927); Besnard and Desplanques (1993, 18–21)

Divorce Per Marriages

Flora (1987, 2:178–181); United Nations (1958, 326–327, 468–469; 1969, 466–467, 682–683; 1977, 468–469, 650–651; 1992a, 508–509, 524–525, 748–749, 754–755)

Urban Population

Tugault (1975, 96–109); United Nations (1968, 186; 1970, 145; 1983, 197; 1992a, 180)

Education

Flora (1983, 1:578–582)

Cinema Attendance

Crisp (1993, 13–14, 67–68); UNESCO (1964, 428–429; 1968, 457; 1971, 718–719; 1972, 802–803; 1977, 985–986; 1983, VIII-16, VIII-17; 1987, 9–14, 9–15; 1989, 9–16, 9–17; 1993, 8–14, 8–15)

Television Licenses

UNESCO (1964, 460–461; 1971, 750–751; 1993, 9–14, 9–15)

GERMANY

First Names

Andersen (1977); Frank (1977); Lukas (1981)

HUNGARY

First Names

Dombai (1974); Kálmán (1978); Virág (1978)

ICELAND

First Names

Tomasson (1975); Kvaran and Jónsson (1991)

Divorce Per Inhabitants

Statistical Bureau of Iceland (1984, 42); United Nations (1969, 682–683; 1977, 650–651; 1992, 754–755)

Household Size

Statistical Bureau of Iceland (1928, 31; 1960, 20; 1967, 79; 1969, 51); Nordal and Kristinsson (1987, 247)

Urban Population

Statistical Bureau of Iceland (1967, 31; 1988, 11)

Education

Statistical Bureau of Iceland (1984, 24–25, 228)

SCOTLAND

First Names

Unpublished data obtained from General Register Office for Scotland, Ladywell House, Edinburgh

Divorce Per Marriages

Dennis (1994, 23); Flora (1987, 2:208–210); United Nations (1958, 470–471; 1969, 682–683)

Number of Persons Per Dwelling

Flora (1987, 2:327)

Urban Population

Dennis (1994, 4, 8–9, 14); Flora (1987, 2:280); Mitchell (1978, 53); United Nations (1983, 199)

Education

Dennis (1994, 88); Flora (1983, 1:629–632)

Appendix 2 • Use of Ethnic Data in Chapter 7

MEXICANS IN TEXAS

The analysis of Mexican naming patterns in Texas is based on all births in Texas for every fifth year beginning with 1965 and running through 1990. The data (obtained through the Texas Department of Health) provide information on whites, blacks, and Hispanics (largely Mexican Americans in Texas and hence referred to as such). Note that all data refer to births occurring in Texas. Excluded are the names of children born to Mexican immigrants before their emigration (as are, necessarily, children born earlier in other parts of the United States). We also know, for each year, the names favored by mothers of Mexican-ancestry who themselves were born in the United States and therefore are at least of the second generation. This group is rather heterogeneous, and moreover, it can not be assumed that the relative frequency of second, third, fourth, . . . nth generation parents is constant over time. This is complicated because there is no reason to assume that names chosen by American-born daughters of immigrants are the same as the names chosen by Mexicans with many generations of residence in Texas (who could indeed go back to a period before Anglo domination). Comparisons between the tastes of immigrants and the tastes of Mexicans of American birth also are based on the assumption that the behavior of the immigrants at a given year describes the earlier behavior of the tastes of the immigrant parents of the American-born mothers (see the issues raised by Taeuber and Taeuber 1967). However, these comparisons do provide us with a

rough measure of shifts in naming preferences between American-born mothers and immigrant Mexican-American mothers. Incidentally, the analysis of
tastes is restricted to mother's characteristics because there is less information
available for fathers.

Ethnic origin is generally a complex and sticky subject, and these data are no
exception. In this case, ethnicity was based on the Spanish surname of the
mothers (as ascertained by the Texas Department of Health, based on listings of
such names) and hence is subject to both errors of inclusion (where a non-
Mexican mother has a Hispanic surname because—among other possible reasons—she is married to a man with such a name) or exclusion (where a Mexican
mother is not labeled, an error that is especially likely if she is listed under a non-
Hispanic husband's surname). These difficulties aside, however, there is every
reason to believe that the vast majority of the cases attributed by ethnicity are
correct—even if some Mexican mothers are excluded and some of the white
parents listed as non-Hispanic (referred to as "Anglos") are in fact Mexican
Americans. All of these difficulties work to understate the intergenerational
shifts toward assimilation observed here. Likewise, the naming behavior of Mexicans who are in Texas solely to have their baby and then return to Mexico,
understates the empirical conclusions reported here.

RESIDENTIAL ISOLATION OF ASIAN GROUPS

As noted in the text, the conclusions about the role of isolation on naming
practices—and the relevance of generation—are strikingly different from those
reported by Watkins and London (1994, 186–185), who find generation to be of
minor consequence in naming choices in the face of the important role of
isolation. They claim that the names chosen by American-born parents scarcely
differ from immigrant changes (hence, the generational gap from the names
given at the same time by earlier whites drops only slightly).

There are enough differences between the studies that at first one is tempted
to see no contradiction. Watkins and London's measurements are different (they
use the index of dissimilarity), whereas a more relaxed measure is in use here
(overlap in the top 20 for each group). Also it is easy to visualize how the
situation early in the twentieth century (their data are based on the 1910 census)
might have generated less pressure against the maintenance of European cultural tastes because the impact of popular culture might be far less invasive and
overwhelming than it is now. A simpler explanation, however, is possible: first,

they misinterpret their data, which actually contradict their conclusion about the role of isolation; second, they err in their delineation of generation such that they are really only talking about the tastes of one generation rather than two.

To capture such interactions, Watkins and London consider the ability of the subjects to speak English, their literacy, and whether they reside in New York City or elsewhere in the United States (because each of these groups had very large and rather isolated populations of compatriots in New York). They also employ such control variables as: length of residence in the United States, gender, age at immigration, and the ethnic origin of the census enumerator (1994, 195). In the full model, every one of these variables—other than residence in New York City—influences shifts in names after arrival in the United States. They do not explain this surprising result for New York, but we should note that it is an important contradiction to the notion that isolation affects naming practices. In the period under consideration, it is hard to think of any location that has as great a possibility as New York City for isolating Jewish or Italians from the naming tastes in the larger society. Their result—in which residence in New York City has no bearing on the naming outcome—is actually harmonious with the conclusion here that residential density has a modest influence on the disposition to use names that are popular among the white population. (In fairness, there is good reason to view their results as highly tentative when we consider that their model, based on eight causal variables, generates an R^2 of .074.)

Second, Watkins and London's procedure underestimates the influence of generational differences on tastes in names. Their first generation consists of people who were born elsewhere and migrated to the United States. The name changes reflect the behavior of the first generation after arrival. What they call "second generation" names, however, are not really second-generation tastes. Rather, they are the names given to American-born children by their immigrant parents, that is, the same first generation. The names given to children tell us something about their parents' tastes, but not the children's tastes. In this case, the names of the second generation reflect the tastes of the same first generation with whom they are being compared. In both cases, it is the tastes of foreign-born parents. So the gap is not really between what they refer to as the "two" generations. Note, then, that their comparison of the gap between native-born Italians (or Jews) and the native whites of native parentage is, in fact, the gap between the tastes of Italian or Jewish *immigrants* when they name their American-born children and the tastes of native whites of native parentage.

In contrast, in this study for both Asians and Mexicans we have the names given by foreign-born parents to children born to them after arrival in the United States and the names given by American-born Asian or Mexican parents to their children. This is a very clear indicator of what the tastes are of immigrants living in the United States and of American-born members of the same group. It is not flawless, however. The "second" generation is not an entirely precise term. It refers to the names given by American-born members of a given ethnic group to their offspring. This category cannot distinguish between different generations of parents—all we know is that they are American-born, but not how far back they go in generations in the United States. This procedure is satisfactory if there is reason to assume that most of the American-born parents are indeed second-generation. As one departs from that condition, there would be a tendency to find a greater gap. In my estimation, the conclusions about segregation based on the Chinese analysis are valid since it is reasonable to assume that the vast majority of American-born parents were themselves of the second generation. In any case, this is a far better approximation of generational differences in tastes than the impossible attempt by Watkins and London to use one generation (the foreign-born) to draw conclusions about intergenerational changes in names.

USING SURNAMES TO ESTIMATE JEWISH TASTES IN NAMES

There are many studies of Jewish naming preferences in the United States. See the references to Jewish names in the annotated bibliographies compiled by Lawson 1987, 1995. Many are anecdotal, others are systematic. This is not the place to review the literature, but many are sound contributions. Kolatch, for example, compiled data on 5,200 children's names obtained from questionnaires sent in 1942 to 49 schools in 38 cities. The same scholar analyzed birth announcements in the mid-1940s in the *New York Times,* comparing children's names with the names of their parents; and repeated a similar examination for the 1966 *New York Times* (Kolatch 1967, 356–361). To my knowledge, however, there is limited information of a systematic nature on the shifts in Jewish naming preferences over a long span in the United States.

The California data, for the period between 1905 and 1984, provide us with such an opportunity because births are reported by the mother's surname. Based on the data reported from a survey of more than a million men and women in the United States, Rosenwaike (1990) determined those surnames with the least error, that is, those surnames with the highest percentage who were Jewish. In particular, he reports a listing of surnames in which at least 75 percent (and often much more) reported themselves as Jewish. The names given to the children of mothers with these surnames are used as an indicator of Jewish naming preferences during this span. The names of other parents (who are also whites of non-Hispanic origin and born in the United States) are used as an indicator of non-Jewish naming preferences. Obviously, there are errors on both sides (some of the "Jewish births" are actually not to Jewish children—even if Jewish is broadly defined; some of the non-Jewish births are to Jews whose surnames are not included in the list used). The latter is not a terribly great problem because the vast majority of non-Hispanic whites in California are undoubtedly non-Jews—notwithstanding a substantial concentration of Jews in metropolitan Los Angeles. At any rate, attribution errors would tend to reduce the observed differences between the groups. The increased intermarriage between Jews and non-Jews means that errors in the determination of Jewish naming behavior will likewise increase over the long run, but again these errors will tend to understate the differences between Jews and non-Jews.

The data do not permit one to delineate American-born Jews by generation—certainly a nontrivial consideration, at least judging by the generational influence found for Asian naming preferences. One might speculate that Jews living in California during this span are of increasing distance from the immigrant generation, hence more assimilated. In addition, there is no reason to assume that the naming preferences of Jews in California are fully comparable with the preferences in eastern and midwestern cities with large Jewish populations. Particularly relevant here is the comparison of Jews with the early naming preferences of California Jews. Notwithstanding the importance of Eastern European Jews in the United States, there is no assurance that tastes in Bialystok are representative of the foreign roots of Jews living in California.

Finally, the reader should note that the naming data are given for broader periods earlier simply because the relatively small number of births in each year obtained through the surname method cannot tolerate finer delineations early in the twentieth century.

Notes

Chapter 1: Tastes

1. In another remarkable study, Simonton (1998) examined temporal shifts in the popularity of 496 operas created over a 332-year span by 55 composers. Although there is some linkage between an opera's initial reception and its later popularity, it does change over time. Not only does the assessment of operas fluctuate, but the magnitude of fluctuation itself varies over time with the period in which an opera is composed.

2. The photo essay in Maeder (1987, 43–51) shows how the portrayals of Cleopatra in movies produced in 1917, 1934, and 1963 were influenced by the aesthetics of each period.

3. See the illustrations and discussion in Grier 1988, chap. 6.

4. There is an extensive literature on this stemming from the work of Bourdieu 1984.

5. Worn but usable objects may be discarded even in the absence of fashion. If the objects simply represent wealth, then an identical item will be purchased as a replacement in order to signify wealth. A raggedy fur coat or a battered luxury car are contradictions that may convey either the former wealth of those now down at the heel or the effort to suggest a status position that cannot be fully reached.

6. For a broader and less focused discussion of various types of mechanisms, see the volume edited by Hedström and Swedberg (1998). However, they do not develop the concept proposed here of internal mechanisms that operate in the absence of external social changes.

7. Of course, it is always relevant to address issues of empirical analysis as well as problems about a theory's logic or clarity.

8. The valuable comments by Lamont and Lareau (1998) on the inconsistencies in the meaning attached to the term are of course a different matter.

9. The literature on first names is enormous, and I do not pretend to provide a full review, for that would be a book in itself. The interested reader should consult two volumes by Lawson (1987, 1995) that provide excellent annotated bibliographies. In this book I confine myself to citing works relevant to the topics discussed.

10. Compare this with the influence of organizations on many elements of culture, e.g., Baker

and Faulkner 1991; Becker 1982; DeNora 1991; DiMaggio 1992; Griswold 1992, 1994; Hirsch 1972; Lopes 1992; and Peterson 1994.

11. Name data are subject to various errors, such as the coding of information reported by the parent, as well as to problems of incomplete registration. Incomplete information is substantial in some nations, but even so, the data sets are far more complete than are most sources used for inferring tastes.

12. To be sure, special steps are needed to deal with spelling variants of same-sounding names, such as *Karl* v. *Carl, Carol* v. *Carole,* and *Sara* v. *Sarah.* (The child's gender is normally reported, so that is not a problem when confronting such androgynous names as *Leslie* or *Robin*—indeed, we can also examine gender shifts over time in the use of these names.) The most common onomastic procedure is to pool different spelling forms of what appears to be the same name—that is, if the pronunciation appears to be identical for the varied spelling forms. This is the procedure used here, although it takes some special programming to get the pooling to work, and some guesses inevitably have to be made about how people pronounce their names. This is sticky, but it is not a major problem, primarily because the really unusual spelling forms are few in number, hence of minimal consequence for the inferred strength of the name or for the estimated distribution of names in a population.

13. For an extensive list of reasons that might be given for choosing a name for one's child, consider de Klerk and Bosch 1995.

14. Smith (1985), for example, employs various data sets to infer the conditions underlying the changes in naming practices in Hingham, Mass., between 1641 and 1880.

Chapter 2: Becoming a Fashion

1. This is plotted on the Scotland graph for the year of 1625, the midpoint of the 50-year span.

2. This is for illustrative purposes; in practice, one would not want to make much of one small case based on a span of two years.

3. The differences are quite modest in Denmark and Iceland—albeit replacement is a tad more rapid for daughters' names.

4. Depending on the nature of the data available for a given location, the list may range from the top 10 to the top 50. This can have a bearing on the likelihood of replacement, but all analyses within a nation are based on a constant number, and so comparability over time within a nation is assured. In the case of France, for example, whatever the influence of dealing with only the leading ten names for each sex (due to the available data), it is the same influence throughout the time period. So the form of the curve is not a statistical artifact.

5. An argument developed in Lieberson 1991.

6. Of course, there were shifts in their rankings among the top 50, but not one dropped out.

7. One-sided $p = .01$ and $<.01$, respectively.

8. See Fischer 1995 for a review of the role of cities in generating subcultures.

9. At first blush, the growth in education appears to lag behind the expansion of fashion—which of course would mean that it could not be a causal factor. However, this is an artifact of the graph's construction because different scales are used for fashion and education. If, for example, the scale for education was expanded (or the scale contracted for fashion), then the line for education would appear to precede the expansion in fashion. The key issue is whether the upward movement in a causal variable is roughly as steep (or steeper) during the same period as the upward movement in fashion.

10. Given the small number of cases, there is little point in trying to sort out the relative influences of urbanization and education. In general, a multivariate approach cannot be justified here.

11. This is inconclusive because data suggest a decline in education that is almost surely due to changes in the enumeration procedures.

12. The drop in the percentage of the population living in areas of 100,000 or more is not necessarily contradictory because by then fashions are well established. See Lieberson (1985, chap. 4) for a discussion of asymmetric causality.

13. There may be a good reason for the fact that education is parallel with schooling later in the century but is much less so earlier. The educational measure is the percentage who pass the university entrance exam. Relatively few were entering universities until after World War II. Accordingly, a more appropriate indicator for earlier would have been a measure geared toward educational developments at lower levels.

14. Based on television data for the United States; unfortunately, a time series for California is unavailable.

15. Again, it is necessary to use national data for movie attendance rather than data specific to California.

16. Adequate radio data were not found for France, Scotland, or Iceland.

17. Of course, even in the most individualistic of societies, deemphasis of individuality is prescribed in some circumstances. That is essentially the case for uniforms, whether they be military, police, postal delivery, restaurant, airline, medical, hotel, and the like. Here the function is to make the person's job or role quickly identifiable to others, and implies a certain expectation that others can have. That is, one approaches the uniform not the person.

Chapter 3: How the Social Order Influences Names

1. This involves, of course, a counterfactual statement that cannot be evaluated.

2. The evidence for these conclusions is strong. Naming choices for California, available monthly for each year, shows that the peak for *Jacqueline* in 1960 was in November, the month when JFK is elected. Likewise, there is a resurgence in November 1963, the month of the assassination.

3. This is a "pushy" analysis, based as it is on net changes in the disposition of a few parents to use a particular name. Rigor is thus difficult. However, the results are consistent with the view that exogenous events will affect the imagery of the cultural attribute in ways that may enhance or contaminate the symbolic attractiveness of the attribute (in this case, first names). The number of baby girls named *Jacqueline* in California in 1968 are as follows: January, 48; February, 40; March, 51; April, 45; May, 41; June, 54; July, 53; August, 54; September, 53; October, 47; November, 34; December, 41. In 1976 the name *Jacqueline* ranked 73d; in 1977 the rank rose to 53.

4. I am indebted to Anne Woodell, chair of the Oakland Parks and Recreation Advisory Commission, for updating my records on recent winners and for explaining that all winners are married.

5. Programs were examined for the 1900–1901, 1910–1911, 1920–1921, and 1930–1931 seasons, but no women were listed as members of the governing bodies. For more recent years, as the number of women increases, the programs were examined more frequently.

6. This discussion is drawn largely from Lieberson and Mikelson 1995.

7. Because the number of white births is substantially greater than the number for blacks, there is a statistical bias toward finding a higher percentage for blacks. However, the level is massively higher for blacks even after this is taken into account. (For a discussion of the problem and the index solution, see Lieberson and Mikelson 1995, 930–931.)

8. Drawing on 1910 census data for Mississippi, for example, Andrew London and S. Philip Morgan (1994) find little difference between the races in the use of unique names. Both

Henry L. Mencken (1963, 628–629) and Newbell Puckett (1975, 135) find that name innovations were once uncommon among African Americans. To be sure, there is reason to believe that usage of distinctive names was increasing before the period covered by the Illinois data. Unusual names are more common among African American college students from 1910 to 1930 than in the years 1880 to 1910 (Puckett 1938). Puckett also reports an increase in unusual names in his comparisons of the pre-1870, 1870–1900, and post-1900 birth cohorts listed in *Who's Who in Negro America.* However, a study of African-American and white college women in the academic years 1931–1932 and 1940–1941 indicates that only a women of either race had unique names (Eagleson and Clifford 1945). For a fuller view, see Lieberson and Bell 1992, 547.

9. Called "Styles" catalog in 1990. The Spring–Summer catalog allows the analysis of hats and gloves without worrying about whether they are being worn for warmth and hence not an issue of formality versus informality. Excluded for men are casual wear, winter hats, ski hats, and baseball caps. The four cowboy hats found in the 1980 catalog were arbitrarily excluded, but even inclusion would not have radically altered the results (the ratio—discussed below— would have been .667 instead of zero in that year). Because the decline in the raw number of men's formal hats could be a function of variations between years in the size of the catalog, the raw data were standardized by dividing the number of hats by the number of pages each year devoted to men's underwear. Only formal dress gloves and dress hats are included for women. Excluded are gardening or other utilitarian gloves, as are caps, hats for warmth, rain hats, and so forth. For standardization purposes, these numbers were also divided by the number of pages of women's underwear of all types.

10. Keep in mind that the shift toward nicknames is understated, if we consider that not all members of Congress have first names that lend themselves to shortening in the customary manner. Examples are: *Paul, George, Ralph, Curt, Austin, Neil, Roger, Dennis, Trent, Jesse,* and *Mark.* The analysis is on the first names of members of Congress reported in various editions of the *World Almanac* beginning with 1888. Comparing these names with official name listings, for the most part one can distinguish a "Fred" or a "Joe" who were born with such names as opposed to a "Fred" or "Joe" whose given name was *Frederick* or *Joseph.*

11. It is conceivable that dissatisfaction with the Establishment after World War I could have started the shift, but obviously the long-term development would reflect some sort of taste mechanism. A war between 1914 and 1918 would itself not have a significant impact on later generations of men who were born after the war and reaching adulthood long after World War I was strongly relevant to them. Limitations in data access prevent me from considering whether the decline had begun before World War I and therefore before any disillusion with older men after that war.

12. California data are especially valuable because they start before World War I, but for almost the entire period those data do not report racial information on the names used. We therefore turn to Illinois in order to consider shifts for blacks.

13. Consider that the Spearman correlations shift only a few points in each period.

14. The antiwar demonstration reached its peak in November 1969, when 250,000 protesters marched in Washington, D.C. American forces in Vietnam had peaked in April 1969.

15. Compared with a single value based on the proportion of all boys (or girls) born in a year who are given one of the 20 most common names for that year (the measure of concentration used above), Spearman correlations may be inherently more volatile. However, I have tried to correct for this by using a five-year moving average.

16. For examples of the difficulty in inferring a causal effect when there are substantial fluctuations in the dependent variable before the event in question, see Campbell 1978 and Haight 1978.

17. Blacks and whites during this period grew progressively apart in their choice of leading names. Around 1920, the Spearman correlation between black and white choices in their top 20 was a shade over 0.6 among boys and 0.4 for girls. By the late 1980s the correlations were approximately zero for boys and −0.2 for girls. (Based on five-year running averages.)

18. Whites in Illinois are compared with all races in California. If anything, given the results for blacks in Illinois, this should not dispose the California decline to occur earlier.

Chapter 4: The Ratchet Effect

1. The issue of fashion being *dictated* occurs later when the success of a new fashion eventually affects the options made available for the remainder of the buying public. At some point, the market for earlier tastes becomes smaller and smaller, thereby affecting the economics of supplying such products as, let alone the image of, say, stores and manufacturers who provide such goods. As a consequence, there are *conservative* retailers who develop a niche by not being too fashionable.

2. Because the study is based on measurements of fashion plates and other pictures that themselves vary in size, Richardson and Kroeber first determine the length of each individual figure to form a base for comparison with these measures—in effect, it is as if pictures of varying sizes were enlarged (or reduced) in different degrees in order to obtain a common standard length of picture, and then the above waist measurements are made.

3. Based on his examination of men's pictures in the *Illustrated London News*.

4. Based on a set of portraits or photographs of each president, shown in the *Encyclopedia Americana* (Grolier 1992, 22:558–559) and President Clinton, who took office after that publication.

5. Again, the "stretch limousine" can work for a special occasion; indeed—like the bride's gown—it marks the special nature of the event (or the person). For daily travel, however, practicality would set bounds.

6. With a large number of fashion elements, it is highly likely that at any given time at least one other attribute will be changing at an unusual rate. Hence these results could be due to chance. However, this consideration is irrelevant here since the point is that—for whatever reason—the period of reversal is usually accompanied by some other relatively substantial movement for another attribute.

7. As we approach the current period, the data are for increasingly shorter spans. This is no great problem because we know that names changed less rapidly in the earlier periods. The similarity between 1700 and 1800 is because there are virtually no changes reported for males and very few for females (Dunkling 1986, 40–41, 44–45). For boys, there are none moving in or out of the top 100, with almost no movements in or out of the top 50.

8. Keep in mind that talk of low points or high points refers only to the years reported. No information is available for the years in between. Although it is unlikely, for all we know, none of the leading names had such an ending in some of the unreported years or, instead, all 50 leading names ended in *a*.

9. Since the initial analysis, a newer volume by Dunkling (1993) has updated his listing of leading names, extending it to 1993 (where 8 of the most popular names given to girls start with a vowel).

10. Dunkling 1993, 47.

11. There are exceptions, of course; starting at the same level in 1918 and 1925, the use of girls' names with a *sh*-sound in it (as in *Ashley*, *Shannon*, and *Latasha*) became more popular among blacks.

12. The sounds are unlikely to have much inherent substantive meaning. They could, of course,

be the product of an association between types of names and sounds; for example, a rise in the popularity of Italian names for boys would increase the occurrence of names ending in *o*. It will be obvious that such connections could not account for the movements in sounds observed.

13. This list is obtained from Reader's Digest Association 1967, 609–612. Analysis of girls' naming patterns is precluded because there are only 15 female names listed in this source.

14. In England and Wales, of the 50 most common names given to girls, 14 and 16 end in *a* in 1700 and 1985, respectively. This compares with 2 and 0 for boys. The gender gap is equally pronounced in California: 10 and 20 of the top 50 girls' names have this ending in 1906 and 1984, respectively. This compares with 0 and 1 for boys.

15. Bathsheba is an unfaithful wife who was David's mistress and whose husband was sent to his death in battle; Delilah is a courtesan who tricks Samson.

16. The decline was essentially due to drop in attendance by Catholics, which then stabilized (Hout and Greeley 1987).

17. As is the case at a number of points, because of limitations in the available data, it is necessary to make an assumption about the comparability of data; in this case the names given to newborn white boys in Illinois compared with the religious trends for the entire United States during this period are a reasonable approximation to the religious trends for white parents in Illinois who are having baby boys in the same span of time. It is not necessary that the actual levels be reproduced but rather that the religious trends be in the same direction, and hence counter to the naming practices in Illinois.

18. Thanks to the excellent work of Currie et al. 1977. Their data on church membership has been divided by the estimated population of Britain in the relevant years. This provides a meaningful set of figures that is not influenced by fluctuations in population size.

19. Changes in church membership in the United States also fail to be associated with shifts in biblical names. Two different series suggest a gradual upward movement through the years, thereby including periods when biblical names do not increase and periods when they do. Drawn from rates of "Religious Adherence" reported in Finke and Stark (1992, 16), and by the ratio obtained between membership in religious bodies and total resident population, 1890–1970 (data obtained in U.S. Bureau of the Census, 1975, *Historical Statistics of the United States: Colonial Times to 1970*, Bicentennial Edition, Part 2, Ser. H 793–799 and Ser. A 6–8).

20. Based on data reported in Greeley (1995, 85) from the 1991 International Social Survey of religion in 16 countries.

21. This is a much more difficult task than meets the eye. A substantial number of respondents appear to use nicknames when referring to their children. It was necessary to clean out the data, making estimates of the actual names of the offspring. Also, because the number of biblical names is enormous, again it was necessary to restrict the analysis to the Reader's Digest list of prominent names. I am indebted to Tom Smith of the National Opinion Research Center for facilitating the plans, for coding, and for steps necessary for the inclusion of first names in the data tapes.

22. "Frequent" means attending at least once a month; "infrequent" means no more than several times a year. Intensity of feeling is divided into three categories: persons answering "Strong," those who are either "Not very strong or moderately so," and those with no religious preference. The relatively small number of cases restricts use of more detailed categories. Bear in mind that these parent data are only for the parent answering the questionnaire—not for both parents.

23. Dichotomized into those born in 1972 or earlier compared with 1973 or later.

24. Fifteen percent of parents with no religion—compared with 3 and 5, respectively, for those whose religious feelings are moderate or strong.

25. See Lowe and Lowe (1982) for a stimulating and radically different effort to account for the results obtained by Richardson and Kroeber (1940). Using concepts in the natural sciences, they employ a formal mathematical model that is then analyzed statistically. This involves: entropy; the existence of inherent aesthetic rules (which I avoid assuming at all); equilibrium points, such that there is a tendency for tastes to return to a certain ideal point; and attributing a greater role to external forces and a greater disposition to connect stylistic changes "to the remainder of the sociocultural system" (538). This is a stretch, in my estimation, being based solely on the fact that the residual variances around the mean differ from period to period.

Chapter 5: Other Internal Mechanisms

1. Barnett (1953) includes a far more extensive and complicated set of innovation models than are appropriate for consideration here.
2. Information about Gaynor drawn from Quinlan 1981, 182; and Siegel and Siegel 1990, 169–170.
3. Because the available California data start with 1905, there is no way of determining the number of years *Mary* was in first place before then. Also, in later times *Mary* intermittently reappears in first place for an additional 10 years.
4. These are *Jane, Jennie, Jessie, Josephine,* and *Julia,* as well as *Genevieve.*
5. The others are *Jacqueline, Janet, Janice, Jean, Jill, Joan, Joanne, Joyce, Judith, Judy, Julia,* and *Julie.*
6. Throughout, I ignore *Carmen* (which appears in the top 100 in 1928 and 1938), which has the same spelling but a different phoneme: *car* as in *carton* versus *car* as in *carry.* I assume that the popularity of *Carmen* reflects the Latina influence in California. In Illinois, which has a considerably smaller Latina population, *Carmen* is not among the 200 most common names used for white girls in 1928 and is tied for rank 195 in 1938.
7. She received a special Oscar in 1939 for her performance (Siegel and Siegel 1990, 168).
8. Figures analyzed for 1916, then 1920, and every 5 years through 1965. The number of girls named *La Verne,* by year of birth, is: 6 (1925); 9 (1930); 5 (1935); 11 (1940); 13 (1945); 15 (1950); 31 (1955); 32 (1960). The highest rank for any of these years is 63.
9. Born in Illinois.
10. There are two fairly common white girl's names beginning with *Lau,* as in *Laura* and *Lauren,* but this is a different phoneme; *Lore* as opposed to the *Lah* sound among blacks.
11. With an increasing number of children given invented names, there will be a feedback effect such that the resistance to the use of such names will decline even more over time.
12. Keep in mind that the criterion for inclusion is that the name must appear in *at least* 5 time points; a name appearing only in one specific year (or 2, 3, or even 4 years) will not be included.
13. Strictly speaking, a survival model is appropriate here because some of the names will take off *after* the period under study and hence the data are truncated. However, we will see that few of these names ever become important, as we go out to at least another 20 years (for those first making the cutoff in 1969) and longer for others.
14. There are two technical considerations to take into account, each biasing the results in opposite directions. The intensity of usage is underestimated because spelling variations based on the same pronunciation are not pooled here. However, because the figures start only with 1930, the actual number of void years is understated for those *La-* names that initially appeared before 1930.
15. See the review of advertising and product failures in Schudson (1984, 36–43), particularly his review of quantitative studies (36–37).

16. It is not entirely correct to view shifts in the symbolism associated with names as entirely a random matter, as we will see in Chapter 7.

17. This account is drawn from the following sources: Dunkling 1977, 129; Dunkling 1993, 71; Dunkling and Gosling 1983, 215; Hanks and Hodges 1990, 258; Kisbye 1981, 601; Stewart 1979, 205; and Withycombe 1977, 235.

18. Based on various data sets gathered by Dunkling 1977, 129, which are not necessarily representative data for either the nation or a constant subarea of the nation.

19. Data are available for 1875 and 1900, but the key period would be to see the usage of *Oscar* somewhere in between, at a point when Wilde was a great success and before his 1895 trial for homosexuality (see Dunkling 1993, 71).

20. Nine million "Sesame Street" toys were sold in 1972 (O'Brien 1990, 210).

21. Mothers' education is used exclusively because data are unavailable on fathers' education.

22. Names favored by women with only a grade-school education is not shown because a strong ethnic factor appears to be operating to distort the results (see Lieberson and Bell 1992, 524).

23. This is not always possible, even though the proposition is valid. See Lieberson 1985, 94–99.

Chapter 6: Models of the Fashion Process

1. This is a useful distinction to employ, although the difference is muddy in some cases between new technological changes that exist as much for fashion as anything else.

2. This is what Coleman calls "double-contingency collective behavior" (1990, 901–903).

3. Taylor continues: "How are we to explain this twentieth-century change? There are really two problems: first, why did the practice decline among the white middle class, and second, why did it increase among the white and black working classes? Perhaps the increase explains the decrease? This is precisely what we propose to argue. Having defined suffixes as status indicators or symbols, we must expect them to follow the same patterns of inflation and circulation which have been observed for other status symbols. What Weber originally identified as the process of status usurpation is now studied as the "trickle effect." Fallers (1954) describes the trickle effect as a "battle of wits" between upper-status persons who attempt to guard their status treasure and lower-status persons who attempt to devalue the status symbolic currency. With the American ideology of equality and in the absence of any legal devices to protect and maintain the value of status symbols, it is a one-sided battle. Over time, the symbols trickle down the status hierarchy and in the process, they cease to have the same value for their original users. The trickle effect is generally assumed to operate in most areas of conspicuous consumption" (1974, 19).

4. The 1990 birth certificates in Texas provide information on parental education, but this is not available for earlier years. Accordingly, because of the association between the month that prenatal care first begins and mother's education, the former is used as a proxy variable. *High* SES refers to mothers first obtaining prenatal care in the first 2 months of their pregnancy; *Low* refers to those first obtaining care in the third or later month. For the 30 most frequent names given to white girls in 1990, the Spearman rank order correlation between the mean level of education of mothers using that name for their daughter and the mean month prenatal care began is $-.97$ (p $<$ .0000); for sons it is $-.94$ (p $<$ .0000). "Popular" is defined as one of the 20 names most frequently given to boys (or girls) by parents of the specified SES category in the year indicated. Note that discussions of period apply only to the year specified; nothing is known about the interim years. Finally, both *Steven* and *Stephen* are allowed separate status in this analysis, although for most purposes names with the same pronunciation are pooled.

5. Respectively, 8 of 29 and 21 of 29.

6. Examples are, respectively, *Lauren, Laura,* and *Lisa.*

7. There is a technical issue here because of the truncation in the data. The *n*'s are too small to take this into account, but I believe that the results are conservative, because the truncation occurs for names that are popular among social classes over a long span of time.

8. In some cases, adults will change their names and their children's first names after migrating to a linguistic setting where their first name is unknown or difficult to pronounce or spell.

9. The relative role of newer cohorts entering and older cohorts leaving is relatively modest in terms of the distribution of tastes.

10. To be sure, there are certain families where a traditional name still has appeal, particularly where one can trace the name to an ancestor. This inclination is probably less widespread, however. Moreover, the use of a name that is appealing for other reasons *and* has the added virtue of being tied to ancestors has to be carefully distinguished from a name used simply because it is traditional or linked to a specific ancestor. In the former case, the search for an appealing name can also have the added value of a remote linkage to an ancestor or tradition.

11. Of course, the issue of naming a child after a relative is a separate matter.

Chapter 7: Ethnic and Racial Groups

1. Henceforth the term *ethnic* includes groups sometimes referred to as *races.*

2. "Remaining white" births is a floating category that includes all of the other white children born to nonimmigrant mothers. For all groups, only the names given by American-born mothers are considered.

3. Based on the naming choices by American-born mothers of each ethnic group compared with the remaining white births to American-born mothers (a floating category, to avoid part-whole problems).

4. Of the other specific groups in table 7.2, *Kevin* ranks 20th for the British, 18th for Germans, 19th among Italians, 15th among Poles, and 17th among Scandinavians. It is even lower among French and Mexican sons.

5. The popularity of *Thomas* was also influenced by Saint Thomas à Becket (Coghlan 1979, 116); also note that *Joseph* is an exception with respect to Irish usage of prominent New Testament names.

6. In order to make this a manageable project, the study uses a list of 10 boys' and 10 girls' names to track popularity shifts over time. Table 7.2 covers 1920 through 1985. In addition, 1916 and 1989 were included because they are the earliest and latest year in the data series.

7. See Appendix 2 for a more detailed review of the data.

8. Bear in mind that the immigrant choices are only for their children born in Texas—this excludes offspring born before parental residence in Texas.

9. At best, *Jesus* ranked 9th in 1970.

10. Except for 1975, the decline in the odds that the son of an American-born Mexican mother (divided by the odds for the Texas-born son of an immigrant mother) will be named *Jesus* is less than the comparable intergenerational decline for *Jose* or *Juan*. In 1975, the decline is essentially the same for all three names. The difference between *Juan* and *Jesus*—the median ratio of odds is .52 for *Juan* and .43 for *Jesus.*

11. Of course, we would want to have data by specific generation of American-born parents of Mexican ancestry in order to have far greater confidence in this conclusion.

12. "Popular" being defined as in the top 20 among the group specified, in this case the Anglos.

13. Of course, features of English and the Latin alphabet are widely known—reflecting its dominance in the world as a lingua franca as well as the significance of English in movies, popular music, television programming, and, more recently, the Internet.

14. To eliminate the influence of other immigrant group tastes as well as the Mexican population studied earlier, included are only those children with a native-born non-Mexican mother.

15. Compared to Mexican immigrants in Texas, Asian immigrants give their American-born children names that are much closer to the tastes popular among native whites—particularly for sons. There are a variety of possible reasons: higher educational levels among Asians; less possibility (or desire) to return to their native country; the greater difficulty for the Asian parents to maintain their traditional names because the disparity from American practices is far greater than the Mexican-Anglo gap; a greater emphasis on assimilation for the children of Asians; or simply that the smaller Asian proportion of the population intensifies interaction with others and hence makes it more critical to have American names. It is impossible to evaluate these factors with the data at hand. One should not make too much of these immigrant differences, however. American-born parents of Mexican origin also have naming tastes that are much closer to those of Anglo parents. The overlap with Anglos is only slightly lower for both sons (11 in 1980, 13 in 1985) and daughters (14 and 11, respectively in 1980 and 1985). Mexican Americans are slower in their shift (particularly among immigrants), but in both cases there is considerable assimilation in naming practices. The difference is probably understated because the Mexican parents of American-birth in Texas are probably more removed generationally from their immigrant ancestors.

16. For every birth, California gives the zip code in which the mother lives. Accordingly, one can determine the number of births to Chinese immigrant mothers living in each zip code. In turn, these zip codes are arrayed from highest (largest number of such births) to lowest (only one such birth). Obviously zip codes without any Chinese births are irrelevant. We then divide this array into two roughly equal halves (in terms of total Chinese births—not in terms of the total number of spatial units). One set of zip codes is labeled "high density," the other "low density." We can analyze the distribution of names used in each subarea. In similar fashion, this procedure is repeated for the births of Chinese-ancestry women who are themselves of American birth (second or later generation).

17. The restriction to Chinese is because of the size of the population such that there is a large number of both immigrant and second-generation members of the population—because each set is subdivided into high and low segregation.

18. This means that the influence of density is, if anything, overestimated because the effect of unmeasured selectivity is not ruled out.

19. The 20th most common name for the daughters of American-born Chinese mothers living in dense areas is given to 13 girls.

20. Bear in mind that state differences exist in the preferences of non-Hispanic whites. The states share only 12 of the 20 most popular girls' names and 13 of the sons' names. The comparisons are based on 1985 births in Texas and births between 1982 and 1986 in California.

21. The average overlap in top-20 boys' names between each of 3 Asian pairs is 15.3. It is also exactly that level for girls, and it is that level for the overlap between each Asian group and native white boys, and again for native white girls. To a surprising degree (such that I rechecked the data several times), the average bond in naming tastes between American-born Asians is the same as their average bond with native whites. There is even a fairly comparable level of variability; the range for each set of 3 indexes (in the order in which the averages are given) are: 14 to 17, 14 to 17, 15 to 16, and 13 to 17.

22. Keep in mind that these data refer to the first names given on birth certificates—not to adaptations of traditional names by immigrants after arrival in the United States in order to have a name that can be remembered and/or pronounced by others and/or "fits in." It is beyond the purview of this study, as well as the available data, to consider the use of a middle

name to continue traditional naming practices while adopting an Americanized name. Discussions with Asian students, however, lead me to guess that this is a common practice.

23. For each of these top-20 names, their frequency was examined for white children born in California to American-born mothers back to 1970, and then back to 1955 for all mothers in California (data not available before 1970 on mother's birthplace and race).

24. Although a formal test is in order for the lags in the names of daughters and sons, it is not possible with the available data. The data for white tastes can be traced back through the years, but comparable data are not available for any of the Asian groups.

25. Based on a random sample of Koreans in Los Angeles, an excellent study by Hurh and Kim (1984) reports that about half of the respondents affiliate with Christian churches before arrival in the United States. The level is even greater in the United States, where close to 70 percent affiliate with Korean Christian churches—Presbyterian being the largest (129–130; sample discussed at 30–34).

26. *Joseph* and *Jonathan* are the only reversals, where they become even more popular in the second generation. This is also the case for *Michael,* but that is a move in the direction of popularity for the name among native white parents.

27. The reader may be surprised by the assumption that *Harry* and *Robin* were diminutive names, because at present they are formal names. There is some reason to believe that they did not have this quality in the 1700s: *Robin* was originally a pet form of *Robert* (Hanks and Hodges 1997, 211; Stewart 1979, 223); *Harry* and *Henry* have the same common origin, but there is evidence that *Harry* served as a pet form of *Henry,* or at least a form of *Henry* for "ordinary" males (Dunkling 1978, 68; Hanks and Hodges 1997, 109).

28. Reported in Puckett (1975, 112ff.) for 1790–1818.

29. Likewise, Gutman reports the prevalence of "Anglo-American" names among ex-slaves (1976, 186).

30. Based on slave names linked to one African root (analyzed in Lieberson and Mikelson 1995, table 4).

31. Because there was a three-way tie for the 20th most popular black name, a computer-generated random assignment procedure picks among the 3. One of the others is *Marion;* had that name been selected there would be even one more overlap in the top 20 in 1940.

32. The ranks are: *Anthony* (21), *Justin* (24), *Timothy* (27), *William* (26), *Brandon* (30), *Jeremy* (42), *Charles* (47), and *Derek* (51).

33. Drawn from Lieberson and Bell 1992, 546–547.

34. This was the Soviet Republic of White Russia before the dissolution of the Soviet Union (also known as Belorussia in the Soviet period).

35. Data are available for later periods, but they are of little use because the post-Holocaust Jewish population was minimal and, moreover, religion was not recorded with the birth data.

36. It is not easy to sort the relative importance of each influence.

37. Note that the Danzig data attests to the Germanic nature of the names chosen, but not to the similarity of these names with those given to Germans who are not Jewish.

38. The nature of the California data on Jews, the assumptions made, and the cautions necessary, are reviewed in Appendix 2.

39. For each population's 20 most popular names for sons and daughters, there are 11 and 10 overlaps, respectively. Obviously this is considerably greater than in Poland, even though the 25 most common names were considered in that case.

40. The choice of *Elizabeth* is complicated because it is an important New Testament name and has other connotations as well. It also has important Old Testament connections, however; *Elizabeth* is the English form of the Hebrew name *Elisheva,* the wife of Aaron and therefore the sister-in-law of Moses (Kolatch 1984, 320).

41. Spearman rank order correlations between year and number of Jewish-Other overlaps for top-20 sons and daughters is, respectively, .01 (single tailed p = .48 and .30, respectively).

42. Beginning with 1970–1971, the overlaps between Jewish and non-Jewish daughters is: 13, 13, 12, 14, 12, 12, 11, 12.

43. The number of overlaps since 1970–1971 is: 13, 13, 13, 12, 12, 13, 9.

44. Bear in mind, however, that rank order correlations based on moving averages also show no persistent upward movement during this span. Using moving averages for 5 consecutive time periods, Spearman is .30 and −.01, respectively for boys and girls (p = .30 and .48).

45. Of the 41 names, 13 are simultaneously popular for non-Jews and Jews, 14 first for non-Jews, and 14 first for Jews.

46. There is a truncation problem for the second period, because there are names that are not yet popular for both groups—only one by 1984. Those names that will eventually also be popular for the other cannot be distinguished from those that will not be popular among the second group.

47. Because this analysis focuses on Jewish naming practices, the Reader's Digest listing of prominent Old Testament men is supplemented with the inclusion of other important names from a Jewish perspective. These are *Benjamin, Jared, Joel,* and *Seth.*

Chapter 8: Entertainment and Entertainers

1. Subjects were allowed to give multiple responses; therefore, if one respondent mentions 5 media forms and 4 mention none, this would be indistinguishable from 5 respondents each mentioning a single media form. Although her links between media, stereotypes, and social class are highly suggestive and merit more work, Vandebosch's own evidence rests on the sources parents indicate as inspiring the names they have given their children. Even though one-third of her responses mention some form of media (television, books, newspapers, magazines, movies, music, sports, and radio), we do not know how many parents mention the media as an influence (as distinguished from the number of responses mentioning media. We do know, however, that 14 percent do mention television.

2. Indeed, I suspect that one of the aesthetic features of a sketch is the ability to convey the scene with the fewest lines and least detail.

3. See Withycombe 1977, 276–277; and Johnson and Sleigh 1973, 130–131.

4. In other words, be able to draw a counterfactual conditional statement about what would have happened if the movie had not occurred (or if Jenny was not the heroine of the movie). A statistical effort is possible, but at this point there is insufficient knowledge to map out the counterfactual curve with any level of confidence.

5. Whether this is a name that a performer takes later on or is the birth name is immaterial because the former option did exist if the name was viewed as unsuitable.

Chapter 9: Broader Issues

1. For example, Bielby and Bielby 1994, Harrington and Bielby 1995, Ferguson 1998, Gronow 1997, Erickson 1996, DiMaggio and Useem 1978, and Peterson and Kern 1996. There may also be *some* overlap between this notion of internal mechanisms and the usage of "field" by Bourdieu 1984 and several followers. As far as I can tell, however, the emphasis is quite different. Mechanisms, as used here, focus on principles that generate cultural change in the absence of further external changes. It is impossible to be conclusive, because Bourdieu intentionally refuses to provide a precise definition—indeed viewing its absence as a virtue (Bourdieu and Wacquant 1992, 95–96).

2. To be sure, there certainly are links between parts of the cultural surface—after all, 11 of the 25 names still end in an *a*-sound.

3. Excellent studies by Zelinsky (1988, chap. 4) and Baldwin and Grimaud (1992) provide a valuable examination of the changing external influences on geographic names in the United States.

4. It is not possible to rule out that some are the surnames of important local settlers, but the correspondence with prominent patriots is too great to name that as the primary cause.

5. For a brief period, the Spanish obtained control of Iowa from the French.

6. Above and beyond the fact that any causal influence should be viewed as a probabilistic matter such that its importance cannot be rejected on the basis of a few settings where it fails to operate.

7. This is a rough version of the succession models envisioned for the social order by human ecologists earlier in the twentieth century. For a classic statement, see Hawley 1950, chaps. 16, 19.

8. The examples are from Morris and Morris 1988, 123, 322, 450−451.

9. For purposes of exposition I am operating as if a cause is either totally asymmetrical or symmetrical; in practice there can be partial asymmetry such that, say, a unit increase in X leads to a unit increase in Y, but then a unit decrease in X leads to a partial unit decrease in Y.

10. The only exceptions being if their own mother tongue were to become a rival or if the new competitor was massively easier to learn.

11. Of course, this is not to say that any and all practices would survive, because age is not the only factor.

12. Even then, it was only in 1924 (about the time when Canadian provinces were shifting) that the right-hand rule was adopted for Italian cities.

13. Not until 1947, two years before it became a province of Canada, did Newfoundland make the change.

References

Abramowicz, Zofia. 1993. *Imiona chrzestne Białostoczan w aspekcie socjolingwistycznym (lata 1885–1985)*. Bialystok: University of Warsaw–Bialystok.

Aczel, Amir D. 1996. *Fermat's Last Theorem: Unlocking the Secret of an Ancient Mathematical Problem*. New York: Four Walls Eight Windows.

Adamic, Louis. 1942. *What's Your Name?* New York: Harper and Brothers.

Alford, Richard D. 1988. *Naming and Identity: A Cross-Cultural Study of Personal Naming Practices*. New Haven, Conn.: HRAF Press.

Andersen, Christian. 1977. *Studien zur Namengebung in Nordfriesland Die Bökingharde, 1760–1970*. Bredstedt: Verlag Nordfriisk Instituut.

Andersen, Otto. 1977. *The Population of Denmark*. Copenhagen: CICRED.

——. 1979. *Denmark: European Demography and Economic Growth*. Edited by W. R. Lee. New York: St. Martin's.

Baker, Wayne E., and Robert R. Faulkner. 1991. "Role as Resource in the Hollywood Film Industry." *American Journal of Sociology* 97(2): 279–309.

Baldwin, Lawrence M., and Michel Grimaud. 1992. "How New Naming Systems Emerge: The Prototypical Case of Columbus and Washington." *Names* 40(3): 153–166.

Baltzell, E. Digby. 1964. *The Protestant Establishment: Aristocracy and Caste in America*. New York: Vintage.

Bang, Gustav. 1976. *Kirkebogsstudier: Bidrag til dansk befolkningsstatistik og kulturhistorie i det 17. arhundrede*. Copenhagen: Selskabet for Udgivelse af Kilder til Dansk Historie.

Barber, Bernard, and Lyle S. Lobel. 1953. "Fashion in Women's Clothes and the American Social System." Pp. 323–332 in *Class, Status, and Power,* edited by Reinhard Bendix and Seymour Martin Lipset. Glencoe, Ill.: Free Press.

Barnett, Homer G. 1953. *Innovation: The Basis of Cultural Change.* New York: McGraw-Hill.

Barthes, Roland. 1983. *The Fashion System.* New York: Hill and Wang.

Becker, Howard S. 1963. *Outsiders: Studies in the Sociology of Deviance.* New York: Free Press.

———. 1982. *Art Worlds.* Berkeley: University of California Press.

Berton, Pierre. 1977. *The Dionne Years: A Thirties Melodrama.* Toronto: McClelland and Stewart.

Besnard, Philippe. 1995. "The Study of Social Taste Through First Names: Comment on Lieberson and Bell." *American Journal of Sociology* 100(5): 1313–1317.

Besnard, Philippe, and Guy Desplanques. 1993. *Un prénom pour toujours: La côte des prénoms en 1994.* Paris: Balland.

Bielby, William T., and Denise D. Bielby. 1994. "'All Hits Are Flukes': Institutionalized Decision Making and the Rhetoric of Network Prime-Time Program Development." *American Journal of Sociology* 99(5):1287–1313.

Blumer, Herbert. 1951. "Collective Behavior." Pp. 167–222 in *New Outline of the Principles of Sociology,* edited by Alfred McClung Lee. New York: Barnes and Noble.

———. 1968. "Fashion." Pp. 341–342 in *The International Encyclopedia of the Social Sciences,* vol. 5, edited by David L. Sills. New York: Macmillan and Free Press.

———. 1969. "Fashion: From Class Differentiation to Collective Selection." *Sociological Quarterly* 10: 275–291.

Bogle, Donald. 1988. *Blacks in American Films and Television: An Encyclopedia.* New York: Garland.

Bourdieu, Pierre. 1984. *Distinction: A Social Critique of the Judgement of Taste.* Translated by Richard Nice. Cambridge: Harvard University Press.

Bourdieu, Pierre, and Loïc J. D. Wacquant. 1992. *An Invitation to Reflexive Sociology.* Chicago: University of Chicago Press.

Braudel, Fernand. 1981. *The Structures of Everyday Life: The Limits of the Possible.* Translated by Miriam Kochan. New York: Harper and Row.

Brooks, Tim, and Earle Marsh. 1985. *The Complete Directory to Prime Time Network TV Shows, 1946–Present.* 3d ed. New York: Ballantine.

Brown, Gary R. 1994. "The Coney Island Baby Laboratory." *American Heritage of Invention and Technology* 10(2): 24–31.

Bryson, Bethany. 1996. "Anything But Heavy Metal: Symbolic Exclusion and Musical Dislikes." *American Sociological Review* 61: 884–899.

Came, Barry. 1994. "A Family Tragedy." *Maclean's* 107(47): 40–46.

Campbell, Donald T. 1978. "Measuring the Effects of Social Innovations by Means of Time Series." Pp. 159–169 in *Statistics: A Guide to the Unknown.* Oakland, Calif.: Holden-Day.

Campbell, Robert, and Peter Vanderwarker. 1994. "The Cyclorama." *Boston Globe Magazine*, June 12, p. 10.

Carmon, Naomi, ed. 1996. "Earlier Immigration to the United States: Historical Clues for Current Issues of Integration." Pp. 187–205 in *Immigration and Integration in Post-Industrial Societies*. London: Macmillan.

Coleman, David, and John Salt. 1992. *The British Population: Patterns, Trends, and Processes*. New York: Oxford University Press.

Coleman, James S. 1990. *Foundations of Social Theory*. Cambridge: Belknap Press of Harvard University Press.

Corrigan, Philip. 1983. "Film Entertainment as Ideology and Pleasure: A Preliminary Approach to a History of Audiences." Pp. 24–25 in *British Cinema History*, edited by James Curran and Vincent Porter. London: Weidenfeld and Nicolson.

Coser, Rose Laub. 1991. *In Defense of Modernity*. Stanford, Calif.: Stanford University Press.

Crisp, Colin. 1993. *The Classic French Cinema, 1930–1960*. Indianapolis: Indiana University Press.

Cross, Gary. 1997. *Kids' Stuff: Toys and the Changing World of American Childhood*. Cambridge: Harvard University Press.

Crystal, David. 1995. *The Cambridge Encyclopedia of the English Language*. New York: Cambridge University Press.

Currie, Robert, Alan Gilbert, and Lee Horsley. 1977. *Churches and Churchgoers: Patterns in Church Growth in the British Isles Since 1700*. Oxford: Clarendon Press.

Cutler, Anne, James McQueen, and Ken Robinson. 1990. "Elizabeth and John: Sound Patterns of Men's and Women's Names." *Journal of Linguistics* 26: 471–482.

Daniel, Clifton, ed. 1987. *Chronicle of the Twenty-first Century*. Mount Kisco, N.Y.: Chronicle.

———. 1989. *Chronicle of America*. Mount Kisco, N.Y.: Chronicle.

Danmarks Statistik. 1925. *Statistisk aarbog*. Copenhagen: H. H. Thieles Bogtrykkeri.

———. 1929. *Statistisk aarbog*. Copenhagen: H. H. Thieles Bogtrykkeri.

———. 1937. *Statistisk aarbog*. Copenhagen: Bianco Lunos Bogtrykkeri.

———. 1942. *Statistisk aarbog*. Copenhagen: Bianco Lunos Bogtrykkeri.

———. 1946. *Statistisk aarbog*. Copenhagen: Bianco Lunos Bogtrykkeri.

———. 1952. *Statistisk aarbog*. Copenhagen: Bianco Lunos Bogtrykkeri.

Davis, Fred. 1992. *Fashion, Culture, and Identity*. Chicago: University of Chicago Press.

Davis, James A. 1958. "Cultural Factors in the Perception of Status Symbols." *Midwest Sociologist* 21: 1–11.

de Klerk, V., and B. Bosch. 1995. "Naming in Two Cultures: English and Xhosa Practices." *Nomina Africana* 9: 68–87.

Dennis, Geoff, ed. 1994. *Annual Abstract of Statistics*. London: Central Statistical Office.

, Tia. 1991. "Musical Patronage and Social Change in Beethoven's Vienna." *American Journal of Sociology* 97(2): 310–346.

de Pina-Cabral, João, with Nelson Lourenço. 1994. "Personal Identity and Ethnic Ambiguity: Naming Practices Among the Eurasians of Macao." *Social Anthropology* 2(2): 115–132.

DiMaggio, Paul. 1992. "Cultural Boundaries and Structural Change: The Extension of the High Culture Model to Theater, Opera, and the Dance, 1900–1940." Pp. 21–57 in *Cultivating Differences: Symbolic Boundaries and the Making of Inequality,* edited by Michèle Lamont and Marcel Fournier. Chicago: University of Chicago Press.

DiMaggio, Paul, and Michael Useem. 1978. "Social Class and Arts Consumption: The Origins and Consequences of Class Differences in Exposure to the Arts in America." *Theory and Society* 5(2): 141–161.

Dodd, Donald B. 1993. *Historical Statistics of the States of the United States: Two Centuries of the Census, 1790–1980.* Westport, Conn.: Greenwood.

Dombai, Mária G. 1974. "Seregélyes Keresztnevei." In *Magyar Személynévi Adattárak.* Budapest: Elte Magyar Nyelvészeti Tanszékcsoport.

Dorbin, Alain. 1986. *The Foul and the Fragrant.* Cambridge: Harvard University Press.

Douglas, Kirk. 1988. *The Ragman's Son: An Autobiography.* New York: Simon and Schuster.

Dunkling, Leslie Alan. 1977. *First Names First.* Ontario: General.

——. 1978. *Scottish Christian Names: An A-Z of First Names.* London: Johnston and Bacon.

——. 1993. *The Guinness Book of Names.* London: Guiness.

Dunkling, Leslie, and William Gosling. 1983. *The Facts on File Dictionary of First Names.* London: J. M. Dent and Sons.

Dupâquier, Jacques. 1984. "La fréquence des prénoms dans le Vexin français." Pp. 357–367 in *Le Prénom, mode et histoire,* edited by Jacques Dupâquier, Alain Bideau, Marie-Elizabeth Ducreux. Paris: l'Ecole des Hautes Etudes en Sciences Sociales.

Eagleson, Oran W., and Antoinette D. Clifford. 1945. "A Comparative Study of the Names of White and Negro Women College Students." *Journal of Social Psychology* 21: 57–64.

Ellefson, Connie Lockhart. 1987. *The Melting Pot Book of Baby Names.* White Hall, Va.: Betterway.

Elley, Derek, ed. 1992. *Variety Movie Guide.* New York: Prentice Hall.

Erickson, Bonnie H. 1996. "Culture, Class, and Connections." *American Journal of Sociology* 102(1): 217–35.

Evans, Cleveland. 1983. "What We Named the Baby." *Ann Arbor Observer* June: 51–58.

Fallers, L. A. 1954. "A Note on the 'Trickle Effect.'" *Public Opinion Quarterly* 18: 314–321.

Ferguson, Priscilla Parkhurst. 1998. "A Cultural Field in the Making: Gastronomy in Nineteenth-Century France." *American Journal of Sociology* 104(3): 597–641.

Finke, Roger and Rodney Stark. 1992. *The Churching of America: Winners and Losers in Our American Economy.* New Brunswick, N.J.: Rutgers University Press.

Fischer, Claude S. 1982. *To Dwell Among Friends.* Chicago: University of Chicago Press.

——. 1995. "The Subcultural Theory of Urbanism: A Twentieth-Year Assessment." *American Journal of Sociology* 101(3): 543–577.

Fischer, David Hackett. 1986. "Forenames and the Family in New England: An Exercise in Historical Onomastics." Pp. 215–241 in *Generations and Change,* edited by Robert M. Taylor, Jr., and Ralph J. Crandall. Macon, Ga.: Mercer University Press.

——. 1989. *Albion's Seed: Four British Folkways in America.* New York: Oxford University Press.

Flora, Peter, Franz Kraus, and Winfried Pfenning. 1983. *State, Economy, and Society in Western Europe, 1815–1975.* Vol. 1. Chicago: St. James Press.

——. 1987. *State, Economy, and Society in Western Europe, 1815–1975.* Vol. 2. Chicago: St. James Press.

Frank, Rainer. 1977. *Zur Frage einer schichtenspezifischen Personnamengebung.* Neumünster: Karl Wachholtz Verlag Neumünster.

Franks, Ray. 1982. *What's in a Nickname? Naming the Jungle of College Athletic Mascots.* Amarillo, Tex.: Ray Franks Publishing Ranch.

Fuchs, Lawrence H. 1990. *The American Kaleidoscope: Race, Ethnicity, and the Civic Culture.* Hanover, N.H.: University Press of New England.

Fujimura, Joan H. 1988. "The Molecular Biological Bandwagon in Cancer Research— Where Social Worlds Meet." *Social Problems* 35(3): 261–283.

Furstenberg, Frank F., Jr., and Kathy Gordon Talvitie. 1980. "Children's Names and Paternal Claims: Bonds Between Unmarried Fathers and Their Children." *Journal of Family Issues* 1(1): 31–57.

Gartman, David. 1994. *Auto Opium: A Social History of American Automobile Design.* London: Routledge.

Genovese, Eugene D. 1972. *Roll, Jordan, Roll.* New York: Random House.

Gerhards, Jürgen, and Rolf Hackenbroch (University of Leipzig). 1998. "First Names and Cultural Modernization: An Empirical Study." Paper presented at the American Sociological Association Annual Meeting, August.

Greeley, Andrew M. 1995. *Religion as Poetry.* New Brunswick, N.J.: Transaction, 1995.

Grier, Katherine C. 1988. *Culture and Comfort: People, Parlors, and Upholstery.* Amherst: University of Massachusetts Press.

Griswold, Wendy. 1992. "The Writing on the Mud Wall: Nigerian Novels and the Imaginary Village." *American Sociological Review* 57(6): 709–724.

——. 1994. *Culture and Societies in a Changing World.* Thousand Oaks, Calif.: Pine Forge Press.

Gronow, Jukka. 1997. *The Sociology of Taste.* London: Routledge.

Guglielmino, C. R., et al. 1995. "Cultural Variation in Africa: Role of Mechanisms of Transmission and Adaptation." *Proceedings of the National Academy of Sciences* 92: 7585–7589.

Gutman, Herbert G. 1976. *The Black Family in Slavery and Freedom, 1750–1925.* New York: Pantheon.

Haight, Frank A. 1978. "Do Speed Limits Reduce Traffic Accidents?" Pp. 170–177 in *Statistics: A Guide to the Unknown,* 2d ed., edited by Judith M. Tanur et al. Oakland, Calif.: Holden-Day.

Hall, John R. 1992. "The Capital(s) of Cultures: A Nonholistic Approach to Status Situations, Class, Gender, and Ethnicity." Pp. 257–285 in *Cultivating Differences: Symbolic Boundaries and the Making of Inequality,* edited by Michèle Lamont and Marcel Fournier. Chicago: University of Chicago Press.

Halle, David. 1993. *Inside Culture: Art and Class in the American Home.* Chicago: University of Chicago Press.

Hanks, Patrick, and Flavia Hodges. 1990. *A Dictionary of First Names.* Oxford: Oxford University Press.

Harrington, C. Lee, and Denise D. Bielby. 1995. *Soap Fans: Pursuing Pleasure and Making Meaning in Everyday Life.* Philadelphia: Temple University Press.

Hawley, Amos H. 1950. *Human Ecology: A Theory of Community Structure.* New York: Ronald Press.

Hedström, Peter, and Richard Swedberg, eds. 1998. *Social Mechanisms: An Analytical Approach to Social Theory.* Cambridge: Cambridge University Press.

Herzfeld, Michael. 1991. *A Place in History: Social and Monumental Time in a Cretan Town.* Princeton, N.J.: Princeton University Press.

Hirsch, Paul M. 1972. "Processing Fads and Fashions." *American Journal of Sociology* 77(4): 639–659.

Hoffman, Mark S., ed. 1992. *The World Almanac and Book of Facts, 1993.* New York: Scripps Howard.

Hoffman, Paul. 1998. *The Man Who Loved Only Numbers.* New York: Hyperion.

Hollander, Zander, and Alex Sachare, eds. 1989. *The Official NBA Basketball Encyclopedia.* New York: Villard.

Hornby, Rikard. 1978. *Dansk personnavne.* Copenhagen: G. E. C. Gads Forlag.

Houdaille, Jacques. 1996. "Les prénoms des Protestants au XVIIe siècle." *Population* 3: 775–778.

Hout, Michael, and Andrew M. Greeley. 1987. "The Center Doesn't Hold: Church Attendance in the United States, 1940–1984." *American Sociological Review* 52: 325–345.

Hurh, Won Moo, and Kwang Chung Kim. 1984. *Korean Immigrants in America: A Structural Analysis of Ethnic Confinement and Adhesive Adaptation.* Rutherford, N.J.: Fairleigh Dickinson University Press.

Jarvie, I. C. 1986. *Movies and Society.* New York: Garland.

Johansen, Hans Christian. 1975. *Befolkningsudvikling og familiestruktur i det 18. arhundrede*. Odense: Odense University Press.

Johnson, Charles, and Linwood Sleigh. 1973. *The Harrap Book of Boys' and Girls' Names*. London: George G. Harrap.

Kálmán, Béla. 1978. *The World of Names: A Study in Hungarian Onomatology*. Budapest: Akadémiai Kiadó.

Katz, Ephraim. 1979. *The Film Encyclopedia*. New York: Harper and Row.

Kincaid, Peter. 1986. *The Rule of the Road: An International Guide to History and Practice*. New York: Greenwood.

Kisbye, Torben. 1981. "Name-Borrowing Mechanisms: The Impact of English Masculine Personal Names on a Major Danish Town Community, 1800–1950." Pp. 599–607 in *Proceedings of Thirteenth International Congress of Onomastic Science*, vol. 1, edited by Kazimierz Rymut. Kraków: Polish Academy of Sciences.

Kolatch, Alfred J. 1967. *The Name Dictionary: Modern English and Hebrew Names*. New York: Jonathan David.

——. 1984. *The Complete Dictionary of English and Hebrew First Names*. New York: Jonathan David.

Kotz, Samuel, and Norman L. Johnson, editors-in-chief. 1985. "Principle of Parsimony." Pp. 578–579 in *Encyclopedia of Statistical Sciences*, vol. 6. New York: John Wiley and Sons.

Kroeber, A. L. 1919. "On the Principle of Order in Civilization as Exemplified by Changes of Fashion." *American Anthropologist* 21(3): 235–263.

Kuiper, Kathleen, ed. 1995. *Merriam-Webster's Encyclopedia of Literature*. Springfield, Mass.: Merriam-Webster.

Kvaran, Gudrún, and Sigurdur Jónsson. 1991. *Nöfn Íslendinga*. Reykjavík: Heimskringla Haskolaforlag Mals og Menningar.

Lamont, Michèle. 1992. *Money, Morals, and Manners: The Culture of the French and American Upper-Middle Class*. Chicago: University of Chicago Press.

Lamont, Michèle, and Annette Lareau. 1988. "Cultural Capital: Allusions, Gaps and Glissandos in Recent Theoretical Developments." *Sociological Theory* 6: 153–168.

Lawson, Edwin D. 1984. "Personal Names: 100 Years of Social Science Contributions." *Names* 32(1): 45–73.

Lawson, Edwin D., ed. 1987. *Personal Names and Naming: An Annotated Bibliography*. Westport, Conn.: Greenwood.

——. 1995. *More Names and Naming: An Annotated Bibliography*. Westport, Conn.: Greenwood.

Lehrer, Adrienne. 1992. "Names and Naming: Why We Need Fields and Frames." Pp. 123–142 in *Frames, Fields, and Contrasts: New Essays in Semantic and Lexical Organization*, edited by Adrienne Lehrer and Eva Feder Kittay. Hillsdale, N.J.: Lawrence Erlbaum.

Lévi-Strauss, Claude. 1966. *The Savage Mind*. Chicago: University of Chicago Press.

Lieberson, Stanley. 1966. "The Price-Zubrzycki Measure of Ethnic Intermarriage." *Eugenics Quarterly* 13(2): 92–100.

———. 1980. *A Piece of the Pie: Blacks and White Immigrants Since 1880.* Berkeley: University of California Press.

———. 1982. "Forces Affecting Language Spread: Some Basic Propositions." Pp. 37–62 in *Language Spread: Studies in Diffusion and Social Change,* edited by Robert L. Cooper. Bloomington: Indiana University Press.

———. 1985. *Making It Count: The Improvement of Social Research and Theory.* Berkeley, Calif.: University of California Press.

———. 1991. "Small N's and Big Conclusions: An Examination of the Reasoning in Comparative Studies Based on a Small Number of Cases." *Social Forces* 70: 307–320. Reprinted (slightly revised) in Charles Ragin and Howard Becker, eds., *What Is a Case?* New York: Cambridge University Press, 1992, 105–118.

———. 1992a. "Einstein, Renoir, and Greeley: Some Thoughts About Evidence in Sociology." *American Sociological Review* 57: 1–15.

———. 1992b. "A Brief Introduction to the Demographic Analysis of Culture." *Sociology of Culture Section Newsletter* 6 (Summer): 21–23.

———. 1995. "Reply to Philippe Besnard." *American Journal of Sociology* 100(5): 1317–1325.

———. 1997. "The Big Broad Issues in Society and Social History: Application of a Probabilistic Perspective." Pp. 359–385 in *Causality in Crisis? Statistical Methods and the Search for Causal Knowledge in the Social Sciences,* edited by Vaughn R. McKim and Stephen P. Turner. Notre Dame, Ind.: University of Notre Dame Press.

———. 1998. "Examples, Submerged Statements, and the Neglected Application of Philosophy to Social Theory." Pp. 177–191 in *What Is Social Theory? The Philosophical Debates,* edited by Alan Sica. Malden, Mass.: Blackwell.

Lieberson, Stanley, and Eleanor O. Bell. 1992. "Children's First Names: An Empirical Study of Social Taste." *American Journal of Sociology* 9(3): 511–554.

Lieberson, Stanley, and Kelly S. Mikelson. 1995. "Distinctive African American Names: An Experimental, Historical, and Linguistic Analysis of Innovation." *American Sociological Review* 60: 928–946.

Lieberson, Stanley, and Mary C. Waters. 1988. *From Many Strands: Ethnic and Racial Groups in Contemporary America—A 1980 Census Monograph.* New York: Russell Sage Foundation.

Lieberson, Stanley, Shyon Baumann, and Susan Dumais. 2000. "The Instability of Androgynous Names: The Symbolic Maintenance of Gender Boundaries." *American Journal of Sociology* 105(5): 1249–1287.

London, Andrew S., and S. Philip Morgan. 1994. "Racial Differences in First Names in 1910." *Journal of Family History* 19: 261–284.

Lopes, Paul D. 1992. "Innovation and Diversity in the Popular Music Industry, 1969 to 1990." *American Sociological Review* 57(1): 56–71.

Lowe, Elizabeth D., and John W. G. Lowe. 1985. "Quantitative Analysis of Women's Dress." Pp. 193–206 in *The Psychology of Fashion*. Lexington, Mass.: Lexington Books.

Lowe, John W. G., and Elizabeth D. Lowe. 1982. "Cultural Pattern and Process: A Study of Stylistic Change in Women's Dress." *American Anthropologist* 84: 521–544.

Lukas, Rainer Friedrich Wilhelm. 1981. *Die Vornamengebung in Schwalmstadt/ Ziegenhain und Gieben von 1945–1975*. Frankfurt: R. G. Fischer Verlag.

Maeder, Edward, ed. 1987. *Hollywood and History: Costume Design in Film*. New York: Thames and Hudson.

Meldgaard, Eva Villarsen. 1990. *Studier i copenhagenske fornavne, 1650–1950*. Copenhagen: Reitzel.

——. 1993. *Navnemode og modenavne*. Vaerløse: Billesø & Baltzer.

Mencken, Henry L. 1963. *The American Language: An Inquiry into the Development of English in the United States*. Abridged ed. New York: Alfred A. Knopf.

Meyersohn, Rolf, and Elihu Katz. 1957. "Notes on a Natural History of Fads." *American Journal of Sociology* 62(6): 594–601.

Michaëlsson, Karl. 1927. *Etudes sur les noms de personne français d'après les rôles de taille parisiens*. Uppsala: Almqvist and Wiksells Boktryckeri-A.B.

Mitchell, Brian R. 1978. *European Historical Statistics, 1750–1970*. New York: Columbia University Press.

Morris, William and Mary. 1977. *Dictionary of Word and Phrase Origins*. New York: Harper and Row.

Mueller, John H. 1951. *The American Symphony Orchestra: A Social History of Musical Taste*. Bloomington, Ind.: Indiana University Press.

National Center for Education Statistics. 1992. *Digest of Education Statistics*. Washington, D.C.: Department of Health, Education, and Welfare.

Nickerson, Colin. 1995. "Canada's Quintuplets Strike Back: Once Gawked At, Survivors Seek Payment for a Stolen Childhood." *Boston Globe*, April 20, p. 2.

Nordal, Jóhannes, and Valdimar Kristinsson, eds. 1987. *Iceland 1986*. Reykjavík: Central Bank of Iceland.

Nuessel, Frank H. 1994. "Objectionable Sport Team Designations." *Names* 42(2): 101–119.

Obermiller, Tim. 1993. "The Secret Life of Languages." *University of Chicago Magazine* 85(5): 32–35.

O'Brien, Richard. 1990. *The Story of American Toys: From the Puritans to the Present*. New York: Abbeville.

Ogburn, William Fielding. 1950. *Social Change with Respect to Culture and Original Nature*. New York: Viking.

Park, Robert E., and Ernest W. Burgess. 1921. *Introduction to the Science of Sociology*. Chicago: University of Chicago Press.

Parker, Peter, ed. 1995. *A Reader's Guide to the Twentieth-Century Novel*. New York: Oxford University Press.

Peary, Danny, ed. 1978. *Close-Ups: Intimate Profiles of Movie Stars by Their Costars, Directors, Screenwriters, and Friends.* New York: Simon and Schuster.

Pedersen, Birte Hjorth, and Lis Weise. 1990. *Danske fornavne.* Copenhagen: C. A. Reitzels Forlag.

Pegg, Mark. 1983. *Broadcasting and Society, 1918–1939.* London: Croom Helm.

Peterson, Richard A. 1994. "Culture Studies Through the Production Perspective: Progress and Prospects." Pp. 163–189 in *The Sociology of Culture: Emerging Theoretical Perspectives,* edited by Diana Crane. Cambridge, Mass.: Blackwell.

Peterson, Richard A., and Roger M. Kern. 1996. "Changing Highbrow Taste: From Snob to Omnivore." *American Sociological Review* 61: 900–907.

Phillips, Roderick. 1991. *Untying the Knot: A Short History of Divorce.* Cambridge: Cambridge University Press.

Puckett, Newbell Niles. 1938. "American Negro Names." *Journal of Negro History* 23: 35–48.

———. 1975. *Black Names in America: Origins and Usage.* Edited by M. Heller. Boston: G. K. Hall.

Quinlan, David. 1981. *The Illustrated Directory of Film Stars.* London: B. T. Batsford.

Rader, Dotson. 1993. "He Turns Shy into Funny." *Parade* May 9, pp. 4–5.

Reader's Digest Association. 1967. *1968 Reader's Digest Almanac and Yearbook.* Pleasantville, N.Y.: Reader's Digest Association.

Richardson, Jane, and A. L. Kroeber. 1940. "Three Centuries of Women's Dress Fashions: A Quantitative Analysis." *Anthropological Records* 5(2): 111–153.

Robinson, Dwight E. 1976. "Fashions in Shaving and Trimming of the Beard: The Men of the *Illustrated London News,* 1842–1972." *American Journal of Sociology* 81(5): 1133–1141.

Rolf, Meyersohn, and Elihu Katz. 1957. "Notes on a Natural History of Fads." *American Journal of Sociology* 62(6): 594–601.

Rosenkrantz, Linda, and Pamela Redmond Satran. 1988. *Beyond Jennifer and Jason: An Enlightened Guide to Naming Your Baby.* New York: St. Martin's.

Rosenwaike, Ira. 1990. "Leading Surnames Among American Jews." *Names* 38(1–2): 31–38.

Rossi, Alice. 1965. "Naming Children in Middle-Class Families." *American Sociological Review* 30: 499–513.

Rozin, Paul, and Carol Nemeroff. 1990. "The Laws of Sympathetic Magic: A Psychological Analysis of Similarity and Contagion." Pp. 205–232 in *Cultural Psychology: Essays on Comparative Human Development,* edited by James W. Stigler, Richard A. Shweder, and Gilbert Herdt. New York: Cambridge University Press.

Schücking, Levin L. 1944. *The Sociology of Literary Taste.* London: Kegan Paul, Trench, Trubner.

Schudson, Michael. 1984. *Advertising, the Uneasy Persuasion: Its Dubious Impact on American Society.* New York: Basic Books.

Seeman, Mary V. 1983. "The Unconscious Meaning of Personal Names." *Names* 31(4): 237–244.

Simmel, Georg. 1955. *Conflict and the Web of Group-Affiliations.* Glencoe, Ill.: Free Press.

——. 1957. "Fashion." *American Journal of Sociology* 62(5): 541–558.

Simonton, Dean Keith. 1998. "Fickle Fashion Versus Immortal Fame: Transhistorical Assessments of Creative Products in the Opera House." *Journal of Personality and Social Psychology* 75(1): 198–210.

Skipper, James K., Jr. 1984. "The Sociological Significance of Nicknames: The Case of Baseball Players." *Journal of Sport Behavior* 7: 28–38.

Small, Christopher. 1987. "Performance as Ritual: Sketch for an Equity into the True Nature of a Symphony Concert." Pp. 6–32 in *Lost in Music: Culture, Style and the Musical Event,* edited by Avron Levine White. New York: Routledge and Kegan Paul.

Smelser, Neil J. 1963. *Theory of Collective Behavior.* New York: Free Press of Glencoe.

Smith, Daniel Scott. 1985. "Child-Naming Practices, Kinship Ties, and Change in Family Attitudes in Hingham, Massachusetts, 1641 to 1880." *Journal of Social History* 18: 541–566.

Smith, Elsdon C. 1950. *The Story of Our Names.* New York: Harper and Brothers.

Søndergaard, Georg. 1979. *General Outline of a Computational Investigation of Danish Naming Practice. ONOMA Bibliographical and Information Bulletin* 23. Leuven: International Centre of Onomastics.

Statistical Bureau of Iceland. 1928. "Manntal á Íslandi 1920." *Statistics of Iceland* 46: 31. Reykjavík: Hagstofu Íslands.

——. 1960. "Manntalid 1703." *Statistics of Iceland.* 2(21): 20.

——. 1967a. "Tölfraedihandbók." *Statistics of Iceland.* 2(40): 31.

——. 1967b. "Tölfraedihandbók." *Statistics of Iceland.* 2(40): 79.

——. 1969. "Manntal á Íslandi 1960." *Statistics of Iceland.* 2(47): 51.

——. 1984a. "Tölfraedihandbók 1984." *Statistics of Iceland.* 2(82): 24–25, 228.

——. 1984b. "Tölfraedihandbók 1984." *Statistics of Iceland.* 2(82): 42.

Steele, Valerie. 1988. *Paris Fashion.* New York: Oxford University Press.

Stern, Jane, and Michael Stern. 1990. *The Encyclopedia of Bad Taste.* New York: Harper-Collins.

Stewart, George R. 1948. *Men's Names in Plymouth and Massachusetts in the Seventeenth Century.* Berkeley: University of California Press.

——. 1979. *American Given Names.* New York: Oxford University Press.

Taylor, Rex. 1974. "John Doe, Jr.: A Study of His Distribution in Space, Time, and the Social Structure." *Social Forces* 53(1): 11–21.

Tebbenhoff, Edward H. 1985. "Tacit Rules and Hidden Family Structures: Naming Practices and Godparentage in Schenectady, New York, 1680–1800." *Journal of Social History* 18: 567–585.

Tenner, Edward. 1989. "Talking Through Our Hats." *Harvard Magazine* 91 (May–June): 21–26.

Tomasson, Richard F. 1975. "The Continuity of Icelandic Names and Naming Patterns." *Names* 23(4): 281–289.

——. 1976. *Premarital Sexual Permissiveness and Illegitimacy in the Nordic Countries.* Comparative Studies in Society and History, vol. 18, no. 2. London: Cambridge University Press.

Tugault, Yves. 1975. *Fécondité et urbanisation.* Paris: Presses Universitaires de France.

Turner, Lorenzo Dow. 1949. *Africanisms in the Gullah Dialect.* Chicago: University of Chicago Press.

Turner, Ralph H., and Lewis M. Killian. 1987. *Collective Behavior.* 3d ed. Englewood Cliffs, N.J.: Prentice-Hall.

UNESCO. 1964. *Statistical Yearbook, 1963.* Paris: United Nations Educational, Scientific and Cultural Organization.

——. 1968. *Statistical Yearbook, 1966.* Paris: United Nations Educational, Scientific and Cultural Organization.

——. 1971. *Statistical Yearbook, 1970.* Paris: United Nations Educational, Scientific and Cultural Organization.

——.1973. *Statistical Yearbook, 1972.* Paris: United Nations Educational, Scientific and Cultural Organization.

——. 1982. *Statistical Yearbook, 1982.* Paris: United Nations Educational, Scientific and Cultural Organization.

——. 1987. *Statistical Yearbook, 1987.* Paris: United Nations Educational, Scientific and Cultural Organization.

——. 1991. *Statistical Yearbook, 1991.* Paris: United Nationas Educational, Scientific and Cultural Organization.

——. 1993. *Statistical Yearbook, 1993.* Paris: United Nations Educational, Scientific and Cultural Organization.

United Nations. 1949. *Demographic Yearbook, 1948.* New York: Department of Economic and Social Affairs, Statistical Office, United Nations.

——. 1958. *Demographic Yearbook, 1958.* New York: Department of Economic and Social Affairs, Statistical Office, United Nations.

——. 1959. *Demographic Yearbook, 1959.* New York: Department of Economic and Social Affairs, Statistical Office, United Nations.

——. 1966. *Demographic Yearbook, 1965.* New York: Department of Economic and Social Affairs, Statistical Office, United Nations.

——. 1969. *Demographic Yearbook, 1968.* New York: Department of Economic and Social Affairs, Statistical Office, United Nations.

——. 1976. *Demographic Yearbook, 1975.* New York: Department of Economic and Social Affairs, Statistical Office, United Nations.

——. 1977. *Demographic Yearbook, 1976.* New York: Department of Economic and Social Affairs, Statistical Office, United Nations.

——. 1983. *Demographic Yearbook, 1981.* New York: Department of Economic and Social Affairs, Statistical Office, United Nations.

——. 1988. *Demographic Yearbook, 1986.* New York: Department of Economic and Social Affairs, Statistical Office, United Nations.

——. 1990. *Demographic Yearbook, 1988.* New York: Department of Economic and Social Affairs, Statistical Office, United Nations.

——. 1991. *Demographic Yearbook, 1989.* New York: Department of Economic and Social Affairs, Statistical Office, United Nations.

——. 1992a. *Demographic Yearbook, 1990.* New York: Department of Economic and Social Affairs, Statistical Office, United Nations.

——. 1992b. *Demographic Yearbook, 1991.* New York: Department of Economic and Social Affairs, Statistical Office, United Nations.

United States Bureau of the Census. 1922. *Statistical Abstract of the United States.* Washington, D.C.: Government Printing Office.

——. 1925. *Marriage and Divorce.* Washington, D.C.: Government Printing Office.

——. 1932a. *Marriage and Divorce.* Washington, D.C.: Government Printing Office.

——. 1932b. *Statistical Abstract of the United States.* Washington, D.C.: Government Printing Office.

——. 1952. *Statistical Abstract of the United States.* Washington, D.C.: Government Printing Office.

——. 1962. *Statistical Abstract of the United States.* Washington, D.C.: Government Printing Office.

——. 1972. *Statistical Abstract of the United States.* Washington, D.C.: Government Printing Office.

——. 1975. *Historical Statistics of the United States: Colonial Times to 1970, Bicentennial Edition, Parts 1 and 2.* Washington, D.C.: Department of Commerce.

——. 1982. *Statistical Abstract of the United States.* Washington, D.C.: Government Printing Office.

——. 1986. *Statistical Abstract of the United States.* Washington, D.C.: Government Printing Office.

——. 1992. *Statistical Abstract of the United States.* Washington, D.C.: Government Printing Office.

——. 1993. *Statistical Abstract of the United States.* Washington, D.C.: Government Printing Office.

Vandebosch, Heidi. 1998. "The Influence of Media on Given Names." *Names* 46(4): 243–262.

Veblen, Thorstein. 1967. *The Theory of the Leisure Class.* New York: Viking. Orig. publ. 1899.

Virág, Gábor. 1978. "Csantavér Keresztnevei (1782–1970)." *Magyar Szemelynevi Adattarak*. Budapest: Elte Magyar Nyelvészeti Tanszékcsoport.

von Nell, Adelheid. 1974. "Les noms de famille et les prénoms en Allemagne." Pp. 5–14 in *Noms et prénoms: Aperçu historique sur la dénomination des personnes en divers pays*, edited by Louis Henry. Dolhain, Belgium: Ordina Editions.

Wallace, T. Dudley. 1977. "Pretest Estimation in Regression: A Survey." *American Journal of Agricultural Economics* 59: 431–443.

Watkins, Susan Cotts, and Andrew S. London. 1994. "Personal Names and Cultural Change: A Study of the Naming Patterns of Italians and Jews in the United States in 1910." *Social Science History* 18(2): 169–209.

Weekley, Ernest. 1939. *Jack and Jill: A Study in Our Christian Names*. London: John Murray.

Whyte, Donald. 1996. *Scottish Forenames*. Edinburgh: Birlinn.

Williams, William Morgan. 1956. *Gosforth: The Sociology of an English Village*. Glencoe, Ill.: Free Press.

Withycombe, E. G. 1977. *The Oxford Dictionary of English Christian Names*. 3d ed. Oxford: Oxford University Press.

Yonge, Charlotte M. 1966. *History of Christian Names*. New ed., rev. London: Macmillan.

Young, Agnes Brooks. 1937. *Recurring Cycles of Fashion, 1760–1937*. New York, N.Y.: Harper and Brothers.

Young, Michael, and Peter Willmott. 1957. *Family and Kinship in East London*. London: Routledge and Kegan Paul.

Zelinsky, Wilbur. 1970. "Cultural Variation in Personal Name Patterns in the Eastern United States." *Annals of the Association of American Geographers* 60: 743–769.

——. 1988. *Nation into State: The Shifting Symbolic Foundations of American Nationalism*. Chapel Hill: University of North Carolina Press.

Znaniecki, Florian. 1952. *Modern Nationalities: A Sociological Study*. Urbana, Ill.: University of Illinois Press.

Index

Page numbers in italics indicate figures
and tables

Aaron, 152, 198, 218, 220
Abbott, 113
Abdul-Jabbar, Kareem, 76
Abraham, 209, 214, 218, 219
Abramowicz, Zofia, 209
Actors and actresses. *See* Entertainers
and entertainment
Ad hoc explanations of tastes, 28–29,
82–83, 90–91
Adam, 179, 181, 218, 220
Adamic, Louis, 177
Adolf, 16, 17, 131–133, *133,* 135, 141,
211
Advertisers' influence, 70, 129–130
A-ending sound, 99, *100, 102,* 106; Afri-
can names, 202; African-American
names, 206; boys' names, *105;* increase
in popularity for girls' names, 99, 101,
106, 245, 247, 254; Mexican-American
names, 189–191, *190*

Aesthetic criteria for tastes, 1–2, 31;
social aesthetics, 8–20
African names: *a*-ending sound, 202;
alteration of slaves' names from, 117;
disappearance of and changes of,
among blacks, 202
African-American names, 172, 200–207;
black nationalism and, 14; compared
with Mexican-American names, 185–
191, *186;* compared with white names,
203–205, *204,* 250–251; concentration
of names, 85; continuity of names, 89;
forms of address between whites and
blacks, 206–207; Illinois, *77, 90,* 183;
invented names, 76–77, 83, 123, 173–
174, 206; *La*-prefix used in, 122–126;
nicknames, 207; postbellum era, 203;
Rebecca and the movie *Sounder,* 249–
251, *250;* sounds in names, 101. *See also*
Slavery
Age: association of name with "old," 163,
165; effect on attractiveness, 162; and
symbolism, 129–130

Alan, 197, *198*

Albert, 163, *214*

Aldrich, 113

Alexander, 179, *198*

Alexis, 259, *259*

Alfred, 214, 229

Ali, Muhammad, 76

Alice, 159, *196, 197, 204, 207, 214*

Alicia, 204, 205

Allison, 139, 140, 180, 196

Alyssa, 259

Amanda, 113, 140, 147, 148, 162, 180, 187, *196, 204, 259*

Amber, 120, *120,* 147, 148, *161,* 196, 204, 205

Amelia, 228

American Association of University Women, 75–76

Amy, 140, 147, 148, *161,* 180, *182, 196, 197,* 217

Ancestors, naming children for. *See* Familial names

Andrew, 151, 164, *179,* 181, *198,* 217

Androgynous names, 259

Angela, 139, 140, 148, 160, 180, *182, 196*

Anglo names compared with Mexican-American and black names in Texas, 185–191, *186*

Animals' names used for college sports teams, 27–28

Ann, 201

Anna, 158, *159, 204, 214,* 245

Annie, 196, 197, 207

Anthony, 164, *179,* 182

Antifashion, 7

April, 149

Ariel, 204, 205

Arthur, 163, *214*

Arts: class differences and, 22; nationalistic movements and, 12–13;

source for rebirth of dormant names, 114. *See also* Entertainers and entertainment; Music

Ashley, 147, 148, 162, *180,* 181, 187, *196, 204, 204,* 217, 259, *259*

Asian-American names, 172, 191–200; assimilation, 192, 193; compared with Mexican-American names, 194–195; dated white names used by, 197, 199–200; density of living area, 192–194, *194;* overlap between white and Asian names, 193, 195–200, *196, 198*

Assimilation, 175–185; Asian-American names, 192, 193; Jewish names in Germany, 211; Jewish names in Poland, 210–211; Jewish names in United States, 212; Mexican-American names, 185–186, 189

Association of tastes with symbols. *See* Symbols

Astrid, 176

Attorneys' telephone listings, 80–81

Automobiles: age of and symbolism, 129; Cadillac, 17–18, 21; colors, 81; design, 17–19, 94; names of models, 28

Awareness: of names versus use of names, 167–168; of new tastes, 169

Barabbas, 105

Baraka, Imamu Amiri, 76

Barbara, 160, 204, 245

Barber, Bernard, 144

Barrie, J. M., 228

Bathsheba, 106

Beards, 96, 127

Becker, Howard, 13, 261

Beethoven, 2, *3*

Bell, Eleanor, 146

Benjamin, 214, *218, 219*

Bergman, Ingrid, 236

Besnard, Philippe, 99, 146

Bessie, 214

Bet, 200, 201, *201*

Betty, 159, 200, *201,* 204

Beverly, 137–138, *159,* 204

Bianca, 204, 205

Biblical names: Hebrew roots of names in England and Wales, 101–104, *103;* Irish use of, 181; Jewish use of, 174–175, 212–221, *217–219;* Korean use of, 174, 199; linguistic influences on choice of, 104–106, *105;* popularity of, 104–110, *105, 107–110,* 217, *217–219,* 219, 242, 244–247, *246;* Puritan use of, 29, 104; religious practices and, 106–108, *107, 108,* 109, *110*

Birth certificate data, 24–25

Blacks. *See* African-American names; Slavery

Blaine, Beverly, 137–138

Blumer, Herbert, 32, 92

Bogart, Humphrey, 130–131

Boston Symphony Orchestra: age of and symbolism, 129; women trustees and board of overseers members, 74–75

Bourdieu, Pierre, 22, 263

Bowling, 127–128

Boys' versus girls' names: biblical names, 247; black names compared with white names, 205; concentration of names, 84–87, *85–86;* continuity in leading names, 87–90; decorative function associated with girls' names, 66; etymological sources of popular names, 101, *103,* 103–104; familial names, 26; invented African-American names, 76; Jewish names, 216, *217,* 220–221; socioeconomic class and name selection, 154; sounds of names, *100,* 101, *102,* 106; turnover rates in names, 36–

37, *37–41,* 41–42, 50, 66; white ethnic groups in Illinois, 177

Brandon, 151, 163, 198

Brandy, 149

Braudel, Fernand, 8, 15

Brenda, 204

Brian, 151, 163, 178, 179, 184, 198

British immigrants, *178–180,* 181

Brittany, 148, 162, 180, 181, *187,* 204, *204*

Bryson, Bethany, 126

Cabot, 113

Cadillac automobiles, 17–18, 21

Caesar, 201, 202

Cain, 105

Caitlin, 178, 180, 184, 204

California: Asian-American names, 191–200; concentration of names, *85;* divorce and turnover in names, 51, *53;* household size and turnover in names, 51, *56; Jacqueline,* 72; Jewish names, 211–213, *214–215, 217–219,* 249–251, *250;* leading names for boys, *85, 87, 87,* 114, 131, 136, 158, *163–164;* leading names for girls, *85, 87,* 114, 120, 158, *159–162,* 258–260, *259;* movie attendance and turnover in names, 61, *63;* radio and turnover in names, 63–64, *65; Rebecca,* 249–251, *250;* television ownership and turnover in names, *59,* 59–60; turnover rates in names, 37, 40, *41–42;* urbanization and education as factors, *47,* 50

Calvin, 71

Canada, 36

Candace, 204, 205

Carl, 176, 211

Carlos, 179, 183

Carol, 117, 120–121, *121, 160,* 204

Carole, 120, *121*

Carolyn, 120, 121, *121*, *160*, *204*, 254

Carrie, 121, *121*, 207

Cars. *See* Automobiles

Carvey, Dana, 26–27

Caspar, 176

Catherine, 139, *140*, 158, *159*, 178, *180*, 196, *204*, 207, *214*, 217, 254

Catholic versus Protestant names, 208–209

Causal hierarchy and names, 261

Cedric, 229

Chad, 152

Chance, 42, 168; association of name with an event, 70

Changes in fashion, 8–10, 257; class imitation and, 14–15, 144–145; "durability-cost principle," 155–156; internal mechanisms and, 14–15; persistence in one direction, 95; slow evolution of, 93–97

Changes in social order, 73–77, 87, 90

Changes in tastes, 4–5, 262–263; ratchet effect, 92–111; and replacement effect, 244–245, 262; slow evolution of, 93–97. *See also* Changes in fashion

Charles, *151*, 153, 163, *214*

Chelsea, 148

Cheryl, 160

Children and infants, treatment of, 11–12

Chinese immigrants, 172, 174

Chinese names. *See* Asian-American names

Christina, *148*, 158, *161*, *180*, 187, 196, *204*, *204*

Christine, *140*, 196

Christopher, *151*, 153, 164, 179, 198, 217

Chrysler automobiles, 18

Church attendance and choice of biblical names, 106–108, *107–108*, 109

Clarence, 163

Class: cultural capital as class differentiator, 22; educational level as factor, 139, *140*; factor in tastes, 7; imitation of higher classes, 14–15, 144–154; middle names, 113, 145; name choices and, 24; snobbery, 127–128; symbols and, 138–141; upper class aversion after adoption by lower class, 144–154, 262; use of *Jr.* suffix, 145

Classical languages, 22; as origin of popular names, 101, *103*, 103–104; slave names taken from, 43, 202

Claudette, 236

Clothing: customs and, 8–9; cyclical reversals in trends, 97–98; fashion as optional component, 33–34; formal wear of hats and gloves, 78–79, *79*; hemlines, 97, 98; length of waist, *94*, 98; pants worn by women, 116; polyester, 128–129; width of skirt, *95*; women's, 93. *See also* Changes in fashion; Fashion

Cody, 151

Colbert, Claudette, 236

Coleman, James, 33, 144–145

Collective behavior, 33, 67–68, 143–144, 154–158

College sports teams, 27–28

Colors, popularity of, 81

Commercial influences, 70, 93

Commonly shared perspective of society, 13

Composers. *See* Music

Concentration of names, 84–85, 87; California, *85*; effect of popularity of name, 157; Illinois, 85, *86*, 157

Confusion of in fashion with what is out of fashion, 95, 97

Congress and use of nicknames, 79–80, *80*

Conrad, 176

Conspicuous consumption, 21, 22

Contamination: of fashion by others who adopt it, 145; of symbols by external events, 126–137, 189, 271

Coolidge, Calvin, 71

Cooper, Gary, 238–239

"Core of culture," 25

Cost of goods: "durability-cost principle," 155–156; influence on tastes, 21–23

Courtney, 148

Crete, 35

Crystal, 139, 140, 148, 161, 180, 187, 196, 204, 205

Cultural aesthetics, 32

Cultural capital, 22

Cultural change, 257–275; causal hierarchy, 261; cultural lag hypothesis, 269–270; cultural surface, 258–260; decline of cultural elements, 270–273; evolution from existing cultural elements, 266–267; maintenance of continuity, 267–270; self-destruction of cultural elements, 273

Custom, 8–9; declining influence of, 42; distinguished from fashion, 34; in naming, 34–36; in settled societies, 32

Cyclical reversals in trends, 97–98; names, 158–165, 159–164

Cyclorama (Boston), 11

Cynthia, 147, 148, 160, 217, 245

Daniel, 151, 164, 179, 181, 182, 198, 199, 209, 217, 218, 220

Danielle, 140, 162, 180, 182, 204, 205, 217

Darius, 205

Darnell, Linda, 253

Darren, 55, 184, 254

David, 104, 151, 153, 164, 179, 181, 182, 198, 199, 211, 214, 217, 218, 219, 220

Davis, Fred, 7, 92

Deborah, 147, 148, 160, 244–245, 245, 247, 251

Debra, 119

Deceased ancestors' names, 23. See also Familial names

Dee, Sandra, 238

Delilah, 106

D-ending sound, 99, 100, 101, 102, 206

Denmark: divorce and turnover in names, 51; English names in, 138, 191; familial names, 35–36, 50; household size and turnover in names, 51, 54; movie attendance and turnover in names, 61, 63; radio and turnover in names, 64, 64; summary of naming practices, 35–36; television ownership and turnover in names, 55, 58; turnover rates in names, 40; urbanization and education as factors, 43, 44

Dennis, 163

Depression. See Great Depression

Derek, 198

Derivative names using stems, 117–122

Design: automobiles, 17–19; new designs, 92–93. See also Changes in fashion; Fashion

Desplanques, Guy, 99

Diana, 196, 197, 259, 266

Diane, 160

Dick, 200, 201

Dickens, Charles, 131, 138

Dietrich, Marlene, 238

Diffusion, 165–171; distinguished from imitation, 169

Diminutive form of names, 117, 118

Dionne quintuplets, 12

Disney. See Donald Duck

Disposition toward uncommon names, 168, 170, 244–245

Divorce rates and turnover in names, 51, *51–54*, 66, 68

Dj-sound beginning name, 119

Dolores, 159, 176, *204*

Dominique, 204, 205

Donald, 16, 131, *132*, 152, *163*, *214*, 217

Donald Duck, 16, 131

Donna, 148, 160, *204*, 217, 245

Doris, 159, 217

Dormant names, 114

Dorothy, 159, *204*, 214

Douglas, Kirk, 5

Dress. *See* Clothing

Driving rules, 267, 269, 271–272

"Durability-cost principle," 155–156

Dutch families in New York, 35

Dwight, 73

Ebenezer, 131

Ebony, 204, 205

Edith, 158, *159*, 214

Edna, 114, 158, *159*

Education: and class differences, 24; influence of, 43–50, 66, 68

Educational level as factor, 139, *140*

Edward, 163, 197, *198*, *214*, 217

Ee-ending sound, 99, *100*, 101, *102*

Eisenhower, Dwight David, 73

Elderly persons, society's view toward. *See* Age

Eleanor, 158, *159*, *204*, 214, 217

Elizabeth, 139, *140*, 148, 158, *161*, 180, 187, *196*, 201, *204*, 207, 212, *214*, 259, *259*

Ella, 207

Ellefson, Connie Lockhart, 189

Elliot, 113

Emi, 195, *196*

Emily, 139, *140*, 147, 148, *180*, *196*, *204*, 259

Emma, 207

Endicott, 113

England and Wales: biblical names' popularity, 104, 107–108, *108–109*, 242; changes in fashion in, 96; *Darren,* 55; divorce and turnover in names, 51, *52*; etymological sources of popular names, 101, *103*, 103–104; household size and turnover in names, 51, *56*; imitation of names favored by upper class, 145; movie attendance and turnover in names, 61, *62*; nuclear family names used for naming, 35; popular boys' names, 134; radio and turnover in names, 63–64, *65*; sounds of popular names, 99–104, *100*; television ownership and turnover in names, 59, *59*; turnover rates in names, 37, *39*, 41; urbanization and education as factors, *46*, 50

Entertainers and entertainment, 223–256; Jewish names influenced by, 220; name changes, 5, *6–7*, 113; persona of performer, 255–256; popularity of names of, 117–118, 166, 230–239, *236–237*; reasons for name changes, 113; riding the curve of a popular name, 231, 234; source for rebirth of dormant names, 114

Eric, 151, 164, 176, *179*, 181, 197, *198*, 217

Erica, 140, 180, 187, *196*, *204*, 205, 217

Erickson, Bonnie, 22, 68

Erika, 197

Erin, 140, 150, 178, *180*, 183, *184*, 196

Eskimos, 34

Esther, 120, *196*, 197, 199, *214*, 247

Ethel, 28, 114, 158, *159*, *204*, 207, 228

Ethnic and racial groups, 172–222; African-American names, 200–207; Asian-American names, 191–200; assimilation, 175–185; fashions in names, 183, 185; Jewish names, 208–

221; joint effect of internal mechanisms and external influences, 173–
175, 222; Mexican-American names,
185–191, 194–195; white ethnic groups
in Illinois, 177–185, *178–180. See also*
African-American names

Etymologies, 101–104

Eugene, 198

Eunice, 196, 197, *199*

European immigrants, 175–185; white
ethnic groups in Illinois, 177–185, *178–
180*

Evans, Cleveland, 252–253

Evelyn, 159, 204, 214, 217

Existing tastes: influence on later tastes,
16, 115, 173, 188, 222; orderly progression of new tastes based on, 93–97,
273; social aesthetics and, 15–17;
source for new tastes among dormant stock, 114

Extended family and choice of names.
See Familial names

External influences, 42–66, 266, 271;
external events and social aesthetics,
10–14, 70–73; joint force with internal
mechanisms, 143, 173–175, 185, 222;
limitations of explanations based on,
81–90; urbanization and education,
43–50

Ezekiel, 165

Familial names, 34–35, 50–51, 55; boys'
versus girls' names, 26; deceased
ancestors' names, 23; durability of
despite popularity factor, 155;
extended family, 24, 35–36, 50–51, 55;
migration's effect on, 67; mother's
maiden name used as middle name,
113; nuclear family, 35–36, 67

Fanny, 207

Fashion: antifashion, 7; collective
behavior model, 154–158; cyclical
reversals in trends, 97–98; definition
of, 31, 92; history of, 9; imitation of
higher classes, 14–15, 144–145; polyester, 128–129; response to "dated" fashions, 3; women's fashion, 93. *See also*
Changes in fashion

Fedoras. *See* Hats

Feminist movement, 73–76, 84, 88, 262

Fictional characters, 224–230; Denmark
and English names, 138, 191; foreign
names, 226; history of influence on
names, 228–230; invented names, 113,
166, 226; movie characters' names,
239–241, *240–241,* 248–251; persona of
character, 255–256; popular names,
226–227; unpopular names, 226

Fielding, Henry, 228

Finnish immigrants, 177–178

Florence, 113, 159, 204, 214, 217

Flower names for girls, 161, 262

Food and foreign cuisines, 2, 115–116

Ford automobiles, 18

Formal wear of hats and gloves, 78–79,
79, 82

Forms of address: between races in the
South, 206–207; Mrs., style of title
and name, 73–76

France: changes in fashion in, 96;
divorce and turnover in names, 51;
divorce rates and turnover rates in
names, *52;* imitation of names favored
by upper class, 145, 146; movie attendance and turnover in names, 62, 63;
pants worn by women, 116; socioeconomic class and name selection,
154; sounds of popular names, 99;
television ownership and turnover in
names, *59,* 59–60; turnover rates in

France (*cont.*)
  names, 36–37, *37*; upper middle class,
    22; urbanization and education as fac-
    tors, 43, *45*. *See also* French names
Frances, 158, *159, 204,* 207, *214*
Francis, 163, 214
Frank, 163, 176, *214*
Franklin, 13–14, 71, *71*
Frederick, 163
French immigrants, *178–180,* 182
French names, 208–209; black prefer-
    ence for, 205; fictional characters, 226;
    geographic names, 260; origin of pop-
    ular names from French language,
    101, 103, *103*
Fritz, 211
Functional changes, 31, 33, 143

Gainor, Laura, 118
Garbo, Greta, 236
Garland, Judy, 122
Gartman, David, 17–18
Garvey, Marcus, 16, 77
Gary, 152, 163, 238–239, *256*
Gay, 228
Gaynor, Janet, 118
Gender difference. *See* Boys' versus girls'
    names
Gender indicated by name, 25, 100–101,
    117, 202–203, 206
General Motors automobiles, 18
Genevieve, 119, *120*
Genovese, Eugene, 207
Geographic names, 260
George, 114, *163,* 200, *201, 214*
Georgia, and names of black females,
    207
Gerald, 163, 217
Gerhards, Jürgen, 68
German immigrants, 176, *178–180,* 181

Germany, 68; Danzig and Jews' names,
    211; turnover rates in names, 37, *38*
Gertrude, 214
Gilded Age, 4
Gina, 180, 182
Giovanni, 176
Girls' versus boys' names. *See* Boys'
    versus girls' names
Gladys, 114, 158, *159, 204, 214*
Gloria, 159, 204
Gloves as formal wear, *79*
Gottfried, 176
Grace, 158, *159, 196, 197, 199*
Great Depression, 13–14, 71, 84, 87,
    88
Greek. *See* Classical languages
Gregory, 152, 163, 217
Greta, 236
Gumm, Frances, 122
Gwendolyn, 204

Hackenbroch, Rolf, 68
Hall, John, 23
Hanks, Patrick, 29
Hannah, 150, 196, 201, 259
Hans, 176, 211
Harding, Warren, 71
Harold, 163, 214
Harry, 163, 200, *201, 214*
Hats, 78–79, *79,* 82–83
Hattie, 207
Hayworth, Rita, 238
Heather, 120, *120, 140, 148,* 150, *161, 180,
    181, 196*
Hebrew origin of popular names, 101,
    103, *103,* 212. *See also* Biblical names
Helen, 159, 204, 207, *214*
Hemlines. *See* Clothing
Henry, 163, 197, 198, 214
Herbert, 13, 70–71, *71*

Hispanic names. *See* Mexican-American names

Historical events: development of fashion and, 16–17; effect on naming, 83–90

Historical preferences for certain names, 28

Hitler, Adolf, 16, 17, 131–133, 135, 141

Hodges, Flavia, 29

Home furnishings, 4

Hoover, Herbert, 13, 70–71

Houdaille, Jacques, 208

Household size and turnover in names, 51, *54*, 55, *56–57*, 66

H-sound starting name, 99, *100*, 101, *102*

Huckleberry, 229

Hugo, 211

Humphrey, 131

Hungary and turnover rates in names, 37, *39*

Husband's first name used by married woman, 73–76

"Iceberg fallacy," 265

Iceland: divorce and turnover in names, 51, *54*; household size and turnover in names, 51, *57*; turnover rates in names, *41*; urbanization and education as factors, *49*, 50

Ida, *214*, 228

"Identity of the invisible heart of a culture," 25

Idiosyncratic historical developments, 15–17, 70–73

Ignorance of naming decisions being made at same time by others, 154, 157, 170

Illinois: African-American names, 76, 89, *89*, *90*, *204*, 204–205; biblical names' popularity, 104, *107*, 107–108,

109, *246*; concentration of names, 85, *86*, 157; influence of movie characters' names, 239; influence of movie stars' names, 238; *Jacqueline*, 72; *La*-prefix used in names, 122; names for boys, *86*, 89, *102*, 104, *107*, *109*, 131, *179*; names for girls, 77, *86*, 90, *102*, 180, 185, *204*, 231, 232, 233, 243, *243*, *246*; *Rebecca*, 243, *243*; sounds of popular names, 101, *102*; white ethnic groups, 177–185, *178–180*

Imagery associated with name, 24, 27–28, 166, 169; fictional names, 224

Imitation: of automobile design, 18–19; distinguished from diffusion, 169; of higher classes, 14–15, 144–154

"In fashion," 32, 95

Incremental replacement mechanism, 114–117

Incubators on exhibit, 11–12

Indian tribes' names used for college sports teams, 27–28

Individual choices, 7, 8, 26–27, 67–68

Infant incubators, 11–12

Influences on name choices, 24. *See also* External influences; Internal mechanisms

Informality: trend in goods and manners, 78; use of nicknames, 79–81

Ingrid, 177, 236

Initials in telephone listings for physicians and attorneys, 81

Intellectual pursuits, 32–33

Internal mechanisms, 112–142, 273; cultural surface and, 258; joint force with external influences, 143, 173–175, 185, 222; social aesthetics and, 14–15, 92–93

Internationalization of names, 113–114, 166; fictional characters, 226

Invented names: African-American children, 76–77, 83, 123, 206, 227; disappearance of, 167, 227; fictional characters, 226; media dissemination of, 166, 227; parental invention, 113
Inventions, 10
Iowa and geographic names, 260
Irish-language origin of popular names, 103, *103*
Irish names, 178, *178–180*, 183, *184*, 185, 239
Irving, 216
Isaac, 209
Italian immigrants, *178–180*, 182
Ivan, 176

Jack, 163, *200*, *201*, *214*, 217
Jackson, Latoya, 126
Jacob, 151, *200*, *201*, *214*, 218, 219, 220
Jacqueline, 16, 71–72, 137, *180*, *204*
Jacques, 208
Jaime, 118, *119*
James, 151, 152, *153*, *164*, *179*, 181, 197, *198*, *199*, 200, *201*, *214*, 217
Jamie, 118, *119*, *140*, *160*
Jane, 117, 118, *119*, *196*, *197*, *201*
Janet, 118, *119*, *159*, *196*, *197*, *204*, 217
Janice, 118, *119*, *160*, 217
Janie, 207
Janis, 118, *119*
János, 176
Japanese-Americans, 172, 174; Japanese names and, 178, 195. *See also* Asian-American names
Jared, 219
Jasmine, *204*, 205, *259*, *259*
Jason, 151, 163, *198*, 217
Jean, *159*, 208, 217
Jeanette, 214
Jeanne, 209
Jefferson, 113

Jeffrey, 151, *153*, 163, 197, *198*, 217, 239
Jenna, 120, *120*
Jennie, 119, *120*, *196*, 197
Jennifer, 117, 119–120, *120*, *140*, *148*, *162*, *180*, 187, 195, *196*, *204*, 217, 231, *232*, 238, *259*, *259*
Jenny, 120
Jens, 176
Jeremy, 151
Jessica, 113, 120, *120*, *140*, *148*, *162*, *180*, 187, *196*, *204*, *204*, 217, 228, *233*, *233–234*, *259*, 265
Jessie, 119, *120*
Jesus, 188
Jewish names, 172–173, 208–221, 242; adoption of non-Jewish names, 174; Bialystok, Poland, 209–210, *214–215*; biblical names and, 174–175, 212–221, *217–219*; boys' versus girls' names, 216, *217*; California, 211–213, *214–215*, *217–219*; Germany during World War I, 211; influence of entertainment industry on, 220; rejection of Jewish names by non-Jews, 249
Joan, *160*, *204*
Joel, *219*
Johann, 176
John, 105, *151*, *153*, *164*, 175–176, *179*, 181, 197, *198*, *199*, 200, *201*, *214*, 231
Jonathan, 151, *164*, *179*, 181, 182, *198*, 217, 218, 220, 239
Jones, Jennifer, 238
Jordan, 135
Jordan, Michael, 135
Jose, *164*, *179*, 183, 188
José, 211
Joseph, 151, 158, *164*, *179*, 182, *198*, 210, 211, 212, *214*, 218, 219, 220
Joshua, 106, *151*, *164*, *179*, 181, 182, 190–191, *198*, 206, 217, 218, 220

Joyce, 159, 204, 217

Jr. suffix, use of, 145

J-sound starting name, 99, 100, 101, 102, 191

Juan, 176, 179, 183, 188

Judith, 122, 122, 160, 204, 217, 244, 247

Judy, 122, 122

Julia, 117, 121–122, 122, 207

Julie, 122, 148, 160, 217

Juliet, 228

June, 122, 159

Justin, 151, 164, 198

Karen, 120, 121, 121, 148, 160, 176, 196, 204

Karina, 121, 121

Katherine, 150, 207

Kathleen, 160, 178, 180, 184

Kayla, 149

Keisha, 124–125

Kelly, 140, 150, 160, 178, 180, 183, 184, 185, 196, 204, 217

Kelsey, 150

Kennedy, Jacqueline Bouvier, 16, 71–72

Kenneth, 151, 153, 163, 217

Kevin, 151, 153, 158, 164, 178, 179, 184, 198, 217, 226, 239

Keyboards, 267, 269

Kiara, 204, 205

Kimberly, 140, 148, 161, 180, 182, 196, 217, 259

Kincaid, Peter, 271

King Oscar of Sweden, 134

Kisbye, Torben, 138

Kisha, 124–125, 126

Kizzy, 76

Kolatch, Alfred, 228

Korean immigrants, 172, 174; biblical names and, 174, 199. *See also* Asian-American names

Kristin, 180, 181, 182, 196

Kroeber, Alfred L., 93, 96, 97, 98

Krystal, 187

K-sound starting name, 99, 100, 101, 102

Kyle, 152, 179, 181, 198

La Verne, 122, 125

Lakeisha, 123, 124, 126

Lakisha, 123, 124, 126

Lamont, Michèle, 22

Lana, 236

Lange, Jessica, 233–234

La-prefix and names of black girls, 122–126, 124–125

Larenia, 122

Larry, 163

Latanya, 124, 126

Latasha, 123, 124, 126

Latin. *See* Classical languages

Latisha, 123, 124, 126

Latonya, 123, 124, 125, 126

Latoya, 123, 124, 204, 205

Latrice, 123, 124, 126

Laura, 140, 148, 160, 180, 187, 196, 217, 245

Lauren, 139, 140, 148, 162, 180, 182, 196, 204, 259, 259

Lavera, 122

Lawrence, 217

Lawson, Edwin, 34

Leading names, changes in, 87–90

League of Women Voters, 75–76

Lee, 113, 136, 136–137, 141

L-ending sound, 105

Lewinsky, Monica, 261, 263–265

Lewis, 176

Lilith, 166

Lillian, 158, 159, 204, 214

Lillie, 207

Linda, 119, 149, 160, 196, 197, 204, 245, 252–254

Lindsay, 180, 196

Lindsey, 150
Lisa, 119, *140, 148, 161, 196,* 197, 217, 245
Literacy. *See* Education
Literature. *See* Fictional characters
Lizzie, 207
Lobel, Lyle, 144
Lois, 159
Lombard, Carole, 120–121
London, Andrew S., 193, 203
Loretta, 204
Lori, 150, 160, 217
Lorna, 228
Lorraine, 204
Louis, 211
Louise, 204, 207
Lowell, 113
Lucille, 204, 207
Lula, 207

Madison, 259, 259
Maiden names of mothers, used as middle names, 113
Mamie, 207
Marco, 182
Marcus, 16, 77, 205
Margaret, 160, 176, 178, *204, 207, 214*
Margret, 217
Mari, 195, 196
Maria, 139, *140,* 158, *161,* 176, 183, 211, *214, 259*
Marian, 159
Marie, 159, 204, 207, 209, 214
Mariko, 195, 196
Marilyn, 159, 204, 217, 231, 252, 254
Marion, 204, 214, 217
Marjorie, 159, 204, 214, 217
Mark, 151, 153, 163, 182, 197, *198,* 217
Marlene, 238
Married women and use of husbands' first names, 73–76

Martha, 114
Marvin, Lee, 137
Mary, 118, 119, *148, 160,* 176, *180,* 181, *201, 204,* 207, 211, *212–213, 214, 259*
Mass media: as influence in choice of names, 24, 42, 55–66, 157, 165–168, 227; internationalization of names, 113–114; secondary role, 64, 167. *See also* Movies; Television
Matthew, 151, 164, 179, 198, 217
Mattie, 207
Max, 211
Media's influence. *See* Mass media
Megan, 139, *140, 148, 162, 178, 180,* 183, *184, 196, 204, 259, 259*
Megumi, 195, 196
Melissa, 140, 148, 162, 180, 187, *196,* 217, *259*
Mencken, H. L., 176, 177, 182
Men's facial hair, 96, 127
Mexican immigrants, *178–180,* 182–183, 185–191
Mexican-American names, 172, 173; *a*-endings, 189–191, *190;* compared with Asian-American names, 194–195; compared with black and Anglo names, 185–191, *186;* influence of existing practices, 188–191
Michael, 151, 153, 164, 178, *179, 198*
Michelle, 140, 148, 162, 180, 182, *196,* 197, *204, 204,* 217, *259, 259*
Mick, 178
Middle names, 113, 145
Mildred, 159, 204, 214
Military figures, 73
Millicent, 165
Miranda, 113, 228
Miriam, 212–213, 247
Mississippi, differences in names between blacks and whites, 203

Misty, 148

Modeling feedback systems in collective behavior, 144

Monica, 160, 180, 261, 263–266

Monroe, Marilyn, 231, 252

Morgan, 113

Morris, 214

Morton, 174

Moses, 105

Mother's maiden name, used as middle name, 113

Movies: attendance and turnover in names, 60, *61–63, 63; Breakfast at Tiffany's,* 169; influence on popular names, 230–241, *236–237, 240–241;* invented names in films, 227; *Rebecca* as character in, 248–251; response to "dated" fashions, 3. *See also* Entertainers and entertainment; Mass media

Mr., as title in the South, 206–207

Mrs., style of title and name, 73–76

Mueller, John, 2, 12, 13, 94

Music: associations and tolerances, 126; changing tastes in, 2–3; innovations in, 94; nationalistic movements and, 12–13; technologic advances and, 10

Mutations of names, 117–126; *La*-prefix, 122–126

Myra, 228

Name changes of entertainers, 5, 6, 113. *See also* Entertainers and entertainment

Names: changes in leading names, 87–90; fictional characters, 226–227; incremental replacement mechanism, 116–117; obstacles to use as indicators of fashion and taste, 26–29; organizational influences on, 23–24; ratchet

effect, 98–104, 165; reasons to study, 23–26. *See also* Popular names

Nan, 200, 201

Nancy, 160, 196, 197, 201, 204, 217

Naomi, 195, 196, 197, 247

Natalie, 259

Nathan, 211, 218

National influences on choice of first names, 23

Nationalistic movements, 12–13

Nelson, 113

N-ending sound, 99, *100, 101, 102, 105,* 254

New designs, appeal of, 92–93

New names, sources of. *See* Invented names; Sources of new names

New tastes, 112–113, 115

New Testament names. *See* Biblical names

New York, girls' names and educational level of mothers, 139, *140,* 146

Nicholas, 164, 179, 182, 198

Nicknames, 79–81; blacks and, 207; college sports teams, 27–28

Nicole, 140, 162, 180, 182, 196, 204, 204

Nightingale, Florence, 113

Noah, 219

Norma, 245

Norwegian immigrants, 176

Nuclear family. *See* Familial names

Nuesell, Frank, 27

Oakland (California) Chamber of Commerce, 73–75

Ogburn, William, 266, 269–270

Old Testament names. *See* Biblical names

Old-country names and immigrants, 175–185, 191, 212

Olivia, 228

O'Neal, Ryan, 239
Orderly progression of change over
     time, 93–98, 273
Organizational influences and names,
     23–24
Oscar, 133–136
Oscar the Grouch, 136
Oswald, Lee Harvey, 136–137, 141
Out of fashion, 95, 162

Pamela, 113, *148, 160,* 217, 228, 245
Pants worn by women, 116
Parental invention of new names, 113
Patricia, 148, 160, 204, 217, 245
Patrick, 178, *179,* 183, *184*
Paul, 151, 153, 163, 197, 198, 199, 217
Peg, 200, 201, *201*
Performers. *See* Entertainers and
     entertainment
Permanence of names, 25
Persona of performer or fictional char-
     acter, 255–256
Peter, 197, 198, 199, 200, *201*
Phillis, 201
Phonemes. *See* Sounds of popular
     names
Physicians' telephone listings, 80–81
Pierre, 208
Polish immigrants, *178–180,* 182
Polish names, and religious influences,
     209–210, *214–215*
Polyester, 128–129
Pope, Alexander, 228
Popular names: changes in leading
     names, 87–90; fictional characters,
     226–227; idiosyncratic events and, 16;
     limit to level of popularity, 157, 244;
     movies and stars as influence, 230–
     241, *236–237;* peak delayed until
     affected population of childbearing

age, 169, 227, 251; picking names to
     avoid popular ones, 85, 100, 157; in
     United States, 101
Portia, 228
Prefixes of names, 117–122
Pregnancy, picking name during, 68
Presidents, U.S., 13–14, 70–73, 96; facial
     hair, 96; middle names of, 113
Pride in ethnic group and choice of
     names, 177
Princess Ingrid of Denmark, 177
Protestant versus Catholic names, 208–
     209
Puckett, Newbell Niles, 200–202
Puritans, 28–29, 104, 131, 242

*Rachel, 140, 148, 162, 180, 181, 182, 196,
     201, 201, 204,* 217, *219,* 245, *247*
Racial groups. *See* African-American
     names; Ethnic and racial groups
Racquel, 236
Radio, and turnover in names, 63–64.
     See also Mass media
Ragna, 176
Ratchet effect, 92–111; fashion, 93–98,
     114–115; names, generally, 98–104, 165;
     popularity of biblical names, 104–109;
     sounds of popular names, 99–104
Raymond, 163, 214
Rebecca, 106, 140, 148, 161, 180, 204, 217,
     242–252, 243
Reflection theory, 273–274
Regional naming patterns in United
     States, 26
Religious influences on choice of first
     names, 23, 24, 34; French names, 208–
     209; Irish names, 181; *Lilith,* 166;
     Polish names, 209–210, *214–215. See
     also* Biblical names; Jewish names
Rhonda, 149

Richard, *151, 153, 163,* 176, *198, 214,* 217
Richardson, Jane, 93, 96, 97, 98
Richardson, Samuel, 228
Rita, 238
Robert, 151, 153, 164, 179, 181, 182, *198, 214*
Robertson, Oscar, 136
Robin, 200, *201*
Robinson, Dwight, 96
Ronald, 152, 163
Roosevelt, Franklin, 13–14, 71
Roots, impact of, 76
Rosa, 207
Rosalind, 228, 229
Rose, 214
Rosie, 214
Rossi, Alice, 26
Royalty: Danish, 177; Swedish, 134
Rules of the road. *See* Driving rules
Ruth, 28–29, 104, *159, 204,* 207, 212, *214,* 219, 244
Ryan, 151, *164,* 178, *179,* 183, *184, 198,* 239

Saints' names, popularity of, 23, 104
Sally, 211
Sam, 200, *201*
Samantha, 149, 162, *180, 204, 259*
Samuel, 198, 199, 209, *214, 218,* 219, 220
Sandra, 149, *160, 204,* 217, 238, 245
Sarah, 106, *140,* 149, 162, *180,* 181, 182, *196, 201,* 204, 207, 209, *214,* 217, 219, 245, 247, *259, 259*
Sary, 200, *201*
Satisfaction with choice over time, 154
Scandinavia: immigrants from, 177, *178–180,* 181–182; popular boys' names, 134. *See also* Denmark; Iceland
Schücking, Levin, 13
Schudson, Michael, 82
Scotland: boys' names, 36; divorce and turnover in names, 51; divorce rates
and turnover rates in names, *53;* household size and turnover in names, 51; household size and turnover rates in names, *57;* turnover rates in names, 37, *38;* urbanization and education as factors, *48,* 50
Scott, 152, 163, 198, 217
Scott, Walter, 229, 249
Scrooge, Ebenezer, 131
Sean, 178, *179, 184, 198,* 217, 239
Secondary influences: mass media, 64, 167; social factors, 69
Segregation: effect on Chinese immigrants' names, 192–194, *194;* effect on Polish names, 210
S-ending sound, 99, *100, 102, 105*
Seth, 219
Seymour, 174, 216
Shakespeare, 120, 138, 191, 228, 229
Shannon, 149, *160,* 183, *184*
Sharon, 160, 196, 197, *204*
Sheldon, 174.
Shelley, 238
Sherry, 217
Shirley, 160, 204, 217, 231, *232, 233*
Sidney, 214, 229
Sigrid, 176
Simmel, Georg, 144
Slavery: alteration of names from African languages, 117; contamination of names used for slaves, 174; fictional characters by Mark Twain, 230; names taken from classical languages, 43, 202; slave names versus free black names, 200–203, *201*
Social aesthetics, 8–20; external events and, 10–14; idiosyncratic historical developments and, 15–17; interaction of influences, 17–20; internal mechanisms and, 14–15; multilayered, prob-

Social aesthetics (*cont.*)
  abilistic, and asymmetrical approach, 19–20, 268
Social class. *See* Class
Social factors, 1–2, 69–91; trends, 77–81
Social interaction, 167–168
Social order: changes in, 73–77, 87, 90; and reflection theory, 273–274
Socioeconomic status: Jewish names and, 220; popular names and, 147–154, *148–153*
Solveig, 176
Søndergaard, Georg, 35
Sons' versus daughters' names. *See* Boys' versus girls' names
Sounds of popular names: boys' names, *102,* 254; England and Wales, 99–104, *100;* girls' names, *102,* 245, 247, 254; immigrants' preference for native language's sounds, 191; influence on choice of biblical names, 104–106, *105;* invented names for fictional characters, 226, 229; Mexican-American names, 189–191, *190;* unappealing because out of fashion, 161
Sources of new names, 113–114; hothouse stage, 167–168; independence from initial source, 161. *See also* Invented names
Spanish place names, 260
Spelling variants of names, 117
Spirit of the age, 12–13
Sports teams, 27–28
Stacy, 140, 150, 196, 217
Stage names. *See* Entertainers and entertainment
Stanley, 174, 216
Stars' names. *See* Entertainers and entertainment
Stephanie, 140, 149, 162, 180, 187, 196, 197, 204, 217, 259

Stephen, 151
Stereotypes, 225
Stern, Jane and Michael, 127–129
Steven, 151, 153, 164, 179, 182, 197, 198, 217
Stewart, George, 29, 36, 104, 213, 228, 229
Stories. *See* Fictional characters
Surnames as first names, 113
Susan, 119, 149, 160, 196, 197, 217
Susie, 207
Suzanne, 209
Swedish royalty, 134
Swift, Jonathan, 228
Symbols: age as factor, 129–130; class as factor, 127–128; contamination of, 126–137, 173, 189, 271; durability of, 155; enhancement of, 126–130, 137–141, 173, 271; pride in ethnic group and, 177; subsets of population and, 138–141, 173

Taft, President, 137
Tammy, 139, 140, 149
Tanya, 124–125
Tasha, 124–125
Taste stems, 117–122
Taylor, 150, 259, 259
Taylor, Rex, 145
Telephone listings for physicians and attorneys, 80–81
Television, 55, 58, *58–60,* 60, 166; invented names on TV shows, 227; *Roots,* impact of, 76. *See also* Mass media
Temple, Shirley, 231, 233, 248
Tenner, Edward, 78, 82
Tennyson, Alfred, 228
Teresa, 149, 160
Texas: Mexican-American names, 185–191, *186;* popular names based on socioeconomic status, 147–154, *148–153*

Th-spelling in names, 99, *100*, 191

Thackeray, William Makepeace, 28, 228, 248

Thelma, 114, *204*, 228

Theresa, 245

Thomas, 151, 153, 163, *179*, 181, *214*, 226

Tiffany, 123, 138, *149*, *161*, 169, *196*, *204*, 205

Timothy, 151, 153, 163, 178, *179*, 198

Tina, *149*, 160

Tisha, 124–125, 126

Tom, 200, *201*, 229

Tonya, 124–125, 126

Toya, 124–125, 126

Tracey, *149*

Tracy, 160, 217

Tradition, 269

Travis, 152

Trice, 124–125, 126

Turner, Lana, 236

Turnover rates in names: cycles, 158–165, *159*–*164*, 183; girls versus boys, 36–37, *37*–*41*, 41–42; movie attendance and, 60, *61*–*63*, 63; popular names and, 85, 158; radio and, 63–64

Twain, Mark, 229, 249

Tyler, 152

Uncommon names, choice of, 154, 157; diffusion as factor, 165; disposition toward, 168, 170, 244–245; media's influence, 227

Unpopular names: fictional characters, 226; public figures, 161. *See also* Contamination

Urbanization, 43–50, 66, 68

Vandebosch, Heidi, 223–224

Vanessa, 113, *162*, *180*, 228, *259*

Veblen, Thorstein, 21, 22

Veronica, *161*, *180*

Victoria, *180*, *259*

Vietnam War, 84, 88, 90

Virginia, *159*, *204*, *214*, 245

Virginia (state), 145

Vivien, 228

Vowel sound ending name, 207

Vowel starting name, 99, *100*, 101, *102*

Walter, *163*, 211, *214*

Warren, 71

Watkins, Susan Cotts, 193

Wayne, John, 231

Wealth: "durability-cost principle" and, 155; as influence on tastes, 21–23; name choices and, 24; tastes expressing, 126

Welch, Racquel, 236

Wendy, 228

West, Rebecca, 252

White Americans' names: compared with African-American names, 203–205, *204*, 250–251; compared with Mexican-American and black names in Texas, 185–191, *186*; overlap with Asian names, *193*, 195–200, *196*, *198*

White ethnic groups. *See* European immigrants

Whitney, 113

Wilde, Oscar, 134

Wilhelm, 211

Will, 200, *201*

William, 151, 153, 163, 176, *179*, 181, *198*, 200, *201*, *214*

Williams, William, 35

Willie, 229

Willy, 211

Winters, Shelley, 238

Winthrop, 113

Women's fashion. *See* Clothing

World War I, 84, 87

World War II, 84, 87

Writers' use of names. *See* Fictional characters

Yellow Pages listings for physicians and attorneys, 80–81

Yiddish, 211–212

Yonge, Charlotte, 28, 228

Young, Agnes Brooks, 96

Yvonne, 204

Z anywhere in biblical name, *105,* 106

Zachary, 151

Zelinsky, Wilbur, 25–26

Znaniecki, Florian, 12